W9-CUG-232

BY ROBERTO CALASSO

THE BOOK OF ALL BOOKS

THE BOOK
OF ALL BOOKS

ROBERTO
CALASSO

TRANSLATED FROM THE ITALIAN
BY TIM PARKS

FARRAR, STRAUS AND GIROUX

NEW YORK

Farrar, Straus and Giroux
120 Broadway, New York 10271

Library of Congress Cataloging-in-Publication Data
Names: Calasso, Roberto, author. | Parks, Tim, translator.
Title: The book of all books / Roberto Calasso ; translated from the Italian by Tim Parks.
Other titles: Libro di tutti i libri. English
Description: First American edition. | New York : Farrar, Straus and Giroux, 2021. |
    "Originally published in Italian in 2019 by Adelphi Edizioni, Italy, as Il libro
    di tutti i libr." | Includes bibliographical references and index.
Identifiers: LCCN 2021028288 | ISBN 9780374601898
Subjects: LCSH: Bible. Old Testament—Criticism, interpretation, etc.
Classification: LCC BS1175.3 .C3413 2021 | DDC 221.6/8—dc23
LC record available at https://lccn.loc.gov/2021028288

Our books may be purchased in bulk for promotional, educational, or business
use. Please contact your local bookseller or the Macmillan Corporate and
Premium Sales Department at 1-800-221-7945, extension 5442, or by email at
MacmillanSpecialMarkets@macmillan.com.

www.fsgbooks.com
www.twitter.com/fsgbooks • www.facebook.com/fsgbooks

10 9 8 7 6 5 4 3 2 1

Thus, book after book, the book of all books would show that it was given to us so that we might try to enter there as into a second world, and lose ourselves there, enlighten ourselves, perfect ourselves.

—GOETHE

CONTENTS

I

THE TORAH
IN HEAVEN

Nine hundred and seventy-four generations before the world was created, the Torah was written. How? With black fire on white fire. It was Yahweh's only daughter. Her father wanted her to live in a foreign land. The presiding Angels said: "Why can't she stay in heaven?" Yahweh answered: "What's that to you?" A king came along and took the daughter for his bride. Yahweh told him: "This is my only daughter I'm giving you. I can't part with her. But nor can I tell you not to take her, because she is your bride. Grant me but one thing: that wherever you go you keep a room for me."

In the solitude before Creation, Yahweh had only his daughter to help. She was Torah, Law, and Hokhmah, Wisdom. His consultant, and his artificer too: she calculated the size of things, took care to plug the waters, marked where the sand should start, sealed the seams of the heavens. Sometimes she served as the open map of Creation. Then Yahweh would watch her in silence.

Wisdom was the artificer, the plane, the tool. But even more often she was his helpmate, at his side. When she was born, "the abysses were yet to be." The waters had not burst forth. And the heavens were still to be raised and hung. Whenever something appeared or was transformed from one thing to another, "I was with him and I arranged all things," *cum eo eram, cuncta componens*, said Wisdom. No one would ever know greater pride or greater awe. As the cycle of marvels was nearing its end, Wisdom was always there in front of Yahweh, playing on the ground. It was Creation's happiest moment, one uninterrupted pleasure (*delectabar per singulos dies*) whose emanation would eventually pass to the sons of men, much abated, much adulterated.

Together with atonement, with Eden, Gehenna, the throne of majesty, the Temple, and the name of the Messiah, the Torah was one of the seven things created before the creation of the world. Eden, a garden, hovered in a place that preceded space. Likewise Gehenna, a valley. Their presence was indispensable, though no one knew how or where they could have existed before the world came into being. For the Torah, on the other hand, the existence or otherwise of the world hardly mattered. She sat on the Father's knee, singing together with the presiding Angels. After hundreds of generations, some of those Angels looked down and saw a man struggling to climb a mountain. With a shiver of nostalgia that anticipated their imminent loss, they asked the Father: "Why do you want to give this carefully guarded jewel to a creature of flesh and blood?" But it was already too late.

It was because the Torah was written with black fire on white fire—Nachmanides, a cabalist of Gerona, believed—that it could be read in two contrasting ways: either as an uninterrupted text, not divided into words—something the nature of fire demands—or in the traditional fashion, a sequence of stories and precepts. Approached the first way, the uninterrupted text became a list of names. Stories and precepts melted away. But other cabalists from Gerona went further. Why insist on a plurality of names? The whole Torah should be read as a single name. The Name of the Holy One. Azriel went so far as to say that Genesis 36, which lists the descendants of Esau and is generally thought an unimportant passage, should not be considered as fundamentally distinct from the Ten Commandments. They were parts of the same structure and all equally necessary.

Wisdom issued from the mouth of the Father in the form of a cloud. "It covered the earth like a cloud." Before the world was created, she raised her tent in the heavens and waited there. She came to the Father in a "pillar of cloud," where he sat on his throne. Tent and pillar of cloud: they would turn up again when

Moses, in the presence of his astonished people, withdrew into the "Tent of Meeting" and immediately afterward a pillar of cloud covered the entrance. That was how Yahweh chose to speak to Moses, "face to face, as a man speaks to his neighbor." Wisdom on the other hand passed from inside the tent to inside the pillar of cloud. It was the first step, the beginning of a never-ending journey. From then on, Wisdom would visit every corner of the cosmos. "I have traveled the circle of the heavens alone, / I have walked in the depths of the abysses. / In the billows of the sea, and across all the earth, / enriched myself among every people and in every nation." Everywhere she went, Wisdom found something to feed on. But she was forever thinking of her tent. She was looking for somewhere to pitch it again. One day the father pointed to a place. "So it was that I settled in Zion," said Wisdom, winding up her story. One day, in the same land, the Son, her brother, would find "nowhere to lay his head."

II

SAUL AND SAMUEL

Saul makes his first appearance on a mission to recover some she-asses that had gone missing. He had a servant from home with him and together they walked a long way. But the asses were not to be found. When they reached Zuf, Saul said to the servant, "My father will have stopped worrying about the asses; he'll want to know where we've got to." They had been walking for three days, after those asses. They had crossed Mount Ephraim, the land of Shalishah and the land of Shaalim. The asses were not to be found. And by now they were disoriented, uncertain how to get home. Then the servant said he'd heard of a seer who lived in Zuf. Perhaps he could help. Saul agreed, but at this point they didn't have so much as a hunk of bread in their bags. What could they offer the seer? The servant said: "I came across a silver shekel. We could give that to the seer and ask him the way." The Bible adds a few words in explanation: "Once, in Israel, when a man went to consult Elohim, he would say, 'Come, let us speak to the seer!'" What today we call a "prophet" was once called a "seer."

Some girls had walked out of Zuf by the city gate to draw water from the well. Fatal meetings tend to happen near wells. As with Rebecca, or Rachel, or with Demeter in Eleusis. On this occasion, as on others, there was a gaggle of girls. They saw the two foreigners climbing toward the city gate. "Does the seer live near here?" the two strangers asked. The girls were eager to help: they could see him right away, but they'd have to hurry, because he was about to leave town. "You must meet him," they said, "before he climbs up the hill to eat, since the people won't eat until he comes. It's he who blesses the sacrifice before the guests eat." Shortly afterward, at the city gate, Saul saw a man leaving the town and asked: "Could you tell me the way to the seer's house?" Samuel answered. "I am the seer." And at once he invited Saul to follow him up the hill: "Today you will eat with me." Then he added: "As for those she-asses you lost three days ago, they've been found." For a priest like Samuel the first thing to do was to make the sacrifice then share out the meat of the sacrifice for people to eat. Saul got the best portion and Samuel said, "Here's what's left, they've served it to you: go ahead and eat! They kept it on purpose for you, when I invited the people to the banquet." The portion is *moîra*, "destiny." Saul's destiny was ready and waiting. They were expecting him.

For anyone not in the know—and no one is in the know—it was the lost asses that led Saul and Samuel to meet. If Saul's father hadn't told his son to look for them, Saul would have stayed at home, in Israel's smallest tribe. He was a handsome young man, a head taller than his companions, and had given no sign of any particular vocation. Thanks to the lost asses, he found himself far from home, not sure of the way back. He was ready to give a silver coin to the person who would guide him.

It was in these circumstances that Yahweh had him meet Samuel. The lost asses were the ruse that made the meeting possible. And the asses would be found. Not by Saul, but—how we don't know—by Samuel himself, the seer who was to make Saul the first king of Israel. Yahweh was, among many other things, an allegorist. The lost and found asses were also the people of Israel who yearned for a king but wouldn't have been able to choose one, if Samuel, the seer, had not anointed him with the oil he kept in a vial.

After the sacrificial meal they went back to the city. Samuel had Saul lie down on a bed on the roof of his house. Then he woke him early next morning and said, "Get up, I'll set you on your way." They left the city together. Samuel told Saul to send his servant on ahead. He must stay behind. He must hear the word of God. Samuel took out a vial of oil and poured it on Saul's head. He said that Yahweh had anointed him as "leader of his people." They were alone, shortly after dawn. Then Samuel told Saul to start walking.

And he mentioned three things that would befall him. The first had to do with the lost asses. In Zelzah, near Rachel's tomb, two strangers would tell him the asses had been found. Thus it was. His father, they said, no longer thought of the matter, he was just worried for his son who hadn't come home.

Other predictions were also soon fulfilled. They were "signs," Samuel had said. And had added: from now on "you will act by accepting whatever offers itself to you." It was a winning strategy. The signs appeared as foretold and Saul understood what Samuel meant when he said, "You will be transformed into another man."

People who had known him couldn't believe it. Was it possible that Saul, Kish's son, that tall handsome boy, was now behaving like a *nabi*, a "prophet," dancing and speaking to the rhythm of harps and tambourines? They said, "But what has happened to Kish's son? Is Saul, too, one of the prophets?" And a gently mocking proverb was born, something people still say today: "Is Saul, too, one of the prophets?"

When Saul had finished prophesying, he met his uncle. It seemed he'd now gone back to being what he was before. In no way was he different from the boy he'd been when he left. His uncle just wanted to know where he'd been, with his servant. "After the asses," Saul said. "But they were nowhere to be found," he added. "So we went to see Samuel." "And what did Samuel tell you?" his uncle pressed him. "That the asses had been found," said Saul. "But he didn't tell him about the kingdom," the Bible observes.

Only Samuel knew that Saul was king of Israel. Now the people must be told. Samuel called them to Mizpah. He reminded them that they had asked for a king and that in doing so they had rejected Yahweh, "who saves you from all adversities and distress." They had dared demand of him: "You must appoint a king over us." So now show yourselves to Yahweh, Samuel wound up abruptly.

All the tribes were there. They drew lots, as Yahweh saw fit. The tribe of Benjamin was chosen. Then they drew lots for the family. And Matri's family was chosen. Now they had to choose which member of the family. They all stood in a line. All except Saul. They asked Yahweh if someone was missing. Yahweh said, "He's hiding among the bags." Now Saul came forward. He was taller than anyone around him. Samuel said, "There is no one like him in all the people." Then the people hailed Saul. He was the first king of Israel.

Saul hid among the bags—something Harpo Marx would do—paralyzed by the *terror of election*, the terror that in the future would afflict his people more than any other, the terror of the drawn lot, the chance, that a moment later might select him. But Saul knew the selection had already happened, when Samuel anointed him. Just that then they had been alone. No one had seen. No one knew. Chance and destiny were about to fuse in his person. An oppressive fusion. Never again would he breathe freely, carelessly, as when he'd walked those remote paths in search of his father's asses. Dreamy and bored, he'd exchanged a few words with his servant from time to time. But that was all. Now nothing like that could happen again his whole life long.

Saul's election as king of Israel was as swift as a simple drawing of lots. But his kingship had no foundation. So Samuel "told the people the law of kingship." But that still wasn't enough. The law must be *written down*. So Samuel "wrote it in the book that he set down before Yahweh." Fitful, inevitable steps. And everything wound up in a book.

Last of the judges, Samuel was also a prototype priest and a prophet before the prophets. Born from the vow of a barren woman desperate for motherhood, he was dedicated to the priesthood before he was born. At twelve he heard Yahweh's voice and did not recognize it. He was asleep in the half-dark of the temple. He thought it was Eli, the chief priest. He ran to him and said,

"Here I am." Eli looked up and said, "Wasn't me, go back to bed." It happened twice more. Same words, same routine. It was hard to imagine Yahweh calling. This was a time when "the word of Yahweh was seldom heard and visions rare." But the old priest, Eli, father of two wicked sons, understood that it had been Yahweh's voice. Then he said to the young Samuel, "If you hear someone calling, say: Speak, Yahweh, for your servant is listening." Silently, Samuel lay down for the third time. And something happened that Scripture describes thus: "Yahweh came in and stood, calling him as before: 'Samuel, Samuel!' And Samuel said, 'Speak, for your servant is listening.'" Yahweh immediately explained that he was going to destroy the line of Eli, the priest Samuel had grown up with, the man who had taught him the rituals of the faith. It was not Eli's fault, but his sons'. They attacked anyone bringing offerings to the temple with three-pronged forks, snatching the best parts of the offerings, "like brigands." Time and again they raped "the women who gathered around the Tent of the Meeting." Others said they just "seduced them with gifts." Eli was old and ponderous, he had judged Israel for forty years, but his words had no effect on his sons. Soon he, too, would be crushed, Yahweh announced. And so it was, shortly afterward. On hearing that his sons had been killed in battle against the Philistines, Eli fell from his seat with a thud. His heavy body lay sideways across the door. He died from a broken neck.

Samuel listened to Yahweh's words. Then he fell into a deep sleep till morning came. And as on every morning, for it was one of his duties, he opened the doors of the House of Yahweh. His only fear was that as soon as they found themselves alone old Eli would ask him what Yahweh had said.

When the elders of Israel came to ask for a king, Samuel was far from happy. He knew his sons were corrupt, even if he himself had made them judges. He remembered the horrors of the sons of Eli, likewise appointed by their father. But this wasn't enough to have him embrace the idea of a king. He didn't think the Jews really understood what a king was. A king is someone who takes more than he gives. This was the idea Yahweh had passed on to him. The people wanted a king because they no longer wanted Yahweh to reign over them. Yet Yahweh had accepted the request, had said, "Hear their voice." It was a kind of abdication, as Yahweh himself had explained: "It's not you they're rejecting, it's me, that my reign over them might end." So Yahweh was relinquishing his sovereignty, even over this very small population. But first he wanted to explain to Samuel what "the law of kingship" meant. That it wasn't a good thing. The people must realize: "He will take your daughters as perfumers, as cooks, as bakers. He will take your best fields, your best vines, your best olive groves, he will take them to give to his servants." A king plunders his subjects before protecting them. This was the law that the people were preferring to Yahweh's law. Samuel repeated what Yahweh had told him point by point. But the people were unimpressed. They listened impatiently, enchanted by an illusion. They said they wanted to be "like all the other nations." They all had kings. Why should Israel be the only one without? "Our king will judge us and march at our head, he will fight our battles." That was what they wanted. A visible, tangible man, predatory perhaps, perhaps greedy, but nevertheless someone the people could follow. "He will fight our battles." Samuel dismissed them at once. He said he would call them together again when he had found someone who could be their king.

Something irreversible happened then in the history of Israel and in the history of Yahweh's relations with Israel. They would no longer be a priestly people, led by those who administered justice, supervised the sacrifices, and watched over the Ark. They would be a nation like other nations, with the advantages and risks, the pleasures and pains that derive from being a kingdom, where everything converges on a single person: the sovereign.

Old and white-haired, Samuel wondered whether, in administering justice "all the days of his life," he had ever damaged or mistreated someone, or allowed someone to corrupt him. Everyone spoke well of him. But Samuel wanted to go over some key events in the past. And key, for Israel, meant Egypt. That's where he started. Everyone must be well aware that Yahweh had "brought your fathers out of Egypt." And that, since then, many were "the blessings that Yahweh has showered on you." Samuel mentioned some of them. But as ever he spoke swiftly, sparingly, in a hurry to get to his final point: "Know then and reflect what a great evil you have committed in Yahweh's eyes by asking for a king!" Yet the king was only a king because Samuel had anointed him. Samuel was determined that they appreciate that a king is *by nature* an evil. To want a king meant to want an evil. Yahweh sent rain and thunder to confirm Samuel's words. From then on, the history of Israel, like the history of the peoples around it, would be told in a succession of kings. But there would always be someone to remind them of the words of Samuel, who had thought kingship debasing, even though he had set it going with his own hands.

On the one hand Yahweh, on the other his people. Then, when required, a few men who knew the law, administered the law, celebrated the sacrifices. Kings? A weakness. Something *other people* needed. That was how Samuel thought of it, one could see it in his face. Thoughts that would haunt the kings of Israel, like a corrosive shadow.

But what were they supposed to do, some wondered, if everything was so compromised? Samuel shook his head. You won't be rejected over this. Just be loyal to Yahweh. And he added: "Don't drift away from him, you'd only be following futile, worthless things that can't save you, because they amount to nothing." So one could still speak of *salvation*. Everyone felt cheered. And went back to hailing their new king.

First and foremost Yahweh demanded *detachment*, required Israel to distinguish itself from *other nations*, whether they be like Egypt or like Canaan. The groove of distinction should be scored as deeply as possible, albeit with an awareness that there would be endless backsliding into old ways. This was why it was so disturbing to give Israel a king. To have a king meant conforming with all the other nations. But the people of Israel yearned for one. Kingship was a debasement that Samuel the priest granted only with a heavy heart. Yet it would be the priests who anointed the king, just as in Vedic India it would be the brahmans who made the *kṣatriya*.

All over the world and throughout history kingship was encouraged by the gods and seen as a necessary connection between men and gods. Which was why it was sacred. Not so for Israel. Yahweh accepted kingship reluctantly, and only because the people wanted to be "like all the other nations." And, even during the first king's reign, Yahweh "regretted making Saul king of Israel." The whole history of Israel from then on would be marred by this fracture, sometimes gaping, sometimes barely visible.

There are no accounts of the first years of Saul's reign, until one day his son Jonathan struck a Philistine chief and killed him. Word went around: "Israel has become hateful to the Philistines." It was the start of a war, but Israel wasn't ready for it. "There were those who hid in caves, thickets, rocks, vaults, and pits." Saul waited, because Samuel had told him to wait seven days. The days passed and Samuel didn't show. Saul saw his men deserting. He decided to celebrate the holocaust he was supposed to celebrate with Samuel. Before embarking on a risky war, he felt he should "sweeten Yahweh's countenance."

No sooner had he done so than Samuel appeared. Once again he had something to criticize. "You've behaved like a fool," he said. "You've disobeyed the order Yahweh, your God, gave you, after Yahweh established that you should reign over Israel forever. Now your reign will not last." So he said and off he went. Whatever you did, you could never get along with Samuel.

"The day of the battle it so happened that none of the men around Saul and Jonathan had either swords or spears. Only Saul and Jonathan had them." Meantime, a company of Philistines was approaching from the Valley of the Hyenas. Without telling his father, Jonathan went off with the young man who was carrying his arms. They ran into the Philistines in a rocky gulley. "Look at the Jews, coming out of the holes where they were hiding," said the Philistines when they saw them. Jonathan was clambering up the rocks. When he came face-to-face with his enemies, he cut them down one by one. Behind him his arms bearer finished them off. Twenty corpses piled up in a tight space. The news of the massacre spread panic among the Philistine advance guard. Many Jews who had sided with the Philistines changed their minds and "turned back to fight beside the Israelites with Saul and Jonathan."

After that, and "for all the days of Saul," there was war with the Philistines. But there was another enemy too, closer in kin, the descendants of Esau. Yahweh had once spoken of these people in terms that had burned themselves into the memory. "Remember what Amalek did to you, along the way, when you came out of Egypt." How could they forget? The Amalekites had cut off their path when they were "worn out and exhausted." Many of the weakest had fallen behind, never to be seen again. And the Jews had feared that the Amalekites meant to kill them all, to cancel the whole caravan from the face of the earth.

Samuel reappeared before Saul. He was Israel's memory. He reminded Saul that he was king only because he, Samuel, had anointed him. He recalled Yahweh's words about Amalek. And said, "Now go and defeat the Amalekites and assign all their possessions to anathema, *herem*: you shall not spare them, but you shall kill all the men and women, the children and newborns, the sheep and oxen, the camels and asses." Not even the asses were to escape.

Saul marshaled his army. Advancing on the Amalekites, he warned the Kenites to keep away. It's the only way to save yourselves, he told them. Nothing was to survive. Then he defeated the Amalekites wherever they were to be found and captured their king, Agag. He ordered his men to kill everyone, "to put them to the sword." Only the king was left alive and "the best of the animals, small and large, the fat ones and the lambs, all that were good." The thinner and weaker beasts had been killed. What to do now with these surviving animals? Saul and his men decided to sacrifice to Yahweh "the finest of the anathema." They thought he would be pleased. After all, the end result would be the same: death, not just of the Amalekites but of all their animals.

It was a mistake fraught with dire consequence. Saul should have been thinking like a theologian or a metaphysician, and instead he was just a soldier. He couldn't see the enormous difference between what Yahweh had ordered and what he planned to do. While Saul was sacrificing the best and fattest of Amalek's animals, Samuel turned up. Saul flinched. Samuel stood in front of Saul, who immediately felt the need to justify himself and said, "I have carried out Yahweh's order." Samuel seemed not to have heard. He looked around as though there was some question in the air. Then said, "What's this racket I hear, this din of small animals and large." Saul explained that the animals had been spared. But hurried to add: "The rest have been killed."

Samuel already knew as much, but wanted to hear it from Saul's lips. He was getting angry. Irked, he reminded Saul that he had been a nobody before becoming king, by the will of Yahweh. So why had he disobeyed Yahweh? Why hadn't he finished off the slaughter? Falling into a bad habit typical of kings, Saul took cover behind his people. "I captured Agag, king of the Amalekites, and I consigned Amalek to anathema. But the people took some small and large animals from the haul, the best of the anathema, to sacrifice them to Yahweh, to your God, in Gilgal." Samuel answered with words that would sink like a wedge into the substance of time. "Do you suppose Yahweh takes as much pleasure in holocausts as he does in obedience to the word of Yahweh? Beware that obedience is worth more than offerings, and submission more than the fat of rams." And he added: "Since you have rejected the word of Yahweh, Yahweh rejects you as king."

This could only mean repudiation. Saul tried to speak the truth: "I was afraid of the people and did what they said." He asked for pardon, but Samuel was not a man for pardoning. He had already turned away. Saul grabbed at his cloak, and tore it. Samuel said, "Today Yahweh has torn Israel's kingship from your back." But could Israel be left without a king? Saul acknowledged all his failings and begged Samuel not to abandon him before his people. Samuel turned away without a word and "Saul prostrated himself before Yahweh."

It still wasn't over. Samuel said, "Bring out Agag, king of Amalek!" Agag came forward, limping. He knew he was a dead man; he said only that death no longer held any "bitterness" for him. Samuel didn't miss the chance to state his case: "As your sword has deprived women of their sons, so your mother among women shall be deprived of hers." And in an instant old Samuel "cut Agag to pieces before Yahweh in Gilgal."

There was nothing for it now but to part ways. Samuel went to Ramah, Saul returned to Gibeath. It was their last meeting. "Samuel did not see Saul again for the rest of his days, for Samuel grieved over Saul after Yahweh repented having made him king of Israel."

In Deuteronomy we read: "Remember what Amalek did to you." An ominous warning that would echo in Jewish ears down the centuries. But nowhere is it written: "Remember what you did to Amalek." Which was quite a lot, when we reflect that not a living creature was spared. As for Agag, their king, he had the privilege of being cut to pieces by Samuel, the priest, who had anointed the first king of Israel.

The decisive words against sacrifice, words that would mark a break with all preceding times and all earlier notions of sacrifice, were pronounced by Jesus, quoting Hosea: "If you knew what was

meant by: *I want mercy, not sacrifice*, you would never have condemned the innocent." It was Jesus's style to present the shockingly
new as a tiny *addition* to some quotation from Scripture. Here it's
striking how he singles out these words from Hosea, which look
forward to a radical rejection of sacrifice, as if the order of sacrifice
could be replaced by some order of "mercy." But even more striking are the words that follow: "you would never have condemned
the innocent." No one had ever dared speak so openly of the even-
tual innocence of sacrificial victims, even equating sacrifice with
condemning the innocent to death. From Abraham's time on, a
victim might at best be spared. The question of its innocence was
not even broached. To do that would amount to replacing the language of sacrifice (offering, slaying) with the language of the law
(condemnation, innocence). And if that were to happen, the consequences would be incalculable—and would ripple out through
time, wider and wider, in never-ending circles.

The distance from Samuel's words to Saul's and Hosea's words
is simply immense, as likewise the distance between Hosea's words
and the words of Jesus. Samuel told Saul he should choose anathema rather than sacrifice, because in carrying out anathema he
would be obeying Yahweh. This already undermined the sacrificial
order by suggesting that sacrifice was not always necessarily pious. Both ruthlessness and piety might be ways to move away from
sacrifice, a practice of its nature inextricably ruthless and pious.
Both Samuel, who condemns to death not just Israel's enemies but
the animals of those enemies, refusing to accept them as sacrificial
victims, and Jesus, who defines sacrifice as a never-ending condemnation of innocents, are both moving against sacrifice, albeit
from opposite directions. And at the same time both go on using
the language of sacrifice and its liturgy.

The fatal decision of the Seventy to translate *herem*, "extermination," as *anathema*, "votive offering" had repercussions across the
centuries that are still unfolding today. When *anathema* then took
the meaning of "curse" and, for Catholics, "excommunication,"

the misunderstandings could only multiply. But looked at together, these distortions and adulterations assume a certain shape, become the very space within which a great part of history has been played out, the part that had its origin in words used in Athens and Jerusalem, and in the place where those two cities met and mingled, Alexandria.

To translate *herem* with *anathema* is a mistake, but metaphysical. It exposes a puzzle as yet unresolved and perhaps unresolvable. On the other hand, to translate the word, as today's scholars do, with *prohibition, ban, Verbot, Bann*, is both elusive and misleading. To prohibit or to ban something implies exclusion, not killing. While *herem* is an injunction to do something thoroughly and completely, to *kill*, to *exterminate*, whatever has been set aside for *herem*.

What is the difference between the Hebrew *herem* and the Greek *anathema*? *Anathema* can be the plunders of war placed for preservation in a temple (but it can also be the tripod, wreath, or bowl that athletes are awarded, or again the robes initiates wear during their initiation); the *herem* is war plunder that must be destroyed, whether things or persons, because otherwise "it would be a trap for you." "*Anatithénai* never had the sense of a ritual that ended with the destruction of the consecrated object."

With *herem*, on the other hand, complete destruction is the only way to avoid the danger of imitation, or gradual assimilation. The same image of the trap is evoked when the Jews are warned "not to agree to an alliance with the inhabitants of the country you will enter, for fear it become a trap for you."

Who was the threat of *herem* meant for? One's closest enemy, you would have thought. But then Isaiah spelled it out: "For God's wrath is turned against all nations / and his anger against all their army; / he has assigned them to destruction and set them aside for the slaughter." It still wasn't enough. Divine fury was also turned against the heavens: "The whole Army of the Heavens will rot.

The heavens themselves will roll shut like a scroll." The aim of the *herem* was to leave nothing behind. Only a scattering of wild animals would survive. Across the earth would stretch "the line of chaos, the plummets of the void."

But Isaiah wasn't the only one to rage against the "Army of the Heavens." Jeremiah foresaw that "on that day," the last day, the graves will open and the bones of the kings, the priests, and the false prophets, indeed all the dwellers of Jerusalem, will be laid bare "before the Sun and the Moon, / and all the Army of the Heavens, / that they loved, that they served, / and behind which they marched, / that they consulted and before which they bowed down." For one last time those bones would be forced to look up at the sky. And destined to be left unburied, aboveground, before becoming manure.

Tells, those mounds of earth scattered all over the Middle East that sometimes yield extraordinary archaeological remains, often started as piles of rubble, slowly covered by sand and soil. And perhaps some were the result of people doing their duty: "You will gather all the spoils in the center of the squares and burn the city with all its spoils, all for Yahweh, your God; it will be a *tell* forever, never rebuilt. And nothing of the *herem* will be left sticking to your hand."

Everything that happened to Saul came as a consequence of the wrongs he'd done. Aside from his disobedience in not completing the slaughter of the Amalekites, there was another incident that weighed on him. At the beginning of his reign, Saul "had expelled the necromancers and soothsayers from the land," as a wise and devote king should. But then, no sooner were the Philistines threatening Israel, and Yahweh did not take the trouble to answer his call, "whether in a dream or with the Urim or through the prophets," than Saul panicked and said to his servants, "Find me a necromancer and I will go and ask her." Clearly one or two were still around, wary and in hiding. But how could the king go to ask help of someone he had persecuted? He decided to disguise himself and set off for Endor with two servants. The necromancer said, "You know what Saul did to all the necromancers and soothsayers." And she meant: "Why have you set this trap for me, to have me die?" Saul didn't even have the energy to keep pretending. He swore that nothing bad would happen to her. Plain and to the point, the necromancer asked, "Who shall I summon up for you?" Saul answered, "Summon up Samuel." Then the necromancer knew she must be dealing with Saul. Because nothing ever happened in Saul's life unless Samuel was looming over him. Saul was at once a king and a man who lived in dread. Who else could be in such a state of subjection to Samuel? Already the summons was taking effect. "An old man in a cloak" appeared. Saul bowed down.

The ghost spoke as sharply and abruptly as Samuel had used to when alive. "Why," he said, "have you disturbed me and brought me back?" Saul explained that he had lost touch with Yahweh and the Philistines were attacking. "You didn't listen to Yahweh's voice and bring down the heat of his anger on Amalek," Samuel replied. And he added a few words that frightened Saul even more: "Yahweh has turned away from you and become your enemy." It was more than enough. Henceforth Yahweh would not speak to Saul, but nor would he forgive him for having resorted in desperation to a necromancer, to find a way back to him. Whatever he did, Saul was doomed, simply waiting for the day when his severed head would be raised up in the temple of Dagon. When Samuel's voice faded, Saul "fell full length on the ground; Samuel's words left him deeply afraid and intensely weak, since he hadn't eaten all day and all night." After a while, the necromancer said, "Your servant heard your voice: I risked my life and took heed of the words you spoke to me. Now you take heed, please, of the words of your servant, and let me bring you a little bread!" But Saul still wouldn't eat. He got up and lay on a bed. Then the necromancer took a calf she kept in the house and "quickly killed it." This time Saul agreed to eat, together with his servants. And they left the same night.

"The spirit of Yahweh withdrew from Saul and an evil spirit that Yahweh had called up shook him with fear." The Lord giveth and the Lord taketh away. It was always his spirits at work. But this didn't absolve those in their thrall.

Kingship was a punishment for Saul. Samuel's curse weighed heavy, the curse of the one man to whom he owed his investiture. Another thing that weighed was the constant feeling that he would one day be toppled by David, the handsome redheaded shepherd boy from Bethlehem, who was also the only one who could chase away the "evil spirit" when he played his lyre. On other occasions the "evil spirit" took aim at David and tried to kill him. It happened a number of times. When David had the gall to ask for his daughter Michal's hand in marriage, Saul at once ordered him to disappear. He must go to fight the Philistines and not come back until he could bring a hundred of their foreskins with him. It was a way of forcing him to go and get himself killed. Another time he threw his spear at David while he was playing his lyre. "I'll pin David to the wall," Saul had said, but he missed. Yet he called David "my son." Step by step, Saul felt he was heading for a gruesome end. Three of his sons were killed in battle on the same day and Saul fell on his own sword for fear of being taken prisoner. When they found him, the Philistines cut off his head, offered his arms in the temple of Ashtaroth, and hung up his head in the temple of Dagon. His powerful body was nailed to the wall of Beth-Shan. Later the people of Jabesh took it down, burned it, and buried his bones under a tamarisk tree.

There is another account of Saul's suicide. In this version he didn't kill himself alone but asked a fleeing Amalekite to kill him. This man later told the story to David and gave him Saul's crown and bracelet as proof. It's as though Saul had completed the *herem*

by proxy, assigning himself to the slaughter, and allowing an Amalekite to survive to tell the tale. David then finished off the job,
killing the last Amalekite who had dared "raise his hand to slay
Yahweh's anointed." Though actually it was Yahweh's anointed
who had asked him to do it.

When Saul ordered David to go to fight the Philistines, David
knew it was a death sentence. But he didn't show it, simply went
off with his men. Saul wouldn't see him again until the day David
presented him with two hundred Philistine foreskins. He wanted
to be on the generous side so that it would be clear how much he
loved Michal. The scraps of mangled flesh were laid on a large tray.
Saul looked grim. For some time a gloomy delirium had seized
hold of him. He'd dreamed of David's head being offered on that tray.
"The hand of the Philistines, the hand of the Philistines . . ." he was
often heard to mutter. He hoped that hand would one day cut off
David's head, as David had cut off Goliath's.

The elect are never simply those who accumulate merits. If that
was the case the world would be one very long, very dull moral
lesson. With its obsessive concentration on what it means to be
chosen, the Bible sets in motion a powerful narrative tension. The
elect are those who make stories happen, move history on. But this
hardly guarantees that they always behave as they should or even
that they be allies with each other. Saul and David were both chosen, but for a long time and in all kinds of ways Saul tried to kill
David. And was simultaneously and irresistibly attracted to him.

From the first, Saul thought of David as an intruder. He wasn't
sure where to place this shepherd boy among his men, who had
very quickly arranged themselves around the young redhead in
concentric circles, as men do in royal courts. David moved inside
an invisible sheath, thanks to some protective power of Samuel's.
Worse, one sensed something alarming about him, something no

one dared allude to. David was not one man alone. Already he was a clan.

David, too, had loved Saul, the man who tried to kill him. And he had loved his son, Jonathan, who loved David "as himself." When father and son were killed in battle on the same day, David mourned them both—and composed a funeral lament that became one of the first poetic texts in Hebrew. He called them "beloved and dear, / never apart in life or death." But only of Jonathan did he say, "Your love was wonderful for me / more so than the love of women."

Between David and Saul, and among their children, it was never clear which prevailed, love or hate. Saul had been dead some time and David had only just survived his own son Absalom's attempt to usurp his throne, when the Gibeonites declared that they were still waiting to avenge themselves on Saul and his family. David, who wanted them as allies, decided to satisfy them at once. He had seven of Saul's sons captured and handed over to the Gibeonites, who "hanged them on the mountainside, before Yahweh."

But when David heard that Rizpah, Saul's concubine and mother of two of these sons, had covered the corpses of the seven hanged men, so that the vultures and beasts of the night shouldn't tear them to shreds, he ordered that their bones be reunited with those of their father, Saul, and brother Jonathan. And he himself took all their remains to the land of Benjamin and laid them in the tomb of Saul's father, Kish, who had once sent off his son in search of some missing she-asses.

III

DAVID

Samuel was still grieving as he thought of Saul, who had now lost his kingliness. But Yahweh spurred him to action. He told him to fill his horn with anointing oil and go to Bethlehem, to Jesse's house. "I've chosen a king from among his sons," Yahweh added.

Samuel took pains to get it right. One by one, he examined the seven sons of Jesse who turned out for him. But each time he knew this wasn't *the one*. Aren't there any others? Samuel asked. There was the youngest, who was out tending the smaller flocks. His name was David and "he had red hair, fine eyes, and good looks." At once Yahweh told Samuel, "It's him, get up and anoint him." Once again, election happened in a flash, with no reasons given. "The spirit of Yahweh descended on David from that day on and evermore." Until that moment, David had had no idea what the "spirit of Yahweh" was.

Saul felt the "evil spirit" darkening his mind. His only wish was to hear a certain kind of music. As soon as he saw David before him, this "fined-eyed" red-haired shepherd boy with his lyre, "he loved him dearly," and appointed him as his armor-bearer. But sometimes David would slip from his mind entirely. Either he was too close or he didn't exist at all. One day David turned up with "the head of the Philistine" called Goliath in his hand, and Saul said: "Boy, whose son are you?" It was as though he were seeing him for the first time.

Abigail was shrewd and beautiful: "*extremely cautious and beguiling*," says the Vulgate, and married to Nabal, a grim, hard man who stubbornly turned his back on the world beyond his pastures and his three thousand sheep and one thousand goats. From time to time David thought back on his times as a shepherd. They told him Nabal was organizing a feast for the sheep shearing. David sent ahead ten young men expecting them to be welcomed as guests. They reminded Nabal that his shepherds had had dealings with other shepherds, including David, their master, and that they had had no reason to complain. It was a ploy to renew an understanding *between shepherds*, in a friendly but subtly threatening way. Nabal looked askance at the young men. Who is this David? he asked. And muttered, "There are so many slaves running away from their masters these days." Why should he share his bread and meat with them? He said "I" and "my" eight times. Insulted and mistreated, the ten youngsters turned their backs on Nabal and went back to David.

A servant told Abigail what had been said and she realized at once that a reckless massacre was in the offing. She and her servants put together "two hundred loaves, two goatskins of wine, five sheep already butchered, five measures of toasted grain, a hundred raisin cakes, and two hundred fig cakes, and loaded them onto some asses. Then she said to her servants: You go ahead, I'll follow." She didn't say a word to Nabal. David, meantime, was already coming for Nabal with his men. He said, "May God strike me down if by tomorrow morning, of all this man's possessions, I leave so much as one man pissing against a wall!"

There was a mountain between David and Abigail. The two columns were headed straight for each other, without knowing it: David's warriors and Abigail's asses with their rich food smells. Suddenly David appeared to Abigail. And Abigail "quickly fell from her ass onto her face and bowed low to David." She spoke at once, at David's feet, saying it was all her own and her foolish husband's fault (both in name and in fact, she said, because Nabal means "foolish"). With the same immediacy that Abigail had fallen from her ass, David dropped his plan. Abigail had spoken blessed words, he said. Now she could go home in peace. And he added a remark that hardly seemed necessary: "I have honored your face," *honoravi faciem tuam.*

Abigail went home and explained what had happened. As Nabal listened, "his heart died and turned to stone." Ten days later he was dead for real. When he got the news, "David sent a messenger to tell Abigail he would take her for his wife." When she heard, Abigail "bowed with her nose to the ground." Then she mounted an ass and set off, followed by five maids and preceded by David's messengers. "She became David's wife. David had also taken Jezreel's Ahinoam. So they both became his wives. At this point Saul had given his daughter, Michal, David's first wife, to Palti, Laish's son, from Gallim."

Time and again David found he had struck people's souls the same way he struck Goliath with his sling: on the forehead. First and foremost Saul, when David, still a young shepherd boy, played his lyre and Saul, tormented by the evil spirit, "felt cheered and was better: the evil spirit left him." But the same thing happened with Saul's son, Jonathan, who "bound himself to David's soul and loved him as himself." Then it happened that "Michal, Saul's daughter, loved David," something her father in the end accepted, even though David still felt "poor and despised."

David possessed a special power: he could make you fall off your saddle, suddenly and fatally in love. This was never clearer than when the shrewd and extremely cautious Abigail saw David and fell off her ass, surrounded by other asses, laden with carefully chosen foods. The feeling between them was immediate. David let her know when he took his leave with the words: "I have honored your face."

Kingly sovereignty came to Israel as a murky necessity brought on by the times. On its first appearance, in Saul and David, there was something shady, feverish, and obscure about it. Whatever the two men did seemed to produce fatal consequences. Often enough they were just trying to obey Yahweh's orders. The moment of maximum friction came with the census. Yahweh ordered David in peremptory fashion: "Go and count Israel and Judah!" But why did Yahweh want a census? "Once again Yahweh's wrath was kindled against Israel and he roused David against them." So the census was a grim calamity that Yahweh was using to smite the Jews.

A way of *obliging them to be guilty*. David obeyed at once, even though Joab, his army commander, warned him that there was something wicked about the project. For two reasons. To count people means identifying them for the forces of evil, singling them out as targets. An invitation to kill. Then because no count is ever complete, and whatever escapes it becomes a danger. As one day a child born in the very place where David grew up would escape a census and with it the regime of the time. But David could hardly have seen so far into the future. He just wanted to obey Yahweh. Nine months and twenty days later, when the census was done and the (incorrect) figures were handed to him, David realized the whole project had been an abomination. He tried to get Yahweh to forgive him for having obeyed his order. But he knew it was no good.

The very next day the seer Gad appeared to bring him the word of Yahweh. One of three things must happen. David could choose which. Seven years of famine, three months of defeats at the hands of his enemies, or three days of the plague. David replied at once that it was better to be killed by the hand of Yahweh than by the hand of men. He chose the plague. Seventy thousand perished.

It was then that David saw an Angel come down from heaven brandishing a sword that he thrust into four of David's sons. "Now seven of my sons are dead," David thought. Meanwhile the Angel was striking down Gad as well, and the elders who were standing beside him. But it's always a detail that really delivers the horror. The Angel wanted to clean his bloody sword on David's robe. Then David felt a shiver in his bones that never ceased unto his dying day.

To undertake a census was one of the worst crimes you could commit. No one knew why. But the revulsion was general. And who had given David the idea? In the second book of Samuel it is Yahweh himself, in the first book of the Chronicles it is Satan: "Satan rose up against Israel and incited David to count Israel." The premise in both cases is "Yahweh's anger," but we are not told the cause of that anger. David was the guilty man, but a man wound up by a powerful agent and aware he was committing a crime. When Joab came back with the results of the census, David immediately begged to be forgiven by Yahweh, who had instigated him. "I have sinned greatly in what I did . . . I've behaved like a complete fool." David wouldn't say anything of the like when he arranged for Uriah the Hittite to be killed, or when he let Saul's seven sons be hanged.

The crime of the census is metaphysical. You are presuming you can know something that must not be known: the measure of life. Just as one day people would be forbidden from planting a field right to the edge, so they were not allowed to know the exact number of the living. At stake was a principle so basic it could not be mentioned. But the consequences were in proportion to its importance.

The ultimate premise of the census is made crystal clear in Exodus: every person counted shall pay a half shekel as a "ransom," *kofer*, for himself: "Anyone counted in the census, aged twenty or over, shall pay Yahweh's levy. The rich man shall not pay more, the poor man shall not pay less than a half shekel as Yahweh's levy, to purchase propitiation for his person." It was a way of reasserting that every life is a debt that needs to be redeemed. And always with the same amount, because it is the life *itself* that has to be redeemed— which has nothing to do with riches or poverty. That was why the census frightened people. Not everyone had the wherewithal to redeem themselves. What if they couldn't pay? The debt could be transformed into a punishment. The census was a cruel reminder that your life was governed by reins held in the hands of an Other, who could leave them loose, for a while, then pull them tight—into a noose.

After Saul's death, David reigned over the house of Judah in Hebron "for seven years and six months." During that time he had six children from six different women. Abigail was the mother of the second son, Khilab. But David hadn't forgotten his first wife,

Michal. To persuade Saul to let him have her he had had to give the king two hundred Philistine foreskins, something he remembered in gory detail. Then one day Saul had taken Michal away, just as one day he had given her to him. And Michal is the only woman in the Bible of whom it is said that she loved a man: "Michal, Saul's daughter, loved David." When the fearsome warrior Abner proposed an alliance with David so that together they might chase Saul's children out of the kingdom of Israel, David said, "Fine, but don't show up without Michal." Who, meantime, had married Paltiel. "Her husband left with her, and went weeping after her as far as Bahurim. Abner told him: 'Go now, go back,' and he went." When David conquered Jerusalem, he added a number of concubines to his women and had another eleven children, one of whom was Solomon.

One nagging thought haunted David all his life. He knew he had been sought out and chosen when he was still a boy tending sheep. And he knew it was his family that would one day produce the Messiah. He knew that Yahweh would protect him to the end, like a shield. Yet he felt Yahweh would never count him among the patriarchs and would never speak his name beside the names of Abraham, Isaac, and Jacob. And David knew that that was as it should be. There was an abyss between those forebears and himself. For one thing, life was not so long, not so dense. David felt it in his bones. He died at seventy, like any ordinary man in these new times. Exhausted. Throughout the forty years of his reign, he had yearned more than anything else to build the Temple in Jerusalem. But Yahweh said no. You can prepare for its building, he had said. You can have tree trunks brought from Lebanon. But it won't be you who builds the Temple, you wouldn't be able to finish the job. Solomon will do it. The question, as ever, was time. And something else too, perhaps. Which was even more irksome, since in the end it would take Solomon only seven years to build the temple.

One day David plucked up courage and asked Yahweh why he was treating him like this. He wanted to know the real difference between himself and the patriarchs. Yahweh said. "I put the patriarchs to the test. You haven't been put to the test. Your test will be a woman." At that time David had still to meet Bathsheba.

When David and Yahweh talked, the exchanges could be terse and fast, above all over military decisions. When the Philistines marshaled their forces in the Valley of Rephaim before Jerusalem, David asked, "Shall I attack the Philistines? Will you deliver them into my hands?" And Yahweh said, "Attack, because I will definitely put the Philistines in your hands." So it was, but soon the stubborn Philistines were advancing once again. Then Yahweh behaved like a tactician and gave David precise instructions on how to beat them: hide behind the balsam trees and launch a surprise attack. Once again, in the end, the Philistines were beaten.

One day, sitting on the ground in the tent of the Ark, David addressed a prayer to Yahweh, a long monologue. It sounded like he was trying to convince himself more than anyone else: Yahweh's favor, he had begun to realize, did not just have to do with a brief moment of time, it stretched out into the future, so that "the house of David will be stable before you." But for how long? That day David found the courage to say, "With your blessing the house of your servant will be blessed forever." *Forever* was the word that hitherto, in those troubled years, you couldn't even think.

So the idea of the Messiah began to take shape in David's mind. And he sensed that Yahweh's favor might go beyond offering protection from a multitude of hostile neighbors, might open a window beyond the brushwood and undergrowth onto something dazzling and vast, whose end one could not see.

It was one of the first days of spring and David was napping on the roof after lunch. Then he got up and began to look around. He heard water splashing, but couldn't work out where. He leaned out and saw "a woman taking a bath and the woman was very beau-tiful to look at." He asked, "Isn't that Bathsheba, Eliam's daughter, wife of Uriah the Hittite?" Right, they said. So David sent his mes-sengers to fetch her. Bathsheba came at once, lay with David, and went home. Shortly afterward, she let David know she was pregnant.

David immediately thought of her husband, Uriah, presently returning from the war. He wanted Uriah to lie with Bathsheba as soon as possible and hence suppose the child was his. But Uriah played humble, he said his men were camped out in open country and he wanted to be near them: "Should I come home to eat, drink, and sleep with my wife while they're out there?" It just wasn't him. David was flustered. Again he invited Uriah to come to eat and drink with him. And he apologized, because of course—he kept repeating—Uriah must be eager to see Bathsheba again. But Uriah didn't want to go home. He slept the night with David's servants.

The following morning David thought up another plan. He gave Uriah a sealed letter and told him to take it to his commander, Joab. Who read these words: "Put Uriah in the front line, where the fighting is fiercest, then withdraw your men behind him so he is struck down and dies." Joab carried out the order and Uriah was killed. When he was given the news, David pretended to be furi-ous and sent a message of consolation to Joab. Bathsheba mourned the death of Uriah for seven days. "When the period of mourning was over, David sent for her and welcomed her into his home. She became his wife and bore him a son, but what David had done was displeasing to Yahweh."

In the genealogy of the Messiah, who was to be a descendant of David's, Matthew mentions only three women in forty-two gen-erations: Tamar, Ruth, and Rahab. A woman who disguised her-self as a prostitute, a Moabite slave, and a prostitute who helped two spies. Matthew goes on to refer to another woman, but doesn't name her: Bathsheba, Solomon's mother. The only thing he says of her is "she was Uriah's." The Moabites, offspring of Lot's incest, were relatives and enemies. Rahab was from Canaan, the first woman that two sons of Israel, on a spying mission, would meet beyond the Jordan, in Jericho. She was the mother of Boaz, who then lay with Ruth and begat Obed, who begat Jesse, father of David. All three of the women Matthew names had lived generations before David. After them came only the unnamed Bathsheba. It was as if, on the female side of his ancestry, the Messiah required the highest possible concentration of the adventurous, the exotic, the erotic, and the clandestine.

Years later, when Israel was sinking into corruption, Yahweh more than once recalled David in these terms: "He served me with all his heart, doing nothing that was not just to my eyes." This in stark contrast to an unworthy present. Young people could thus imagine the recent past of David's time as a rule of justice governed by a resolute, unbending king. Nothing could have been further from the truth. His whole life, David was racked by doubts. He seemed condemned to love people who wished him dead. First King Saul, then his own son Absalom. Or people who ended up despising him, like Michal, Saul's daughter. Or conversely he would find himself being saved by someone he loathed, like Joab.

But behind the massacres, the humiliations, and the betrayals, David was well aware that one episode stood out, etched deeper into the memory, with a sharper, brighter light than any other. Yahweh himself was obliged to mention it when once again he chose to recall that "David had done what is just in the eyes of Yahweh and never did anything but what he was ordered to all the days of his life." Really "all the days"? At that point Yahweh felt he had to add: "Except in the matter of Uriah the Hittite."

But Yahweh hadn't talked about this to David. Time passed. One day the prophet Nathan came to visit his king. He spoke of this and that. Then, for no apparent reason, he began to tell a story.

There was a rich man, he said, and there was a poor man who had just one little lamb. He had bought it and "he reared it and fed it together with his children; it ate the same bread and drank from the same bowl and was like a daughter to him." A traveler came along, a guest of the rich man, who had no desire to reduce the number of his own flocks. So he took the poor man's sheep and fed it to his guest. David reacted to the story with his usual impetuosity. Such a man, he said, deserved death. "Then Nathan said to David: 'That man is you.'" The razor edge of those four words together with the story that came before looked ahead to other stories that in times far in the future Jesus would tell—stories people called *parables*.

David realized he would be condemned. Calamities of many kinds were about to fall upon him. He heard Yahweh's voice: "I will take your women from under your eyes and give them to your neighbor, who will lie with your women under the gaze of this sun." But Yahweh did not explain that that "neighbor" would be one of David's sons: the fabulously handsome Absalom, with the wild hair.

There was more. Soon after he was born, David and Bathsheba's son fell ill. David fasted and slept on the ground, hoping these privations would help the child. But after seven days the baby died. "David noticed his servants were whispering among themselves and understood his son had died."

Those in the household who expected David to be even more desperate were wrong. David perfumed himself, bowed to the ground in the House of Yahweh, and asked to be served lunch. He seemed his old self, glowing with power and good looks. His servants couldn't understand. David said his weeping and fasting had been an attempt to save his child. But why fast now? "Do you think I could bring him back? It is I who am going toward him, he will not come back to me." This was a writer speaking. "Then David consoled his wife Bathsheba and went to her and lay with her and she bore a child and called him Solomon and Yahweh loved him." Through Nathan, Yahweh let David know as much, after which David gave Solomon another name as well: Jedidiah, "beloved of Yahweh."

Shortly before his death, David composed a song that ended with a list of "David's brave men" (and later became Psalm 18). Many of the entries are followed by detailed descriptions of the men's most glorious exploits. Others, at the end, are simply named. There were thirty-seven in all. The last on the list was Uriah the Hittite, Bathsheba's husband, whom David himself had ordered to be killed.

Throughout Saul's and David's reigns, war was constant, war without and war within. As if a ceaseless tempest were blowing around the lives of the first two men to have received the royal anointment. Both were "men of blood," burdened with guilt, though this hardly explained the whirlwind that followed them constantly about. For forty years David had wanted to build a temple, because his people had never had one, they were still sacrificing "on the heights." But he wasn't allowed. Yahweh had told him: he would only be able to prepare for the building. Every time he planned to start the work proper, something violent would distract him. By virtue of the same despotic will, no sooner had Solomon become king than everything calmed down. The hostile peoples who had harried and encircled them melted away. To the point that Solomon had the temerity to marry the Egyptian pharaoh's daughter, as if an alliance with their ancient oppressor were something obvious, which hardly deserved mention. And Solomon at last set about building the Temple, made from cedarwood and whole, uncut stones. "In the House, while it was being built, there was no sound of hammers or shears or other iron tools."

David was to *prepare* the Temple for Yahweh, but not to build it, as Moses was to point toward the Promised Land, but not to set foot in it. For years David piled up building materials in Jerusalem: big stones, "nails for the doors of the gates and the hinges,"

cedarwood, and metal, mainly bronze, "in quantities beyond measure." David told everyone, "My son Solomon is a delicate boy and
the House of Yahweh must be very great . . . so I am preparing
things for him." But David knew full well that this wasn't the reason why he didn't dare start the building. And one day he confessed to Solomon: "My son, I would have loved to build a House in
the name of Yahweh, my God; but Yahweh spoke to me and said:
'You have shed a great deal of blood and fought great wars: you
shall not build a House in my name, because you have shed much
blood on the ground before me.'" David did not point out that he
had shed all that blood in Yahweh's name and on his instructions.
He merely added that Yahweh had announced the birth of the son
he was talking to and said that he would be "a man of reconcilia-
tion." So the son's father couldn't do anything but pile up stones
and nails. And wait. But he didn't hesitate to tell Solomon, and
proudly, how many gold and silver talents he would have at his
disposal. Then David dismissed his "delicate" son.

The Ark was terrifying. Taking it from place to place was always a risky operation. So it was when David decided to move it
from Baalath to Jerusalem. Uzza drove the cart. Around the Ark
was a great clashing of tambourines and sistra. David and "all the
house of Israel" danced along. But all at once the oxen pulling the
cart broke loose and Uzza had to hold up the Ark to stop it falling. This was too much for Yahweh. The Ark must not be touched.
So Yahweh struck Uzza and he fell to the ground and died, beside the Ark. David realized he'd better be more careful. The Ark
stopped in Obed-Edom. But three months later David decided to
make another attempt to have it brought up to Jerusalem. More
dancing, more din. David whirled around, wrapped in a linen
loin cloth. When at last the Ark entered Jerusalem, "Michal, Saul's
daughter, looked out the window and saw King David, twisting
and turning before Yahweh, and in her heart she despised him."
There were holocausts and communion sacrifices. And everyone
was given meat and bread to celebrate. When it was over David

went home. Michal greeted him with her princess's sarcasm. It hardly seemed decent for a king to be dancing in the crowd with no more than cloth around his loins, a cloth that kept slipping "in full view of serving maids and men." David was livid and told her he had bared himself before Yahweh. And Yahweh had chosen him—he reminded her—"in preference to your father." As far as the serving maids were concerned, David had no trouble coming down to their level. On the contrary, he would have more children with them. And none with Michal, who "had no more children unto the day of her death."

In Jerusalem, David had a house made of cedarwood, as Yahweh had promised: "I will build you a house." David was puzzled: the king had a house, but not the king's god, because the Ark was still sheltered in a tent. But this was not to worry him. Yahweh quickly cleared the matter up, appearing at night to the prophet Nathan: "The fact is I haven't lived in a house since the day I brought the children of Israel out of Egypt; I went about in a tent, a shelter." And Yahweh had never complained. Whether in a tent or a house of cedarwood, it hardly mattered. What counted was timing. In David's reign the time had not yet come for Yahweh to have a house. But it was approaching. The task would fall to one of David's sons. Yahweh didn't say which, but that was the first time that he alluded to Solomon.

One day the Jebusites, who lived in Jerusalem and were descendants of the children of Heth, claimed that their ancestors had given Abraham the Cave of Machpelah only on condition that their descendants would never be forced to leave Jerusalem.

David must have remembered this when he attacked Jerusalem. Capturing the city in daring and miraculous fashion was not enough for him. He chose to do what Abraham once did. He offered money for this other piece of land, the entire city: six hundred shekels. Every tribe of Israel paid its part. And the Jebusites left David a receipt as proof of sale.

Jerusalem is far from being the native home of the Jews. Jerusalem is the city the Jews bought from the Jebusites. But as with the Cave of Machpelah, where Sarah was buried, the previous owners asked that they never be forced to leave Jerusalem. So Jerusalem was always going to be a mixed society where past and present owners lived together.

David found the forty years of his reign harrowing and glorious. The torment was greater than the glory. Fighting the Philistines meant fighting them over and over again. No respite, ever. Each victory was a breathing space between one war and the next. His sons were many and much-loved. And all potential conspirators against their father. The most dangerous was the most handsome: Absalom. David sensed his people were more and more attracted to Absalom, less and less to himself. Something very similar had happened to Saul, when he persecuted David, in vain. But David didn't persecute Absalom. Instead he chose the ultimate humiliation: he left Jerusalem of his own free will, "barefoot and with veiled head," his last loyal followers beside him. The son he had chosen to succeed him, Solomon, was still too young and had replaced another son who had died a baby because Yahweh's wrath had come down upon him. That son, whose name we don't know and whom David had not initially wanted to recognize, was connected to the most despicable thing he had ever done, when he had given Uriah the Hittite a sealed letter containing instructions that Uriah himself was to be killed. Uriah was a respectful, courageous soldier who would never have suspected the motive behind that letter, would never have broken the seal to read it, never have attributed to his master, David, the one thought that in fact obsessed him: to take Uriah's wife, Bathsheba, from him. Who would then be the mother of Solomon, as though to cancel out the dead son and everything that had happened before his birth. All this formed the premise to the opening of the first book of Kings, one of the strongest openings that have ever been written: "King David was old, advanced in years. They covered him with clothes, but he could not get warm."

Absalom was riding on a mule, alone. His thick, bushy hair caught in the branches of a majestic oak. The mule kept going. Absalom couldn't free himself. He was left dangling. A group of enemies arrived. They filled him with spears and arrows, like a dummy used for target practice.

When news of Absalom's death reached David, those around the king thought he would be relieved and feel safer. It was the end of a bloody war of uncertain outcome. But David wept. He walked back and forth saying, "Absalom, my son, my son, Absalom, why didn't I die in your place. Absalom, my son, my son!" He gazed with hatred on those around him. One by one those who had fought for David and saved his life slipped away, as if ashamed. Only Joab, the mighty soldier, had the courage to face him and say, "Now I know that if Absalom were still alive and we were all dead, it would be a good day for you!"

Having returned to Jerusalem, David made a decision with regard to the ten concubines he had left behind to look after the house, women Absalom had appropriated "in plain view of all Israel." David moved the ten concubines to a place on the edge of town. He didn't want to see them anymore. "He provided for them, but no longer went to them and they were segregated there until their deaths, living the lives of widows."

After Saul's death and the death of Saul's seven sons whom he had consigned to the Gibeonites to be hanged; after the death of his own son, Absalom, who had tried to take his throne; after the near constant wars with the Philistines, stretching right back to the time of Samuel, also dead now, the man who had sought him out when he was no more than a redheaded shepherd boy tending a few sheep near Bethlehem and chosen him and anointed him king, setting him up for a glorious destiny; after these wars so like one another that David would get them mixed up, the events of a victorious cam-paign being easily muddled with others that had ended in defeat: only then, at last, "David felt tired." On one occasion they had saved him just as Ishbi-Benob was about to split his chest with a heavy spear. On another, quite suddenly, "David had a wish and said, 'Who will bring me water to drink from the well near the gate of Bethle-hem?'" Nothing could have been more dangerous, since Bethlehem had been occupied by the Philistine advance guard. Fight one's way through enemies to fetch a little water? A crazy, impossible idea. But three "brave men" who were with David, and whose names have not come down to us, didn't think twice. They cut a passage through the Philistine lines, drew the water from the well, and brought it to David. But David didn't want to drink it. He said it would be like drinking the blood of his three brave men. He got to his feet and poured it on the ground, as a libation for Yahweh. It was the most sublime and mysterious moment of his long, cruel, tormented reign. It was also the moment that revealed and redoubled in the now aging king, a burning thirst for the water of the well near the gate of Bethlehem where in times past he had tended his sheep. One day a descendant of his, born in Bethlehem, would speak of "living water." It was the water of David.

When David called together all the tribes of Israel to make a formal announcement that he would not be building the Temple of Yahweh because he had shed too much blood and hence the task would pass to his son Solomon, he spoke a few words to his son that the young man would remember when he asked Yahweh to grant him "a heart that understands." The words Solomon used that day were not so different from those his father had spoken to him: "As for you, Solomon, my son, know God your father and serve him with a perfect heart and eager soul, because Yahweh searches all hearts and finds out every kind of thinking."

Solomon, son of David and Bathsheba, possessed a supreme wisdom and his father had been anointed king by Samuel. But the last words this father said to his son were neither mild nor generous. David ordered Solomon to kill Shimei, whom he himself had spared years ago. Despite which, the awful curse that Shimei had pronounced when David left Jerusalem in the hands of his son Absalom, the son who was coming to depose him, was still ringing in his ears. Shimei had the look of a "dead dog," but his voice was all the more piercing for it, and his presence all the more obsessive. He moved across the mountainside, in the same direction as David and his men, but at a distance, as if in mocking counterpoint. "He went on, parallel with him, cursing him, throwing stones, throwing dust." That dust, that countless dust, had drifted out across David's memory and still swirled there from time to time. Even now, at death's door. And while it was true, David thought, that one day he had told Shimei, "I will not slay you with my sword!"—and once his word was given it could not be taken back—nevertheless nothing prevented Solomon from slaying him with his sword. With a little inventiveness, revenge can strike even after pardon has been granted. So that "intolerable curse" would not be left unpunished. And David would be able to go "the way of all the earth" with a quieter mind. Shimei was the last person David spoke of before dying. He told his son, "You shall bring his gray hair down in blood to Sheol." Then David died. They buried him in the city, which was now called the "City of David."

Toward the end of his life, David was always cold, even when everyone said the air was scorching hot. His servants covered him with heavy blankets, but they didn't warm him. So they searched for a young girl to look after him. She would need to be very beautiful, and they searched all over the kingdom for her. "She shall sleep on your breast and my lord will be warmed," the servants would tell him. They chose Abishag the Shunamite. "She became the king's helpmate, always at his service, but the king did not know her."

David had many sons and there was always one planning,

like Absalom, to take his father's throne. The most stubborn and flagrant was Adonijah, son of Haggith. Handsome as Absalom, he shared his traits and followed his footsteps. The sage, Nathan, warned Bathsheba that Adonijah was plotting with Joab and others. The giveaway was always a sacrifice. And right then Adonijah was eating and drinking with his accomplices, after sacrificing "bulls, fat calves, and sheep in great quantities." Nathan hadn't been invited—nor Bathsheba with her son Solomon. But wasn't it Solomon whom David had chosen as heir to his throne?

Bathsheba went to David and found him alone with the Shunamite. Then, as if by pure chance, Nathan arrived too. When they had told him what was going on, David ordered them to put Solomon on his mule. He must go down to Gihon, where "Zadok the priest and Nathan the prophet would anoint him king over Israel." It was a return to the origins. Neither people nor soldiers need be present. It was like that day, in Zuf, in the early morning and in complete solitude, when Samuel had anointed King Saul. David added, "Then come back here with him and he will go to sit on my throne."

David's "last words" were a song that ended with a description of something he hadn't been: a just king. The just king must be "like the morning light when the sun rises, / a cloudless morning, / and makes the grass shine on the earth after the rain."

In the last years of his life, David preferred studying to fighting. Yahweh had told him he would die on the Sabbath. Every Sabbath, David would immerse himself entirely in the Torah, because he knew that the Angel of Death cannot strike a person studying the Torah. His attention was keen, fluid, constant. From the garden came a sound. David raised his head and his eyes were flooded with a dappled glow. The garden was in full bloom. What was that sound? Some kind of call? Still deep in thought, David got up from the table and walked slowly to the window. He gazed ahead as he went down the few stairs that separated him from the garden. His foot slipped and he fell, banging the back of his head on a stone. His lifeless body lay there in the sunshine, because it was the Sabbath and no one could touch him. But soon four eagles glided around him to shade him with their wings, as if beneath a black tent.

IV

SOLOMON

Solomon was the first king of Israel who was able to look at the world and study it. He was not beset by nagging concerns and did not have to fight one war after another. He had been anointed king at twelve, shortly before the death of David, his father. And soon a general calm had spread out around him, something that seemed to depend more on nature than on men. Of course certain debts contracted in King David's years needed to be settled first. So Solomon had Adonijah killed, and Joab, and Shimei. The brother, the warrior, and the man who cast the curse. Two to obey his father, David, one with sudden and peremptory decisiveness. All were struck down by the hand of his chancellor, Benaiah. Each time, the spilled blood was kept in a triangle of king, chancellor, and appointed victim. And there it had to stay. Outside that triangle, Solomon didn't want any clutter. Only thus, he explained to Benaiah before dispatching him to kill Joab, "would Yahweh grant peace to David, his descendants, his house, and his throne, forever." And the chronicler concludes, "So royal power grew stronger in Solomon's hands."

Solomon killed his half brother Adonijah, Haggith's son, because of the Shunamite. A grown woman now, and beautiful at that, she knew David's bedroom better than anyone, "but the king did not know her." Bathsheba couldn't stand her. She had been David's wife, concubine, and daughter without being any of the three. So Bathsheba was not unhappy when Adonijah asked her to persuade Solomon to let him have "Abishag the Shunamite as his wife." It would be good to be rid of her at last.

Bathsheba came to Solomon, sat on her queen mother's throne, and said, "I have a little request for you." A few words were enough: "That Abishag the Shunamite be given to your brother Adonijah." But was it really a "little request"? Solomon's response came back in a flash: "You may as well ask me to give him the throne, since he's my older brother and already has Abiathar and Joab, son of Zeruiah, on his side." Solomon remembered all too well when he had been twelve years old and his father had sent him away from Jerusalem, on a mule, to have him anointed king, while in the cities his older brother Adonijah was already making communion sacrifices to celebrate his seemingly legitimate rise to power. He was the elder son, and many felt that David no longer had the energy to make decisions.

Later Adonijah had resigned himself and accepted Solomon's anointment. But now, if he was going to ask for the Shunamite . . . Abishag was sovereignty itself in the eyes of Solomon, who instinctively understood feminine power. He owed his birth to it. To deprive him of the Shunamite was to deprive him of his kingship. It was the worst possible offense. He said, "Adonijah will be killed this very day." But kings don't kill. They have someone do the job for them. So Solomon "put the matter in the hands of Benaiah, son of Jehoiada, who struck him, and he died."

"Peace," *shalom*, was part of Solomon's name. His father, David, on the other hand, had known nothing but war. Father and son were opposites in everything. David had always been tormented by bad dreams. It was a strange expression spoken to him in a dream that brought Solomon all his luck. He was still a boy who "doesn't know how to come and go" when he dreamed that Yahweh said, "Ask me what I must give you." Solomon answered listing all the reasons he had to be thankful to Yahweh. And now, he said, he was "in the midst of your people, that you chose, a numerous people that can't be numbered or counted, it's so numerous." A shrewd observation, with the implication that Solomon would never repeat his father's great mistake, the census. But now he must make the wish that Yahweh would grant. And Solomon chose something no one had ever asked for before. He said, "Give your servant a heart that understands." Who had ever heard of such a wish? Everyone wished for long life, riches, revenge. There was nothing more wearisomely predictable than human wishes. No one had ever dared to wish for something so strange as to understand— and, more mysterious still, something as indeterminate and impersonal as "a heart that understands." The Seventy translated *kardían akoúein* as the capacity to "listen to the heart." Neither David nor Saul would ever have asked for anything like this. Then Yahweh made a move that was supremely divine: he *gave in surplus*. And answered Solomon thus: "Even that which you have not asked, I shall give you: both riches and glory." Without that *surplus*, on one side and the other, earth and sky, asymmetrical and indomitable, there could be no regular or effective traffic with the invisible.

Defining Solomon's "intelligence and wisdom," the first book of Kings says that his "heart was vast as the sand on the seashore." And the Seventy speak of a *chýma kardías*, a "liquid mass of the heart." It was a *latitudo cordis*, as the Vulgate rather wonderfully put it, that included both the discrete and the continuous. The liquid mass and the grains of sand. It was exactly what the Jews had lacked in so many dramatic situations. But now they could rival the Orientals, and above all the Egyptians. Even outdo them. "Solomon's wisdom was greater than that of all the children of the Orient and all the wisdom of the Egyptians." And hadn't Moses been an Egyptian? Like the rest of the world, Israel had always been in awe of the wisdom of the Egyptians, the *prisca Aegyptiorum sapientia* that Giordano Bruno would one day lay claim to. After all, when Israel had its first king, Egypt was already on its twenty-first dynasty.

But from this point Israel would bow to an even greater wisdom. Greater, too, than that of its own wise men in the past. Who had they been? The first book of Kings mentions Ethan, Heman, Calcol, and Dara. The first two supposedly composed two Psalms, but not much else is known of them. Solomon, on the other hand, wrote a great deal—or rather "spoke": he spoke words that would one day be *read*. His father had composed a few songs, but Solomon "spoke three thousand proverbs and one thousand, five hundred songs." It wasn't all. Solomon had also spoken—and this was quite unprecedented—"of the trees, from the cedar of Lebanon to the hyssop that grows on the walls." No one before him had tried to turn their attention *to trees*. And animals: "quadrupeds, birds, reptiles, and fish." Perhaps David would have liked to try something similar, as he would have liked to have built a proper house for the Ark, but hadn't been able to "because of the wars with those who were all around him." Thus Solomon justified his father to Hiram, king of Tyre, who had been David's friend. There was another reason for telling him that: Hiram's son was a great architect. Solomon meant to give him the task of building the Temple. He added: "And now order the felling of many cedars of Lebanon." The work would be well paid, "because we don't have men who can fell trees the way the Sidonians do."

Jerusalem was looking more and more like a warehouse: big squared stones, stacks of beams from Lebanon, heaps of metal brackets, and, so they said, silver and gold, were "common as stones," in the city. Everyone knew why. David was constantly reminding people that his son Solomon was "a delicate boy" and that he, David, was doing the groundwork for him as thoroughly as possible. Not only did he order all the materials for the Temple, he also prepared the project down to the last detail. Although Solomon would be celebrated for centuries as an outstanding architect, right down to the times of Villalpando and the Masons, he didn't design the Temple, only executed his father's design. His privilege was to be on the right side of the barrier of blood that had stopped his father, David.

No sooner was all ready than Solomon chose to add something of his own, something no one else could bring to the project. He wrote right away to Hiram, king of Tyre: "Send me a man skilled in working gold, silver, bronze, and iron, purple, crimson, and indigo, and who knows how to make engravings. He will work alongside the experts I have with me in Judah and Jerusalem, the men my father, David, had trained." Clearly local "experts" weren't expert enough. An artificer's hand was required. This early move already suggested what Solomon's great gift to his people would be: the *aesthetic*, something sovereign, but of a kind of sovereignty hitherto unrecognized, even distrusted.

Hiram, king of Tyre, immediately sensed what Solomon was after and wrote that he would send him Huram, "son of a woman who belongs to the daughters of Dan, though his father is from Tyre." Jewish mother and foreign father. Huram, the king went on, "can engrave any engraving and execute any design." Alongside the scribes and the guardians, the singers and the ministers, a new figure would now be at work in the Temple: the artificer. Then the cautious Hiram added, "It's time that my lord sent his servant the grain, barley, oil, and wine he spoke of." The first contract for *a work of intellect* was thus clinched.

In Solomon's Temple Huram was responsible, among other things, for "the two columns, the moldings of the capitals at the top of the two columns, likewise for the two nets covering the moldings at the top of the columns, the four hundred pomegranates for the two nets, that is two rows of pomegranates for each net to cover the two moldings of the capitals at the top of the columns, the ten stands and the ten bowls on the stands; the one Sea and the twelve oxen beneath it; the cauldrons, the shovels, the forks." The list was finicky and clumsy, because this was new territory. No one had ever listed the things an artificer makes before. One thing is clear though: Huram was allowed to link his name to Yahweh's temple, while those who later worked in so many Gothic cathedrals remain nameless.

When Solomon spoke of trees, it was the first time in the history of the Jews that vegetable nature had been mentioned *for itself*. And it was a distant, foreign nature. Solomon wanted to tackle the cedars of Lebanon right away, with a view to the Temple he was about to build. He drew up a complex agreement with Hiram, who would arrange for the felling and cutting of the trees. They would be sailed down toward the kingdom of Israel on big rafts. Without the cedars it wouldn't have been possible to build the Temple. But they used big stones, too, for the foundations of the House. Whole stones, untouched by "hammers or shears or other iron tools." Inside, the building was all cypress and cedarwood. The walls were sculpted, with "Cherubim, palms and flower garlands within and without." All clad in gold. Over twenty years, the time it took to build the Temple and the king's palace, Hiram supplied Solomon with "as much cedarwood, cypress wood, and gold as he wanted." In return, Solomon offered Hiram twenty towns in Galilee. When Hiram went to visit them "they did not please his eyes." Raising the issue with Solomon, he was sarcastic: "What kind of towns have you given me, my brother?" He called them Kabul, a name that sounded like *ke-bal*, "mere nothings." And Hiram recalled all the gold and cedars he had sent to Solomon. A hundred and twenty gold talents. Four tons. And how many cedars? Solomon called his palace "Forest of Lebanon."

Built by Solomon over seven years, four hundred and eighty years after leaving Egypt, the Temple inside displayed walls of polished cedar sculpted here and there in garlands and colocynths. "Not a single stone was to be seen." The altar, a cube, was clad with gold. Two Cherubim, their spread wings touching the walls, were placed at the center of the "inside of the House." Made from olive wood and clad with gold, these identical Cherubim were about sixteen feet high. On the walls, in bas-relief, were other Cherubim, palm trees, and entwined flowers, while the capitals of the two columns sprouted lilies. Yet more Cherubim, palm trees, and garlands in bas-relief adorned the doors. And Cherubim appeared next to oxen on the supports of a huge basin that was the one Sea. Everywhere surfaces rippled up in images. Far from being forbidden, they were abundant. And just as it was said that Solomon the builder had more knowledge than "all the sons of the Orient and all the wisdom of the Egyptians," so the Temple seemed to gather into itself all the images of the Orient, as if a vast ocean current had washed them up as ornaments, cornices, and rails around that supremely frightening object that occupied the center of the center: the Ark of the Covenant. Anyone daring to get close would have noticed that the Ark contained nothing beyond two bare stone slabs with inscriptions. Moses had put them there, on Sinai.

The job of building the House of Yahweh was never done. David had arranged for every detail, but it wasn't enough. Solomon only got the work underway "in the second month of the fourth year of his reign." There was always something missing. But finally the day came when the Ark was carried "to its place in the sanctuary of the House, the Holy of Holies, beneath the wings of the Cherubim." The long poles so often used to move it stuck out in front of the sanctuary like a woman's breasts, certain Talmudists would one day observe. When the hundred and twenty priests came out of the Holy of Holies, "trumpeters and choristers united in a single voice to praise and glorify Yahweh" and then "the House was filled with the cloud of the Glory of Yahweh and the priests could not go on with their ministry because of the cloud, for the Glory of Yahweh had filled the House of God." All rules and duties faded in the presence of that cloud. It recalled the continuous, the primordial indistinct, without which the marks inscribed on the stone slabs, the only presences within the Ark, could never have unleashed their power.

Solomon was the first to find his voice: "Yahweh has said he resides in a cloud and I have built a House as your dwelling, a place where you can live, forever." He could hardly have been clearer: god is in the cloud, but men can build, give shape to, a place where that cloud can reside, or a tiny part of it, in the same way that they articulate words to celebrate he who is within the cloud. Everything takes place between cloud and House—and everything that happens is a consequence of that, which is to say, history.

Having uttered these few words, Solomon made a gesture: "he reached out his hands." In the middle of the space outside the temple he kneeled in front of everyone. "And he reached out his hands toward the heavens." Then Solomon said there was just one question to be asked: "Will God, in truth, dwell upon the earth with man?" Can it be true that the uncontainable Glory will agree to dwell in the cramped cell that the Temple reserves for it? There is no answer, Solomon said, but prayer, in the hope that Yahweh may hear "the cry and the prayer your servant raises before you."

"When Solomon had finished praying, fire descended from the heavens, devoured the holocaust and the communion sacrifices, while the Glory of Yahweh filled the House." The second book of the Chronicles states that that day, "King Solomon sacrificed twenty-two thousand oxen and a hundred thousand rams. Thus did king and people consecrate the House of God." The figures are hardly plausible, but there must have been a large number of victims since "the bronze altar that Solomon had made could not contain the holocaust, the oblation, and the fats." What is certain is that the holocausts must have been devoured by the fire of Yahweh. Until that happened the House could not be considered consecrated. A blood sacrifice was necessary—and implicit. Countless animals had to be killed. And most of them completely burned up. They had to *disappear*. If Solomon really was a master of riddles, a reputation that would reach the distant ear of the Queen of Sheba, this was very likely the first—or the last—of the riddles.

In line with the *latitudo cordis*, the "vastness of heart" he had asked for and been granted, Solomon enormously extended Israel's horizons. There was no trace now of that narrow-mindedness whereby every discussion bounced back off the names of the surrounding peoples, for the most part enemies. Even Egypt had seemed far away, except when the Exodus was remembered. But now, having dealt with the unavoidable vendettas, Solomon had married the Pharaoh's daughter, a woman born in the home of all idolatry. And no one seemed to have made any objection. People could breathe the wide-open air again.

Once he had finished building the Temple, Solomon addressed Yahweh and his people, often speaking of "all the peoples of the earth," not an expression his father had ever used. He even spoke of someone that most people had never heard of: "the foreigner who will come from a distant land because of your Name" and will even pray to Yahweh. At this point Solomon boldly asked for something unheard of, and in a voice that might have sounded like it was giving an order: "You will listen in the heavens, which are your dwelling, and will act in everything according to the stranger's invocations, so that all the peoples of the earth might know your Name." It was as if Solomon were daring to tell Yahweh how he should behave with "the foreigner"—and even the "stranger," *allótrios*, as the Seventy translated. Because one must think of "all the peoples of the earth." Yahweh would have to make his Name known among them.

Yahweh was not taken aback by such boldness, which he had preordained. And his response was equally blunt. For a second time he appeared to Solomon in a dream, as he had in Gibeon. He said he had heard his prayer outside the Temple. He reassured Solomon that he would support Israel if it obeyed his laws. But "if you turn away from me," he warned of two calamities. "I will uproot Israel from the surface of the land I have given it": that was the first and most obvious. While the second referred to "all the peoples of the earth," as if Yahweh meant to reply directly to what Solomon had dared suggest. And another terrible prospect opened up: "Israel will become an object of satire and sarcasm among all peoples." Or so it runs in Édouard Dhorme's cautious translation. The Hebrew word is *mashal*, "stories," "similes." But also "wisecracks," "jokes." The chosen people risked becoming the butt of jokes "among all peoples." But Yahweh was as subtle as he was threatening in that dream. The same warning, in almost

the same words, had been pronounced hundreds of years before by Moses, at the time of the Horeb alliance. Moses, too, had
warned: the Jews could become an object of derision "among all
the peoples."

The Queen of Sheba had stepped out in the early morning to
salute the sun. The sky suddenly darkened. A flock of hoopoes
was circling around. One glided along beside her. It had a letter tied to its wing. The queen opened it and started reading. It
came from someone she'd never heard of, a king called Solomon.
And it was an invitation to visit him. Threatening, though. If the
queen refused, Solomon would invade her kingdom. "Demons
will choke you in your beds," he wrote. The queen consulted her
counselors. They'd never heard of Solomon either. But she decided to accept his invitation, sending magnificent gifts in advance. She took six thousand boys and girls with her, all dressed
in purple, all born the same day. And she gave them a letter to
announce her arrival. The journey would take three years, traveling as fast as possible.

When the Queen of Sheba reached Jerusalem from Qitor, the
city of incense, King Solomon already had hundreds of wives
and concubines, not to mention his first wife, who was the Pharaoh's daughter. Every evening, in hundreds of rooms, women
would have meals prepared for him, in case he should visit. And
now, after three years on the road, a queen was about to arrive,
a queen no one knew much about, except that she reigned over
a distant land, and was very beautiful and probably a witch.
Solomon's spies had told him that the foreigner had already
committed a serious faux pas. Solomon had sent his chancellor,
Benaiah, son of Jehoiada, to meet her. Partner of interminable
chess games, Benaiah was so utterly loyal that Solomon had entrusted him with the task of killing his half brother Adonijah,
and indeed two other men. If Solomon wanted someone killed,

the only person for the job was Benaiah. Who was famous for his radiant beauty. As soon as the queen saw him, she had climbed out of her chariot, eyes sparkling, sure that Benaiah must be Solomon. When she realized her mistake, as if to apologize, she turned to the nobles in her entourage and said, "If you haven't seen the lion, you have at least seen his den." That news reached Solomon too. "Quick-thinking lady," thought the king. But he was nettled. He decided he must come up with something that would surprise the queen from the East once and for all. Something so extraordinary that she would never again get Solomon mixed up with someone else.

As soon as they told him her procession was arriving, Solomon moved to a glass palace that he had had built for the occasion. Soon the palace was surrounded by camels laden with spices, gold and jewels, and pearls and parrots from Ophir.

At last the queen's chariot appeared. She got down in silence, a beautiful woman of a beauty hitherto unknown. Dazzled by the shimmering reflections, she thought Solomon's palace must be made of water and that the king sat in the center, motionless on the waves. Then with superb, studied grace, coupled with the candor of a child, the queen lifted her jewel-encrusted dress to reveal a slim, dark, nervous foot. With his encyclopedic eye, Solomon registered a light and charming down of hair. He hid a smile. He thought, "Time to strike." He decided that only a certain rude brusqueness would do for such an occasion. And said, "Your beauty is a woman's beauty, yet you have a down of hair like a man." The Queen of Sheba ignored the remark. She said, "I've heard a lot about your wisdom. Can I ask you some questions and expect the answers?" Solomon nodded. Then to satisfy their spectators the Queen of Sheba and Solomon set about asking and answering a series of tiresome riddles, things they had both known since childhood. While they were speaking, they studied each other. By now they were aware that everything had been decided the moment the Queen of Sheba raised her dress so as not to get it wet and Solomon, already under her spell, had named that barely perceptible down of dark hair on her foot.

It wasn't just to have him solve a few riddles that the Queen of Sheba and her motley caravan had come from afar to visit Solomon, but because she felt drawn by an irresistible attraction to every splendor. She "went in to meet Solomon and told him all that was in her heart," but immediately afterward turned her regal and controlling eye on "the palace he had built, the food served at table, the living quarters of his servants, the manners and clothes of his ministers, the cupbearers, and the holocausts celebrated in the House of Yahweh." Everything that appeared, in whatever shape or form, was the aesthetic. When the Queen of Sheba had studied every detail "it took her breath away." Which is the effect the aesthetic has, indeed must have. If there are no moments when the things that appear before us take our breath away, then the world is lacking something essential, even for he who follows the way of Yahweh.

The Queen of Sheba's arrival in Jerusalem is told twice in the Bible, with almost the same words: in the first book of Kings and in the second book of the Chronicles. Every variation is precious. After the Queen of Sheba had put Solomon to the test, in the first book of Kings she says: "In both wisdom and goodness you exceed the account I had heard of you. Happy are your women and happy these servants who are ever beside you to hear your wise words!" In the second book of the Chronicles, the Queen of Sheba says: "Happy your subjects and happy these servants of yours who are ever beside to hear your wise words." The women, the wives and concubines, have been removed. But the same thing happens in the Vulgate, where the passage from the first book of Kings is translated: *"Beati viri tui, et beati servi tui, qui stant coram te semper et audiunt sapientiam tuam."* The omission of the women—a sensitive matter in the case of Solomon, since it will be the women who lead him astray—begins within the Bible itself and gets its stamp of approval in the Vulgate. By the time we get to Luther, a confirmation is inevitable: "*Glück-lich sind deine Männer und deine Grossen.*" The women have gone, but to compensate, instead of "the servants" here we have "*die Grossen,*" "the dignitaries." As for King James: "Happy are thy men, happy are these thy servants." At least the servants are still there.

The Queen of Sheba arrived in Jerusalem at the head of a long procession of camels laden with "spices, gold in great quantities, and precious stones." She lived as a guest in Solomon's palace, though for how long no one says. Then she left to return to her own kingdom. The whole thing might seem no more than a pro-tracted hallucination. And many stories were indeed made up about that visit. Until one day Jesus said something no one had thought before. He said that at the end of time the "Queen of the South" (which is what he called her) would rise to her feet and judge those Jews who had not understood who Jesus was. *Regina austri surget.* Matthew and Luke use almost the same words: the Queen of Sheba would condemn those "scribes and Pharisees"—meaning the better-educated Jews—who surrounded Jesus and demanded, "We want to see a sign from you." Someone who asks for a sign is someone incapable of recognizing what they should. And failing to recognize is the first of all crimes, the one from which all the others proceed. But why should it be the "Queen of the South" who passes judgment? Matthew and Luke both reply, "Because she came from the ends of the earth to hear the wisdom of Solomon." The long journey was essen-tial. The scribes and Pharisees had never undertaken, nor wished to undertake, anything of the kind. So now that foreign woman would get to her feet and condemn them. None of the figures who appear in the Apocalypse can match her, for majesty and mystery. At last it was clear why that oriental queen, with her remote and singular beauty, had one day, long ago, traveled even unto Jerusalem.

The Song of Songs is attributed to Solomon, but on the flimsiest of premises. Still, even if we go back as far as Abraham and beyond it's hard to see who else the book could be associated with. "Happy are your women," the Queen of Sheba had said, because Solomon had practiced his wisdom partly—some said mostly—on women. Like Krishna and the *gopi*, they shared a complicity no one could profane. It might play out in pasture or palace, without the smallest rift between one place and another. Touch, smell, and voices were the things they talked about. Bodies, nothing but bodies—and the emotions bodies give rise to.

One wonderful thing about the Song of Songs is that, from the opening words, you never know for sure who is speaking. "Your breasts (*mastoí, ubera*) are sweeter than wine," we read in the Seventy and in the Vulgate. And immediately one supposes the Beloved man is talking to his Beloved woman. But there are those who believe these words are spoken by the woman to the man. In which case, in Giovanni Garbini's version, the "breasts" become "tendernesses," and in Guido Ceronetti's, "caresses." Robert Alter gives a generic "loving."

Even the number of voices is hotly disputed: we go from two (the Beloved man and his Beloved woman—or Solomon and the Shunamite) to many, organized in various groups: mistresses of the harem, shepherds of Sulam, the Shunamite's brothers, girls of Jerusalem. In many places it's not clear whether the person speaking is Solomon or the Shunamite. Or where the various groups get involved. The book is a prodigious, enchanted composite that matches the mobility and subtlety of eros. No one knows if the text was actually composed as we now have it, or whether—like the rest of the Bible—it is the product of laborious compilation. Either way, the result is a kind of text that simply didn't exist before this, and that very likely no one could ever have thought up intentionally.

The Song begins and ends in lovemaking ("that he kiss me with the kisses of his mouth / because your tendernesses are sweeter than wine . . . Come in, my beloved, and be like a fawn / or a young stag / on hills of spice"), displaying a boldness not even the Alexandrians, for all their famed audacity, ever matched. And what unfolds in the book "has all the feverish inconsistency of dreams," says Ceronetti, or of eros in action. To describe bodies, one spoke of fruits and perfumes. The "hills of spices," or rather fragrances, were parts of the female body. And the woman "who lies in the garden" reminded Garbini of the Aphrodite *en kepois*, "in gardens," a famous statue, long lost, by Alcamenes, that Pausanias claimed was "one of the great beauties of Athens."

Thanks to the powerful physicality of the Latin language, Jerome's translation remains the most daring, far more so than the secular attempts. You need only take it word for literal word: *Statura tua assimilata est palmae, et ubera tua botris*, "Your stature is like a palm and your breasts like bunches of grapes." *Juncturae femorum / tuorum sicut monilia / quae fabricata sunt manu artificis*, "The joints of your thighs are jewels / fashioned by the hand of an artist." *Ascendam in palmam / et apprehendam fructus ejus*, "I shall climb on the palm / and pick its fruits." *Laeva ejus sub capite meo / et dextera illius amplexabitur me*, "His left hand under my head / and his right will embrace me."

At the moment of maximum intensity of the Song of Songs the Shunamite reappears. So far the lovers have remained nameless—we don't know even how many there are. *Reverte, reverte*, "Come back, come back," says the Vulgate now. And the name Shunamite is another thing we can't be sure of: perhaps it derives from Sulam, a small village in the land allotted to Issachar, in which case she's a country girl; perhaps it is a corruption of Solomon itself, or

Shelomoh; perhaps "peace," *shalom*, or "wholeness" as expressed by the root *š-l-m*, is at the origin of both. In any event, the lover who enters the "hills of fragrances" reminds us how, for Solomon, to lose the Shunamite meant to lose his sovereignty.

The Romans were besieging Jerusalem and the Jewish factions went on slaughtering one another inside the city. Which would soon be captured. The Temple destroyed. Rabbi Johanan ben Zakkai felt there was an urgent need for a place of study, a *yeshiva*, beyond the bloodbath. He slipped out of the city in secret and asked the Romans for permission to set up a school at Iabneh. There were pressing questions and the right answers must be found: once the one and only Temple, which admitted of no lesser or remote temples, was destroyed, how could the people make up for the absence of all those rituals, those ceremonies? "Innumerable questions arose also from the cessation of the temple worship, for which there was no rule or precedent, and about which an authoritative decision was necessary if there was not to be endless perplexity of conscience and confusion of practice."

It was then that the High Court (Beth-Din) met at Iabneh. One could hardly call it the Sanhedrin because it was no longer a national council with political powers. But the arguments continued to rage, above all between the Shammaites and Hillelites. Could Ecclesiastes and the Song of Songs be admitted into the biblical canon? Or not? A vote was held, which the Hillelites won, and the two books were admitted. Many of us would like to know what was said in those discussions, of which no trace remains. And other decisions loomed. The Sirach was not admitted to the canon, and "the passages in the Tosefta, which report this decision name specifically 'the gospel' (*euangélion*) and the books of the sectarians (or heretics), among which, in the context, it is fair to presume that Christian writings are at least included."

Thus the Song of Songs and Ecclesiastes, the two books of the Bible least concerned with religious authority, become the closing seal of a Scripture that has now turned outward, to the indefinite, and the ever vaster territory of the diaspora among the *goyim*.

The Song teems with *hapax*. If a translator were to find equivalents, his text would be full of words that no one had seen before. Including numerous Graecisms and thirty or so Arabisms. Other neologisms refer to the facts and objects of ordinary life.

It's hard to grasp the sense of so many *hapax*. Are they exclusive to the Song simply because a huge quantity of profane texts have been lost forever? Or was the author of the Song an eccentric juggler, who loved twisting old words and bringing in unusual ones? Or could both explanations be true? We will never know, because no other text in the biblical canon has been so determinedly subverted—and in this respect Jewish and Christian exegetists were in perfect agreement, each obeying the same imperative: de-eroticize the Song. Masoretic vocalization came to their aid, allowing scholars to confuse or cancel many words that had to do with the physical or the physiological, especially those referring to the female body. But paradoxically this process of adulteration only made the Song even more astonishing. Compared with Theocritus and certain Greek epigrammists, on whom it feeds and draws its inspiration, the Song boasts a formal boldness that transgresses every classical rule. The word is immersed in a fragrant cloud that contrasts with the sharp lines, univocal semantics, and clarity of mise-en-scène that distinguish the Alexandrians, rather as if Athens and Jerusalem had met in a bedroom.

Within the Bible, the Song of Songs looks like a splinter driven into some chemically alien geological strata. Not a single mark of respect or devotion is shown to superior powers. Even less is there any hint of rejecting anything. It is self-sufficient, sealed off in its own cosmopolitan vocabulary where the words wait to be identified like small exotic birds. We still do not know on what possible grounds the Song could have been allowed into the biblical

canon. If it is true, as the Seventy-two Elders said to Simeon ben
Azai, that the Song "dirties one hands," it should nevertheless be
acknowledged that it does so *enormously*, and in spectacular fashion. Which is why, from Origen on, scholars silenced the text,
allegorizing it. This despite the fact that the Song insinuates that
it can do without *any* further meanings. And certainly without
Israel. "The girl in the Song is not Israel. She is a soul," Simone Weil
insisted. *A* soul, not the soul. And again: "She is a walled garden,
my sister, my betrothed, a closed well, a sealed fountain." An absolute, physical, unique entity, unrelated to and cut loose from everything else. The book speaks in coded episodes and never explains
a thing.

The Song of Songs is drenched in erotic excitement, or rather
it is nothing but that. The eroticism is constant, without distrac-
tion or deviation, from first to last. There is nothing comparable
in the literatures of the West. One has to look to the Orient, to
India for anything similar. At least there we find Jayadeva's *Gīta-
govinda*, Kalida's *Kumārāsambhava*. But in those cases the lovers
are gods—Krishna and Radha, Shiva and Parvati. The lovers in the
Song are nameless, and often one cannot tell who is speaking.

In the last phase of his life, Goethe spoke of the "Orient" in
terms that had little to do with either history or geography. It was
the word or seal that led there where one breathed "the air of
the patriarchs"—and the Bible, which Goethe referred to as "the
oldest collection" of "oriental poetry," seemed to him the book that
more than any other allowed us to approach that air.

One would have expected Goethe to have illustrated these ideas
with examples from "the five books of Moses," as the Pentateuch
is called in Germany. But no. With one of those short, sharp shifts
typical of his later writings, which veer back and forth between
the obvious and the wildly daring, and without the slightest preparatory hint, Goethe demonstrates his thesis citing the two erotic
high points of the Bible: the Song of Songs and the book of Ruth,

which he thought "the most charming tiny entirety," at once "epic and idyll," that has ever come down to us.

Why liken two books apparently so different from each other? Because their only subject is eros. The one—the Song—saying everything, making the marvelous manifest, fusing literal and metaphorical to the point that they become interchangeable (exactly the opposite strategy to that adopted over the centuries by both Jewish and Christian allegorists in relation to the Song). The other—the book of Ruth—hiding everything.

The one narrating, as Goethe would have it, "the ardent impulse of young hearts that seek each other out, find, rebuff, and attract each other," in a never-ending night of love. The other having as its only, never acknowledged subject the union between a rich peasant, half drunk and half asleep after a day's harvesting, in his barn, on a heap of barley, and the young foreign maid curled up at his feet; what happened, that is, between these two when, "in the middle of the night the man shivered and turned. And there was a woman lying at his feet." In any event, that night Ruth conceived Obadiah, a necessary link in the genealogical chain that would end in the Messiah.

Goethe compares the texts as examples of supreme erotic intensity. Though both, over the course of time, had been found wanting: the Song for its shapeless abundance of events and their tangled interconnection, the book of Ruth for going to the opposite extreme, its "irrepressible charm" depending on having cloaked the only thing that happens in an "incomparable reticence." In both cases readers would come along who felt the need to *impose order*, specifying exactly what was going on. To no avail, Goethe observed: with regard to the Song, "time and again the well-intentioned and the lovers of order were lured into attempts to find meaningful connections or to introduce them, but always leaving the readers who came after them none the wiser." Yet something similar happened with the book of Ruth, when some scholars could not resist "the crazy idea of bringing details and paraphrase" to the event that the text never acknowledges.

As Goethe saw it, these two examples showed how the biblical Orient, in the superb foreignness of its forms, refused to adapt to the canons of his contemporaries. The consequences were not merely literary: "Thus, book after book, the book of all books could show how it was given to us that we might try to enter there as into a second world, where we lose ourselves, enlighten ourselves, perfect ourselves." This was the condition under which one could once again savor "the air of the patriarchs." But Goethe was also suggesting *a way of reading,* that can still be usefully applied two centuries after the publication of the *West-östlicher Divan.*

The Song of Songs and Ecclesiastes are the only two books in the Bible where the name of Yahweh does not appear. This was the reason, John Barton claimed, for the long dispute over their position in the canon. At last, a treatise in the Mishnah observed: "All Holy Scriptures defile the hands. The Song of Songs and Qohelet defile the hands" (*Yadaim,* 3, 5). Behind the apparent differences, there must have been a deep complicity between the two books. They were made up of words written under an empty sky, a sky free of Yahweh's ubiquitous gaze. Words that rang true, without anyone to guarantee them.

That centuries after his supposed existence the Song and Ecclesiastes were both attributed, falsely, to Solomon, suggests a profound perspicacity. These books were the missing rocks in the stony agglomerate of the Bible: pleasure affirmed for pleasure's sake, impermanence for the sake of impermanence. And only Solomon, of all the many biblical figures, could have asserted both perennial emptiness and momentary fullness. He was the only one you could imagine saying, "I have set my heart to study and examine with wisdom all that is done under the heavens: it is an evil occupation that God has given men to busy themselves with." That "evil occupation" mockingly translated into human terms the majesty of Wisdom, Yahweh's familiar spirit who measures the universe. It was another way in which the inversion of heaven and earth could show itself. The knowledge of "all that is done under the sun" had not prevented Solomon from being "not altogether" with Yahweh in his old age. Knowledge did not bring him asymptotically closer to God. But it did intensify the power of the unknown, which increasingly became an object of reverence. This was hardly acceptable to the Bible's ecclesiastical editors. Yet on two occasions it was precisely this that slipped through their fine mesh, in the mutable, multiple voices of the Song, and the one clear voice of Ecclesiastes: "Calmness avoids great mistakes," said Qohelet.

One thing the Song and Ecclesiastes share is the determined avoidance of any linear development. From the very first syllables, they are books that stay obsessively on theme—pleasure and the dissolution of anything that purports to be permanent. All is there in the first note they strike. Which is then modulated, but nothing more. In the teeth of numerous commentators who claim that the achievement of the Bible is to give direction to time, these two books, late in the writing and belatedly accepted into the canon, deny such a direction, ridicule it even, and each from quite different but equally unassailable positions.

No book is as stubbornly anti-messianic as Ecclesiastes. If "all words weary, / there will be no more speaking." The idea of the last word is eliminated. Just as nothing can be added or taken from the Torah, so it is with the world's unfolding: "I know that everything God does is forever. / Nothing to add, nothing to take away." No question of a people in need of nurture, no suggestion that performing this or that sacrifice could be of any importance. "Whether a person sacrifices or not, the outcome is the same." No goal is better than any other. There are no winning arguments. Such was the foundation of Solomon's wisdom, which couldn't be mentioned, otherwise it would have seemed just banal assertion.

It would be hard to imagine anything more hostile to Ecclesiastes than Proverbs, aside from its wonderful chapter 8. Ecclesiastes says things that are sometimes obvious, but irrefutable, which is why they hit so hard. Proverbs speaks, endlessly, of things as they should be. Ecclesiastes declares the futility of all success. Proverbs tells us that the good succeed and the evil fail, despite all evidence to the contrary. Ecclesiastes twists the knife with every verse; with every verse Proverbs papers the cracks. Both books were falsely attributed to the same author: Solomon.

From the start, with his very name—"He who speaks"—Qohelet is a voice. It's not clear where he's speaking from, or to whom. Whether he's illustrious and powerful or a nameless nobody hardly matters. He speaks about the things that happen to everyone, and that everyone knows about. But that's what is so unnerving. Nobody wants to hear a single voice naming all those things in one place. It's too much. It's a teeming emptiness, mirror image of the Song's plenitude. Everything is "puff," *hevel*. But whether that means a destructive wind or the breath that gives life we're never sure. It's both one and the other.

What is Wisdom, "artificer of all things"? And how did it come about that Solomon could say: "I have loved and sought after her since my youth; / I tried to have her for my bride / and I fell in love with her beauty"? Words that traveled through time to settle at last in the book that bears his name. Again in that book Solomon describes Wisdom as though sketching the portrait of an admirable woman: "Blessed and intelligent is her spirit, / one, many, subtle, / mutable, precise, pure, / bright, inviolable, benevolent, penetrating, / unshakable, charitable, friend to man, / still, safe, calm, / all powerful, watching over everything / and pervading all spirits / that are intelligent, pure, and very subtle." The capacity of Wisdom to shine through everything is extraordinary, because it is "an exhalation of [divine] power," and a "pure emanation of the glory of the Omnipotent." Everything that takes place between Solomon and his innumerable women includes within itself that Wisdom of which Solomon said, "I decided to have her as the companion of my life."

Circuibam quaerens ut mihi illam assumerem, "I encircled her seeking to make her mine": words of intense eroticism to describe the pursuit and wooing of Wisdom. At once one was trapped in a vicious circle: it was a quest that could not bear fruit *nisi Deus det,* "unless granted by God." But only Wisdom would allow you to grasp that. When you haven't yet achieved Wisdom, you need to be illuminated by a gift that presupposes the possession of the Wisdom you seek. *Hoc ipsum erat Sapientiae, scire ejus esset hoc donum,* "It was the mark of Wisdom to appreciate that that gift came from her." A contradiction that offered no way out. So one resorted to prayer. And discovered that that was the way out. "I turned to the Lord and spoke to him, from the depths of my heart," *et dixi ex totis praecordiis meis.*

Solomon behaves quite differently from the patriarchs, Abraham, Isaac, Jacob, whose wives were chosen from the family circle. "As well as Pharaoh's daughter, King Solomon loved many foreign women: Moabites, Ammonites, Edomites, Sidonians, Hittites, from among those nations Yahweh spoke of when he told the children of Israel, 'You shall not go among them and they shall not go among you, because they would most surely ravish your heart to follow their gods!' but Solomon bound himself to them through love. He had seven hundred princesses as wives and three hundred concubines. His women ravished his heart." So, when Solomon was old, "his women ravished his heart to follow other gods and his heart was no longer altogether with Yahweh, his God, as David his father's heart had been." It wasn't just Ashtoreth—that is, Astarte—whom Solomon worshipped, but Milcom, Camos, and

Moloch as well. All around Jerusalem the hills and heights were dotted with stelae, wooden simulacra, and altars. Solomon "did the same for all his foreign wives who burned incense and sacrificed to their gods."

Wherever it appears in the Bible, one senses that the condemnation of idolatry is strictly connected to the condemnation of sex. But only in *The Wisdom of Solomon* is this link made explicit: *Initium enim fornicationis est exquisitio idolorum*, "The fashioning of idols is the beginning of fornication." The hands that gave shape to an inanimate material were the same that caressed a woman's body. So men "trusted their eyes, because what is visible is beautiful," and immediately fell into that "trap for men's feet." If we turn it on its head, the biblical condemnation could be read as an incandescent glorification of everything that is visible and palpable and that takes shape before our eyes.

There was a deep affinity between idols and foreign women. In both cases the terms of the condemnation were the same. Foreign women pointed the way to the idols—and the idols increased the interest in foreign women. Solomon followed them time and again, but any young man might come across a soft-speaking foreign woman "as he walked toward her house, at dusk," and find himself looking at a woman "adept at capturing souls." A woman "*garrula et vaga, / quietis impatiens, nec valens in domo consistere pedibus suis,*" insidious at every corner, in every square, able to ensnare "with her eyelashes." *Apprehensumque deosculatur iuvenem*, "Having grabbed the young man, she kisses him on the mouth," and whispers: "I have just celebrated a sacrifice / and performed my vows; / so I came out to find you / to try to see you and I have found you. / I have spread my bed with the colored linens of Egypt; / I have strewn myrrh / aloes and cinnamon." And at last the invitation: *Veni, inebriemur uberibus, / et fruamur cupitis amplexibus donec illucescat dies*, "Come, let us get drunk on my breasts / and enjoy, embraced in desire, / until dawn." At once the young man follows her "like an ox led to the sacrifice." Thus admonished the book of Proverbs.

Inanna, Ishtar, Astarte, Atirat, Anath, Astoreth; queens of many kingdoms; virgins, libertines, mothers, warriors; known by the children of Israel under the name Asherah and in the shape of carved wooden simulacra, standing on hilltops, at irregular intervals, near leafy trees, with power to attract and lead astray; then uprooted, cut down, broken up, burned; their ashes scattered in the valley of Ben-Hinnom, which is scored by the river Kidron, not far from Jerusalem, toward the southeast, where the mass graves are and the rubbish heaps.

Asherah, the naked goddess of the many names, mother of Anath or Astarte in the letters of Tell el-Amarna, empress of the Sea, queen of Tyre and Sidon, where she was called Ashtoreth, was a constant obsession for the children of Israel. Raising their eyes to the hilltops, they would see the familiar graven images in the shape of nude women, sometimes holding up their breasts with their hands. None of those images have survived, but we do have hundreds of small clay figures made in the same shapes, like wicked *teraphim*.

Even before the children of Israel set foot in Canaan, Yahweh ordered them: "You shall destroy their Asherah," as if goddess and images were the same thing. It was a key precept, and Yahweh explained: "Because Yahweh is called Jealous: he is a jealous God." So it wasn't enough to crush the seven peoples of Canaan. Their Asherah must be broken up and burned. Even trees were condemned, because the Asherah and "the stelae, which Yahweh, your God, abhors," were set up next to them. But it was a rule the children of Israel were reluctant to obey, even back in the times of the judges: "They abandoned Yahweh and served Baal and the Astartes."

When it came to the kings, the first to accept and introduce the cult of the Asherah was the wise king, Solomon. He even raised up images himself on "the heights opposite Jerusalem, south of the Mountain of Destruction," "in honor of Ashtoreth, abomination of the Sidonians." This was one of the reasons why it was said of Solomon that "his heart was no longer altogether with Yahweh." *No longer altogether*: an unusual construction. Of other kings it was said that they walked with Yahweh or that they did that which was evil in the eyes of Yahweh. Partial obedience was not an option. Solomon was the only king to whom the Bible grants the privilege of being "no longer altogether" with Yahweh. And the first book of Kings suggests the reason why that was so: Solomon had *bound himself by love* to many women.

The immediate and inevitable consequence of Solomon's inclination was his acceptance that the divine was many: "So Solomon followed after Ashtoreth, goddess of the Sidonians, and after Milcom, abomination of the Ammonites." To worship Asherah meant to worship other gods too. But it wasn't Solomon who introduced Asherah into the Temple that he had built with the help of Hiram, king of Tyre, a city devoted to the goddess. It was his son Rehoboam. Solomon's Temple stood for three hundred and eighty years. For two hundred and thirty-six years Asherah had a place in it and was worshipped there. For one hundred and forty-four years she was excluded from it and considered an abomination. Thirty-five years after Rehoboam, Asa removed the goddess. Joash brought her back, until, a century later, Hezekiah removed her again. Twenty-seven years went by before Manasseh brought her back again. Seventy-eight years later, Josiah removed her: "He had Asherah taken out of the House of Yahweh and out of Jerusalem to the river Kidron, where he burned her to ashes and threw the ashes on the tombs of the children of the people." It still wasn't enough: "He destroyed the houses of the sacred male prostitutes who were in the House of Yahweh and where the women weaved linen for Asherah." But when Josiah died, Asherah was brought back once more. And there she would stay until the first destruction of the Temple, in 586 B.C.E.

As late as the times of Lucian, the priests of Sidon could still remember that before being dedicated to Astarte—or Asherat in Phoenician, Asherah in Hebrew—their temple had been dedicated to Europa. A Roman coin from Tyre shows a veiled Europa standing beside two baetyls with a tree between them, while a bull emerges from the sea. The name *Europa* was written around the edge.

The goddess, whom a text found in Ras Shamra described as "creator of the gods" and whom the children of Israel were forever coming across up on the hills, and forever persecuting, had one day fled to a beach in Sidon, where a bull rose from the sea to carry her off. Until at last she could lie back, breasts exposed, between the branches of a huge plane tree in Gortyna, on the island of Crete. It was only the first stage of a journey that would eventually bring her to the continent she couldn't know she would give her name to, and with it a new chain of stories.

Even as she crossed the sea on the back of her divine bull, Europa was spelling out new names for her celestial relatives. She let vowels burst forth from choked Semitic roots. She had once been a tree between two standing stones, rounded at the top. Now she sank down into another tree, a plane whose rustling leaves spoke a new tongue, akin to that of the oak of Dodona, voice of Zeus, her abductor.

Alongside a loathing for the Asherah, even in the form of statuettes, and likewise for the stelae standing in the earth, Yahweh did not hide his condemnation of trees. It wasn't enough to suppress man-made images, certain elements of nature had to go too, as if they were guilty in and of themselves. Trees were among them. Without trees, nature could hardly survive, yet a tree was an enemy: "You shall not plant any Asherah for yourself, nor any tree, beside the altar of Yahweh, your God, that you have made for yourself, and you shall not raise up any stelae for yourself, which Yahweh, your God, abhors."

Solomon had wished for "a heart that understands." He then reigned for forty years until, in his old age, "his heart was no longer altogether with Yahweh." The first book of Kings underlines this question of age, without making clear whether it is a mitigating or an aggravating factor. Solomon himself, of course, had been the child of David's old age. Yahweh wished to punish Solomon for his crimes, but again, *not altogether.* He would take his kingdom from him. Or rather from his son, "because of David, your father."

The last years of Solomon's reign were turbulent. Jeroboam, Solomon's servant, "raised his hand against the king." But did not prevail and "took refuge in Egypt, near Shishaq, until the death of Solomon," who, at last, "lay with his fathers and was buried in the City of David, his father."

Solomon, like his father, had been a writer-king. Not only is he attributed with writing the Proverbs and the Song of Songs, but also the book of the Acts of Solomon, annals of the kingdom of the children of Israel, now entirely lost. Despite having been punished by Yahweh, it was accepted that "King Solomon was the greatest of the kings of the earth, both for riches and wisdom . . . The king acted in such a way that money, in Jerusalem, became common as stones and cedars as numerous as the sycamores in the plain."

V

WICKED HEIGHTS

After Solomon's death and the schism that split the children of Israel into two kingdoms—Judah and Israel—the same things went on happening, over and over. War was never-ending: "There was war between Asa and Baasha, kings of Israel, all their days." With the reliability of a pendulum, outrage and massacre swung back and forth from one camp to the other. Baasha "destroyed the entire house of Jeroboam, he left not a single living being of Jeroboam's alive, obeying the word that Yahweh had spoken through his servant Ahijah the Shilonite." A few years later Baasha would be on the receiving end of these words inspired by Yahweh and put in the mouth of Jehu: "I will wipe out Baasha and his house, I will make your house like that of Jeroboam, son of Nebat. Those of Baasha's family who die in the city will be eaten by the dogs, and those of his family who die in the fields will be eaten by the birds." But when Ahab became king and reigned over Israel for twenty-two years, war was declared on Yahweh himself.

"Ahab did more than all the kings of Israel before him to vex Yahweh, God of Israel." Eminently wicked, Ahab was not only a destroyer, but a builder too. He founded many cities. And built himself a "house of ivory," which the Bible does not describe. But nor does it cancel all record of it, leaving us an idea to dream on. Ahab married Jezebel, daughter of the king of the Sidonians. "He served Baal and bowed down before him," hardly distinguishing between the beautiful Jezebel, "who seduced him," and the "dirty idols" that she worshipped.

But one person cast a persistent shadow over his life: Elijah the prophet. At the beginning of his reign, Elijah foresaw a drought. Ahab told him to go and hide himself in the bed of a remote dry river valley and get the crows to feed him. Hoping never to see him again. But Elijah came back. "You is it, Israel's doom monger?" was

Ahab's greeting. Elijah said it was Ahab bringing disaster. And he proposed an experiment. He claimed he was the last surviving priest of Yahweh; all the others had been killed. While Baal had four hundred and fifty priests. To see which of the two faiths was true, which the more powerful, debates were no use, but sacrifices were. He suggested they prepare two sacrifices, one that he would celebrate, alone, to Yahweh; the other to Baal, celebrated by his four hundred and fifty priests. They should bring a young bull, cut it up, and place its flesh on some wood. But without lighting the fire. "The god that answers with fire will be the true God." They accepted.

For hours the priests of Baal hopped and danced around the altar they had prepared. When it was nearly noon, Elijah said mockingly, "Shout away, shout away, he's a god: he must be busy, or off somewhere, on his travels; maybe he's sleeping and you can wake him up!" The priests went on dancing. In a frenzy, they cut their arms and drew blood. Something else that was supposed to attract the god's attention. To no avail. Evening came and—as the Bible reports—"no voice, no answer, nothing of note." Pieces of meat laid on chunks of wood. The earth trodden down all around. Insects buzzing in the humid heat.

Then Elijah called upon the people to rebuild the altar of Yahweh, "which had been destroyed." With his own hands he placed twelve stones one beside the other. The same number as the tribes of the sons of Jacob. Then they prepared the ceremony, following the rules in every detail. Three times they poured water on the wood from four jugs. They let the water drain from the altar and gather in a pool. When it was time for the offering, Elijah spoke to Yahweh, God of Abraham, Isaac, and Jacob. He asked for an answer. Fire fell from heaven, "devoured the holocaust and the wood, the stones and the dust, and dried the water left in the pool." The people bowed down, in worship. But Elijah rebuked them: "Seize the priests of Baal: not one must escape!" And they seized them. Elijah had them led down to the dry bed of the Kishon and there he cut their throats." Such was the end of the four hundred and fifty priests of Baal. Then Elijah spoke to Ahab. He told him to eat and drink, because soon it would rain. From far away, beyond Mount Carmel, came a rumble of thunder. Suddenly a wind rose.

Elijah had challenged Ahab to the supreme test: fire. Not that anyone must pass through a fire; they must cause it to fall from heaven. No test could have been more reckless. None could have given a more definite result. To set it up, a sacrifice had to be prepared. There was no question, as Elijah saw it, of the test's taking place outside the ceremony. The priests of Baal must abandon themselves to their ridiculous dances. Elijah must follow the rules to the letter, placing the stones side by side, the wood, the water jugs, exactly as prescribed in the times of Moses. Only in that way, Elijah believed, could the ultimate test be carried out. Only then would it be clear who was the real god, Baal or Yahweh. At the same time, in those tense, jittery hours, Elijah spoke of sacrifice with scandalous sarcasm. Was Baal perhaps asleep, he wondered, or off on a trip. But couldn't someone have said the same of Yahweh? Of course. And how many times had Yahweh failed to answer a call . . . That was why, when the preparations for the sacrifice were complete, Elijah said very little to Yahweh, focusing on these three words: "Answer me, Yahweh." There was no need for dances, or blood, or special robes. There was an abrupt, intimate request, together with three names—Abraham, Isaac, and Jacob— one of which evoked a boy who had *not* been sacrificed, thanks to Yahweh's last-minute intervention. What mattered was to affirm sacrifice, and at the same time to hint at something beyond it. Elijah's sarcasm laid bare that underlying assumption. At the same time, Elijah didn't hesitate to behave like a sorcerer calling for rain. "And it came to pass that little by little the heavens darkened with clouds and wind, and there was a great rain."

Communion sacrifices and holocausts were celebrated in the House of Baal. Communion sacrifices and holocausts were celebrated in the House of Yahweh. There were prophets of Yahweh.

There were prophets of Baal. Of course the two doctrines were different. But certain practices were the same: killing this or that animal, burning them, eating their flesh, in the House of Yahweh, in the House of Baal.

Jezebel had a plan: to dispose of the prophets of Israel and substitute them with the prophets of Baal. But Obadiah, her husband, Ahab's master of ceremonies, was still faithful to Yahweh and managed to hide a hundred prophets in two caves, where they were fed on bread and water. Meantime the drought intensified. Elijah chose this moment to tackle the "four hundred and fifty prophets of Baal and the four hundred of Asherah." For now he could say: "I am the one remaining prophet of Yahweh."

Every prophet spoke as if he were the only one, whereas in fact there were dozens of them. And they knew that in places not too far away there were hundreds of other prophets worshipping gods with other names. But they all celebrated sacrifices. The pride in being unique would pass from Elijah to his partner Elisha, who one day sent word to the king of Israel: "Come to me and know that there is a prophet in Israel!"

Nobody terrified Elijah so much as Jezebel. When, one by one, he had cut the throats of the four hundred and fifty priests of Baal on the dry bed of the Kishon, "the river of ancient times" that flowed at the foot of Mount Carmel, girding the mountain now like a sash of blood, Elijah knew that the game with the queen was far from over. The very next day Jezebel sent him a message: "May the gods treat me as they do now or even worse, if by this time tomorrow I have not made your spirit like one of theirs." By "theirs" Jezebel meant her gutted priests. And the queen had used the formula of the oath, calling upon her gods.

Elijah had to get out at once. He headed south, toward Egypt. In Beersheba he even said goodbye to his servant. He needed to be alone, against her alone. He kept going into the desert, as if intending to follow Moses's footsteps in reverse. After a day's walking, he sensed the futility of what he was doing. After all, he was just a lone man fleeing from a woman. He didn't have a people after him, only terror. Now he wanted to die. Why go on, if he didn't have the mettle of his ancestors? Then he fell into a deep sleep, beside a gorse bush. He woke with the sensation of being lightly touched. An Angel of Yahweh pointed to a piece of bread and a jug of water beside the gorse bush. The bread was still warm, freshly baked. The water was cool. Exhausted, Elijah ate, drank, and fell asleep again. And again the Angel woke him. In his weariness that delicate presence was the only thing he was aware of. Again he remembered Moses. For forty days and forty nights he walked across the desert to God's mountain, Sinai. And there, like the prophets pursued by Jezebel, he hid in a cave.

Now Yahweh decided to speak to him. Only now, only in this utter desolation could he give him instructions. Elijah came to the opening of his cave, covering himself with his cloak, the only thing he had. A strong wind was rising. It seemed it must uproot the rock itself. Elijah waited for Yahweh in the whirlwind. But he wasn't there. Then he felt the earth tremble. Again he waited for Yahweh. But he wasn't there. A fire roared up and encircled him. Once again, Elijah supposed Yahweh was about to show himself. But he wasn't there. Elijah felt alone, as he had that first night when he'd wanted to die. Then he heard "the sound of a light breeze." *Sibilus aurae tenuis*, as the Vulgate put it. That was what Yahweh sounded like, he realized, overwhelmed by the obviousness of it. Wrapped in his cloak, he stepped out into the open and at last heard a voice, that might have seemed mocking, for it said: "What are you doing here, Elijah?" Yet it was only thanks to his long flight, and because his desperate escape had reduced him to such a state of exhaustion, that Elijah was able to recognize Yahweh in the barely perceptible sound of the breeze. But already Yahweh was giving instructions: he must cross the desert again, this time to Damascus; then anoint Hazael as king of the Arameans, then anoint Jehu king of Israel and then Elisha as prophet and successor of himself.

Ahab's depraved insolence was contagious. Dozens of his sons would make such behaviour the norm. There were now only seven thousand men in Israel who had not knelt before Baal. Yahweh had to move fast, using signs as effective as they were invincible: a prophet's cloak, the sound of a light breeze, a few drops of anointing oil. Elijah hurried to climb down from Sinai. But it would be three years before Ahab was struck down.

Ahab and Jezebel were a grim couple. They always agreed about everything. One day Ahab was in an evil mood. Jezebel asked why. Ahab said, "Naboth won't sell his vineyard, the one alongside our house. He won't take money, or even another vineyard in exchange." Jezebel said, "But aren't you king of Israel? Let me handle this." Jezebel wrote a few letters using Ahab's signature and seal and sent them off to the elders. They should put Naboth "at the head of the people." And let everyone recognize him. Then two shifty characters must testify against him, saying that he had "cursed God and the king." Didn't the law require that there must be at least two witnesses and they agree on all points? The letter ended with this order: "Then have him leave the city and stone him, till he's dead." The elders obeyed. The two men sat in front of Naboth and said he had cursed God and the king. "They had him leave the city, they stoned him and he died."

Like Europa before her, Jezebel was a Sidonian princess. She wasn't carried off by a bull from the sea. But the king of a bordering country bowed down before her gods. Jezebel became his queen. While Ahab was building an "ivory house," Jezebel celebrated the rites of Asherah, Baal's consort, before the sacred trees. By her request, for as long as she was queen, those trees were planted all over the heights of Palestine. Sometimes simulacra of Asherah were no more than posts thrust in the ground. You could see them from afar.

The divinity the biblical texts call Asherah, but also many other names, was anything but a harmless creature. A tablet found in Ugarit describes her up to her knees in the blood of slaughtered enemies, while their torn limbs buzz around her head like locusts.

Like all gods, she sought out temples and sanctuaries to dwell in. Welcoming her into the House of Yahweh in Jerusalem was bound to cause upheaval. "The Virgin Anath washes her hand, / the Protectress of peoples [washes] her fingers. / [She washes] her hand in the blood of *š²mr*, / [She washes] her fingers in the *mmˁ* of the *mhr*." Charles Virolleaud, who deciphered this tablet, wasn't sure how to translate *mmˁ*, which could indicate "bowels." But he adds: "However, it's more likely that *mmˁ* is the name of an organic liquid, like blood itself: perhaps, as with the Assyrians, there was already a distinction between dark blood and bright blood."

Elijah appeared to Ahab the day the king decided to take possession of Naboth's much-coveted vineyard. He was alone, sure that no one could witness his pleasure. Instead Elijah was suddenly right there before him. As always he didn't waste words. And, as always, he attributed them to Yahweh. The prophet said, "Taking over, now that you've murdered him, are you?" And he added two more messages, part curses, part threats, springing directly from Yahweh. One message was for Ahab: "In the very place where the dogs lapped up Naboth's blood, the dogs will also lap up your blood." The other was for Jezebel: "The dogs will eat Jezebel against the wall of Jezreel." Then the prophet withdrew, and for three years nothing more was seen of him.

Elijah and Jezebel clashed as opposite and parallel powers, each recognizing the other, fearing the other—each desiring to destroy the other. Elijah came from an obscure village on the borders of Canaan; his parents' names are never mentioned. Jezebel was the daughter of a king and married a foreign king. Elijah was one of the first prophets of Yahweh; Jezebel claimed to be a prophet ("*se dicit propheten*," according to the Apocalypse) of Baal and Asherah. Jezebel persecuted and killed the prophets of Israel; Elijah put to the sword four hundred and fifty prophets of Baal. Elijah was a hairy man, "dressed in fur with a leather belt," and owning but one cloak; Jezebel knew all the cosmetic arts and thought them sufficient to seduce the very worst of her enemies. Elijah would appear before Ahab as a kind of bogeyman, to remind him of the law; Jezebel whispered to Ahab how he might exploit the law to get rid of anyone standing in his way.

Israel was at war with the Arameans again. Ahab was struck by an arrow that found a chink in his mighty armor. He stood motionless as the blood flowed down his body. Crouched on his chariot two armor bearers held him up like a broken statue, knowing that victory depended entirely on the presence of the king. Ahab died that evening, feet drenched in blood that slopped back and forth on the floor of the chariot. He was buried in the city of Samaria, on whose gate he had ordered these words to be carved: "Ahab denies the God of Israel." His chariot was washed in the city's pool. "The dogs lapped his blood and the whores bathed in it, according to the word that Yahweh had spoken."

If ever there was a being you could liken to the Saptarishi who watched over Asia from the starry heights of the Ursa Major, it was Elijah, first among the prophets in Canaan. He never saw the sea. Rather, his sea was the desert. Elijah had the kind of contact with the elements that the kings of Israel always lacked. He looked on the kings with scorn and infuriated them as if he were calamity itself, always ready to disappear, always lurking in ambush. He could call up fire—and doing so twice reduced to ashes the soldiers that Ahab's son Ahaziah sent against him. He had a certain intimacy with water too. But it was the scorching and the arid that were closest to his genius. He vanished on a chariot of fire while walking and talking with Elisha. Interrupting their conversation. And was seen no more, he was not touched by death.

Over the centuries, many claim to have seen Elijah wandering the world, as others say they see Harun al-Rashid roaming the backstreets of his city. They recognized him under the disguises of an Arab, a knight, a Roman dignitary, a prostitute. He stood accused of administering relations between earth and sky in a somewhat cavalier fashion. Once he brought Rabbah bar Abuha up to Paradise, a man so poor he couldn't afford to study. Elijah let him gather up some leaves fallen from the trees of heaven into his ragged cloak. This wasn't allowed and the rabbi had to drop them there and then. But when he got back to earth his cloak still gave off the fragrance of Paradise. He managed to sell it for an excellent price and could at last settle down to studying the Torah. To achieve the impossible you need no more than a cloak. Elijah knew that.

Elisha copied certain traits from Elijah and would have liked to be his equal. He had the privilege of being present when Elijah vanished "in a whirlwind." The two were walking and talking, as on so many other occasions, when Elisha saw "a chariot of fire and horses of fire came between them." All that was left of Elijah was his cloak. But it was a powerful cloak. Elisha had seen Elijah beat his cloak on the waters of the Jordan and the waters had opened. Allowing them to cross and keep their feet dry. It was a re-play, in miniature, of what had happened with Moses and the Red Sea. Elisha went back to the place with Elijah's cloak in his hands. Once again he stood by the Jordan. Why not try? He beat the water with Elijah's cloak. The Jordan went on flowing. But the cloak was soaked. Elisha was puzzled. He said: "Where is Yahweh, God of Elijah?" The waters parted. But only because Elisha had spoken the name Elijah.

Elisha was always accompanied by "the sons of the prophets," orphans of the men who had been killed by Jezebel. Their children had survived and gathered around the one prophet, which, after Elijah vanished on the chariot of fire, could only mean El-isha. And the children of the prophets multiplied. One day they said to Elisha, "The place where we live beside you is too small for us now. We're going to Jordan, where each of us will take a beam of wood and build a place to live." This was the pulse of events: a small group multiplied, then was wiped out; but at least *one* voice survived, and around that voice another small group would form and grow. That was the back and forth of the story of Israel.

Elisha had inherited Elijah's grouchiness. And likewise a way he had with the elements. The citizens of Jericho told him the city's water was unhealthy. Elisha "went to the source of the water and threw in some salt." And the waters became pure again. But not everyone considered him a benefactor. When he climbed up to Bethel a swarm of boys surrounded him, jeering: "Climb on up, baldie! Climb on up, baldie!" Elisha looked up, sent them a withering look, and cursed them. Then "two she-bears came out of the forest and tore apart forty-two of the boys."

For Jesus it was essential that some of his miracles also be quotations. It showed that he was following in the footsteps of the prophets. Lazarus was brought back to life, as Elisha had brought back to life the son of Zarephtah's widow, or Elisha the son of the rich woman of Shunem. In this case Elisha behaved like an expert thaumaturge: "He went in, closed the door, and prayed to Yahweh. He lay on the boy, put his mouth on his mouth, his eyes over his eyes, his palms on his palms, and lay facedown on him until the child became warm again. He walked back and forth around the house again, then climbed on him and lay over him again. At which the boy sneezed seven times and opened his eyes." Likewise the Gospel multiplication of the loaves recalled a similar miracle of Elisha's during a famine in Gilgal.

Though hardly on a par with his teacher Elijah, Elisha was nevertheless so powerful that, as Ecclesiasticus claims, "his body prophesied even in the sleep of death." After Elisha's death, bands of Moabites began to sneak into Israel. One day a group of men were going to bury someone. They ran into one of these bands. So they threw the dead man into Elisha's sepulcher. They had dug down in the earth first, so that the corpse "touched Elisha's bones." That was all it took. "The man came back to life and got to his feet." We are told no more. We don't know who the resuscitated man was. Nor what happened to the Moabites, nor to the friends of the dead man, who had already run off. The text moves on to another subject. We're left with the radiating power of Elisha's bones, which, though disturbed in "the sleep of death," emanate life at the merest touch.

There are many affinities between the Vedic seers, the rishis, and the biblical prophets. Their first concern was to watch over the order of the world to make sure it did not degenerate too drastically. When that happened, frequently enough, they would step in, sometimes in a blazing fury. The Vedic seers were said to swing back and forth between wrath and lust. The prophets mentioned lust only insofar as it was to be deplored and persecuted. When it came to wrath they were specialists. While for the rishis an occasional conflict with a king was no more than another episode in the primordial and canonical tension between Brahmans and Kshatriyas, something in itself salutary, the prophets had only ever accepted the kings grudgingly, because the people demanded them. They never conceded any intrinsic legitimacy to royalty. It depended entirely on anointment, which they could grant or otherwise as they chose.

In Vedic India, anointment was the focal point of a complex ritual in which the king was consecrated. In Jewish history it happened quite suddenly, in some out-of-the-way place, far from others, in response to the inspiration and command of a "man of God." Saul, the first king, was anointed by Samuel, in Zuf, early in the morning, with no witnesses. Solomon was hurried out of Jerusalem on a mule and anointed by Zadok the priest. A measure taken in an emergency because his half brother Adonijah was about to have himself proclaimed king, was already celebrating, in fact, with a banquet. By the time we get to the sons of Ahab, anointment actually occurred indirectly, through a third person. Elisha summoned one of the sons of the prophets and told him to go to Ramoth. There he must look for Jehu, who had no idea what was about to happen to him. Jehu was with his brothers.

Elisha's envoy must take him "into a separate room." Elisha wound up: "Then you take your vial of oil and pour it over his head and say, 'Thus said Yahweh: "I have anointed you king of Israel!"' Then you open the door and run for it, without waiting a moment longer."

A frenetic, spasmodic, almost clandestine scene: quite the opposite of Vedic anointment, which came at the climax of a meticulously celebrated ritual. But that moment would mean extinction for the house of Ahab and open the way for Yahweh's revenge against Jezebel. When Elisha's go-between had run off, Jehu went back to his brothers, who were baffled. "Everything all right? Why did that madman come after you?" Jehu didn't repeat everything the stranger had said, just a few words: "Thus said Yahweh: 'I have anointed you king of Israel!'" No one objected, no one doubted it was true. They rushed to strip off their cloaks and lay them under Jehu's feet. "Then they blew a horn and cried, 'Jehu is king!'"

The last time the two met, Elijah had told Ahab: "I will sweep you aside and pluck from the house of Ahab even the man pissing against a wall, the slave and the free man of Israel." It wasn't so much a question of striking Ahab in person, but of wiping out his entire lineage. Yahweh wanted to take his time over it, though. He let Ahab's reign go on and for three years even the wars ceased. When they began again, he let Ahab die fighting on his chariot. The curse would fall above all on his children, and Jehu was to be the executioner.

It was the elders of Samaria who, to please Jehu, gathered up the seventy heads of Ahab's sons in two big baskets and had them delivered to Jezreel. "The messenger went in and told him, saying, 'They have brought the heads of the king's sons.' Jehu said, 'Leave them in two piles by the city gate until morning.'" These eloquent heads would serve to convince his people to go on and kill "all those of the house of Ahab still in Jezreel, all his dignitaries, his close friends, his priests, so that no one be left alive."

Jehu was not so much an expert in killing as in having others kill. The only one of Ahab's sons he killed with his own hands, piercing the man's heart with an arrow as he fled, was Jehoram. As for Ahaziah, king of Judah, Jehu sent other men to kill him.

Jehu had just completed these two assignments when he arrived in Jezreel to tackle the toughest challenge of all: Jezebel. The queen was waiting for her sons' murderer. She had taken great care over her makeup that day. She appeared at the window of her room *pompeusement parée*, as Racine would one day write. She had "prettified her head." Her face, which time had not spared, still radiated a certain splendor. Her expression, looking out and greeting Jehu, was brazen and cold. "Coming to make peace, murderer?" she asked—and quickly added a scathing comparison: Jehu, she said, was like Zimri, the slave who had killed his master.

It all happened very fast. Jezebel leaned out the window, as if offering her body. Behind her, in the shadows, were three eunuchs, always at her side. Jehu looked up and, as if giving a prearranged signal, shouted, "Who is with me?" For a second you could see the eager arms of the eunuchs as they grabbed the queen and pitched her down onto the flagstones below. Jezebel's blood spurted onto the stuccoed walls as horses stamped on her with a sudden fury. Poker-faced, Jehu walked into the palace. He ate and drank. Then said, "Deal with that abomination and put her in a grave, since she was a princess." And he moved on. But this time his orders couldn't be obeyed. The dogs had got there first. All that was left of Jezebel were "her skull, her feet, the palms of her hands." The legendary body of the queen was gone. "It'll make good dung for the fields," someone punned; *zebel*, in Aramaic, means "dung." Now no one could say: "This is Jezebel!"

It wasn't enough to display the heads of the seventy sons of Ahab in Jezreel "in two piles before the city gates till morning." It wasn't enough to cut the throats of the forty-two brothers of Ahaziah "near the pit of Beth-Eked." There were the people themselves, who were now followers of Baal. Jehu decided to trick them. He said, "Ahab served Baal a little. Jehu will serve him a lot." It seemed like the prelude to some grandiose celebrations: Jehu announced "a great sacrifice to Baal: anyone who doesn't take part will die." If only to cover their backs, the people came running. They crowded into Baal's temple, filling every nook and cranny. Jehu had taken care to supply the same clothes to all Baal's followers. He was admirably scrupulous: he asked for a careful check that "only those who worship Baal" were in the temple. Then the communion sacrifices and holocausts began. Meantime the temple was surrounded. No one was to leave alive. No one did leave alive. "Then they destroyed the altar of Baal and they destroyed the House of Baal, they turned them into toilets that are still around today."

The man who had plotted all this was not even one of Yahweh's faithful. Jehu "rid Israel of Baal," but went on worshipping "the golden calves in Bethel and in Dan." It was just a change of idol. All the same, Yahweh rewarded Jehu, because he had been "the agent of his revenge"—as Racine would write—and had carried out his word and exterminated the house of Ahab. Otherwise, Jehu fell into the same sins as Jeroboam. "It was at this time that Yahweh began to cut Israel down to size." The kingdom shed piece after piece. Nevertheless Jehu managed to reign for twenty-eight years.

"Seeing that her son Ahaziah was dead, Athaliah set about destroying the whole royal lineage." Now Ahab's family had been exterminated, the other royal family had to be exterminated too: the family of David, which Yahweh was stubbornly keeping alive. Since Athaliah had married Jehoram, a descendant of David's, the people she would have to kill were her own grandchildren. Here the second book of Kings doesn't offer a detailed account. But Racine fills us in: "The room was full of slaughtered princes. / Dagger in hand, the implacable Athaliah / Spurred on her barbarous soldiers, / And proceeded to carry out her murders." She didn't want people ever to say she hadn't been a worthy daughter to her mother, eaten by dogs. Yet one child was saved from the massacre: Joash. They took him into the House of Yahweh as an orphan, "while Athaliah reigned over the country."

Athaliah had wanted nothing less than to *imitate Yahweh*. She felt it was the only proper response. As Yahweh had decided to wipe out the house of Ahab, so Athaliah would wipe out the house of David, snuffing out the last "lamp" that Yahweh had always wanted to keep alight. For sure this was not an undertaking of the same order. It hadn't been easy to heap the heads of the seventy sons of Ahab in two piles. Athaliah only had to kill the children of her son Ahaziah, who had died aged twenty-three. It was a baby hunt.

Always at his most vibrant when writing lines for wicked women, Racine presents Athaliah as a *dame* of the night. Her hatred for the house of David was theological: "I have a horror of David; and of the sons of that king, / Even though born of my blood, they are foreign to me." Athaliah, too, was acting in obedience to a higher duty, as she confessed to her devoted Abner: "What I did, Abner, I believed it was my duty to do." A fatal formula that came tumbling into history, endlessly repeated by mouths both holy and foul.

"As for Athaliah, she was put to the sword in the House of the king." That is all the second book of Kings has to say about the end of the "haughty Athalia." After which sovereignty passed to a child. "Joash was seven years old when he became king." And he would rule for forty years, in Jerusalem.

But the families were inextricably tangled. It's true that Joash was the one surviving descendent of the house of David, but likewise of the house of Ahab. The biblical text overlooks this detail; not so Racine's Athalia, that "great soul" and bloodthirsty queen who chooses to remember the boy just before the sword runs her through. What could she wish for Joash, that rather petulant boy who had nevertheless charmed her to the point that she would have liked to take him with her? After all, he was, as she had discovered, her grandson, hence blood of her blood. "Faithful to Ahab's blood, which he got from me, / Following his grandfather's footsteps and the likeness of his father / The loathsome heir of David will / revoke your honors, profane your altar, / And avenge Athalia, Ahab, and Jezebel."

Little Joash grew up and in the first years of his long reign did not stray from the paths of Yahweh, at least "so long as the priest Jehoiada was his teacher." But Yahweh couldn't be satisfied with a people who were merely docile and obedient. There was still an ongoing calamity: the heights, the hilltops where once the Jews, too, had celebrated communion sacrifices and holocausts. Worse, since Solomon had built the temple, there was nothing on those heights but idols, engraved stones and sacred trees. A seething parallel life, impervious to change. Meantime the House of Yahweh was falling apart. While the Asherah that Ahab had raised in Samaria was still standing. It was said that the priests in Jerusalem were keeping the money donations for themselves.

Hazael, king of Aram, had Jerusalem surrounded, and Joash stooped so low as to offer him "all the gold in the treasures of the House of Yahweh and the House of the king." But it didn't end there. After Hazael, his son Ben-Hadad came along. There was no escaping him. But Yahweh didn't want to be tough on Israel. He let the people slip out of the city. "They lived in tents as they had years ago, and even before that." They went back to the times of their nomadic past. But that didn't mean "they turned away from the sins that the house of Jeroboam had made them sin. They went on doing them."

Elisha was old and ill, Israel oppressed by the Arameans. Joash went to whine to the man of God. Elisha hadn't lost his faith in the simple gesture and the word. He had walked long enough with Elijah to know how powerful they were. Joash repeated the words Elisha had said to Elijah shortly before he vanished in the whirlwind. Then Elisha found a bow and put it in Joash's hand. He told him to open an east-facing window and ordered: "Shoot!" Joash shot the arrow. Then Elisha said, "Yahweh's victory arrow!" And now another order: "Take the arrows and strike them on the ground." Joash struck them on the floor three times. Elisha wasn't happy. With one of those angry looks that struck fear into everyone he said, "You should have struck them five or six times, that way you would have beaten Aram until he was quite destroyed; now you will only beat him three times."

Not long after that, Elisha died. Now it was the Moabites' turn to launch raids of conquest on Israel. But bit by bit, Joash managed to drive out the Arameans, under their leader Ben-Hadad. "Joash beat him three times and won back the city of Israel."

Joash, son of Ahaziah, reigned for forty-years, according to the most reliable estimates. The second book of Kings remarks: "However, the heights remained as before: people still made sacrifices and still burned incense on the heights." Amaziah, Joash's son, reigned for sixteen years. The second book of Kings notes: "But the heights remained as before: people still made sacrifices and still burned incense on the heights." Then Azariah, son of Amaziah, reigned for thirty-four years. Once again the second book of Kings remarks: "However, the heights remained as before: people still made sacrifices and still burned incense on the heights." Of Joash, Amaziah, and Azariah, it was said that "they did that which was right in the eyes of Yahweh," albeit with a few reservations. All the same, the wicked heights were as before.

Hezekiah became king when he was twenty-five and reigned in Jerusalem for twenty-nine years. Although the Asherah were finally torn down during his rule, Judah went on swinging back and forth, pendulum-like, always spending somewhat longer on the dark side. Manasseh, son of Hezekiah, became king when he was twelve and reigned in Jerusalem for fifty-five years. His first

concern was to "make an Asherah like the one Ahab, king of Israel, had made." So "he bowed down before all the Army of the
Heavens and served her." That wasn't all: "He placed the idol of
Asherah that he had made in the House of which Yahweh had said
to David and his son Solomon: 'In this House and in Jerusalem,
which I have chosen out of all the tribes of Israel, I shall put my
name forever.'" So Astarte, the naked goddess, wasn't worshipped
only up on the heights, but inside the Temple of Yahweh.

After Manasseh came his grandson Josiah. He had become king
at age eight and in the eighteenth year of his reign "he tore down the
houses of the sacred male prostitutes that were in the House of Yahweh and where women wove linen for the Asherah." Then the Asherah
was removed from the temple and "he had it burned in the scrub of
the Kidron and reduced to ashes and the ashes thrown on the tombs
of the children of the people," the common burial ground. If the Asherah was burned, it must have been made of wood. But it is fair to
doubt whether these images were simple poles, as most commentators
claim. They were carved from wood and often took the form of the
naked goddess, who was then clothed with linen woven in the houses
of the sacred prostitutes. The ceremonial dressing of the goddess was
a constant characteristic of this cult, as for Artemis in Ephesus, or for
Devi in so many Hindu temples.

At the time the House of Yahweh wasn't just run down; over
the years so many illegitimate superfetations had been introduced
as to make it barely recognizable. Some of them get a mention
only when Josiah orders their destruction. "He removed the horses
that the kings of Judah had dedicated to the Sun, at the entrance
to the House of Yahweh, near the room of the eunuch Nathan-
Melek, which was in the annexes, and he had the chariots of the
Sun burned in the fire."

The wicked Manasseh ruled almost as long as Queen Victo-
ria one day would. Whatever could upset Yahweh, he did it. But
his grandson Josiah, who ruled for thirty-one years, undid it all

again, crime by crime. Something happened to mark the break between the two reigns. A book was found, the Book. "The great priest Hilkiah said to Shaphan the scribe, 'I have found the book of the Law in the House of Yahweh.' Then Hilkiah gave the book to Shaphan and he read it." So *the book* wasn't on display in the House of Yahweh. They had come across it, unexpectedly, while repairing some damage to the Temple. And the scribe *read* the book at once, as if it were something new. What's more, Shaphan the scribe went to Josiah and said, "'Hilkiah the priest has given me a book,' and Shaphan read it to the king." Josiah listened and, "when he had heard the words of the book of the Law, he tore his clothes." Finding a book that is the Book, as a priest; reading it, as a scribe; listening to its words, as a king. This is the primary reading scene. And it happens when the book has already been forgotten, half buried in rubble in the House of Yahweh.

More than any claims with regard to the uniqueness of Yahweh, or any denunciations of the "filthy idols," what gives us a measure of the insuperable distance between Jerusalem and her many, noisy neighbors is *reading*, the decisive power of reading a book. Which in this case was Deuteronomy, a summary of the entire Law of Moses. And Deuteronomy, in Hebrew, is *debarim*, "words." Right from the start, "to be Jewish was to be bookish," Simon Schama observed. The act of reading was not part of the theology. It was its prerequisite. The entire Bible was founded on this premise.

Josiah chose an unusual way to proceed. He said, "Go and consult with Yahweh for me, for the people and for the whole of Judah, about the words of the book that was found." And the first move was this: a delegation including the priest who had found the book and the scribe who had read it went to see "Huldah the prophetess, wife of Shallum, keeper of the wardrobe, son of Tikvah, son of Harhas. She lived in Jerusalem, in the new city." A prophetess, like Miriam, Moses's sister, and a very few others after her, Huldah already seemed to know about the discovery of the book and the king's reaction. She said Josiah should be aware that Yahweh had been on the point of unleashing his rage and had held back only because the king had "listened to the words that are in the book," and because his "heart was stirred." Reading had had an effect at the last possible moment. The delegation "passed on the answer to the king."

Then Josiah decided to summon an assembly not just of the priests and the prophets but of everyone who lived in Jerusalem. All without exception must be present. Standing on a dais, "he read out loud for their ears all the words of the book of the Covenant that had been found in the House of Yahweh." There were thirty-four chapters.

Josiah read the entire scroll of Deuteronomy that had been found in the ruins of the temple "before all the men of Judah and to all the inhabitants of Jerusalem, to the priests and the prophets, as well as all the people, from the least to the greatest." Those who listened might well have supposed that the Law took up the whole horizon, to the ends of the earth. But what had happened before the Law? Going back in time, before the kings, before the judges, before the conquest of Canaan, before the years in the desert, before their bondage in Egypt, there had been the patriarchs: three men, Abraham, Isaac, Jacob. Everybody descended from them, because to be "children of Israel" meant to be children of Jacob.

The law couldn't have been passed on and put in writing on a scroll if there hadn't been the twelve tribes to apply it; and the twelve tribes brought together the descendants of a single family, the family of Jacob, Abraham's grandson. Before Abraham, the only name they knew was his father, Terah, who had known nothing of Yahweh. Israel existed only insofar as Yahweh "loved your fathers," who had been a father, a son, and a grandson: Abraham, Isaac, Jacob, and no one else.

VI

THOSE WHO
WENT AWAY

In the beginning, Abraham was just another name among the many descendants of Shem, as was Nimrod among the descendants of Ham: "Terah begat Abram, Nahor and Haran. Haran begat Lot . . . Abram and Nahor took wives. The name of Abram's wife was Sarai and the name of Nahor's wife was Milcah . . . Sarai was barren and bore no children." This was all that was known of Abraham when he set out to follow his father, Terah, and his caravan, leaving Ur for Canaan, a place he had never seen. Terah stopped halfway, in Haran, where eventually he died.

Down to the time of Terah, Abraham's relatives and clan did not recognize Yahweh. "They served other gods." It was then, said Yahweh, that "I took your father, Abraham, from over the river and had him go toward the land of Canaan." It was a sudden and irreversible decision, a separation with no return from every previous land and people. The separation and the journey: two traits that would mark out the children of Israel forever.

Ur of the Chaldees, the city Abraham left, had at its center "a huge sacred enclosure, an irregular quadrilateral whose sides measured 380 meters to the northeast, 248 meters to the northwest, 400 meters to the southwest, 197 meters to the southeast." There dwelled the moon god Sin with his "great lady" Ningal, whose cult was celebrated by a priestess who was the god Sin's wife and lived in a sanctuary called *bit-gipâri,* "country house." Among its ruins were leafy branches and fruit.

The same cult was celebrated in Haran, where Terah's caravan stopped. Haran was a sort of smaller Ur and there was a constant back-and-forth between the two. "Their point of departure was the same: Ur of the Chaldees; and likewise their main way station, Haran of the Arameans. But while the star that guided one group of these shepherds or these errant warriors was the moon divinity, *Sin* or *Sahar*, the other group followed a higher light."

Between Adam and Noah there were ten generations, and much degeneration. And between Noah and Abraham ten more generations, and more degeneration. Degeneration was what generations mainly did. Yahweh hadn't created a stable world. The natural tendency of the world was to the worse. But with an occasional shake-up, when someone was chosen and Yahweh became his "shield," so that the world might go on.

Aside from a sequence of names we are told nothing of the descendants of Shem in the generations preceding Abraham. The last story the Bible tells before Yahweh's words to Abraham is the account of the Tower of Babel. Yahweh had come to the conclusion that it wasn't a good thing for "men to form a single people and have a single language." To understand one another too easily was fatal. Certain obstacles were required, an opaqueness, if life on earth was to be bearable. A breathing space was needed, or simply an empty space, between one tribe and another. People would have to be *dispersed*, something that would one day be called *diaspora*. From then on, Yahweh kept quiet until he spoke to Abraham.

Here are the first words Yahweh said to Abraham: "Go away from your land, from your country and from the house of your father toward the land that I will show you." But Abraham was already in the midst of a journey and wasn't altogether sure what his country was; his father's house was a temporary affair, where they had stopped on the way. As for the destination, Canaan, it was hardly new to Abraham. Terah had chosen it, before Yahweh intervened: "Terah took Abram, his son, and Lot, Haran's son, his grandson, and Sarai, his daughter-in-law, wife of his son Abram, and had them leave Ur of the Chaldees to go to the land of Canaan. They got as far as Haran and stopped there."

The only thing that mattered was separation, going away.

Wherever he was, for whatever reason, Abraham had to *go away*. As for the destination, Yahweh would show it to him. No calling could have been sparer, vaguer, more unsettling and untimely. Abraham was seventy-five. He had no children and had done nothing of note in his life to date. And now Yahweh spoke to him as though to the father of a people: "I shall make a great nation of you, I shall bless you and make your name great. You shall be a blessing: I shall bless those that bless you and curse whoever curses you; in you all the families of the earth shall be blessed."

Lekh-lekha, "go away," had a specific meaning. Comparing the expression with other occurrences, Umberto Cassuto came to the conclusion that "in each case the reference is to someone (or something) who goes alone (or only with those who are specially connected with him) and breaks away from the community or group in whose midst he was till that moment." It is the ordeal that gives rise to the individual. At the time, for Abraham, it was just an order to leave Haran and head for Canaan. But this was already his father's plan. It wasn't the destination that was new, but the separation. All he had to do now was complete the last part of the journey. Given this modest requirement, Yahweh's grandiose promises might have seemed excessive. But one day Abraham would hear the same word, *Lekh-lekha*, in quite different circumstances, when he was told to leave his house together with his son Isaac and go to the land of Moriah, where he was to offer the boy "as a holocaust on one of the mountains which I will say to you." Again it was a matter of *going away*. And going to a place that wasn't clearly specified, "which I will say to you." The destination was hardly important, what mattered was the *separation* from another place. The path of this separation was not something you could know, only that there would be moments of great pain. That was another thing Yahweh had in store for Abraham.

In the beginning, the Jews were *those who went away*, following Abraham. No one forced them to go, no one was pursuing them.

They were obeying a call. But before Abraham's life was over they would also become the people who were *chased away*, escorted by Pharaoh's guards back to where they had come from. This constant back-and-forth, between escape and expulsion, would continue throughout their history, until it formed the very fabric of their stories. The Jews *go away* (from Ur of the Chaldees) or they are *chased away* (from Egypt). Movement without respite. Two variations of separation. Without *separation*, of one kind or another, there can be no Jews.

Abraham was the first to receive grace regardless of merit. Noah had received grace before him, but Noah was "upright, perfect among his contemporaries." He "walked in the company of Elohim." His merits were so remarkable because all around him the earth "had grown corrupt." No one had heaped up so many reasons for God to favor him. It was the basis for the grace he received. For his part, all Abraham had done for seventy-five years was follow his father. Nothing marked him out, except his having married a very beautiful woman, who had born him no children. And he was still following his father, Terah. They were rich, seminomadic herdsmen and their movements from one land to another were part of the normal order of things. Abraham was neither king nor priest, nor even the head of a household. Nor was he especially devout. But Abraham was the only one Yahweh chose.

There hadn't always been kings, judges, priests, prophets. Once there were only caravans, moving and settling. Then they moved off again and settled again. Around them, as far as the eye could see, were other, similar settlements. Taking care to avoid too much contact. From farther still came rumors of kingdoms, empires. The oldest and strongest was Egypt. Each caravan was commanded by a patriarch and organized according to kinship and servitude. Yahweh chose to show himself to one caravan, or rather, he asked Abraham to leave his father and form his own caravan.

He wasn't interested in the inhabitants of the kingdoms. They all worshipped a throng of other gods.

For a long time people found it hard to accept that nothing should be known of Abraham, the patriarch, until, in his old age, Yahweh spoke to him. Among the Bible's many omissions, this seemed one of the most glaring. So the *midrashim* set about filling this gaping hole with excessive zeal. Abraham's early life becomes a string of miracles: he was born, they recount, narrowly escaping a slaughter of babies, grew up in a cave feeding on milk sucked from the little finger of his own right hand. Wise at ten days old, at twenty days he was already giving his mother lessons in theology. Persecuted from birth, he was thrown into a fiery furnace and survived. He acquired a special abhorrence for idols, chopping them up with an axe on many occasions. Even the twelve that his father, Terah, worshipped. There's not a word of any of this in Genesis. The *midrashim* had decided to fill the Bible's empty space with a wealth of stories taken from several mythological traditions. But what makes Genesis special, powerful and unique, was precisely this empty space.

When he read out Deuteronomy to the inhabitants of Jerusalem, Josiah found these words: "My father was a wandering Aramean and went down into Egypt, dwelling there with a few others, but there he became a great people, powerful and numerous. Then the Egyptians mistreated us and oppressed us, and forced hard labor upon us. So we cried out to Yahweh, the God of our fathers, and Yahweh heard our voice, saw our hardships, our sufferings, our oppression. Yahweh brought us up out of Egypt with a strong hand and outstretched arm, in the midst of great terror, among signs and wonders. Then he brought us to this place and gave us this land flowing with milk and honey. And behold I have brought the first fruits of the soil that you gave me, Yahweh."

This was the Bible's underlying tonality, hidden beneath all the others. With regard to these words, in his commentary on Deuteronomy, Gerhard von Rad would note, "in a synthesis reduced to the bare essentials, they do no more than state the *bruta facta*." It was an extraordinary lesson in style and a precious legacy for the children of Israel. There would come the day when Franz Kafka, too, would do no more than state the *bruta facta*.

Yahweh's choice of Israel implied the passage from direct analogy to inverted analogy. The foundation of order, on earth, had lain in the interconnection between a people—equivalent to all mankind—certain powers, and a sovereign, who then were made to correspond with celestial powers—also known as gods—and to the celestial sovereign. This was that sacred sovereignty that had been so perfect, enduring and well structured in the Egypt of the pharaonic dynasties. There were similar structures in Mesopotamia, Iran, China (the Son of Heaven), and in Vedic India. Between earth and heaven there was a direct analogy. The sovereign on earth corresponded to the sovereign in heaven, both were at the apex of an order.

Choosing Israel, Yahweh settled on the opposite, an inverted analogy: the smallest would become the greatest, the last would take the place of the first. Israel was "the least numerous among the peoples." And in the beginning Yahweh didn't even choose a people. He chose a nomadic patriarch, who had no land and no descendants. Abraham was the opposite of the Pharaoh. Only with his grandson Jacob would the story of his family become the story of Israel, since Israel was the name given to Jacob.

For a long time Israel would steer clear of kingship, in line with the nature of Yahweh's choice. When finally it was accepted, it was as a concession to decadent times. And the decision to establish the institution was made by a priest, Samuel, reluctantly.

Abraham came to Canaan with "his wife, Sarai, and Lot, his nephew, all the goods they had acquired and the servants they had taken in Haran." They were a caravan arriving in a densely inhabited land, as Genesis immediately makes clear: "The Canaanite was then in the land." Yahweh appeared to Abraham again and said, "I will give this land to your descendants." The vision occurred by the oak of Moreh. Abraham built an altar there, the first altar mentioned after the one Noah built to celebrate the first holocaust.

What else had to be done? For the moment there was no question of conquering the Promised Land. They just needed to find some empty territory where they could settle. Abraham and his family moved on, to Bethel. There Abraham built another altar. Those stones marked his path. But Canaan wasn't as yet the land running with milk and honey that Yahweh would one day describe to Moses. On the contrary, there was a severe famine. So the caravan moved on again, toward Egypt, the oldest of empires, the land that could withstand all the shocks of time.

One can leave Egypt or "come up out of" the country, as the Bible invariably puts it, in several ways. One day Moses and his people would choose the heroic way, crossing the desert and fighting off the attacks of the Amalekites. But the first *exodus from Egypt*, Abraham's, was hardly heroic. Rather than leaving, Abraham was escorted back to the border by Pharaoh's men. He and Sarah had become unwelcome guests.

It all began when, taking refuge in Egypt with Sarah, Abraham passed her off as his sister. Sarah was ravishingly beautiful and Abraham was afraid that as a foreigner whom nobody knew he might be killed by the first man who wanted to possess her. The Pharaoh had good informers, who soon let him know of the arrival of this foreign beauty and her brother. It was very odd that a woman of mature beauty should be unmarried. But there was no time to lose: "The woman was led to the Pharaoh." As a result, the Pharaoh took pains to treat this foreigner whom nobody knew with great generosity since he was the only relative of the woman now living beside him. The gifts flowed and kept flowing: "Small animals and large, asses, manservants and maidservants, she-asses and camels." A settled caravan.

In a typical omission, the Bible doesn't tell us over what period of time the Pharaoh was heaping gifts on Abraham or when exactly the "great scourges" were unleashed on Egypt. Whatever the truth, Pharaoh was quite sure: if Egypt was suffering it was because of the beautiful foreigner living in his palace. Or rather, because of her alleged and hardly credible brother. So "the Pharaoh called Abraham and said, 'What have you done to me? Why didn't you tell me she was your wife? Why did you say, 'She's my sister,' so that I took her as my wife? Here she is! Take her and get out of here.'" Then the Pharaoh ordered his soldiers to escort Abraham out of Egypt, "with his wife and all his belongings," including the rich gifts he had received. An "admirably humane" response, Simone Weil thought. As for Abraham, he emerged from this period of his life much wealthier than before. At the end of the day the deceit had been profitable.

In Genesis, Sarah is the first woman of whom a man says that she is "very beautiful." Before that we had heard only that "the daughters of men" had appeared "beautiful" to the "sons of Elohim," celestial powers. Sarah's beauty is at once linked to fear. It was because of her beauty that Abraham was afraid the Egyptians would kill him and devised the ploy of passing her off as his sister. But the *midrashim* offer an alternative version of events. Abraham supposedly said to Sarah, "The Egyptians are very sensual, and I will put thee in a casket that no harm befall me on account of thee." The border tax collectors asked Abraham what was in the casket. "Barley," said Abraham. "No," said the tax collectors, "it must be wheat." Abraham agreed to pay the price on wheat. The tax collectors weren't satisfied. "It must be pepper," they said. Again Abraham complied. When the tax collectors realized that Abraham was willing to pay up even if they said the casket contained precious stones, they demanded that it be opened. Sarah came out and lit up all Egypt with her beauty. The tax collectors and officials fought to buy her, each outbidding the other. Meantime, the news had reached the Pharaoh, who sent a party of his guards to bring her to his palace.

The Pharaoh regretted having returned Sarah to her fake brother. But he was in a hurry to be rid of those troublesome herdsmen. He despised Abraham and worshipped Sarah. He decided to keep up a connection with her, in the form of his daughter Hagar, "for he preferred that his daughter become the servant of Sarah than reign as mistress in another harem."

Accustomed to being served in a palace, Hagar had to get used to serving in a caravan whose tents were constantly on the move. Then they settled in Canaan and ten years went by. One day, "Abraham went to Hagar and she conceived." Their child would be called Ishmael.

Among the many causes of bafflement scholars come up against in the Bible one of the most glaring is the fact that there are three occasions in Genesis when a man tries to pass off his wife as his sister. Abraham does it twice, with the Pharaoh and with Abimelech, king of the Philistines, and his son Isaac once, again with Abimelech.

Cassuto acknowledged how incongruous the three stories were, above all for their proximity: "It is surprising to find three such similar stories narrated in one book as three successive episodes; and it is even more astonishing that the characters who act and suffer in the second narrative are the same as in the first, and that those of the third are none other than the son and daughter-in-law of the first pair, as though the four of them had been incapable of learning the moral of the first incident, nor even the lesson of the recurrence of events in the second episode."

When in difficulty, biblical scholars often end up supposing that there are three different sources: "as a rule, the section [in Genesis 12] is assigned to the Yahwist, chapter 20 to the Elohist, and the story in chapter 26 to another stratum of the Yahwist." But this division, based on fairly shaky criteria, could equally well be used to show how easily biblical philology can become imaginary philology, deployed mainly to help the philologists wriggle out of a tight spot. Cassuto himself suggested as much, and objected that, even were we to accept the hypothesis of the three sources, there would still be the question, "why did the final editor find it necessary to incorporate all three accounts in his book?" And here Cassuto added a valuable reflection, worthy of a real philologist this time: "The difficulty remains unresolved, the responsibility of a redactor not being less than that of an author." This claim has far-reaching consequences: more than the Yahwist, the Elohist, and the Chronicler, the main author of the Bible could be thought of as the unknown Final Redactor, who thus becomes responsible for all the innumerable occasions of perplexity that the Bible is bound to provoke in anyone.

Even if we accept Cassuto's hypothesis, there is still the question of the episode itself: why did Abraham twice resort to the trick of presenting his wife as his sister (a trick his son Isaac then inherited from him)? Answering this question, both Cassuto and the imaginary philologists fall into a trap. To understand Abraham's behavior we need to remember that "the Bedouins are accustomed to tell lies in order to extricate themselves from trouble or to achieve their desire, and Abram was still afflicted by one of the faults of the Bedouin character; only in the future would he succeed, little by little, in purifying himself completely." So even Abraham the patriarch is explained in terms of the faults of the Bedouin character. For a would-be Jewish patriarch the road to purification is long indeed.

Abraham is the only person in the Bible to be called "the Jew," *ivri*. It happened in the context of a war. Not for the first time, the armies of four kings had lain Canaan to waste and, in Sodom, had taken a number of prisoners including Lot, Abraham's nephew. Abraham mustered three hundred and eighteen men from among his relatives, servants, and members of his clan to attack the foreign soldiers. Not to defeat them, which would have been too much to hope, but to harry them and gain some advantage. So Abraham recovered some booty, and likewise his nephew, Lot. It was then that Genesis calls him "the Jew." The word didn't denote a people, but a certain kind of person, to be found all over the Middle East. Von Rad defines them as "a fluctuating underclass of destitute people, very likely unattached to any family unit and constituting a danger to these states." Meaning to the Babylonians, the Assyrians, the Hittites, and the Egyptians.

At the end of these skirmishes, Abraham found himself face-to-face with a mysterious figure: Melchizedek, king of Salem and priest of the Most High. Abraham was head of a clan that owed allegiance to no king. He himself was not a priest. But on meeting Melchizedek, who introduced himself bringing "bread and wine," Abraham immediately recognized the two supreme forms of authority, united—something rare—in the same person. And so offered him a tenth of the booty he had just captured, as if fulfilling a duty to a higher power.

Who was Melchizedek? Over the centuries there have been any number of answers. Often contradictory and incompatible, but always agreeing on one point: Melchizedek's appearance has something abrupt and solemn about it that remains entirely without justification. Many Bible commentators thought they might make the scene somewhat less unfathomable by presenting Melchizedek as a king of Canaan with a special affinity to Abraham, insofar as he worshipped the Most High. But this actually intensifies the strangeness of the meeting. It would be the only occasion on which one of the patriarchs not only recognizes a god who is not Yahweh, but bows down to him. And who could Melchizedek's Most High be? There was no scarcity of sovereign gods, but they always came together with other gods and other customs. How could Abraham, who had gone away in order to follow Yahweh, not only accept them, but worship them?

Up to and including Abraham, everybody we meet in the Bible

comes burdened with a genealogy. Melchizedek is the exception. We know nothing of his forebears. For Christians this would one day become a mark of divinity. "Without father, without mother, without genealogy," the Epistle to the Hebrews would define him. And the text adds that Melchizedek "had neither a beginning of days, nor end of life." René Guénon sees in him "the point of connection between the Hebrew tradition and the great primordial tradition." This prompted the idea that the bread and wine he brings—but hasn't *sacrificed*, it seems—is the first and most powerful foreshadowing of the Eucharist. And in fact bread and wine had never hitherto been brought together in such stark and grandiose prominence.

"After these events the word of God came to Abraham in a vision," Genesis says. But what events are we talking about? Of the appearance of Melchizedek. It is as if this mysterious figure were the precondition for all investiture. Only *after* Abraham had recognized Melchizedek's dual sovereignty would Yahweh tell him, "Be not afraid, Abraham, I am your shield. Your reward will be very great." But Abraham was feeling old and childless and dared to observe to Yahweh: "My servant will inherit my goods." He was a nobody and risked disappearing without trace. And so "on that day Yahweh made a covenant with Abraham," announcing events still distant in time.

The pact between Yahweh and Abraham took place among animals cut in two and still bleeding: a heifer, a she-goat, a sheep, a turtledove, and a pigeon. Vultures wheeled around the carcasses. Abraham chased them off. Then, toward sunset, he fell into a tormented sleep. Dimly, he saw a dark future. Yahweh spoke of "four hundred years of servitude and oppression." When night came on, "a smoking brazier and a torch of fire passed among the pieces of the victims." To make a covenant one has to cut something—the victims—and pass between the remains. The parts of the sacrificed animals are arranged at the two ends of the altar. But how can you pass through an altar made of stone? With fire. Then Yahweh spoke again and "made a covenant with Abraham" that would one day be called the "covenant between the pieces." To which Yahweh soon added another condition: a *cut* must be made in the body of every male, "even the foreigner you have bought with money": circumcision.

Circumcision was to be a sign of the covenant made on a man's body, distinguishing him from all those who did not belong to the covenant. But circumcision had been in use among the Egyptians since the most ancient times. Herodotus claims the practice had passed from them to other peoples, as far as distant Colchis. So how could the Jews distinguish themselves from the subjects of the nearest and most powerful kingdom that worshipped endless gods? It could be done only if the covenant that circumcision signaled were to become the foundation of everything. And that foundation implied killing and blood. In the modern world a pact is a formal understanding requiring a written text and two signatures. But between Yahweh and Israel, from Abraham onward, it demanded bloodshed. The contracting parties must cut a sacrificed victim in two and pass between the halves of a bleeding body. No bloody sacrifice, no pact. And the two parties were so much part of this sacrifice that they had to pass *between the pieces*, as if they were themselves the victims. Dhorme claims this happened "so as to identify with the victims and share their destiny, in the event that either party violate the commitments undertaken." Such an interpretation is immediately a way of transferring the rite into a juridical context that can guarantee the consequences of an act. A modernizing, euphemistic explanation. Far more important was the premise behind the act itself: the killing of a victim and its blood. Without that first act, in which an animal—a "calf they cut in two," as Jeremiah puts it—was killed, the pact itself couldn't be made.

What is this repeated and absolutely necessary act in the account of the first covenant between Yahweh and Abraham? The act of cutting. Something *must* be cut. In Genesis 15 some animals have to be sacrificed; they must be cut in half. In Genesis 17 it is the foreskin of every male. Two actions performed in order that blood, which is life, be shed. Only then can the covenant come into being. There are no other rules, no doctrine to obey. Just two actions, two cuts, and a promise of boundless expansion: for one man, Abraham, who will become a people.

Yahweh never set out the Ten Commandments for Abraham. Nor the precepts of Leviticus and Deuteronomy. Yahweh gave him just four commands: *separate* yourselves—you and your family— from the caravan of Terah, your father; *cut*, ritually, a covenant with your god; *remove* a part of your body and those of your men, with circumcision; *leave* your home and go to Mount Moriah together with your son Isaac. Each time, something had to be separated from something else. And the separation was understood as final, because of Isaac, Yahweh said, "offer him as a holocaust," and holocaust meant total destruction. There is not a hint of verbal doctrine in these commands. They were four acts to perform. The doctrine was implicit. Four hundred years of oppression would follow, something Yahweh saw fit to let Abraham know. At the end of which the doctrine would be manifested in a different way: etched in tables of stone and proclaimed in the desert.

For a certain time, after birth, man, like an animal, like a tree, is not to be touched: seven days, then circumcision: "At eight days old every male among you will be circumcised"; likewise an animal is to stay beside its mother for seven days, after which it can be sacrificed: "When a calf or lamb or kid is born, it will stay seven days with its mother and from the eighth day it will be acceptable as an offering to Yahweh"; likewise a tree is to produce fruit for three years without anyone picking it. Then the fruit will be offered to Yahweh and, only later, eaten by men. Every life is a deferment of the moment when that life will be cut, sacrificed, eaten: through circumcision, sacrifice, the act of eating. Actions that injure and annul a former wholeness.

This rule didn't apply only to men, but to life itself, vegetable, animal, human. Rather, the rule defined life. This was the toughest doctrine that Yahweh chose to reveal to Abraham and to all those who *went away* with him.

It was Abraham's ninety-ninth birthday when Elohim told him he must circumcise himself and all the males in his house; and that his name would no longer be Abram, but Abraham, as Sarai would henceforth be called Sarah; and that she would bear him a son called Isaac. Abraham laughed. Never before was there any mention of his laughing. It's not clear whether out of pleasure or for the sheer unlikeliness of what he had heard. His immediate response was not for the son thus announced but for the life of the son he already had and who was now thirteen, as if Abraham already foresaw that some months later he would be abandoning the boy together with his mother, in the desert, with a bit of bread and a goatskin of water. "Abraham said to Elohim, 'So long as Ishmael may live in your presence.'"

But there was no time for reflection. Elohim demanded that the entire house of Abraham be circumcised that very day. The patriarch's friends were baffled. Aner told Abraham that being circumcised at a hundred was torture. Eshkol said that once they had been circumcised their enemies would find it all the easier to recognize them. Abraham decided to circumcise himself with his own hands. And he made sure Ishmael was circumcised at once. Then it was the turn of the others in his household, amid much blood and wailing. Three days later, in a blistering heatwave, Abraham was still suffering from his circumcision. He was sitting outside his tent, in a place he loved, among the oaks of Mamre, in Hebron. "He raised his eyes and saw three men before him." Two were angels, one was Yahweh himself; they said they were wayfarers.

The announcement of Isaac's birth was repeated when the three strangers appeared in the dazzling midday sunshine. Exemplary host that he was, Abraham was at once concerned that they have something to eat. One of the strangers asked where Sarah was.

Abraham replied that she was inside, in the tent, unseen. Then Yahweh said, "I will come back at the same time next year and then Sarah, your wife, will have a son."

Sarah was spying on them from the darkness of the tent. She laughed silently, so as not to betray herself. And thought, "Now that I'm shriveled up and my husband is old, am I to give myself to pleasure?" The Seventy cut these words, but Jerome translated: *Postquam consenui, et dominus meus vetulus est, voluptati operam dabo?* Sarah, at this moment, chose to remember that to conceive a child you first had to give yourself to "the work of pleasure." Then Yahweh asked Abraham, "Why did Sarah laugh?" Something he hadn't asked when Abraham had laughed. And Sarah was so bold as to deny it, as if a tent were shelter enough. Then Yahweh insisted, "No! You laughed." They were the only words Yahweh and Sarah ever exchanged, a sort of family quarrel, no less intimate than those between Yahweh and Abraham.

One might ask what it was that set Abraham apart from others. Perhaps his capacity to ask the simplest, most tiresome, unavoidable questions, not of other people but of Yahweh himself. In the beginning, when Yahweh had ordered him to leave Haran, Abraham had obeyed without a word. But after reaching Canaan and having fought the first skirmishes and battles, worn out and childless as he was, when Yahweh started repeating, as if Abraham didn't already know, "I am Yahweh who brought you out of Ur of the Chaldees to give you this land for your own," he answered, "Oh, Lord Yahweh, how can I know that I will possess all this." It was his *doubt concerning election*, the most powerful of all doubts. His question could have been seen as skeptical and insolent, attitudes for which Abraham has been criticised down the ages. But Yahweh didn't see it that way. At once he ordered that preparations be made to seal—or "cut," but it amounted to the same thing—the first covenant with Abraham.

More than twenty years later the time would come for another question, and this time Abraham himself was shocked by his boldness: "So I decided to talk to my Lord, I who am dust and ashes." This was the difference that mattered: if dust and ashes were not in a position to address their Lord, then they might as well stay as they were and all history would be natural history. But if they could speak, then election and a consequent intimacy with the Lord were possible.

In fact Abraham had now become his Lord's confidant, to the point that immediately after decreeing the total destruction of Sodom and Gomorrah, Yahweh had said, "And can I then hide from Abraham what I am about to do?" At that moment Abraham was taking his leave of the two angels and sending them on their way as good manners demanded. He didn't know that his nephew Lot and all the inhabitants of Sodom and Gomorrah had been sentenced to death. It was then that Abraham risked asking God the biggest of questions: "Are you really going to have the just perish with the wicked?" In that case what difference would there be between the justice of Yahweh and a tidal wave?

The exchange that followed between Yahweh and Abraham was based on a wonderful equivocation that both speakers were aware of. Abraham's understanding was that if in a city there were fifty just men, then that city should be saved. And from Yahweh's answers it seemed he agreed: "If I find fifty just men in the city of Sodom, I will pardon the whole area for their sake." But Abraham knew that wasn't going to happen. There weren't fifty just men to be found. So he lowered the bar to ten. It was a match between two experienced players, each capable of playing the other's game, to the point of becoming accomplices rather than opponents. Abraham wanted to save Lot and his family. Eight people, including four daughters and two husbands (two daughters were still unmarried). Abraham knew that Lot was not a just man, but a judge in a town where all the laws were unjust. And he knew that by appealing to the existence of some just men he could save his own. Yahweh didn't contest Abraham's criterion, even in its most demanding formulation, that is, that the existence of such and such a number of just men would be enough to save the whole "area." But he knew he was going to destroy Sodom. Like two able negotiators they arrived at the number that both wanted to hear: ten. At that point Yahweh broke off the game and destroyed Sodom. But Lot and his family were saved.

Two strangers arrived at the gates of Sodom. Lot, who lived nearby, invited them to his home. He was taking a big risk because in Sodom you didn't welcome guests, you robbed them. Initially, the two strangers turned him down. They said they'd sleep in the open. But Lot repeated his invitation. He offered them unleavened bread, as in the times of his nomadic life. Sodom was full of people spying on one another. Soon enough news got about that two strangers were in town. Around Lot's house things started getting noisy. A crowd formed. They wanted the two strangers, no doubt to kill them. Lot appeared at his door. He said, "I have two daughters no man has ever touched, I'll send them out to you and you can treat them as you wish." But lynching and raping weren't going to be enough. The crowd wanted Lot himself. In the end he, too, was a stranger. They wanted to break down the door. It was the beginning of the destruction of Sodom. A dazzling light stunned the aggressors. Then the two Angels said to Lot, "Rise up, take your wife and the two daughters who are here, if you don't want to perish for the city's crimes." So Lot was saved. He wasn't a just man, he hadn't hesitated to offer his two daughters to the crowd who'd surrounded his home, but he had given shelter to the Angels. A little later, after a firestorm had descended from the sky and burned up the city, Abraham "went, early in the morning, to the place where he had stood before Yahweh." It offered a commanding view of the plain. Abraham "looked toward Sodom and Gomorrah, and the area all around, and saw smoke rising from the earth like the smoke from a furnace."

What would have happened if the Angels hadn't dazzled the aggressors with a supernatural light? In the book of Judges another story gives us a good idea, because in places it follows word for word the story of what happened around Lot's house in Sodom.

There was a Levite, "in those days," innumerable days after the times of Abraham, who had a concubine, a woman from Bethlehem. The concubine left him to go back to her father. Four months later, her husband went to find her, to bring her home. "With him he had his servant and two asses." The concubine's father was pleased to welcome him. They ate and drank together for three days. The Levite wanted to get back home with his concubine, but her father kept finding reasons to have him stay. Finally, the fifth day, they set off. Toward evening they left their route to spend the night in Gibeah because the inhabitants were Benjaminites. The city square was empty. No one welcomed them.

But the Levite saw an old man coming home from the fields. The man asked who they were and invited them to his house. They ate and drank. Then they heard some noise outside. A crowd had surrounded the house. Words were exchanged with the old man: "Send out the man who's in your house so we can get to know him," the aggressors said. The old man came outside and said, "'No, my brothers, please, no violence. This man came to my house, don't do anything bad to him! Here is my daughter, a virgin, and he has a concubine! I'll send them out and you can rape them and do everything you want with them. But don't do anything bad to this man.' The aggressors wouldn't listen. So the man took his concubine and pushed her out into the crowd. They knew her and abused her all night . . . When it was almost morning, the woman fell at the door of the man's house where her master was staying and lay there till daybreak. Her master came out in the morning and opened the door of the house. As he was getting ready to resume his journey, he saw the woman, his concubine lying at the entrance to the house, her hands gripping the threshold. He said, 'Get up and let's go!' But there was no reply. So he put her on his ass, then returned to his own land. The man went into his house, took a knife, picked up the concubine, and cut her to pieces, bone by bone, twelve pieces that he sent throughout the land of Israel."

The other tribes of Israel organized a retaliation and attacked the Benjaminites. The inhabitants of Gibeah were "put to the sword." A column of smoke rose over the town.

Abraham's concubine, Hagar, twice found herself wandering in the desert. First when she was pregnant and Sarah was giving her a hard time. Hagar was afraid the older woman would put a jinx on her. She fled toward her father, toward Egypt. But found only desert. When at last she came across a well, the Angel of Yahweh appeared to her. He called her "Sarah's maid," not Pharaoh's daughter, but he wanted to save her and spoke of a race that would be born from her, of countless descendants. For the moment, though, Hagar would have to go back to her mistress and humble herself "under her hands." The Angel also told her what her son would be called: Ishmael. He added that he had appeared because Yahweh had "heeded your humiliation." This didn't quite add up. Yahweh had sent his Angel because he had heeded Hagar's humiliation and now he was ordering her to accept even more humiliation. But Hagar now spoke directly to Yahweh. She called his name and said, "Wasn't it here that I saw the trace of he who saw me?" Then she went back to Abraham's house.

Fourteen years passed. At last, utterly implausible as it was, Sarah had given birth to Isaac. And one day Ishmael was playing with his little half brother. Sarah's face darkened. She saw the two sons of Abraham as equal heirs, her son and the "son of this servant." It was out of the question. Abraham was upset. But Elohim quickly intervened and said, "Don't be anxious for your son and your maid!" He should listen to Sarah, to "everything she will say." Then Elohim wound up: "As for your maid's son, I will make a nation from him, too, because he is your offspring."

These were great expectations, but for the moment Abraham would have to abandon Hagar and her son, Ishmael, in the desert. "Abraham rose early, took some bread and a goatskin of water, gave them to Hagar, then lifted her son onto her shoulders and said goodbye." Once again Hagar found herself wandering in the desert. This time her son wasn't in her belly, but on her shoulders. And this time she knew there was no way back. When the water in the goatskin ran out, Hagar decided to sit still until she died of thirst. But she didn't want to have Ishmael beside her and hid him behind a bush. Then she moved on, "a bowshot away." She said to herself, "Just so long as I don't have to see my son die!" She wept.

And once again the Angel spoke. He said Elohim had heard a voice. Not hers, but Ishmael's. Hagar must get up and take her son's hand. Once again she heard tell of a "great nation" in the future. By now obedience was a habit. She walked along holding Ishmael's hand. And, as if earlier she had been blind, she saw a well. "She filled the goatskin with water and gave it to the boy to drink." They were saved. Ishmael "lived in the desert and became an archer. He lived in the desert of Paran and her mother chose him a wife who came from Egypt." When Sarah died, Abraham married Hagar, who bore him six more children. They grew to be idolaters.

What took place between Sarah and Hagar after Hagar gave birth to Ishmael corresponded point by point to what the Code of Hammurabi laid out in paragraphs 146 and 147: "If a man has taken a wife and she gives her husband a maid and the maid bears children; if, later, this maid feels she is her mistress's equal, because she has borne children, her mistress cannot sell her for money, but shall impose the mark of servitude on her and count her among her servants. If she has not born children, her mistress can sell her for money." Ur of the Chaldees had been left far behind, but its laws were still very much alive. Abraham certainly wasn't going to repudiate them. Yahweh had made a covenant, but he hadn't as yet prescribed any laws. For ordinary disputes, Abraham had to turn to the laws of his fathers: Hammurabi law. When Sarah came to him because she felt her maid was insulting her, Abraham said, "'Look, your maid is in your hands: do with her whatever seems fit in your eyes.' So Sarah humiliated her and [Hagar] ran away."

Isaac was *not* Abraham's firstborn. Yet Yahweh called him "your son, your only son, the one you love." The firstborn was Ishmael, "the maid's son," born as a *substitute*, after Sarah had prompted Abraham, "Go to my maid, perhaps you will have a child through her."

But only Isaac had been announced by Yahweh. And one day Abraham would arrange for his death, as previously he had arranged for Ishmael's. In Ishmael's case there was no question of a holocaust; he was treated as a goat, a scapegoat, sent off into the desert to die.

On two mornings thirteen years apart, Abraham "rose early" and went through the motions that heralded the death of his two sons: Ishmael and Isaac. For Ishmael, "the maid's child," and for his mother, Hagar, the concubine, the Egyptian, he prepared a goatskin of water and a bit of bread; for Isaac, the son of Sarah, his wife, he saddled an ass and split the wood that would be needed for the holocaust. Abraham knew that that bread and water wouldn't last long in the desert of Beersheba, where he meant to send Hagar and Ishmael when he parted from them. They would die of hunger and thirst. Abraham knew that the wood he cut that morning would serve to burn up Isaac completely on the summit of Mount Moriah. But Abraham remembered the words that Elohim had spoken to him: "It is with Isaac's name that your descendants will be known. As for your maid's son, I will make a nation from him, too, because he is your offspring." Something wasn't clear: if both children were to die before procreating, and if Abraham himself was to be the instrument of their deaths, how on earth could they found not just one nation, but two? Throughout the three days in which Abraham was walking toward Mount Moriah with Isaac and two servants, then at the end just with Isaac, these thoughts tormented him. They went on and on. As Kierkegaard wrote, "from the ethical point of view, we describe Abraham's behavior saying that he planned to kill Isaac, and from the religious point of view, that he planned to sacrifice him."

Back bent under the wood for the holocaust, while his father held "the knife and the fire," after three days walking, Isaac spoke these indelible words to Abraham: "Father mine, here is the fire and the wood, but where is the ram for the holocaust?"

Kierkegaard made the sharpest of distinctions between the story of Abraham and Isaac and the many other instances where parents sacrifice sons and daughters, whether in the Bible or in the stories of the ancient world (Jephthah's daughter, Iphigenia, the daughters of Erechtheus). In the case of Abraham and Isaac the sacrifice would bear no *fruit* (fulfilment of a vow, placation of divine wrath, salvation of a city). On the contrary, sacrificing Isaac would actually prevent the fulfilment of a promise that Elohim himself had made. If Isaac died before having children, he could hardly produce descendants constituting a people numerous as the stars in the sky. After thirty years living in the glow of that promise, Abraham's entire life would be rendered null and meaningless. And in fact Elohim never told Abraham that the sacrifice had a purpose. And no one besides Abraham knew what Elohim had asked of him.

It's true that many years later Yahweh would tell Moses, "Consecrate unto me every firstborn: man or beast, whatever creature opens her womb among the children of Israel is mine"—and Isaac, albeit born after Ishmael, was Abraham's divinely legitimized firstborn. In fact Elohim had called him, "Your son, your only son, the one you love, Isaac." *To belong to Yahweh* meant to disappear from the world, as happened when a body was completely burned up. But right afterward Yahweh had said to Moses, "Every firstborn ass you shall redeem with a lamb and, if you do not redeem it, you will break its neck. Every human firstborn among your children you will redeem." That law was given the very night in which the children of Israel were to go out of Egypt. But there was no doubt it had been valid since time began and for all time. Even if Yahweh had given Abraham only the law of circumcision.

The new word was *redeem*, the possibility of one thing *substi-*

tuting for another. If a lamb could substitute for an ass, it could certainly do the same for a man. This was the miracle that would allow people to avoid the ongoing loss of their firstborn children. But before that became routine, one man and his son had to have the experience—and the *terror*—of that miracle. And that man must never dare to suppose that it had been him who invented the miracle. This was what mattered: to recognize that only a divine miracle could form the basis of a law that would one day be applied every day. Witnessing that miracle was the *test* to which Abraham and Isaac were subjected.

After the Angel of Yahweh had stayed his hand as he made to cut Isaac's throat, Abraham could have hurried back down Mount Moriah with a lighter heart. Instead "he raised his eyes and saw a ram, its horns caught in a bush." No sooner had he seen it than "Abraham went to take the ram and offer it as a holocaust in place of his son."

It is this aspect of the story that commentators most often overlook: one can hardly question the fact that the animal that so miraculously appears must be killed. One can hardly suppose that Abraham will climb down from Mount Moriah without celebrating a holocaust. The ram with its horns trapped in the bush might have been a stray or an apparition of divine origin. Abraham could have worshipped it, or paid no attention. Instead he felt he had to kill it. Not to eat its meat, but to burn it, "in place of his son." About this substitution questions might, indeed must be asked. Not about the killing.

To Isaac's concern that there was no animal to sacrifice, Abraham had answered, "Elohim will provide the ram for the holocaust." Divine power guaranteed that in any event an animal would be killed and burned on Mount Moriah. Isaac's doubtfulness is so poignant because it has to do with a matter that admits of no doubt. Isaac knows that come what may an animal is going to be killed. And he knows that he himself could substitute for the animal. It is this ploy of substitution that is all-determining.

Will man substitute for animal or animal for man? Whichever it is, substitution always goes hand in hand with killing. Even when a sound—a word—substitutes for a thing, the act of killing is implicit. Substitution—forever uncertain and arbitrary as it is—is based on something certain: the kill.

If, after three days of thoughtful walking toward Mount Moriah, after dismissing the two servants who had walked with them, so that they wouldn't be witnesses, after heaping the firewood around his son Isaac, bound on top of the altar, whom that wood was going to burn—if Abraham at this point had begged of Yahweh the grace to substitute Isaac with a ram that he could look for on the mountainside and if Yahweh had agreed, then from that day on Abraham could have claimed that he had been the first to propose *substitution*. And in so doing he would have failed the trial to which Yahweh was subjecting him and hence proved himself unfit to be the founding father of the children of Israel. Substitution must come as a gift from Yahweh, not an invention of man. If Abraham had been able to substitute Isaac with a ram, if Abraham had counted on the fact that the Angel would stay his hand, then from that moment on everything would be open to substitution with everything else. And no one would have objected, since substitution is a constant companion of the mind, starting with the word, which is based on substitution. If this substitution had been understood as a purely human device, Yahweh himself, in the end, would have been made redundant. Men knew they could go a long way with substitution and hardly needed help. Yahweh chose to destroy any such illusions at once, in the cruelest and most effective way. Thus Abraham confirmed his role as the first of the patriarchs.

"Then Abraham reached out his hand and took the knife to cut his son's throat." Just as he had decided to grasp the knife, so an instant later he would have decided to plunge it into his son's body. But that didn't happen. Abraham had stripped himself of the sensation of free will. He no longer felt able to want anything.

He had recognized that something else was acting through him. Abraham's achievement was not total obedience, but the ability to suspend the rarest of the gifts that Yahweh entrusted to Adam: the sensation of free will. A slippery gift, necessary for living. But for now the matter in hand was not living, but recognizing. Whether free will exists, no one can say for certain. But everyone can claim to have the sensation of free will. A precious sensation that makes life liveable and offers the foundation on which every order rests, however fragile a foundation it may be. The trial Yahweh put Abraham through was drastic, obliging him to recognize the necessary illusion to which man is subject: that of attributing free will and the power of substitution to himself.

According to the *Sifte Kohen*, the *Book of the Priest's Lips*, published in Wandsbeck in 1690, some time after Isaac had set out together with Abraham and the two servants, Satan appeared to Sarah dressed as an old man and asked her where Isaac was. "'He went with his father to be instructed in the laws of sacrifices,' was her reply. 'No,' rejoined Satan, 'he himself is the sacrifice.'" Those words answered the question that, at that very moment, Isaac was asking Abraham, about the ram for the sacrifice, which he couldn't see.

In the case of Ishmael, Elohim "heard the boy's voice"; in the case of Isaac he recognized his mute "Terror." Both were saved in the nick of time. It wasn't just Hagar, or just Abraham who persuaded him to intervene. It was the two boys themselves, condemned without knowing why.

The *doubt concerning election* that so violently assailed Abraham is the most corrosive and irrepressible of doubts. It is the doubt on which Kafka would one day build *The Castle*. And would never finish building it, since this is a doubt that one can never resolve. But more than anyone else Kafka captured certain of its traits. "An Abraham who comes without being called!" he wrote in his Abrahamic letter to Klopstock. What could be more ex-cruciating? What would be more likely to make you an object of derision? Kafka imagined a school where "the teacher plans to ar-range things so that the reward of the best pupil is at the same time the punishment of the worst." The smartest and the dumbest of the class would have to be involved. But what if the two were—necessarily, inextricably—the same person?

Other possibilities came to mind: "I could imagine another Abraham, who for sure would never manage to become a patri-arch, nor even a rag-and-bone man: this Abraham would be more than willing to carry out the requested sacrifice, keen as a waiter, but would never manage actually to make the sacrifice because he can never get out of the house, he's indispensable, the house-hold depends on him, there's always something that needs sorting out, the house isn't in order, but if the house isn't in order, if that condition isn't satisfied, he can't go out, the Bible itself explains as much when it says: 'He put his house in order,' and Abraham already had everything and more; if he hadn't had a house, where would he have brought up his son, which shelf could he have kept his knife on?"

"He put his house in order": words that, as Kafka would have it, we should find in the Bible. Only they're not there. In Genesis we read, "Abraham rose early in the morning, saddled his ass, took his two servants and his son Isaac, split the wood for the holo-caust, got to his feet, and set off toward the place Elohim had men-tioned." Nothing about the house.

The Italian translator of Kafka's letters went to check the story of Abraham in the Bible and couldn't find the words "He put his house in order." Puzzled, he wrote to Max Brod, who "politely in-formed him that the words turned up in a Bach cantata: *Bestelle dein Haus, denn du wirst sterben*, "Put your house in order, for you shall die." And in fact Kafka had written: *Er bestellte sein Haus*, "He put his house in order." Bach was putting to music a verse from Isaiah: "In those days Hezekiah fell mortally ill. The prophet Isaiah, son of Amos, went to him and said, 'Thus says Yahweh: Put your house in order, for you shall die and will live no more.'" An example of Isaiah's abruptness, but also his ability to set up a U-turn. For shortly afterward with the same abruptness he tells Hezekiah, "Thus says Yahweh, God of your father David: I have heard your prayer, I have seen your tears. And behold I will add fifteen years to your days." It wasn't a simple thing to do: the shadow must retreat ten steps "and the sun retreated ten steps along the steps that it had traveled along." The course of nature, that is, or rather of time, would have to be altered. That was what it took to move the death of just one man. Hezekiah understood, and tried to offer an explanation: "For Sheol will not glorify you, / nor death celebrate you. / They that go down into the abyss / hope no more in your faithfulness. / The living, the living, it is he that praises you."

Kafka's transposition of Isaiah's words to the story of Abraham, whether intentional or otherwise, amounted to an application of Bloy's rule, whereby every verse of the Vulgate could be applied to every other verse. "He put his house in order," could be said of Abraham because the following words were "For you shall die and will live no more," words spoken to Hezekiah, who had been struck down, as Abraham was struck down, by a mortal illness and was destined, like Abraham, to live beyond that illness.

Abraham finds his counterpart in an isolated, rugged figure who arrives much later in the Bible: Job. If Abraham was grace without the justification of merit, Job was "dis-grace" without the justification of guilt. The one calls to and demands the other. If this wasn't the case, everything that happened would present itself as the result of a precise accountancy. Instead the bottom line doesn't add up, since calculation ignores the initial back-and-forth of grace and dis-grace.

We hear very little of either Abraham or Job before they are touched respectively by grace and dis-grace. Of Abraham's first

seventy-five years we know nothing aside from his family relations. Of Job we hear only that he did no evil. Neither man, in
his previous life, had been conspicuous for his merits or demerits.
Each could perfectly well have died without leaving any trace, like
so many others, the one as a member of a numerous seminomadic
clan, the other as a rich, much-loved landowner. Just that, from
a certain point on, their stories break away from all others. They
become the story of grace and dis-grace.

For Job's seven sons and three daughters life was one long party:
every day they invited one another to their homes, the three sisters included. So every day of the week was a feast day. Their father,
"blameless and upright," not only "kept away from evil," but did
not want evil to get anywhere near his children. How could he be
sure of that? In the midst of all that eating and drinking, might not
one of them be having nasty or even wicked thoughts? As soon as
the last day's partying was over, Job called his children together
and celebrated a holocaust on their behalf. An animal burned on
an altar would make up for shortcomings that might or might not
have been committed. It was the only way to guarantee the pu-
rity of what was perfect. Then at once the feasting could start over.
"They ate and drank wine in the older brother's house."

Meantime Job waited, as always, for the moment when he
would perform the next sacrifice. So the cycle could begin again.
That was the moment when Satan suggested to Yahweh that he put
Job to the test. For Abraham the test had had to do with one unique
and unlikely being, Isaac. For Job it involved all his offspring and
everyone connected to him. But in Job's case it went even further.
It wasn't enough to deprive him of everything he had; his body was
to be ravaged. "Skin for skin. To save his life a man will give everything he has." So said Satan, with sovereign succinctness.

If we are to believe the words Yahweh spoke to Satan, Job was
"a blameless and upright man who fears Elohim and keeps away
from evil." Not only was Job careful to do no evil himself, he also

took care that his seven sons and three daughters did none. So when his children came back from their parties, "he rose early to offer holocausts, the same number as his children, because Job said to himself: 'Perhaps my children have sinned and cursed Elohim in their hearts.'" Certainly, Yahweh had "put a hedge" around him. All the same, Job felt the need to take precautions just in case his children sinned. It was as if he foresaw what might at any moment happen. There was something beyond the power of holocausts. Pure evil, evil that is not the consequence of sin.

To Satan's mind, Job was an example of the kind of person who can spend his entire life close to evil without ever being touched by it, as though there were "a hedge around him, around his house and all that he possessed." And Satan, who was constantly busy in every corner of the earth, wasn't going to accept this. He knew the world too well. He knew it doesn't allow for hedges that can't be torn down from one moment to the next. Satan said as much to Yahweh, in the presence of "the sons of Elohim." Satan could mix with them, because he was one of them.

In their presence Yahweh could hardly adduce arguments that might dispel the mystery surrounding the fortunes of the wicked and the sufferings of the righteous. Those arguments were not to be known. Men must live inside that mystery without expecting to be told what was behind it. So Yahweh spoke with an epiphany that would expand beyond all boundaries. Nothing less was required. Simone Weil talked about it in a few words that she underlined in her Notebook XI, written in Marseille in 1942: "*The order of the world is made for us, to have us accept suffering, and it reaches out to the things we don't know, because it is useful to us only in so far as it is outside us, indifferent to us. Job.*"

The just man who suffers and the man who is chosen. Job and Abraham. To understand them, we must see them together. The one is the condition and premise of the other. The way the world is constituted demands the presence of both. If grace only came as a benediction, never as a condemnation, the world would be run by sovereign beings who pass through it unscathed. But that's not how it is. Beings touched by grace find their mirror image in just men who suffer for no reason. Their justness does not help them escape their doom.

How else could the world work? Like a company whose efficient employees are rewarded at the end of the year, while the less efficient are regularly assigned the more miserable jobs? So goes the secular world machine. Alternatively, we could imagine evil striking quite randomly, careless of the good and the bad. In which case fortune would favor those who have temporarily avoided evil's blows merely thanks to statistical probability. So goes the scientific world machine. But these two machines are not enough to explain how a world containing both Abraham and Job is constituted. For that we must turn to the Bible.

When Job found his body covered with sores "from the soles of his feet to the top of his head," and tried to scratch them with a broken pot, sitting on a heap of ashes, his wife, for whom he had never celebrated any holocausts, came out with the toughest words he had heard yet: "Still clinging to your perfection, are you? Curse Elohim and die." Words that nullified Job's life and any life based on merit. Job replied in the only way that was appropriate, without talking up his perfection or claiming it could weigh in the balance. "If we accept the good from Elohim, should we not also accept the bad?" Before Job, Abraham, too, had found himself in a situation that prompted the same question. But then it was a question of a sacrifice. A situation with a possible way out. A ram could turn up to take the victim's role in place of his son. But the question also arose with regard to existence itself, at its simplest, and Job gave words to it. It was not so different or distant from what Nietzsche would one day say of the eternal return: if we

accept an instant of existence, we must accept existence in all its
instants.

Job decided to take issue with Yahweh, but he didn't complain
of the deaths, all at once, of his ten children or the loss of all their
belongings. Rather, he spoke of something that everyone felt and
no one dared mention: divine oppression. For Yahweh, he said,
men's lives are like "the days of a mercenary," who longs only for
his service to end. Everyone, Job said, felt Yahweh was spying on
them and weighing them up at every moment. Why did Yahweh
bother "to frighten a leaf in the wind / and harass a straw," since
that was how men in general must seem to him? The ultimate question was "What is a man that you pay him so much attention?"
And why "have you made me your target?" It was something he
felt continuously: "Shaddai's arrows are inside me," and it is "their
poison my spirit drinks."

By now this was the only tone Job could take: "I bring my
flesh between my teeth, / and hold my life in my hand." Even if he
knew he was "like a moth-eaten cloak," Yahweh never loosened
his grip on him: "You watch every step I take / and study all my
footprints."

Yahweh's response is astonishing: he doesn't deny any of Job's
claims; on the contrary, he accepts that they are sound. And
evokes an epiphany to "make manifest to him the beauty of the
world."

With time men had cut themselves some space among the animals. Some they had taken into service—flocks and herds—living
off their produce. Others they kept with them in their houses. The
predators they emulated, in the hunt, to the point of hunting down
the predators themselves. But there was always one predator, supreme and invisible, whom they couldn't escape. No one dared
name him, until Job said, "You hunt me, like a leopard." As well as
a hunter, Yahweh could also be a severe and sharp-eyed overseer:
"When are you ever going to take your eyes off me / and give me

time to swallow my spit?" asks Job. A sleepless guard like this was enough to ruin your life. "Move away from me so I can cheer up a bit," he insists. The heaviest weight men had to bear was this omnipresent divinity always looming over everyone, as if they were no more than hired soldiers. It was one of the undeniable truths that Yahweh chose never to mention, but allowed Job the privilege of bringing out into the open.

His torments over, Job found himself with fourteen sons and three daughters, fourteen thousand sheep instead of seven thousand, six thousand camels instead of three thousand, a thousand pairs of oxen and asses instead of five hundred. Everything had doubled, except the daughters, who stuck at three. And once again there were holocausts. Only this time it wasn't Job who was obliged to celebrate them. Now it was up to his three comforters, whom Yahweh accused of not having "told the truth about me as my servant Job did." Now Job "will plead on your behalf," Yahweh added. Sublime sarcasm.

What was missing in all this? The hedge. Surrounded by a teeming wealth of new possessions, Job knew that he could not and must not think of building hedges. For sure, his fourteen sons were not the seven who had died. But divine justice doesn't deal in equivalents, because equivalents are just something men invented, a sham. Divine justice can only be an exchange of surpluses, from the invisible toward the invisible.

Job's three new daughters were called Dove, Cinnamon, and Beauty Case. People said, "in all the country no women were as beautiful as Job's daughters." That was the surplus.

The foundation stone of the Promised Land was a tomb, one that Abraham was absolutely determined to buy. We even know the price he paid: four hundred shekels, about four and a half pounds of silver.

Sarah was dead and Abraham was mourning her. Then he rose up and said these words to the sons of Heth, "I am a guest settled in your country. Grant me land for a tomb among you, so I can put my dead in the tomb out of my sight." The sons of Heth were not enthusiastic. They preferred to offer a gift rather than sell. A gift can be canceled, a sale can't. And they were all more than ready to give a gift to this "prince of God." But Abraham was determined and dogged. Not only did he want to buy a small piece of land to bury Sarah, but he knew which piece. The Cave of Machpelah at the bottom of Ephron's field. He asked the sons of Heth to persuade Ephron to accept. The bargaining began. Abraham wouldn't let it be, he was stubborn. Ephron repeated the same old answers. Giving him a field, and even the cave at the bottom of the field, was not a problem for him. On the contrary . . . Abraham wouldn't back down. He spoke resentfully, as if Ephron were proposing something mean, not a gift. He kept on saying the words *money*, *property*, that the others tended to avoid. Then Ephron fell into the trap. He said, "Listen, my lord! Four hundred shekels' worth of land, what's that between you and me?" Now the price was out there. All that remained was to weigh out the silver before watching eyes. Finally Abraham could claim to be the owner of a piece of land, in the darkness of a cave. There he laid Sarah's body. Genesis gives a whole chapter, the first, to the six days of the Creation. And a whole chapter, the twenty-third, to the bargaining for the purchase of Sarah's tomb.

Abraham's purchase of the Cave of Machpelah is told in such painstaking detail because it touches on a crucial principle. For the children of Israel, if a thing is sacrosanct, it must be bought. Which is the opposite of the common notion that the most important things have no price. The point was as decisive as it was delicate. Rabbi Yudan Bar Simon stated the situation clearly with regard to Jacob's purchase of the piece of land in Salem where Joseph would one day be buried. "This is one of the three places that the nations of the world cannot cheat Israel and say, 'They were seized by you through fraud.' They are: the Cave of Machpelah and the Temple and the grave of Joseph." It's something we must keep in mind every time we approach the tangled relationship between the Jews and money.

After Sarah's death Abraham lived another fifty years almost. He married Keturah—another of Hagar's names, according to the rabbinic tradition—and had six more children with her. Nearing death, his main concern was to guarantee that his lineage survived intact. So "he gave Isaac all that he had." But he didn't forget the children of his concubines. He gave gifts to all of them along with an invitation to go elsewhere. Abraham, "while still alive, sent them away from his son Isaac, eastward, toward the land of the East." Dying, Abraham asked to be alone with Isaac, "his son," Genesis insists, though Isaac was only one of his eight sons. But the only one Abraham had agreed to sacrifice.

As the years passed Abraham felt more and more strongly that he could not accept the fact of death. The idea of being resurrected at the end of time was no consolation. He just wanted to go on living the way he was.

Yahweh knew and didn't want to upset him. But he was eager for Abraham to put things in order: the tomb for Sarah, the other members of the family and himself, then the division of the inheritance. To get Abraham used to the idea of dying Yahweh made use of the Archangel Michael and of a dream Isaac had. When the Archangel Michael arrived, Abraham took him for a foreigner and got ready a bowl to wash his feet. Then he said, "I sense I will never wash a passing guest's feet in this bowl again." The archangel disappeared and told Yahweh he hadn't had the heart to announce Abraham's death to him. But there was a sort of conspiracy of premonitions. During the night Isaac ran to Abraham shouting. He wanted to hug him one last time, after the dream he had just had. While his father had taken the Archangel Michael for some unknown foreigner, Isaac had recognized him at once. Then Michael made up his mind to announce Abraham's death to him. And added some words that would have had a familiar ring to Abraham: "Now, therefore, Abraham, set thy house in order, for thou hast heard what is decreed concerning thee." After all, one day he would rise again, "for then all flesh shall arise." Abraham looked at him and said, "Now I know thou art an angel of the Lord, and wast sent to take my soul, but I will not go with thee, but do thou whatever thou art commanded." No one had ever said such a straightforward no to an archangel. And it was only one of many refusals. One day, when Abraham was sitting under the oaks of Mamre, Yahweh sent Death to him, in person, all dressed up and looking lovely. The two spoke, but in the end Abraham said, "I will not go with thee." Not knowing where to turn, Yahweh decided to take the patriarch's soul "as in a dream, and the Archangel Michael took it up to heaven." Genesis doesn't say a word about all this, merely recording that Abraham died at a hundred and seventy-five years old "in contented old age, old and full of days."

Abraham was dead, once again there was famine, and Isaac resolved to go down, as his father once had, into Egypt. Yahweh stopped him and said, "Stay in the land that I will say unto you"— and it was Canaan, where Abraham had come. Then Yahweh said a few words that amounted to his posthumous verdict on Abraham: "Because Abraham listened to my voice and observed my precepts, my statutes, and my laws." *Mitzvot, huqqot, torot*: three words that brought together Yahweh's various commands. And words that drew attention to the most puzzling aspect of the life of the patriarchs. Abraham had listened to Yahweh's "voice," but the only precept he had been given was the rule of circumcision. Of the other six hundred and twelve *mitzvot*, not a word. Only seven generations later, on Sinai, would Yahweh announce those precepts to Moses. So how did the patriarchs manage before then? How had they been able to observe precepts that they knew nothing about?

For many years, many centuries, Talmudists were vexed by the question. Answers went from one extreme to another. Some thought Abraham was already observing all the precepts of the Torah—even those of the oral Torah. Others traced knowledge of the Torah right back to Adam. Since the Torah existed long before the world began, it must have illuminated the world right from the start. The book of Proverbs says, "Because the precept is a lamp and Torah a light." Others again disagreed. They supposed the patriarchs had observed only some of the *mitzvot*. But which? A crucial question loomed. The Torah comes before the world and gives it shape and energy. If the Torah didn't exist, the world would fall apart. But the Torah was revealed on a particular day and in a particular place, a mountain in the desert. Many years before that day Abraham "circumcised Isaac, his son, when he was eight days old, as Elohim had ordered him." And this was the only one of the *mitzvot* that Genesis tells us Abraham observed. Either it omits to tell us about the others, or there was nothing to tell. All we know is that Abraham listened to Yahweh and Yahweh "put him to the test." So one could live within the Law before the Law had been announced. But only on this condition: you had to be chosen, touched by grace. And put to the test. The long story of the patriarchs, full as it is of setbacks, intrigues, and treachery, guaranteed that, over the course of time, grace precedes law, even though the Torah is ever latent and sustains the world.

We know very little about Isaac. When he was a child his older brother, Ishmael, would play with him, until he was sent off into the desert. When he was old and blind he loved to eat the meat of the hunt. He greatly increased his possessions, as did his father, Abraham, before him. He had two children from the sterile Rebecca, as Abraham had had him from the sterile Sarah. Like Abraham, he tried to pass off his wife as his sister, to the same person, King Abimelech. His whole life seems one of repetition. But when his son Jacob came to swear an oath, he swore on "the Terror of his father Isaac." That moment at least had been unique, something no one else would ever go through. It was Isaac's secret, and he passed it on to his son Jacob. As for his father, Abraham, he had witnessed that terror. It was the link that tied together father, son, and grand-son. So one could speak of "the God of Abraham, the God of Isaac, and the God of Jacob."

Between Isaac and Rebecca it was love even before first sight. To go toward her future husband, whom she had never seen, Rebecca refused to stay home even ten days or so. Abraham's servant was impatient. He said, "Don't make me wait. Yahweh has made my journey a success, let me leave and get back to my master." They asked Rebecca, "Do you want to go with this man?" And Rebecca said, "I'll go."

They set off. Arriving at the well at Lahai-Roi, "Rebecca raised her eyes and saw Isaac, she jumped off her camel and said to the servant, 'Who is that man walking across the field toward us?' 'My Master,' the servant said. So she took her veil and covered herself."

A few words were enough to describe what happened next. "The servant told Isaac everything he'd done. Isaac had her go into the tent that used to be his mother, Sarah's, and took Rebecca and she became his wife. He loved her and so Isaac was consoled for his mother's death." No love story since has been faster or more effective.

Every time Yahweh promised a people numerous as sand on the seashore, every time he looked forward to building "a nation, even a group of nations," from a single family, without fail the woman from whom this people was supposed to be born turned out to be sterile. It happened to all three generations of the men who for centuries would be invoked as patriarchs: to Abraham with Sarah, Isaac with Rebecca, Jacob with Rachel. Sarah was Abraham's wife and half sister; Rebecca was Isaac's wife and the daughter of his cousin Bethuel; Rachel was Jacob's wife and his cousin. Everything had to stay in the family, among its separate households. And pre-cisely with regard to family, sterility was a crime, a serious crime, like abortion. But in each case sterility at last relented, with a mi-raculous birth.

The protracted sterility of the matriarchs was the basis for election. The more unlikely the birth, the more imminent the election. And the closer the punishment that the sterile matriarch felt looming over her. Of the three wives, Rachel was the most candid in acknowledging this when she said to Jacob, "Give me children or I'm going to die." And when Joseph was conceived, she said, "Elohim has taken away my shame."

That Yahweh chose the Jews not because of their merits but because of a promise he'd made to three men singly—Abraham, Isaac, and Jacob—and again not because these men had any special merits, at the start, that led to their being chosen, is the basis of every theory of grace from St. Augustine to Pascal. This is the trait that distinguishes the Bible from the first Egyptian, Mesopotamian, and Phoenician texts. Here at last we have an irreducible difference.

The equivalent of election in the life of the community was primogeniture. Never was this clearer than when Rebecca gave birth to Esau and Jacob. With twins the entirely arbitrary basis of primogeniture came close to being revealed. Precedence didn't depend on timing, but on the position the two embryos assumed in the mother's womb. All the same, the privilege of primogeniture remained absolute and was the only basis for establishing the legitimacy of a dynasty. If Jacob had not persuaded Esau to surrender that privilege, Israel would never have been Israel, which is to say the descendants of the sons of Jacob. Who were soon to split up, as Jacob had had to split up with Esau, but Israel nonetheless would continue to exist. Esau on the other hand had "sold his birthright to Jacob," because he didn't recognize it. Or rather, he disowned it with the strongest argument that, one day, in other circumstances, would be used against grace: "Here I am about to die! What use is my birthright to me?" The two paths would never be reconciled: "Esau ate and drank, then got up and left. So Esau scorned his birthright." Jacob had won the primogeniture with a trick. But it wouldn't be valid unless accompanied by his father's blessing. So

Jacob won that blessing by deceit. And the blessing was the seal of election.

Troubled and humiliating as it was, Jacob's life was marked by two miraculous events that both happened in the same place: Bethel. The first time when he went to look for a wife at the house of his maternal uncle Laban, while also fleeing from his twin, Esau, who had sworn to kill him. The second when he was returning to his father's house with two wives, their maids, and twelve children and once again found himself alone, in Bethel. It was there that twenty years before he had discovered how one could reach heaven. The men of Babel had tried to do it some time before, without success. To Jacob the secret was revealed. And it was simple. There was a ladder "planted on the earth, whose top touched the heavens." Certain beings, who all looked alike, were climbing up and down. Between Yahweh and the earth, then, there wasn't just a vast empty space, as inevitably one tended to suppose, but a series of steps, that you could go up and down. The proof was the constant silent movements of those beings: the Angels.

When Jacob woke up and lifted his head from his pillow, he said, "In truth Yahweh is in this place and I didn't know." The presence of Yahweh reminded him of the terror of his father, Isaac. Jacob "was afraid and said, 'How terrible is this place! What is it but the House of Elohim and Gate of Heaven.'" Many had searched for that gate, in vain. Jacob had been allowed to come across it with no effort at all. Yet his first reaction was fear. Then, without a word, he chose to celebrate the moment, raising up a stele and pouring oil over it. The place was mysterious and perhaps only the first people to live there had known why. Now it was called Bethel, but once it had been Luz, Almond. That almond was the perfect splinter of heaven thrust down into the earth.

In his commentary on Genesis, Gerhard von Rad remarks, "the story of Bethel is directly juxtaposed with the account of the fraud, which is to say immediately after Rebecca advised Jacob to flee." And he can't hide his embarrassment that at Bethel "it was a fugitive swindler who received this word of grace." It is one of those abrupt, impenetrable, unjustifiable episodes that stand out in the Bible and with regard to which, von Rad admits, "however much we attempt to enter into the story, we will never be able to make the incomprehensible comprehensible."

Most of all, Isaac was concerned that his son Jacob not marry a Canaanite. Things had to stay in the family. His instructions were peremptory: "Get up, go to Paddan-Aram, to the house of Bethuel, your mother's father, and take for your wife one of the daughters of Laban, your mother's brother." The only possible choice, for Jacob, was between Leah and Rachel, Laban's daughters. He got both. But in Laban's house he also experienced twenty years of harassment, trickery, and subterfuge, both as tricked and trickster. Laban and Jacob spent the time swindling each other. The demon of pettiness never let up goading them. In the end Jacob left, secretly, with his two wives, six children from one and one from the other, "many sheep, maids, servants, camels, and asses." And above all the *teraphim*, the precious household idols that Rachel had taken from Laban and hidden in the basket on her camel. Laban caught up with them. He told Jacob that everything he had with him was stolen: "Everything I'm looking at is mine," starting with the daughters whom Jacob was now taking away like "the spoils of war." Laban was furious and would have killed Jacob had not Elohim warned him in a dream, "Take care not to speak either good or evil to Jacob!" So Laban held back, but there was something that riled more than anything else: the loss of the *teraphim*. He knew that it was a disgraceful thing to worship idols in the open; all the same, without those little idols hidden away in the dark of his tents, life was in danger of falling apart.

It was Rachel who had taken the *teraphim* from her father, without telling Jacob and knowing full well the gravity of what she was doing. She hid them in her camel basket and sat on top. When her father was looking for them, feverishly, in vain, rummaging among Jacob's pots and pans, Rachel asked him to excuse her if she didn't get up to speak to him; she was menstruating, she said. Meantime, Jacob spoke as if it were him being mistreated. He said to Laban, "Now you've finished fingering all my things, what have you found of your own?" Nothing, Laban had to admit. Rachel watched, poker-faced, sitting on the *teraphim*. Only two things could happen between Laban and Jacob now: either one killed the other, or they came to some agreement. It was Laban who made the offer: "Let's make a pact, you and me, and let there be a witness between you and me!"

They called on the God of their ancestors, of Abraham and Nahor, to judge between them. Then "Jacob swore on the Terror of his father, Isaac."

When Rachel sat on her camel basket to hide the *teraphim* she'd stolen from her father, Laban, not getting to her feet in his presence and pretending she was menstruating, to keep the *teraphim* hidden, we could say she saved the life of her husband, Jacob, whose name Yahweh would soon change to Israel, "He who fights." For if Laban had found the *teraphim*, this spiteful, violent man would have treated his son-in-law as a thief to be slain. It wasn't the first time they'd almost come to blows. But Rachel saved the situation by lying to her father and not telling Jacob what she'd done. A double deceit that allowed Jacob to challenge Laban to search for his "gods," convinced as he was that no one had taken them. So Jacob managed to get away without a fight. And above all the caravan got away, taking with it, in the camel basket, the little gods that Rachel hadn't wanted to leave at home. Gods that would play a part—contested by some, supported by others—in the future vicissitudes of Israel.

Biblical scholars have never managed to agree as to what these *teraphim* looked like or were used for. The only thing that seems certain is that they were statuettes. But how big? Michal, Saul's daughter, put one in her husband's bed to have people believe it was David sleeping: "Then Michal put one of the *teraphim* in the bed and where his head should be she put a bag of goat's hair, then covered it all with a cloth." But other passages suggest smaller, easily portable *teraphim*. They must have had a human form and belonged among the things around the house. This has led many scholars to liken them to the Lares and Penates of the Romans. However, any connection with ancestors is hypothetical. The *teraphim* are often associated with divinatory practices, and as such condemned. But no one has established what those practices involved. Whatever the case, the *teraphim* had all the characteristics of the much-deplored idols. They were fetishes, guarded and venerated in tents and homes. And the rabbinical literature described them as such, including them in the category of *shameful things*.

In the final frantic round of bargaining with Laban, a man wholly and incessantly bent on improving his own position, Jacob twice mentioned the "Terror of Isaac," an expression that does not appear anywhere else in the Bible. The first time was in his heated reconstruction of the twenty years he had spent with Laban: "If the God of my father, the God of Abraham and Terror of Isaac, had not been on my side, you would have sent me away with empty hands. Elohim saw my distress and all the work I was doing, and last night he announced his decision." In fact, Elohim had appeared in a dream, a few hours before, both to Jacob and to Laban. He had told Jacob to rise up and *go away*, the same command he had once given to Abraham. *Those who went away* were not only to leave Ur of the Chaldees, but their blood relations, too. Speaking to Laban, Jacob used words never heard before, claiming that it wasn't only Elohim supporting him, but also the "Terror of Isaac"; on the one hand a divine being, on the other the momentary experience of a man, his father. Never before had two such elements been put together. The intense, overwhelming sensations that Isaac had felt when he saw his father pick up the knife to sacrifice him now had the power to guide and protect the life of his son Jacob. Who otherwise would have had to leave Laban "with empty hands," canceling out the life of twenty years. And to have found himself "with empty hands" would have been the worst possible scenario not only for Jacob, but for Elohim, too. Having empty hands meant having nothing to offer.

Shortly afterward, Laban and Jacob stood together before a pile of stones that henceforth would mark the boundary between their territories. The moment required a celebration. Laban said, "May the God of Abraham and the God of Nahor be judges between us!" The text adds that he was referring to the "God of their father." A gloss that betrays Laban's indifference to the divine. The two fathers had in fact worshipped incompatible gods, since Nahor was an idolater. But all that mattered to Laban was obedience to some generic superior authority. Which authority was hardly important.

"Then Jacob swore by the Terror of his father, Isaac." This was the second time the expression was used. If Jacob broke his oath it would not be Isaac suffering the consequences, but a momentary, searing experience. If that experience were to be annulled, everything else would be wiped out with it. A thing we swear on must inevitably be an *ens realissimum*. To deny it would mean denying everything. But if the oath was kept, the "Terror of Isaac" would become a mark of identity for the children of Israel, a name Jacob was to be given just a few hours after swearing the oath. Thus the "Terror of Isaac" was imprinted on all his descendants.

On the way back to Canaan, when they arrived in the city of Shechem, Dinah, Jacob and Leah's very young daughter, the only girl after six boys, "went out to look at the daughters of the town." It so happened that Shechem, "prince of the town, saw her and took her, coupled with her, and raped her." At once "his soul attached itself to Dinah, Jacob's daughter, he loved the girl and spoke to the girl's heart." Then he went to his father and asked, "Get me this young girl for my wife." It won't be easy, his father said, after what you've done. It was more likely the brothers would come looking for revenge.

Jacob soon heard of the outrage. Master of deceit and delay, he decided to keep quiet. Leah's six sons were out with the flocks. When they came back and were told what had happened they were furious and wanted to attack Shechem's family at once. But their father, Jacob, had been talking to Hamor, Shechem's father, who proposed that he give Dinah to his son as his bride. After which, Hamor said, Jacob and his family would become owners of the town. It would all be theirs.

Here Genesis doesn't say whether it was Jacob who suggested a ferociously mean trick to his sons, or whether it was the boys who thought of it and Jacob who didn't do anything to stop them. They told Hamor, yes, they would accept, but only on one condition, "if you become like us, circumcising all the males among you." Only then, they added, "will we become one people." Their plan was as simple as it was cruel. They might as well have said to the inhabitants of the city of Shechem, "Become like us, cut your bodies with the mark of belonging to our religion, that way it will be easier for us to kill you while you are suffering and helpless."

Shechem so wanted Dinah, and his father, Hamor, so wanted to please his son that they accepted. Now all they had to do was persuade the town's inhabitants. Only a few refused and went into hiding. Otherwise the city was suddenly full of sore, limp men. "Simeon and Levi, Dinah's brothers, picked up their swords, went fearlessly into the city, and killed all the males. They put Hamor and Shechem, his son, to the sword, took Dinah back from Shechem's house, and left." It was only the beginning of the massacre and devastation. "They captured all their riches, all their women and children, and looted everything there was in their houses."

Rachel had stolen the *teraphim* from her father, Laban, and hid them carefully and shrewdly because she knew they were a precious possession, to the point that it would have been a mistake to set off on their journey without them. Thus, in the clash between Jacob and Laban, the fact that Laban didn't find the *teraphim* that Rachel had hidden made it possible to reach an agreement and get out of a situation that was looking more dangerous by the minute. One can live in opposition to idols, but one can't live without them. That was why Rachel had to steal the *teraphim* from her father. Without those *teraphim* Jacob would have been lost. And with him the struggle with the idols. Rachel risked falling into contradiction, but trusted in wisdom.

When, however, on the way to Canaan, the caravan with the *teraphim* stashed in the basket of Rachel's camel approached Bethel, Jacob gave a firm order: "Remove the foreign gods that are among you, purify yourselves and change your clothes." It wasn't simply the usual cleansing on approaching a sacred place. Rather, they were finally to free themselves of these "foreign gods." And those gods were nothing more than some small objects hitherto worshipped in every tent.

Bethel was the place where the Gate of Heaven and the ladder with the Angels climbing up and down had appeared to Jacob. There the *teraphim* became once again what they had always been, incompatible with the heaven that one could reach through Bethel. "So they gave Jacob all the foreign gods they had with them, as well as the rings they wore on their ears, and Jacob buried them under the terebinth tree near Shechem." It was an anxious moment, because the caravan was expecting a revenge attack after the massacre that Jacob's sons had perpetrated in Shechem. But getting rid of the *teraphim* helped, otherwise what happened soon afterward would be incomprehensible: "They set off again and a supernatural terror came upon the nearby towns, so that the children of Jacob were no longer pursued." Once again terror is associated with Jacob and saves him. The *teraphim* would reappear, many centuries later, on the desk in Freud's study. And they went with him to London, last barrier between him and the world.

Jacob spent his whole life deceiving and being deceived. Deceit covered him like a spiderweb that went on spinning itself all on its own. Now, twenty years on, he was going to see Esau again. "He felt a deep dread and was distraught." He remembered the last words he had heard him say: "The days of mourning for my father are at hand and then I will kill Jacob, my brother." Maybe the time had come.

"That night he got up and took his two wives and their two maids, with their eleven children, and forded the Jabbok. He took the children and had them cross the river, then his belongings. At which point Jacob was left alone." It wasn't something that happened often, what with all those children, wives, concubines, servants, and animals always around him, always pestering. And that night was unlike any other. Jacob spent it locked in a wrestling match, without a break "until dawn," with a mysterious being, and at last he won. When the being tried to wriggle free, Jacob told him he wouldn't let him go, unless the other blessed him. The being asked, "What is your name?" as if he didn't know whom he'd been fighting. Jacob said his name. And the being said, "You will no longer be called Jacob, but Israel, because you fought with Elohim as with men and won." Now it was Jacob's turn to ask his opponent's name: "Tell me your name." He didn't wait for an answer. "I have seen Elohim face-to-face and saved my life." From that day on people spoke of the "children of Israel." There were eleven of them, born from two wives and the wives' maids. The twelfth, Benjamin, was on the way. Now the family was about to enter the world, much as when Abraham made his unhappy journey into Egypt. And they would never again step out of the world, though always retaining their *family aura* in every place and every situation.

That night was a watershed moment. The following morning, Jacob found himself with a heavy limp and a new name. No one, least of all he himself, could guess the meaning of that fight. But one thing he was sure of: he had managed to get himself blessed, or rather he had forced the other to bless him. And this time it had not been a trick, as when he had pretended to be Esau to wring a blessing out of his father.

For a long time, Israel meant "children of Jacob." Yet it was still Abraham that the family turned to as their father. Jacob, if anything, was the procreator, the one who with four women had generated the twelve fathers of the tribes of Israel. All his life had been a story of women, from the moment his mother, Rebecca, had dressed him up in his brother Esau's clothes to get the blessing of Isaac, the blind father.

The most mysterious moment in Jacob's life was the fight with the angel. Why did they fight? Which of the two was in the right? As his name suggests, Jacob is the "supplanter" (from *aqab*, "to supplant," an action that could be understood as violent usurpation). In Hosea this is the *precedent* behind the struggle with the angel: "In the womb he supplanted his brother / and as a man he fought with God, / he fought with an Angel and won, / [the Angel] wept and asked for mercy." This is Dhorme's translation. But in the Seventy it is Jacob who weeps. Because he had won? Because of the sciatic pain consequent on the fight? But if we read it the other way around, how had Jacob managed to make the Angel weep? Jacob would never impress for his good works, but for his awesome closeness not just to Yahweh, but also to the powers surrounding Yahweh. He proved able to fight "with Elohim as with men." Was that a good thing or a bad thing? It was both, cause for glory and for guilt, but in any event it was the exploit that founded Israel. From Jacob came the name of what Yahweh would call "his people," the people with whom he was so often in conflict. And what was this man's first claim to glory? "Israel served for a woman, / for a woman he looked after [the flocks]." The only achievement on offer was the long years when Jacob served Laban and shepherded his flocks with the sole aim of winning Rachel's hand. His whole life, from the start, had something elusive about it, something anomalous and unexplained.

Unlike the first mythographers, the editors of the Bible were not trying to offer an account of world order. Rather, they told the story of a people who took the name of a single man: Jacob. And the story of that people, like Jacob's, was one long sequence of triumphs and reversals, of conning and being conned. Obsessive and repetitive as the lives of individuals tend to be. But always with certain peculiar and recognizable traits. So that, for all its many editors and the different times and styles of its writing, the Bible as a whole assumed a quality of compactness and simultaneity, as though it were the likeness of a single person. Every verse settled down beside the others, all necessary, all equal in their belonging to the Bible.

From the opening of Genesis on, any number of sentences in the Bible begin with the word *vav*, "and." Translations often ignore it or respect it only sporadically, or perhaps replace it with a "thus" or a "meanwhile." But *vav* is a way of marking time. Everything that happens is presented in rough, jagged blocks, juxtaposed in an unstoppable parataxis. And the secret of parataxis is that it allows you to proceed without explanations. Motivations are rarely clarified. Not because the text denies that one thing is consequent upon another, but because every single event appears encased in a tangle of earlier events that can never be unraveled. The biblical *vav* has a function as important as, albeit quite different from, the word *iva*, "so to speak," in the Veda. Just as *vav* puts every event on the same level, so *iva* allows the Vedic texts to affirm that each and every thing is also "so to speak" *something else*. Binary choices that prove decisive in the way we name the things that happen.

"Here comes the dream master," said Jacob's sons when they saw the figure of their brother Joseph appear in the distance as they were out grazing their flock at Shechem. The sentence conveys the long-accumulated rancor that would lead to the decision to kill him. Joseph was doubly odious: he was their father's favorite, and his own favorite. He brazenly interpreted dreams that left his brothers dumbstruck. Worse, he interpreted them to glorify himself. Only their father, Jacob, had once dared contradict him, when Joseph recounted a dream in which the stars revolved around him. The sun and the moon were his father and mother. "But your mother, Rachel, is dead," Jacob said. "How could she bow down?"

It was a way of lightening the mood, given the sulky silence of the other sons. But when he was alone Jacob noted down the dream in all its details, including "the day, the hour, and the place" in which it happened.

Abraham's descendants didn't set foot in Egypt until Joseph, Jacob's son, arrived there as a slave in a caravan of Ishmaelites. Joseph was handsome "in body and face" and possessed one extremely rare quality: "Yahweh made everything he did a success." But, when he was seventeen, Jacob's other sons, jealous and utterly fed up with his arrogance, threw him into a dry well, to kill him. Then they decided to sell him as a slave to a group of Midianites who sold him on to the Ishmaelites. In Egypt he did time in prison, thanks to the calumny of a powerful woman. But even in prison his flair for watching over others emerged, as it had years before when his father, Jacob, had given him the job of spying on the suspect behavior of his brothers. And in the end Pharaoh, with generous words, gave him the responsibility of watching over his empire. "Only with regard to the throne shall I be greater than you." Nothing could explain these events were it not for one quality in which Joseph excelled: he knew how to make sense of dreams. His brothers called him "the dream master," exactly as they were preparing to kill him. There was something indomitable and overbearing about this quality, something that freed its possessor from the natural order of things. Every so often, Joseph felt obliged to remind others of this. One day he said to his brothers, "You do realize, don't you, that a man like me is capable of divining things?" It was the only reason Pharaoh would confer on him the task of governing his country, setting no limits on his power.

We have no record of any disagreements between Joseph and the Pharaoh, despite the fact that Joseph seemed more and more the Pharaoh's shadow, to the point that people said of him, "Even though you are like the Pharaoh." No one objected to the immense power accumulated by Joseph, the one Jew who also had an Egyptian name: Zaphenath-Paneah. When speaking to the Pharaoh, Joseph would occasionally refer to Elohim, who was not one of the Egyptian gods. And there was no need for the Pharaoh to name his own gods, worshipped as they were by everyone. Yet he recognized that "the spirit of God" was at work in Joseph. He agreed to all of Joseph's requests with regard to his family and had the entire clan—sixty-six of them—come along from Canaan. He didn't object when Jacob, now an old man, blessed him. And he granted the family as a whole "a property in Egypt, in the best place in the country, in the land of Ramses." Yet they spoke of themselves as shepherds, and "every shepherd is an abomination in Egypt."

Joseph swore to his father, Jacob, that he would respect his wish to be buried in Canaan in the Cave of Machpelah, beside Abraham, Sarah, Isaac, Rebecca, and Leah, and he kept that promise, with the Pharaoh's help and approval. As for himself, he died at one hundred and ten years old, while his father had made it to one hundred and forty-seven. We are not told in what way or how deeply he was mourned: "They embalmed him and laid him in a sarcophagus in Egypt." Four generations on, leaving Egypt, Moses would take Joseph's bones with him.

With regard to the story of Joseph, Jon D. Levenson offered this sober comment: "Human nature, the story makes clear, is not constituted so as to facilitate the acceptance of chosenness." The whole Bible story seeks to establish as right and just what appears unacceptable to us, sparking off frequent, stubborn rebellions. What is unacceptable, insofar as it provokes our instinctive rejection, could be described as unnatural. In this sense election— Levenson's "chosenness"—is about as unnatural as you can get. But without election, which is the first form of grace, the entire Bible would have no ground to stand on. Before telling us how the world was made, the Bible first established who was looking at it.

Immediately election appeared as the first, inescapable fact. The Bible story was founded on "chosenness."

Evil as an occasion and instrument of the good is an essential device in the process that is election. Joseph ventures to say as much when he tells his brothers, "You planned evil against me, Elohim planned to turn it to good." If evil and good were to proceed in parallel, like two players competing to score the most points, life on earth would conform to a predictable and governable accountancy. But the moves of the two players mesh in such a way that, whether meant or not, the achievements of the one can promote the goals of the other. Evil can lead to good just as good can lead to evil. Each is constantly exposed to thrusts that may help or hinder and whose origin and intention remain obscure. This was the vision Yahweh chose to inscribe in the story of men, and in particular in the story of the nomadic family to which Joseph belonged.

Joseph was the first and perfect example of the assimilated Jew, more than capable of improving on the models he was assimilating. He substituted for the Pharaoh—and the Pharaoh was glad to be substituted for—in an essential function: the government of the country and the administration of huge sums of money. He achieved this position for one reason: the wise men and sorcerers who counseled the Pharaoh did not share his ability to interpret dreams.

Centuries later, when the Jews had been carried off from Judea to Babylon, a story unfolded that parallels Joseph's in Egypt. Daniel was one of the "young men without blemish, of handsome appearance, wise, educated, intelligent, and able to behave properly in the king's palace," who were chosen by Nebuchadnezzar to "be taught the writing and language of the Chaldeans." For three years these men were schooled and taken care of. Every day some of the king's food and drink was set aside for them. But Daniel persuaded the head of the eunuchs to let him live entirely on vegetables and water. Meantime, the four young men from the kingdom of Judah had been given new names. Daniel was now called Belteshazzar, "Protect the life of the king." Clearly Nebuchadnezzar put a great deal of faith in these handsome young Jews. Daniel stood out among them for his ability to "understand all visions and dreams." When the four young men from Judah found themselves competing with the wise men of Babylon, they won. Nebuchadnezzar "found them ten times better than all the soothsayers and sorcerers in his kingdom." It was as if the king could sense that his kingdom and all the wisdom it had accumulated were coming to an end. There was an ill-concealed resentment in his dealings with *his* wise men. He had begun to suspect they weren't up to the job.

Nebuchadnezzar was tormented by dreams; he couldn't get to sleep for fear of them. That was when he got so impatient with the wise men from Chaldea. He had called them together and ordered them to interpret his dreams, but without telling them what he had dreamed. If they couldn't do it, he added, "you'll be cut to pieces and your homes reduced to dung heaps." The wise men didn't know what to say. Interpreting, as they saw it, meant studying certain signs: words, entrails, stars, miracles. How could they interpret something sealed away in the king's head? They said, "No one on earth could do what the king is asking." It wasn't only the wisdom of the Chaldeans that had its limits, but human wisdom in general. And they said, "What the king is asking is very difficult; no one is capable of explaining these things to the king if not the gods themselves who dwell where creatures of flesh cannot go." This reasonable answer was the pretext for Nebuchadnezzar's flying into a rage. "He ordered all the wise men of Babylon to be put to death."

At this point it looked as though the grim caprice of a single king was about to obliterate once and for all a huge body of knowledge that had been accumulating on cuneiform tablets of stone for more than two thousand years. One by one the wise men of Chaldea were arrested, and Daniel and his companions were among them, since by now they had Chaldean names and were considered part of the group. But Daniel pleaded for a stay of execution. And decided to act. He asked his God to let him know "the matter of the king." As things stood, there was only one way that was going to happen: he must dream the king's dream. So it was. Then Daniel was able to tell the king exactly what the king himself had dreamed.

Daniel introduced an innovation that changed everything: the dream could be understood only through the dream, as myth can be understood only through myth. There was no need now to refer to manifestations in the visible world: configurations of stars, the organs of sacrificial victims, the flights of birds. Everything unfolded within the one element, as though in a single watery mass, where Nebuchadnezzar's mind could flow into Daniel's. But this was hardly what the Chaldean king and the young Jew talked about. Nebuchadnezzar was astonished, but above all eager to hear the meaning of his dream. And Daniel explained everything, one detail after another, weaving together the story of the imminent ruin of Babylon with that of other kingdoms that would appear and disappear over the coming centuries. Then Nebuchadnezzar "bowed down before Daniel and ordered that he be brought gifts and perfumes." Finally the king was satisfied. The fact that his dream spelled his own downfall was less important than that finally the dream had a meaning. So Nebuchadnezzar appointed Daniel "governor of the whole province of Babylon and chief over all the wise men of Babylon." Who were still alive. Daniel had gone to Arioch, Nebuchadnezzar's first minister, and told him, "Don't put the wise men of Babylon to death. Take me to the king and I will give the king the interpretation." Because that was all Nebuchadnezzar in his angst-ridden insomnia really wanted: an interpretation. Many generations later, a Viennese Jew, Sigmund Freud, would take up Daniel's role once again.

When Jacob arrived in Egypt, the Pharaoh asked him, "How many are the days and years of your life?" Jacob said, "The days and years of my wanderings add up to one hundred and thirty years. The days and years of my life have been short and evil." Even in his mother's womb he'd been trouble. He had bought his twin brother's birthright for a bowl of lentil soup and a bit of bread at a moment when Esau was tired from hunting. He had let his mother, Rebecca, dress him up in Esau's clothes so that his blind father, Isaac, would bless him. He had left Canaan in a hurry when Esau threatened to kill him. On the road to Paddan-Aram he had dreamed of a ladder resting on the earth and reaching to heaven with Angels going up and down. He had spent twenty years with his uncle Laban, years of hard labor, humiliated as a poor relative forced to submit to his master's whims. His wages had been altered ten times. He had had twelve children from four women. To have the eleventh, from Rachel, the woman he loved most, he had had to serve Laban fourteen years to get her, then wait another six before her womb opened. Heading back to Canaan with his caravan he had spent all night wrestling with a creature, dislocating his hip in the process, and when it was over, at dawn, the creature had told him, "You will no longer be called Jacob, but Israel, because you fought with Elohim as with men and won." He had seen Esau again, still anxious that his brother meant to kill him. Instead he succeeded in showering him with gifts. In Shechem he had nothing to say about the massacre that two of his sons, Simeon and Levi, perpetrated when, to avenge their sister, Dinah, they killed the men of the city, all suffering from the circumcision to which the brothers had persuaded them to submit. In Bethel he ordered the members of his caravan to bury under a terebinth tree "all the foreign gods they were carrying with them, and the rings they wore in their ears." He was there when Rachel died giving birth to Benjamin and he buried her on the road to Bethlehem. He had to disown his concubine Bilhah, who had taken Rachel's place in his bed, when his firstborn, Reuben, slept with her. For years, back in Canaan, he believed that the seventeen-year-old Joseph, Rachel's son, had been torn to pieces by a wild beast. When Canaan was stricken by a famine, he set out for Egypt with "his sons and the sons of his sons, his daughters and the daughters of his sons, all the family," which amounted to "sixty-six persons, not counting the wives of the sons of Jacob." He was reunited with Joseph, who "threw himself on his neck and wept for a long time on his neck." Then Joseph, who was now a powerful figure in Egypt, introduced him to the Pharaoh. "Jacob blessed the Pharaoh," and told him that he had lived one hundred and thirty years, but without achieving "the days of the lives of our fathers." After which he lived a further seventeen years. The Pharaoh let Joseph set his father and brothers up "in the best place in the country, in the land of Ramses." There "they bore fruit and greatly multiplied." When Jacob felt death was at hand, he asked Joseph to go back to Canaan. He wanted to be buried "in the Cave of Machpelah, the field Abraham had bought from Ephron the Hittite as a burial ground, opposite Mamre."

Old and blind, Jacob found himself in the same situation as his father, Isaac. He had to bless not two sons, but two grandsons, children born in Egypt from the son "he loved more than all his sons, because he was the son of his old age": Joseph. He didn't know the boys, and when Joseph brought them to him, he said, "Who are these two?" His father had placed Manasseh, the firstborn, by Joseph's right hand, so that he might be blessed first. But Jacob didn't hesitate. He placed his hand on the head of Ephraim, the younger brother. Joseph said, "Father, not like that. This is the firstborn. Put your right hand on his head." But his father refused and said, "I know, son, I know." He himself had been blessed, in his brother's place, by a blind father who didn't know what he was doing. Now Jacob chose to repeat the mistake, but knowingly. That moment put a closing seal on the age of the patriarchs. Their job was done. The sovereignty of election, and hence the rights of the firstborn, had been reaffirmed, but also reaffirmed were certain corrections to which these rights were subject, as had been the case with Isaac, with Jacob himself, with Joseph, and now with Ephraim. The right of the firstborn was an image of grace within the law. But grace could also act alone, quite independently. In any event, Ephraim wouldn't be another patriarch, just the son of one of the twelve sons of Israel, founding fathers of twelve tribes. Jacob called them all together and told them "what will happen to you in the course of time."

They were fiery words, alternating enigma and rejection. They looked forward to the future, but at the same time they evoked the past, particularly its open wounds. Jacob began with his first-born, Reuben, an intemperate man "foaming like the waters," who had lain with Bilhah, his father's concubine. "And Israel had found out." Jacob commented: "Then you fouled my bed, mounting up." *Ne crescas*, "Don't spread yourself further," was the father's final verdict.

Next came Simeon and Levi. They had been the leaders in the Shechem massacre, attacking and slaughtering the men of the town, still helpless after their circumcision. Jacob had said nothing so far about the rights and wrongs of that exploit. Now he spoke: "Simeon and Levi are brothers, / their knives weapons of violence . . . They killed men in their anger, / and in their fury they cut the heels of young bulls." Yet the descendants of Levi, the Levites, would be the priests, privileged in matters of religion. Nevertheless, their father said, "May my soul avoid their counsel. / May my heart keep away from their assembly." Moses's decision not to grant the tribe territory would be a further judgment passed on them: "I shall disperse them in Israel." Even within Israel there was a diaspora.

Now it was Judah's turn. Jacob acknowledged that his descendants would form a kingdom. It would last "until the one comes to whom belongs / and is due the obedience of the peoples": a presentiment of the Messiah. Then came the other sons, their destiny sketched in totemic emblems. Issachar a "bony donkey," Dan "a snake on the road," Naphtali "a hind set free," Benjamin "a wolf that tears its prey." At last it was Joseph's turn, and Jacob showed that as well as foreseeing the future ages of Israel, he was also a theologian, capable of looking back to the very origin of origins, and that he knew that all things had arisen from the waters. He pronounced a blessing reserved exclusively for Joseph: "Blessings of the Heavens on high, / blessings of the Waters gathered below, / blessing of the breasts and of the womb," *benedictionibus uberum et vulvae.* Tehom, the Waters, Yahweh's cosmic adversary, at last uniting with the Heavens to bless. So ended the age of the patriarchs.

All that remained was to speak of tombs and burials. Scrupulous in every detail, Jacob said he wanted to be buried "in the cave in the field of Machpelah, opposite Mamre, in the land of Canaan, the field Abraham bought from Ephron the Hittite as a burial ground." Abraham and Sarah were buried there, and Isaac and Rebecca. And there, Jacob added, he had buried Leah. Then he reminded them, "The tomb there was purchased from the sons of Heth." There were just two people who didn't make it into that tomb: Rachel, the beloved wife, who died giving birth to Benjamin and was buried near Bethlehem. And Joseph himself, who would die in Egypt and whom the Egyptians honored in line with their own traditions. But Jacob had thought of a place where Joseph's bones could be laid. He told him, "I have given you, over and above your brothers, a ridge that I took from the hand of the Amorite with my sword and bow." That ridge was in Shechem. It was here Joseph's bones would be laid, "in the plot of land Jacob had bought from the sons of Hamor, Shechem's father, for a hundred coins." Shortly after that purchase, Jacob's sons had killed Hamor and Shechem together with all the men of the place, the third day after their circumcision. Jacob had said nothing when his sons were planning the massacre, but afterward he spoke to Simeon and Levi, who had led the attack: "This is a calamity you have brought upon me, making me hateful to the people of the land, the Canaanites and the Perizzites. I have only a handful of men with me and they will unite against me and I will be

destroyed, together with my family." For all response, Simeon and
Levi said, "Are we supposed to stand by while our sister is treated
like a whore?" This was the place where Joseph's solitary bones
would now be laid.

There was just one moment when Egypt and Israel acted together in perfect accord. On Jacob's death, "Joseph ordered his servants, doctors, to embalm his father and the doctors embalmed
Israel." Jacob was to be treated like an important Egyptian dignitary. The embalming took forty days, "then the Egyptians
mourned him for seventy days."

Joseph informed the Pharaoh that Jacob had made him swear
to bury him in Canaan. The Pharaoh approved. It was a good opportunity to gratify the man who had become essential to the government of Egypt. An immense procession gathered. "Joseph went
up to take his father to his grave and all the Pharaoh's servants
went up with him, the elders of his house and all the elders of the
land of Egypt, all Joseph's household, his brothers and his father's
household. All they left in the land of Goshen were the young
children, the flocks and the herds. Horsemen and chariots went up
with them. It was a grand caravan."

At last they crossed the Jordan. The people of Canaan
watched them file by and said, "This is the solemn mourning of
the Egyptians!" So Jacob, last of the patriarchs, was escorted to
the Cave of Machpelah, in "the field Abraham had bought from
Ephron the Hittite." For Jacob to be buried as he wished a long
journey had had to be undertaken, across the desert. Jewish guests
and Egyptian hosts had walked together behind his embalmed
body.

After the funeral rites, Joseph went back to Egypt, as he had
promised the Pharaoh he would. He lived to see the birth of
Ephraim's and Manasseh's grandchildren. And asked them to
swear an oath in his presence: "You will take up my bones from
this place!" They embalmed him, "and laid him in a sarcophagus

in Egypt." Generations were to pass before a man called Moses took it upon himself to carry the bones toward Canaan. Nothing is said of those years. Pharaoh succeeded Pharaoh as they always had. Until there came "a new king who had not known Joseph." Then quite suddenly everything changed.

VII

MOSES

When the children of Israel—which is to say the children of Jacob and their servants—arrived in Egypt they were no more than a clan about seventy strong. In Egypt they became a people embedded in another, much larger people, who nevertheless, with time, began to fear they would be replaced by these guests whom they had started to think of as "stronger and more numerous than ourselves." This was the opinion of a Pharaoh who came to power long after Joseph was dead and forgotten. He saw the Jews as a threat. He asked two midwives, Shiphrah and Puah, to kill every Jewish male child they delivered. The girls could be spared. But the two midwives refused. They said the Jewish women were tough and could give birth without their help. So "the Pharaoh gave an order to his entire people: 'Every male child born must be thrown in the Nile, but you can let the girls live!'" The Pharaoh's proclamation became the calamity at the origin of all calamities for the children of Israel. From then on, every action on their part had to be considered in the light of what they had been through. Every action was a reaction to that first fatal persecution.

Of all the baby boys thrown in the Nile one was rescued from the water, in a wicker basket, by a woman who had gone to bathe in the river with the Pharaoh's daughter. It was the Pharaoh's daughter who gave the boy the name Moses and the unknown child "became a son to her." Nothing else is said of this period of Moses's life, which lasted forty years. Time and again, for centuries, people would claim that Moses had been initiated into the knowledge of the Egyptians, growing up in the Pharaoh's palace, isolated from the world.

One day he stepped out of the palace, "went to his people and saw the burdens they had to bear. He also saw an Egyptian who struck a Jew, among his brothers. He looked around, saw there was no one about, struck down the Egyptian, and buried him in the sand." The next day, Moses went out again. He saw two Jews arguing and decided to judge between them. "He said to the more brutish of the two, 'Why are you striking your companion?' And the man answered, 'Who made you the prince and judge between us? Are you planning to kill me, perhaps, the way you killed the Egyptian?' Moses was afraid and said to himself, 'Obviously everyone knows.' The Pharaoh heard about it and tried to kill Moses. Moses fled from the Pharaoh and went to live in the land of Midian. He sat down beside a well." *Killing* and *election*. In two days the two words that were to dominate Moses's life had taken on form and weight.

Yes, you can kill people, but the truth will out. You can act as a judge, but there will always be someone who casts doubts on your authority. Law and vengeance are ever and everywhere active. All his life, Moses would be involved with both.

After killing the Egyptian overseer, Moses spent the next forty years as a refugee in Midian. He looked after sheep in the wilderness. As with others, his fate was decided by a well. Seven sisters came to get water for their father's flock. "Then some shepherds turned up and chased them off; but Moses stood up for them and watered their flock." To the seven sisters, Moses appeared as "an Egyptian" who had "saved them from the shepherds." They didn't know that he was on the run because he had committed a murder. The father of the seven sisters was a priest, Jethro, who worshipped the gods of the place. He decided to welcome this stranger into his house and "gave Moses his daughter Zipporah." A name that means "fledgling." "Long days" went by and the Pharaoh died. No one remembered the murdered overseer. No one was going to look for the murderer now.

Meantime, in Egypt, the children of Israel were bemoaning their fate and "the groans from their slavery rose to Elohim." Then their God "recognized them," but did not speak to them. He saw a shepherd with his flock and a bush in flames. All that was required now was for this shepherd to make up his mind to approach the blazing bush, which was not burning up. Moses approached. He wondered, "How come the bush isn't burned to ashes?" There had been another miraculous bush, where a ram got his horns caught in a tangle, then appeared to Abraham and Isaac. When Moses heard Yahweh's voice, he answered exactly as Abraham had, "Here I am." Then for the first time Yahweh said that he wanted "to free his people from the hands of the Egyptians and have them come up out of Egypt to a vast, beautiful country, a land flowing with milk and honey, the land where the Canaanites and the Hittites, the Amorites, the Perizzites, the Hivvites, and the Jebusites live." A few words and Moses's entire life stretched out before him. At once, like Abraham, he was afflicted by *doubt concerning election*. Moses said, "Who am I to go to Pharaoh and take the children of Israel out of Egypt?" And how would the children of Israel recognize their God, if they no longer even knew his name? The answer settled the question. "Elohim said: 'I am who I am.' You will speak thus to the children of Israel: 'I am has sent me to you.'" Never again would the one God speak so clearly and so inscrutably about himself. But at once he proceeded to give detailed orders. The children of Israel must be told to "proceed for three days in the desert and sacrifice to Yahweh." It was assumed that the Pharaoh would not allow this. But Yahweh would take care of that and strike him. After which, he added, the Pharaoh "will send you away." There was no need, however, to be anxious: "You won't be leaving empty-handed. Every woman will borrow from her neighbor and from the mistress of the house, articles of silver and articles of gold, and clothes; you will dress your sons and your daughters, and strip Egypt bare."

Moses spent forty years in Egypt, forty in the land of Midian, forty in the desert. The main drama of his life came when two thirds of it were well over. And "Abraham was seventy-five when he came out Harran." Yahweh tested men who had already seen a lot of life. Though what exactly they had seen we are never told. Everything pointed toward the moment when they were *put to the test*. Which for both Abraham and Moses meant a barren landscape, and a bush. Moses saw a bush and a flame that did not consume it. Abraham saw a ram whose horns had got caught in a bush. Before Moses's eyes, "the bush burned, but was not devoured by the flame." No one had ever seen the like. Before Abraham's eyes, a solitary ram had its horns tangled in the briars. It was unusual, but hardly unheard of. To Abraham, the bush appeared when he "lifted his eyes," right after hearing the voice of the Angel "from the heavens on high." Moses had "approached" the bush. As the Vulgate has it: *Dixit ergo Moyses: Vadam et videbo visionem hanc magnam*, "Then Moses said, I shall go and see this great vision." There was a movement and a recognition of the miracle. All Abraham had to do was lift his eyes. The ram wouldn't be freed, but would take his son's place on the firewood that Abraham himself had split and, after three days' march, had given to Isaac to carry. Everything was clear, no words were required. The sacrifice was still absolutely necessary, something that couldn't be avoided. An action that would go on being performed, forever. But to Moses Yahweh said, "I am the God of your father, the God of Abraham, the God of Isaac, and the God of Jacob," pronouncing the three names Pascal would one day keep sewn in his jacket. Then right away he spoke of his "people who are in Egypt," and he ordered Moses, "Go! I am sending you to the Pharaoh, you will bring my people, the children of Israel, out of Egypt!" This time we have a single, unrepeatable event, located in a particular time and place. At last and definitively, the children of Israel make their entry onto the stage of history.

Moses left the land of Midian for Egypt with his wife, Zipporah, and his son, Gershom. They stopped in a camp and there Yahweh "tried to kill him." But Zipporah grabbed Gershom, picked up a sharp piece of flint, and, without a moment's hesitation, circumcised him. Then she threw the scrap of bleeding foreskin onto Moses's testicles and said, "Now you are my husband in blood." Immediately afterward, Yahweh "let him go": he let Moses live.

Why did Yahweh decide to kill Moses after speaking to him from the burning bush and telling him of his rescue mission? And why did he change his mind after Zipporah sliced their son's foreskin? How could Zipporah know what she had to do to prevent Moses from being killed? Why did the son's bloody foreskin touch his father's genitals and the scene end at that very moment? We don't know, but Umberto Cassuto, having observed that prior to the voice speaking to Moses from the burning bush the biblical text always uses the name Elohim and never mentions Yahweh, approaches the question with sober erudition, thus: "Apparently the Torah intended to intimate thereby that since they were in a foreign land, the children of Israel were unable to preserve their spiritual attachment to Yahweh, the God of their fathers, or their knowledge of Him, to which their ancestors had attained in the land of Canaan. Although there remained with them the knowledge of God, that is, the general belief in the Godhead, which is shared also by enlightened people among the gentiles, yet it was not the concept of the Deity that belongs specifically to Israel and finds expression in the name Yahweh." That divine specificity demanded circumcision and its blood. Without it, and without its being performed on Moses's firstborn, how could Moses plead the cause of the children of Israel before Pharaoh?

Hugo Gressmann, 1913: "Since the story tells of a divinity attacking a man, what we have is a saga. That it is extremely old one can see from the story's brevity: just three verses; next from its style: subject and object remain undeclared, but must be assumed by the listener or reader—hence the equivocations that have dogged this saga up to the present day; then from its content, which seems to us aberrant and even repellent; and finally from its self-sufficiency: it has no need to connect up to any other stories whether before or after, but stands out like a primordial erratic boulder from everything around it and every other species."

Gressmann's description is impeccable, but did the episode really have no connection with what comes before and after? If we put ourselves in the position of R (which is how biblical scholars refer to the Final Editor of the Bible, the most ignored and most decisive of all its authors), perhaps something may come to light: at the very least the reason this fragment of an archaic, unrelated text was not edited out, but on the contrary left in a crucial position, right before the meeting of Moses, Aaron, and the Pharaoh.

Reading any text, but especially the Bible, sometimes all one need do is lift up ones eyes. Then the "primordial erratic boulder" of Gershom's circumcision can pick up light from another direction. In the three verses before this story Yahweh once again told Moses what to expect in the future; he used his words sparingly, but introduced one that was new: *firstborn*. "Then you will say to the Pharaoh, 'Thus spoke Yahweh, My firstborn son is Israel and I have told you: Let my son go so that he can serve me! But you have refused to let him go, and so I will kill your firstborn son!'"

What he was announcing, then, was a deadly clash between firstborn sons. And immediately afterward we have the story of the circumcision of Moses's firstborn. Is there then some connection, however obscure, between these verses? When, some forty years later, Joshua approached Canaan, his first concern was that all the males be circumcised. The practice had been abandoned for those born in the desert, and everyone else, with the exception of Caleb, was dead. As the children of Israel prepared to set foot in the Promised Land there had to be a visible sign of their primogeniture. Which meant the one sign Yahweh had imposed on Abraham: circumcision.

In their four hundred and thirty years of bondage in Egypt, the children of Israel cried out more often to Elohim, a diffuse and all-embracing divinity, than to Yahweh, an imperious and jealous god. In fact, from the last chapters of Genesis through to the first of Exodus and right up to the revelation of the burning bush, the Bible names only Elohim, neglecting Yahweh. Now Moses, Yahweh's chosen one, was heading back to Egypt to carry out his mission of setting Israel free. It was time for circumcision to show up again—in the most disquieting fashion—as the mark of primogeniture. Zipporah understood in a flash. And moved with lightning speed. That scrap of her son's foreskin touching his father's genitals was the most effective way of persuading Yahweh to withdraw his lethal attack.

For both Hugo Gressmann and, a century later, Robert Alter, the meeting between Yahweh and Moses during the journey toward the Pharaoh "is the most enigmatic episode in all of Exodus." The details of the scene remain forever obscure. Yet one aspect stands out and is undeniable: there is an attempt to kill someone, and a circumcision that heads off that attempt. Indeed is the *only way* to head it off. The deep and secret connection between killing and circumcision is thus brought into the open. And as always, the positioning of the text is eloquent. In the space of just a few verses, the Pharaoh's son is threatened with death and Gershom is circumcised. What is at stake in each case is a lineage, a people. If no blood is shed, if the principle of part-for-whole doesn't come into play—the foreskin being the only part of the male body that can be removed without mutilation—then killing is inevitable. The elect are also and always the ones who got away.

The Pharaoh listened to the peremptory commands that Yahweh had dictated to Moses, but he wasn't altogether sure who Yahweh was. He knew plenty of gods, both in Egypt and beyond. But Yahweh was new to him. Before responding to the threat, the Pharaoh wanted to have this point cleared up: "Who is Yahweh and why should I heed his voice and let Israel go? I don't know Yahweh, so I won't let Israel go."

This was the worst possible insult for Yahweh, the only one that could never be expiated: that someone should not recognize him.

And this, even more than the destiny of a people, was the matter of contention in the nerve-racking negotiation that now followed between the Pharaoh and Moses. Who, however, right from the start had insisted that what was at stake was the death of the firstborn, and all firstborn male children.

Now one begins to see what unleashed Yahweh's terrifying attack on Moses, that night, camped in the desert. Zipporah's reaction proved a dazzling augury. Circumcising the young Gershom and throwing his bloody foreskin on his father's genitals was the only thing that could have saved Moses. A move that more than any other foreshadowed the events of the now imminent night when the children of Israel would smear lambs' blood on the doorposts of their houses, as Zipporah had smeared her son's foreskin on Moses's testicles.

The way the Pharaoh looked at it, Yahweh wasn't even an enemy god. He didn't exist, he didn't add up. Egypt was used to assimilating gods and had been witness to ferocious struggles between gods. The country was full of shattered idols and vandalized engravings. Whether there were many gods or just one was a question people had been asking since time immemorial and something priests still argued about. The divine was one and many, that was the doctrine. It was just a question of choosing how to present it.

The Pharaoh even began to mock: if you Jews want to have a feast in the desert, "go ahead at your own expense," he said. Later, he summoned some officials and gave them tougher rules for dealing with the Jews: "They're slackers, that's why they cry out and say, 'Oh, we'd really like to go and sacrifice to our God!'" To the Pharaoh's mind, Yahweh was mainly an excuse.

From the start Moses and Aaron looked like trouble. On the one hand there was Egypt, the oldest and most glorious of empires, founded on repetition; on the other two pesky brothers, ready to challenge illustrious priests in trials of sorcery. They claimed to speak on behalf of a tribe of laborers, slaves like so many others. And here they were accosting the Pharaoh, as if they were equals. They spoke of a god no one had heard of and who presumed to show no respect to anyone.

The scribes who watched over the heavy building work to which the Jews were subjected looked daggers at Moses and Aaron when they came out of their meetings with the Pharaoh. "Thanks to you we stink as far as the Pharaoh is concerned." Insisting on this celebration in the desert had been a mistake. An excess of zeal that simply made the Jews an object of spite. Moses passed on the complaints to Yahweh. "Ever since I went to speak to the Pharaoh in your name, he has done nothing but harm these people and you haven't really freed your people!"

Yahweh was a god who wanted to defeat other gods. And Egypt was home base for the gods. Hence he chose to have a numerous but enslaved people challenge the Pharaoh and his priests. It was the earthly equivalent of the clash in the heavens between Yahweh and those other powers that had bossed the scene for so long. What mattered was to force the Pharaoh to recognize an alien and execrated god. Who was nevertheless the god who was going to kill his firstborn son. Threatening the Pharaoh's firstborn with death went far beyond the arrogance of someone who wished to strike at the intimate circle of a powerful man. The Pharaoh was himself son of the supreme god. To kill off his line of descent was a way of bringing about the extinction of the gods. Yahweh, that unknown god that Moses spoke about, wasn't planning merely to protect his enslaved people, but to declare a divine war. That's how Pharaoh saw it and that is why, as the Bible never ceases to remind us, his heart hardened.

The whole battle between Moses and the Pharaoh centered on one issue: primogeniture. In Canaan and Ugarit, among the Phoenicians and the Carthaginians, it was an ancient and powerful belief that the firstborn should be sacrificed, like the first fruits, as an offering to the divine of whatever is the *primum*, whether vegetable, animal, or human.

Only Egypt, which, as Herodotus would observe, differed from other countries in everything, had neither cults nor rites that revolved around primogeniture. In Egypt the Pharaoh's firstborn was just the natural heir to a power that was already divine. And now this god no one had heard of came along, the god of a numerous tribe of menial laborers, and claimed that, if he wasn't obeyed, the Pharaoh's firstborn would be killed, as though in some court conspiracy.

From the Pharaoh's point of view, the Jews were a community of foreign workers settled mainly in the area of Goshen. Their job was to mix clay to make bricks, making sure to stick to the required delivery times. Nothing else. And now this odd couple, Moses and Aaron, had turned up to speak on their behalf. They wanted permission to hold a feast, with sacrifices, in the middle of the desert, for a god of theirs who seemed to be at once rather more and rather less than all the other gods. They said, "We would like to go for a three-day walk and sacrifice to Yahweh, our God." Like so many other gods, this Yahweh could perfectly well have been welcomed into Egypt. So why were they insisting on worshipping him far away, in the desert? The Pharaoh didn't get it and their insistence made him more and more irritated.

Being believed in could wait, what mattered for Yahweh now was to be recognized. Above all recognized as different from other divine powers. Who might or might not have names, but always operated in the invisible. And the invisible meant the heavens. For Yahweh the earth became a device, a stratagem, in his war against the *spiritalia nequitiae in caelestibus*, "the wicked spiritual powers in the heavens." But it was a device that could backfire. Hence his anger when even his own chosen people failed to recognize him. Now it would be their job, with Moses at their head, to have him recognized by the foremost representative of his enemies: the

Pharaoh of Egypt. The ten plagues that swept the country were the answer to the Pharaoh's defiance, when his heart "hardened." Then his firstborn son was killed. This meant the ancient, ever solid reign of Egypt could no longer count on its survival, while *other* firstborn sons had escaped its grasp.

When Moses reported the outcome of his meeting with the Pharaoh, Yahweh said he would unleash "signs and miracles on the land of Egypt." And he added, "I will have my armies, my people, the children of Israel, come out of Egypt, with the help of terrible punishments." It was the announcement of what would be the exodus. And in the same speech Yahweh revealed his prime objective: "So the Egyptians shall know that I am Yahweh." Not only among men, but among the gods, the principal struggle is for recognition. Through Moses, Yahweh had sought to be recognized by the Jews, who were crying out from their exhaustion in Egypt. Through a series of calamities, Yahweh would be recognized by the Egyptians. The whole earth hitherto had lived in a state of inferiority to Egypt. Egypt had been there first, ages before any other power. Everything was ephemeral, beside Egypt. And now a minor people subjected to menial tasks would elude the Pharaoh's grip. To come out of Egypt was to come out of the world. To go where? As for Abraham, the command was *Lekh-lekha*: "Go away."

In the battle between Moses and the Pharaoh, the disproportion between what was asked—that a people hold a feast in the desert—and the punishments inflicted, starting with the waters of the Nile turning to blood, was immense. It was as if two stubborn card players were refusing to cut their losses whatever the cost. Never mind the money on the table, what mattered was to wear out the opponent.

Only when the punishment went beyond dreadful and became a degrading mockery, his palace and bed leaping with frogs, did the Pharaoh decide to cut a deal and said to Moses and Aaron,

"Pray to Yahweh to free me and my people from these frogs and I will let your people go and sacrifice to Yahweh." They were still talking about that miserable feast. No one had said anything about the Jews leaving Egypt for good, let alone being liberated. Like two tough negotiators, Moses and Aaron agreed with the Pharaoh that by the next morning a certain number of the frogs would return to the Nile. The others would die. They were heaped up all over the place and "the earth stank."

But the Pharaoh soon went back on his promise; it amounted to admitting defeat. Next came the plague of mosquitoes. Once again the Egyptian sorcerers tried to reproduce the miracle. Had they succeeded, they would have seen it as just another trick, one for the repertoire. But since that wasn't the case, an overwhelming unknown power must be at work. Next came the plague of flies, which infested all of Egypt, with the exception of the land of Goshen, where the Jews had settled.

Had the Pharaoh asked himself why Yahweh was inflicting so many, as it were, partial scourges, rather than a single, total, and definitive scourge, Yahweh was ready with the answer: "If I had stretched out my hand at the start and struck you with the plague, you and your people, you would have been wiped from the face of the earth; but here is why I have let you survive: to show you my power and to spread my name throughout the entire world." The clash that was reaching its climax was not between a tribe who wanted to hold a feast in the desert and the Pharaoh, but between Yahweh and the whole world—because Egypt was the world—a world reluctant to recognize Yahweh, a world faithful in its attachment to old traditions, along with their miracle men, their sacred animals, and their gods. More than just bringing the Jews out of Egypt and returning them to Canaan, these events were to constitute a first announcement that the name of Yahweh would become known worldwide. And in opposition to what went on worldwide.

Four times, in the days of Yahweh's plagues, the Pharaoh gave way to Moses, even asking forgiveness for having "sinned against

Yahweh, your god," about whom he knew very little. But four times he changed his mind. Yet his counselors, who loathed Moses, advised the Pharaoh to give him what he wanted, if only to be rid of him. They said, "How long is this man to be a snare for us? Send these people away and let them worship Yahweh, their God! Do you still not see that Egypt is finished?" The Pharaoh had seen it only too well, which was why he wouldn't give in. In this fractious quarrel over an unlikely feast in the desert he foresaw the decline of his kingdom, founded as it was on immutability. After thousands of years, Egypt risked ruin because a bunch of stiff-necked foreigners were insisting on worshipping their god in the middle of the desert. It was unthinkable.

One day, exasperated, "the Pharaoh summoned Moses and Aaron and said: 'Go and sacrifice to your God in the land!'" He hadn't pronounced the name Yahweh, but he had accepted that the Jews might celebrate their ceremonies *inside* Egypt. Similar concessions had been made often enough for other foreign gods. But Moses dug in: "We will walk into the desert for three days and sacrifice to Yahweh, our God, there, as he instructs us." It was partly a question of caution, he explained: "If we make a sacrifice that is loathsome to the Egyptians where they can see it, don't you think they will stone us to death?"

The Pharaoh was at his wits' end. He went so far as to agree to the feast, "but not too far away." And he demeaned himself by asking his opponent, Moses, to intercede with Yahweh on his behalf. This was when the Pharaoh found himself forced to recognize that Yahweh existed. But at once, again, he changed his mind. Precisely because he had recognized Yahweh, he must go on fighting him. All the wisdom and ancient history of Egypt demanded it of him. To give way now would mean to give way forever.

The plagues kept coming. They struck down the livestock, but only the animals of the Egyptians, not those of the Jews. There were hideous boils. Still it wasn't over. Each time Pharaoh would give way, and each time, once again his heart would harden. He knew that the fight over this stupid feast in the desert was a question of life or death. At last the final exasperating provocation came. That day Pharaoh dropped the role of the negotiator with his back to the wall. He looked at Moses with hatred and said, "Get out of my sight. Take care never to come back to see my face again, because that day will be your last." Moses answered, "You've said it, I'll never see your face again."

The fight was entering its last round. And Yahweh's ultimate goal was about to be revealed, a goal that had nothing to do with the Jews celebrating a feast in the desert. "I will wipe out all the gods of Egypt, I, Yahweh!" This was a ferocious war of the gods.

The feast had never been anything but a pretext. Yahweh warned Moses: something unheard of was about to happen. After which, "when [the Pharaoh] lets you go, it will be for good: in fact, he will chase you out of here." What could be worse than all the calamities so far? A cull. On the day Yahweh named, a day already marked out by other prescriptions, the day when all the Jews, to save themselves, were to smear their doorposts with the blood of a "perfect lamb, male, born that year," since only with such blood on the door would the Destroyer pass over that house, on that day, or rather that night, everything took place, blow by blow, exactly as Moses had been warned: "It came to pass in the middle of the night that Yahweh struck down every firstborn in the land of Egypt, from the firstborn of the Pharaoh on his throne, to the firstborn of the prisoner in his cell, and every firstborn of every animal. The Pharaoh rose, in the night, he and all his servants and all the Egyptians. A great wailing went up in Egypt, for there was not a single house where someone had not died." Then, his firstborn son dead, the Pharaoh "called Moses and Aaron in the night and said: 'Get up, and get out from among my people, you and the children of Israel, go and serve Yahweh as you have said! Take your animals with you, large and small, as you have said, get out and bless me.'" Once again, as with Abraham, the Pharaoh was behaving impeccably. But his predecessor had not gone so far as to ask to be blessed. He just said, to Abraham: "Here's your wife! Take her and go."

The children of Israel left Egypt at the expense of all the first-born, men and beasts, in the entire country. From the Pharaoh's household to the most miserable of cattle sheds, death was in the air. Exodus does not dwell on the massacre. All attention is con-centrated on the bloodied doorposts of the houses of those for-eigners who, in the middle of the night, were getting ready to flee. But the firstborn Egyptians died that night, the night the children of Israel departed, and died without knowing why. If it was a new plague, why did it kill only them? From that night on, the idea of returning to Egypt became an abomination for the Jews. Yet as early as the seventh century B.C.E., on the island of Elephantine in the Nile, there was a flourishing community of Jewish merchants, who kept up contacts with their relatives in Judea, writing letters on papyrus, which time and the dry climate have preserved.

As the hours approached when the Destroyer would kill all the firstborn, men and animals, in Egypt, Yahweh was busy prepar-ing the Jews for what was about to happen. And right away he ex-plained that they must keep in their memory every detail of that "night of vigil," the bunch of hyssop that was to be dipped in the lamb's blood, the sandals, the loincloth, the staff they must hold in their hands as they ate the lamb with bitter herbs, "in haste." Finally the unleavened bread, the only bread they were allowed to eat, and the leftovers, which must be burned. All details of a fe-verish, bloody night when the moon was full, details that already belonged to "an eternal rite." For the first time an event, shapeless and accidental as every event is, coincided with a rite. Not a ques-tion of repeating something immemorial, but rehearsing over and over a tiny splinter of time

Pesah is a word that the Seventy felt was untranslatable. Hence the transliteration in *Páscha*, from which the Italian *Pasqua*, the English Easter. The basic meaning of the word had to do with the passing over—in order to save—the houses of the Jews, by marking them with blood on the doorposts. Something that happened just once, on a certain night. And that fact became the one Jewish rite that has been preserved intact down to the present day, even in times of utter profanity. A rite that distinguished itself from all others, in that it didn't require priest, or temple, or altar. And from the beginning it was a celebration in the family, though Exodus 12:27 defined it as *zevah*, a "sacrifice."

Where some are chosen others must be lost. This is the dramatic basis of election, a truth glossed over, obliterated, and canceled out time and again in the biblical commentaries. It is also the first mystery of Passover: the connection between the salvation of the Jews who escape and the killing of Egypt's firstborn, humans and animals. As Roland de Vaux succinctly puts it: "The tenth plague . . . is strictly tied to Passover and Passover is strictly tied to the liberation from Egypt. In the same night in which God struck down the firstborn of Egypt, the Israelites celebrate Passover and this rite preserves them from the plague. Exodus 12:13, 23, 27."

But shrewd as he was at grasping the essential drift of the texts, de Vaux was equally adept at evading that drift, when it suited; and he must have been well aware that to pin down the connection between the salvation of the Israelites and the killing of all firstborn Egyptians would have consequences beyond his control. So, no sooner has he recognized what Exodus very clearly *says* than he hurries to deny it, on the basis of a slipshod anthropological reconstruction. This obliges him, initially, to deny the quite extraordinary novelty that the Bible introduces here, nothing other than the founding of a rite on events that occurred on a certain night in a certain year. With academic haughtiness, de Vaux deigns to explain that the rite must always be thought of as *preceding* the event: "Passover is a feast of nomadic or seminomadic herdsmen, as its essential elements indicate: it is celebrated outside a temple, with neither priest nor altar." And he goes on: "It is a pre-Israelite sacrifice" that has "close links to the sacrifices of pre-Islamic Arabs."

With this claim he cancels out—or uncouples—the connection between the Passover and that certain night when the Destroyer "passed over" the Jews because the doorposts of their houses had been smeared with blood, while Egypt's firstborn on the other hand were killed: "If the Passover dates back before the exodus from Egypt, its connection with the Tenth Plague is casual or at least fortuitous: the departure of the Jews happened to take place at the time of the Passover." So the whole feverish account of Exodus had to do with the merest coincidence: it just so happened that the Jews found themselves fleeing the very night of their ancient feast. Here, with the patience and penetration of the great scholar who knows how things really stand, all that is revolutionary and profoundly disturbing in the biblical account is taken apart, piece by piece. This was a serious claim to make, one that goes against all the textual evidence. So just a few lines later, de Vaux himself feels obliged to remind us that the Bible describes things *quite differently*: "In fact, in Exodus 11:5–8; 12:31–33 (J), a cause-and-effect connection is established between the Tenth Plague and the Exodus from Egypt, but later the connection is no longer clearly expressed: Psalm 105:36–37 only juxtaposes the Tenth Plague and the Exodus; likewise Psalm 78:51–53." But if "later the connection is no longer clearly expressed," that was only because there was no need, since it had already been expressed with such terrible, unequivocal clarity right from the start.

Memory of the exodus would be renewed year after year in the *pesah* and every single day in the minds of the faithful throughout the whole of Jewish history. It was a memory of supreme dramatic tension. But with a little anthropology you can ease and defuse whatever tension you like. Here again is Roland de Vaux, in person, speaking from the height of his authority: "The historical memory that this story [the book of Exodus] transmits can, ultimately, be summarized thus: one spring, at the time of the feast that celebrated the abundance of their herds before they left for their summer pastures, and just when a scourge was devastating Egypt, the Israelites came out of Egypt led by Moses in the name of their god, Yahweh." Everything has been returned to the ordinary, the usual—business as usual we might say—disturbed only by the scourge that devastated Egypt and from which the Jews fled.

But there are details that don't add up: Why do the Jews head for the desert, rather than their "summer pastures"? And why does blood have to be smeared on the doorposts, if they are to be saved. Here, too, de Vaux has an explanation, albeit witless: transhumance: "This is a crucial and dangerous moment, there are many perils along the way, no one knows the state of the pastures and the young animals are particularly at risk. These dangers are personified in a demon, the Destroyer, *mashhit* who is named in Exodus 12:23 (J), and it is to protect themselves from him that people smear their houses, or previously tents, with blood." All is explained away and a ferocious struggle dissolved in the understandable worries that surround any departure, in any place and any age: "The practices of the herdsmen became those of travelers about to depart, Exodus 12:122 (P), the fact that the bread is unleavened is the sign of the haste of this departure, Exodus 12:34, 39 (J)."

The sacrifice of the first fruits, often reckoned the most primitive and harmless of sacrifices, idyllic almost, includes in its category the sacrifice of the firstborn, the most demanding and cruel sacrifice of all. Rather than an agrarian ceremony, it is a recognition that singles out the *primum*—any *primum*—as that part of life that is most exposed, privileged, and at the same time doomed. The *primum* can never be left unscathed. And its supremely dramatic condition is passed on to the chosen one, the *elect*, last heir of the *primum*.

Chapter 12 of Exodus tells of the slaughter of the firstborn Egyptians. Chapter 13 opens with Yahweh giving this instruction to Moses: "Whosoever opens a womb among the children of Israel,

whether of human or of animal, the offspring is mine." This proximity is eloquent. Yahweh demands, everywhere and in whatever
form, a precious quota of the world he has created. He could take
by killing, as he did in Egypt. Or by saying it "is mine," as with
the children of Israel. There are various ways, ritualistic and otherwise, in which he can insist that what is his be returned to him. But
in any event it will be *his*, payable on demand.

That the offer of the firstborn was connected to that of the first
fruits and consequential upon it is something that, immediately
after announcing the Ten Commandments, Moses confirms as
one of the fundamental precepts: "You shall not delay to offer me
your surplus and your juice. You shall give me the first of your
children."

The firstborn are the first fruits, the surplus of life, the most
precious part, which must be offered to the divine, because one
cannot approach the divine *with empty hands.*

The sacrifice of the firstborn, a perverse variant of the sacrifice of the first fruits, was not a universally acknowledged idea.
The Egyptians knew nothing of it, while the Semitic people who
lived around them practiced it. There was nothing special in the
Jews' attachment to this form of sacrifice; what was new was their
transformation of the *firstborn* into the *elect.* This had enormous
consequences, though always remaining within the metaphysic of
sacrifice.

The firstborn was the *natural* elect, as the first fruits were the
natural sacrifice. But Yahweh preferred the unnatural elect, the second born, or the son of the second wife: Isaac, Jacob, Joseph. All
born to women thought to be sterile. Another sign of their separation from the ordinary course of nature. But when it came to striking the Pharaoh, he chose to kill the firstborn. Egypt was another
name for nature.

In Genesis the rule of primogeniture is affirmed then over-
turned, again and again: neither Isaac nor Jacob, nor Joseph, nor

Ephraim were firstborn sons. In Exodus, primogeniture is instituted within the twelve tribes of the children of Israel. The firstborn
would be the Levites.

From Adam on, Genesis tells the story of individuals. Exodus the story of a community. In Genesis what matters above all
is grace, in Exodus the Law. But to grasp the significance of the
firstborn one must go back to the beginning, long before Moses
and the Law. Abel was *not* the firstborn, but offered the firstborn
of his flock. Clearly the privilege and benefits of the firstborn
were already recognized. And likewise the fact that they must
be killed. Yahweh chose Abel's offering, granting him his grace.
Cain was the firstborn, he had seen that Yahweh had accepted
the offering of the firstborn, but his grace had gone to the second born, Abel. Cain's reaction was to turn against the order of
primogeniture. If Abel had received the grace due to primogeniture from Yahweh, he should get the punishment too. So Cain
killed him.

With regard to the Passover, Moses took care to instruct every Jewish father how to answer their children's questions: "When
tomorrow your son asks, 'What is this?' you will answer, By the
strength of his hand Yahweh brought us out of Egypt, from the
home of slavery. Since the Pharaoh did not want to send us away,
Yahweh killed all the firstborn in the land of Egypt, the firstborn of
men and of animals: therefore I sacrifice whatever male breaches
the womb and ransom every firstborn of my children."

He could hardly have made things clearer, or at the same time
more elusive. In particular with regard to leaving Egypt, where
he does not say that the argument with the Pharaoh wasn't about
the Jews leaving Egypt for good, but rather about a circumscribed
trip to celebrate a feast in the desert. And there is a contrast he
doesn't explain, when he says, "I sacrifice whatever male breaches
the womb and ransom every firstborn of my children." What was
the connection between sacrifice and ransom?

Moses had alluded to it shortly before, with reference to asses: "You shall ransom every firstborn ass with a lamb and, if you do not ransom it, you shall break its neck." Every firstborn faced one of two options: either to be exchanged with an animal that would then be sacrificed (the lamb), or to have its neck broken. The Vulgate is illuminating here, throwing a Christ-like light on redemption: *Primogenitum asini mutabis ove; quod si non redemeris, interficies*, "If you do not redeem it, you will kill it." The alternative is between killing and redemption: the "ransom" that in Exodus is still a simple exchange becomes, in Jerome's translation, a "redemption" that looks forward to the Gospels. But redemption was already implicit in the ransom, because the firstborn animal went on living. However, there had to be an exchange. And the exchange presaged the killing of *another*.

"So they set off from Ramses, the first month, the fifteenth day of the first month. The day after the Passover, the children of Israel departed, with hands raised, under the eyes of all Egypt, while the Egyptians were burying those whom Yahweh had struck, all the firstborn. Even their gods Yahweh had executed." Over the centuries, two elements came to be removed from this spare, terrifying description: Egypt's firstborn, who were in the process of being buried, and their gods, who that night had been *executed*.

"Toward Ramses" or "The March Toward Ramses" are alternative titles for the fourth chapter of Kafka's novel *Amerika*.

Among much else America is the place where the names of certain towns may *substitute* the names of others. So we have Athens, Venice, Memphis. So, too, Ramses substitutes for another Ramses, in Egypt. In a Yiddish play by Moshe Richter that Kafka saw just a few months before writing the chapter "The March Toward Ramses," the main character's servant says, "What is the difference between Pithom and Raamses and Brooklyn and New York? There they fed us clay and bricks, and here they feed us machines and pressing irons."

Kafka was always careful to leave no trace of what he was up to. Nor was he inclined to give his characters names with obvious meanings. On the contrary, he reduced the surnames of the protagonists of *The Castle* and *The Trial* to a single letter. All the same, you can't help wondering when you run into some of the names, like Count Westwest in *The Castle*, or the Hotel Occidental in *Amerika*. And in one case the evidence is underlined for us, as in Poe's stolen letter: Ramses. The name even appears in the chapter heading: "The March Toward Ramses." For no apparent reason. At no point in the novel do we learn why Karl Rossmann should march *toward Ramses*. Yet if we concentrate our attention on the name Ramses we soon see it is sufficient to give definition to an undefinable novel: *Amerika* is the story of an attempt to come out of Egypt.

Like Josef K, like K, Karl Rossmann is very likely a chosen one, an elect, and certainly doomed. He is the one *because* he is the other. Like the Ks, he flounders among the endless complications such a condition involves. He is stubborn, waiting for something. He wonders if he will ever arrive in Ramses, the place from which they "departed."

Therese, the typist at the Hotel Occidental, says to Karl Rossmann, "I'm not always typing though, I also have to run a lot of errands in town." "But what's the town called?" asks Karl. "Don't you know?" she says. "Ramses." "Is it a big town?" Karl asks. "Very big," she answers. "I don't enjoy going there."

The meeting in the Clayton Hippodrome, where Karl is present, is one of the many stops along his peregrinations, while the grand theater in Oklahoma is an indefinably remote location, such that not even two days of nonstop train travel will get you there. About the theater in Oklahoma nothing absolutely certain is known. There are rumors that it is "almost boundless."

The Clayton Hippodrome, on the other hand, was a moveable specter, a still impure amalgam, burdened with dross, compared with what was to appear in Oklahoma. It's the same image that the children of Israel had of Canaan when still in the desert. As they were running to catch the train for Oklahoma, Karl realized for the first time that no one, himself included, *had any luggage*: "In fact the only luggage was the pram that now, pushed along by his father at the head of the crowd, kept bouncing up and down. What destitute, disreputable people had gathered here, yet he had been welcomed and protected so generously! And they must have been very dear to the transport supervisor," an occasional Moses.

"Only the Old Testament sees—don't say anything about this yet." Kafka, *Diaries*, 1916.

At first the Pharaoh supposed the children of Israel would lose their way, the desert would swallow them up. But reports from patrols sent ahead to scout told him the Jews had changed direction and were still on the edge of the desert. So the Pharaoh changed his mind. Now the Jews' departure appeared to him "merely as the escape of slaves from their masters." He had two options: to bring them back to the place they'd left and set them to work again, since in the end they were useful, or to destroy them. The Pharaoh mobilized his troops in haste, with their chariots. But once again, he had not guessed he was merely doing Yahweh's will: "Yahweh hardened the heart of the Pharaoh, king of Egypt, so that he rushed off to follow the children of Israel."

All at once, "the children of Israel raised their eyes and, lo, Egypt was marching after them." A moment of terror prompted the first rebellion against Moses. "They were very frightened and cried out to Yahweh. Then they said to Moses, 'Was it because there weren't enough tombs in Egypt that you brought us here to die in the desert?'" In Egypt tombs made up a huge, ornamented parallel world with the pyramids above ground and enough subterranean chambers below to accommodate all the children of Israel. Instead they were about to leave their bones in the desert sands.

Moses had always run up against fierce resistance, even before leaving Egypt. And now they reminded him, "Isn't this exactly what we said to you before, in Egypt? Let us serve Egypt, because it's better for us to serve Egypt than to die in the desert."

No sooner had the Pharaoh's troops appeared on the horizon than the pillar of cloud that moved ahead of the children of Israel during the day now moved back behind them, separating them from the Egyptians and making them invisible. But ahead of them, when night fell, the column of fire appeared. Cloud and fire made two barriers, separating them from the rest of the world.

But how long could this last, some were wondering? A strong wind rose from the east, whipping up the Sea of Reeds. Toward the end of the night the waters parted. In the middle was a strip of dry land. They crossed it between two walls of water. "The children of Israel went into the sea with dry feet and the waters were a wall to the left and to the right of them." So that day the children of Israel escaped from the Egyptians, who were pursuing without being able to see them. Henceforth, in whatever circumstances, *crossing the sea with dry feet* would remain their supreme aspiration.

Once they had crossed the Sea of Reeds, the children of Israel chanted the Song of the Sea, which ended with the solemn words: "The Lord shall reign forever." But who could ever have doubted it? Certainly not the Pharaoh and his army, who sank "to the bottom like stone." The Egyptians were also-rans like so many others on this earth, walk-ons who appeared and disappeared. The real enemy was Raab, Prince of the Waters, of the *mayim kabbirim,* the "great waters," and his powerful allies: first and foremost Leviathan, the coiled snake, and the great rivers. All ready to swell, flood, and spread out beyond their established limits. It was a struggle that had been going on since time began, before even

Egypt existed, let alone the children of Israel. And the outcome was always in the balance. Once Yahweh had been obliged to tie a reed around Leviathan's nose as a kind of muzzle. But sometimes he played with Leviathan. Then swiftly resumed his endless struggle with Raab and his allies.

The children of Israel defeated the Egyptians without having to fight them. But even Yahweh hadn't struck them directly. His enemy was the waters. Since the world began they had been his most powerful antagonist, one that threatened to overwhelm every attempt to establish order. But now Yahweh did something unheard of: he violated the very order he himself had instituted—the necessity that governs the world—so that an earthly tribe could cross the waters *with dry feet*. What was overruled with that decision was the hitherto intact sovereignty of the waters. Until then there had been much talk of the sporadic and deadly rebellions of the waters against their Creator. But now it was the waters who succumbed to an attack from which they would never recover. Or not for so long as there was anyone alive who could claim to have crossed them *with dry feet*.

After coming close to dying, first of hunger, then of thirst, and after Moses had risked being stoned to death, the first enemy the children of Israel encountered in the desert was Amalek. "Then came Amalek and fought Israel at Rephidim." Not just any old enemy, the children of Israel would gradually realize, but *the* enemy. For the moment, though, the only thing to do was fight these people. But how could Moses, who was in his eighties now, lead his men onto the battlefield? His power lay in his staff, the same staff that had made water spring from the rock in Meribah. He passed his command to Joshua, a name that comes out of nowhere, and took up position on a hill, with Aaron and Hur. Moses knew the outcome of the battle depended on him: "When Moses raised his hand, Israel was stronger, but when he lowered his hand Amalek was stronger." After hours and hours, "Moses's hands grew heavy." Then Aaron and Hur propped him up against a stone and held up an arm each. This composition of three motionless figures was visible from far away. And that's how they stayed till sunset. So Israel was saved from the Amalekites. But it must have been a close-run thing, because it was then that Yahweh spoke a few terrible words to Moses, and ordered him to write them down, "to be remembered in the book." Those words were: "I will wipe out the memory of Amalek utterly from under the heavens."

Right from the start the Amalekites presented themselves as an *eternal enemy*, one suspected of seeking to exterminate the children of Israel altogether. Moses had spoken of "Yahweh's war against Amalek for generation after generation." This helps us understand why it was such a serious crime on Saul's part when he spared the king of the Amalekites, Agag, whom Samuel then cut to pieces. After which, many generations would go by before, in Persia, the children of Israel found themselves having to kill the ten sons of Haman, a distant descendant of Agag. One day, in a *midrash*, Rabbi Eliezer would warn, "if anyone from any of the nations of the world comes to convert [to Judaism], they [the Jews] must accept him, but from the House of Amalek, no one will be accepted."

With the Amalekites it wasn't enough to plan for the future. One had to look back to the past as well. Their founding patriarch, Amalek, had been Esau's grandson, son, that is, of Eliphaz and the concubine Timna, a Horite. Hatred of the Amalekites was thus *a family affair* that went right back to the hunter with the red hair, Isaac's firstborn. Every now and then, with a sort of twitch, people would remember as much. And as happens in families, there were mixed feelings. Deuteronomy decreed, "You shall not abhor the Edomite [another of Esau's descendants], because he is your brother." The children of Esau were what the Jews would have been had Jacob not taken Esau's place. They would always be nearby, like a double lurking in the shadow. The perfect enemy had to be someone close to you, so close as to be mistaken perhaps for the people he was attacking. And nothing was as close to the children of Israel as the children of Esau. Just as the children of Israel were set apart from other peoples, because they were Yahweh's elect, so the Amalekites were set apart among the children of Esau: "If one excluded the bastard Amalek, there were twelve tribes, which is clearly deliberate." So wrote Eduard Meyer, pointing out that Esau's descendants were the mirror image of the twelve tribes of Israel. And like the children of Israel divided in two, between the children of two women, as between Leah and Rachel. But to those twelve tribes one had to add the "bastard Amalek," who was out on his own, the sort everyone shuns. The Amalekites were people who stabbed you *in the back*, came at you from behind, with deadly and carefully planned raids. They took advantage of their enemy, striking where he was weakest. Hence the Amalekites couldn't be thought of as just another people, to be crushed in battle and later subdued. They were a perpetual enemy, whom you went on and on fighting "for generation after generation." It wasn't enough to defeat them. They would have to be eliminated. Point by point, this characterization corresponded to what would later be said of the Jews in anti-Semitic literature. It didn't really require much effort on the part of the anti-Semites to find the essential traits of *their* enemy, the Jews themselves, in Jewish descriptions of the Amalekites. All the characteristics of the Amalekites—kinship with their enemies, nomadism, devious attacks, aiming at the enemy's weakest point, refusing face-to-face warfare, endurance over time (Haman the descendant of Agag)—were all applicable to the Jews as seen by the anti-Semites. The root of the arguments against the Jews was right there in what the Bible said about Amalek.

In the desert, for a while, Moses behaved like Abraham, God's chosen one who solved all the problems of his clan. But now the clan had grown to a people, the children of Israel. And between individual and people some mediation is required. Moses didn't grasp this himself, it took his father-in-law Jethro to tell him.

Jethro had come on a visit, with his daughter Zipporah and Moses's two sons. A great deal had happened between them without our being told. Zipporah had been repudiated by her "husband in blood" and had gone back to her father with her two boys.

But apparently there was no resentment. Jethro was treated as the wise old man of another tribe. He was welcomed with all possible ceremony and in the evening "offered a holocaust and sacrifices to Elohim." Jethro wanted to see how Moses was living. The following morning, "Moses sat to judge the people and the people were beside Moses from morning to evening." It was enough for Jethro. He said to Moses, "What is it you're doing for your people? Why are you sitting here on your own, while all your people are standing around you from morning to evening?" Then he added, "It's not right, what you're doing." This was the voice of politics, speaking through Jethro, something Moses knew nothing about. You might avoid being a king, as all the other peoples wanted. But being a judge—the one and only judge—was hardly an improvement. As Jethro saw it, power ought to be broken up into the smallest possible parts, power not over a thousand, but over ten.

Looking into the future of the children of Israel, Jethro had foreseen the weaknesses of the period of the judges, and indeed the period of the kings. "Moses listened to his father-in-law's ideas and did everything he said." Those exhausting assemblies where Moses would sit all day and judge the people standing in line after line before him would be no more. "Then Moses took his father-in-law back and he set off for his own country."

During the exodus from Egypt, Moses had an Ethiopian wife. Her name is not recorded. All we know is that her presence provoked a strong aversion in Moses's brother and sister, Aaron and Miriam. So much so that they wondered, "Was it only through Moses that Yahweh spoke? Didn't he speak through us, too?" Because Miriam and Aaron were also prophets. As they saw it, this Ethiopian wife was enough to put Moses's leadership in doubt.

The gift of prophecy turned into a family feud. Then, "suddenly," Yahweh summoned the three into the Tent of Meeting. Something extremely serious was to be announced, once and for all. Not all prophets are equal, Yahweh told them. To some "I appear in a vision, speak in their dreams." But with Moses, Yahweh went on, things were different: "He is trusted in all my house. I speak to him mouth to mouth and in visions, not by enigmas." That Miriam and Aaron hadn't understood this and had dared to speak against Moses, using his Ethiopian wife as an excuse, was offensive. "So Yahweh's wrath was kindled against them and he left."

Nothing more is said of the Ethiopian wife. Yet it was because of her that Yahweh chose to reveal the abyss between Moses and all the other prophets. That expression "mouth to mouth" in particular had a solemn and mysterious ring. The episode would prove a torment—one of many—for the commentators. Was there a connection between the Ethiopian wife and Moses's privileged position as prophet? Or was that connection fanciful, due merely, as Martin Noth would claim, to the juxtaposition of two separate attempts to arrive at a definitive edition? If the latter, all embarrassment was dispelled and the Ethiopian wife could sink back into the obscurity from which she had emerged in such a bright flash, like a walk-on in a peplum.

But it wouldn't be so easy to set aside Moses's relationships with the women of Cush. In *Antiquities of the Jews* Flavius Josephus reports that Moses had had an Ethiopian wife, but before the exodus. Favorite of Thermuthis (the Pharaoh's daughter who had brought him up) and loathed by the scribes, who had intuited his future as a ruinous subversive, Moses had been given the task of fighting the Ethiopians who had invaded Egypt and were sacking the country. Thermuthis hoped the appointment would bring glory for her adopted son, while the scribes were counting on him dying in the war. Moses attacked the Ethiopians when they least expected it, pushing them right back to their capital city, Sheba, or Meroe, as the Egyptians called it.

On the city walls Princess Tharbis saw Moses leading the Egyptian troops in the siege and "fell terribly in love with him. Overwhelmed by this passion, she sent the most loyal of her servants to him to propose that he marry her. He accepted the proposal, but on condition that the city surrender." And so it was. "Moses thanked God, celebrated the marriage, and led the Egyptians back to their own land." But this unexpected victory merely unleashed the irreversible hatred of the scribes against him. They feared he meant to exploit his success to "revolutionize Egypt." Moses discovered that the Pharaoh was planning to kill him. It was then that he took refuge in the city of Madian, alone, "deprived of any supplies, proudly counting on his capacity to resist." From that point on nothing more was said about the Ethiopian bride. And one day the Queen of Sheba, who again remains nameless, would set out with her caravan from the land of Cush, in search of a remote king of the Jews: Solomon. She had a few questions to ask him.

Moses entered the cloud and began to climb Mount Sinai. He wouldn't see any other humans now for forty days and forty nights. The first thing Yahweh said to him had to do with a "levy"—or "first fruits," *primitias*, the Vulgate gives—which was to be asked of anyone willing to give spontaneously: "Gold, silver, and bronze, indigo, purple, and crimson cloths, fine linen and goat hair, red-dyed sheepskins, dolphin hides and acacia wood, lamp oil, balsams for anointing oil and aromatic incense, lapis lazuli and other precious stones for cloaks and breastplates." A sumptuous list of miscellaneous materials to be brought together for some purpose that was not immediately clear. But Yahweh quickly explained: "They will make a sanctuary for me and I shall dwell among them." The Ark. At first it seemed an impressive, overembellished fetish at the center of which would be placed an as yet unknown object: "the testimony I will give you," something to be protected and watched over by two solid-gold Cherubim with spread wings. But weren't these Cherubim images? Images more precious and imposing than the crude little statues of goddesses that Moses had ordered must be abhorred. Extremely detailed instructions were now given with regard to the colors and dimensions of the Dwelling's drapery, which again were to be decorated with Cherubim, "the work of artists," Yahweh specified, twice. Moses was expected to take notes, like some expert decorator or carpenter. The longer the description went on, the clearer it became that the Dwelling would feature two indispensable elements: the Tent and the Tablets. But nothing had been said as to what these Tablets actually were.

How to construct the Ark, using which materials, cut to what sizes; how to dress the priests, in what colors and fabrics; how to choose the sacrificial victims, how to arrange them on the altar and how to sacrifice them; how to apply perfumes and anointing oils; how to cleanse oneself; how to behave in the event of a census; how, above all, to celebrate the Sabbath, for on the seventh day Yahweh had "breathed." For those who didn't observe the rules there was the death sentence.

Sparing no detail, Yahweh chose to give all these instructions before handing over "the two Tablets of the Testimony, tablets of stone written with God's finger." Without the liturgy, the vestments, and the crushed powders of the perfumes, without the various prohibitions and the contact with certain woods and metals and cloths, the Tablets that Yahweh himself had written would not have been understood. Moses listened to all the instructions. Days and nights went by. Meantime, at the foot of the mountain, outside the cloud, the people were getting restless. Some thought Moses had vanished forever, like a mirage. In which case, what to do? They said to Aaron, "Make us some gods to walk before us." Then Aaron asked everyone to hand over the gold earrings they all had, men, women, and children. He melted them down and made a gold animal, a calf, like so many you saw in Egypt. Then he built an altar and said, "Tomorrow is a feast day for Yahweh!" He didn't mean to lead the children of Israel back to other beliefs, just to keep them quiet. One day they would realize that Yahweh was something else.

When Yahweh spoke the "ten words"—the commandments—he was up on the mountain "in the midst of the fire, the cloud, and the fog," so that there could be no distinct image of him. He spoke "out loud and added nothing." While for the secondary instructions, Yahweh had been more than generous with his specifications and comments, when it came to the ten words he "added nothing." These words were of a different kind. They were axioms. All precepts must follow from them, and all must be traced back to them. But the ten words themselves were not to be justified. Only accepted. The same way the world must be accepted, at every moment. To announce those words was to make them operative. Then, Moses said, Yahweh "wrote them on two tablets of stone and gave them to me." So they would become part of the world.

Aaron had organized the collection of all the gold earrings of the sons and daughters of Israel and had forged the statue of the golden calf himself. Then the people said, "Here are your gods, Israel, that brought you out of the land of Egypt!" No one doubted that there had been divine assistance, as no one doubted that it had been right to leave Egypt. What they doubted was Yahweh. The people preferred to recognize other gods and attribute the help they had received to them. "The following morning they arose, offered holocausts and brought communion sacrifices; the people sat to eat and drink, then got up to play." These were things they could perfectly well have done for Yahweh. But now Yahweh's name was left out. And then, at Yahweh's feasts, you did not talk about *getting up to play.*

"Leave this to me": these were the most terrible words Yahweh ever said to Moses, and the most intimate. The Tablets of the Law were still intact. What Yahweh meant to do right then—his *this*—would have meant the end of the children of Israel: "let me wipe them out and cancel their name from under the heavens."

To convince him not to, Moses broke the Tablets of the Law and "fell down" before Yahweh for forty days and forty nights, "because Yahweh had spoken of wiping them out." It was the supreme, unwitnessed act of dedication on the part of Moses toward the children of Israel. In those forty days Moses did not shrink from inviting Yahweh to remember "his servants Abraham, Isaac, and Jacob," those remote patriarchs who had lived four centuries before, and whom he now named as close relatives, but slipping in the most subversive of doubts: "For fear that the people of the country you brought us out from might say, 'This happened because Yahweh wasn't able to take them into the land that he had promised.'" To wipe out the children of Israel would be an admission of impotence in regard to Egypt, first of all enemies. Something Yahweh would never have allowed.

When Moses came down from the mountain, holding the Tablets of the Law, he heard a murmuring that soon became a din. Then he saw a golden statue, a calf, and a swarm of people whirling around it, dancing.

Later, when he had broken the Tablets and destroyed the golden calf, after scattering its dust on a *water of malediction* and making the children of Israel drink it, Moses asked Aaron, "What did this people do to you that you induced them to commit such a terrible sin?" Then Aaron came out with a remark that was all the harsher because it referred to the people whom Yahweh thought of as his firstborn: "You know the people, how they dwell in evil!" It was very much the same thought Yahweh himself had had before the flood: "He saw that the wickedness of man on earth was great and that the thoughts of his heart had always been directed toward evil."

But equally Moses knew that "the people had gone wild because Aaron had let them go wild." He didn't ask him to help, but summoned the Levites and told them, "Go back and forth from door to door in the camp; kill your own brother, your own friend, your own kin." In the end "about three thousand men" were killed. It was the day of the Levites' investiture, said Moses, "in that each went against his son and his brother, so that today Yahweh might give you his blessing."

The golden calf (or bullock?) was a *farewell to Egypt*. It had been forged with earrings and other precious objects that the children of Israel had borrowed from the Egyptians. Now they were returning them, cast together in that last sacred animal, alone in the desert.

Moses had all those who had taken part in the loathsome celebration killed. But what about the others, those who had not rebelled against it? Moses punished them with an injunction as cruel as it was shrewd: they must give up all their jewels—the last beloved souvenirs of Egypt that had not been used for the golden calf. They would be the first people to have *no ornaments*: "And the children of Israel stripped themselves of their ornaments, from Mount Horeb on."

The sheer number of jewels handed over was so overwhelming that a group of wise men went to Moses to tell him, "The people are overdoing it, handing in more than is needed for the work that Yahweh has ordered us to carry out." At which Moses announced that the levy had been called off and "people should not hand in anything else. What they had was enough for all the work that had to be done, more than enough."

Stripped of their most precious belongings, the children of Israel were ready to resume their march. But first the Tent of Meeting had to be set up in line with all Yahweh's many instructions. When they had finished, Moses blessed them. The one task remaining was something that only Moses could do: place within the Ark the two Tablets of the Law, written this time in his own hand. And so he did.

If Aaron had instigated the crime, was everything that Yahweh had said of him and his descendants to be annulled and swept away with them in the slaughter? Moses chose another way. He circumscribed the slaughter and did not punish his brother, Aaron. Yet in his anger he had broken the Tablets written on both sides in Yahweh's hand. Now he wrote out another two himself, copying word for word what was written on the first Tablets.

Then he began to repeat to the children of Israel the words that Yahweh had spoken with regard to his Dwelling. One by one, those words were spoken again, but outside the cloud. The sizes, the materials, the colors. So began the seven days in which Moses would consecrate Aaron and his children, as if nothing had happened. The priest is a go-between; the person who actually assumes the role is not important, but the rite is "eternal for him and for his descendants after him." At the end of the ceremonies, "Moses and Aaron went into the Tent of Meeting, came back out, and blessed the people. Then the Glory of Yahweh appeared to all the people. And a fire roared up before Yahweh, devouring the holocaust and the fat upon the altar. All the people saw it: they yelled for joy and fell on their faces."

Such are the closing words of Leviticus 9. Then there is a lapse of time, how long we do not know. Then the narrative resumes: "The children of Aaron, Nadab, and Abihu each took a brazier and started a fire inside, adding incense and offering before Yahweh an alien fire that [Yahweh] had not asked of them. Then a fire issued from before Yahweh and devoured them, they died before Yahweh. Then Moses said to Aaron, "It is as Yahweh said: 'I will be sanctified in those who come close to me and I will be glorified before all the people.'" And Aaron was silent." What was that "alien fire"? The Bible does not say, but we can assume it was one that had not been lit according to the rules, as if—when it came to fire—one was free to behave *in another way.*

No further comment was required. Then Moses summoned two sons of Aaron's uncle and asked them to take the two corpses "outside the camp" as soon as possible. Aaron had other sons who would replace the two killed, but without dressing in mourning for their brothers. Priests were not expected to show their feelings.

Lest Yahweh be provoked "against the whole community." Then Aaron's descendants could get on with the role assigned to them. The one absolutely crucial thing was that the "eternal rite [go on] for your generations, so that one might discern between the sacred and the profane, the pure and the impure." The golden calf was no longer an issue.

"Yahweh spoke to Moses after the death of Aaron's two sons." He did not want to pass over their crime. But he did not speak of it directly. He asked Moses to summon Aaron and instruct him in the rite of the scapegoat, with which he was to be entrusted.

Two goats were taken and stones were cast to establish which belonged to Yahweh and which to Azazel. This was followed by a propitiatory killing of a bullock and of the goat that belonged to Yahweh. Finally it was the turn of the scapegoat, the one belonging to Azazel: "Aaron shall place his two hands on the living goat's head and confess over it all the sins of the children of Israel and all the misdeeds arising from their sins, and he shall put them on the head of the goat and let it go free, led by a man chosen for this, in the desert. And the goat shall take all their crimes with it into an arid land. Then the man will free the goat in the desert."

Even after the ablutions, after dressing once again in "the robes of sanctity," having sacrificed the bullock of expiation and the goat belonging to Yahweh, and having sprinkled the altar with their blood, seven times, Aaron was still a guilty man, like all the others, albeit detached from all the others. And this was why he was entrusted with another ceremonial act of the utmost potency: confession. With his hand laid on the head of Azazel's goat he would put into words "all the sins of the children of Israel," things he knew only too well. Clearly there were some things no blood of a sacrificed animal could remedy. The blunt power of the word was required. But pronounced while touching the head of an animal. And that animal must then be abandoned in the desert, like the words of the confession, which were to be pronounced and cast away into an "arid land."

Life in the desert. One day a man was surprised "gathering wood on the Sabbath." He was arrested but no one knew what to do with him. "Then Yahweh said to Moses, 'The man must be condemned to death: the whole community must stone him with rocks outside the camp.' Then the whole community made him go outside the camp, they stoned him with rocks, and he died, in accordance with Yahweh's instructions to Moses."

The desert was a laboratory where for forty years the children of Israel carried out an experiment on themselves. There were no other peoples now, nor other forms of nature. What had so far been a shapeless tribal mass must now become a single entity: no longer the children of Israel, but Israel. At the beginning of the second year Moses, like Descartes in the *Regulae ad directionem ingenii*, ordered the crucial first step: the *enumeration*, which in his case corresponded to a *census*. After which the space had to be organized: at the center was the Tent of Meeting, which the Levites would watch over. To the east, Judah, together with Issachar and Zebulun. To the south Reuben, with Simeon and Gad. To the west, the children of Joseph and Benjamin. To the north Dan, with Asher and Naphtali. This is recounted at the beginning of the book that, from the translation of the Seventy on, is called Numbers, though in Hebrew the title is *In the Desert*. *Numbers in the Desert*: an ambitious, unsettling association that no one before had ever hazarded. Finally we begin to see the reason for that famous feast "three days' march into the desert," which had so irritated the Pharaoh for the mindless stubbornness of the request and ended up unleashing so many plagues. The point was not the feast, but the desert. It was to be a first experiment in separation from everything, an exercise in nullifying all that was prolific in nature, forgetting the vast waters of the Nile and above all those animals that turned up and were worshipped in every corner of Egypt. The weaning of the children of Israel in the desert was a weaning away from nature. They hated the manna, greasy biscuits that left the mouth dry. What they missed most of Egypt was the food. They had been slaves, but well-fed slaves. They said, "Who will give us meat to eat? We remember the fish we ate for free in Egypt, and the cucumbers and watermelons, the leeks, the onions, and the garlic!" Yahweh was always reminding the children of Israel that it was he who had brought them out of Egypt. But now the children of Israel muttered, "Why did we come out of Egypt?"

The idea behind the years in the desert was not to liberate a certain number of kindred tribes from a condition of bondage within an ancient empire, so that they could then migrate to a smaller territory, already portioned out in small kingdoms, where they would have to fight to win themselves their own land. This would be the version of future historians. Yahweh had quite different plans: those years of extreme isolation had been a long exercise—Yahweh explained to Israel—"to humble you, to put you to the test, to know what was in your heart." If they survived— and above all if they did not attribute a happy outcome to themselves, but to Yahweh, since "it is he who gives you the strength to gain wealth for yourselves"—then all the promises that their numbers and happiness would be multiplied would come true. If not, if they were so exasperated as to "go in search of other gods," Yahweh would take appropriate measures: "I shall scatter you among the peoples and few of you will be left among the nations where Yahweh will lead you." It was the first intimation of the diaspora.

The day he announced the ten words and wrote them on two tablets of stone, Yahweh was a voice, while the mountain "was scorched with fire right up to the heavens in shadows of cloud and fog." And in all this "you saw no image." The enemy was the image itself, any image, "for fear that you might be corrupted and forge an idol, an image of some giant or other, a male or female figure, or the figure of some animal that lives on the earth, the figure of some bird that flies in the heavens, the figure of some reptile on the ground, the figure of some fish in the waters beneath the earth." This still wasn't enough: "For fear that, raising your eyes to the heavens, when you see the sun, the moon, the stars, the whole Army of the Heavens, you might be overcome, you might bow down before them and serve them." It was a perfect description of something Moses knew all too well: Egypt. And Egypt stood in for "all the peoples under all the heavens" whom Yahweh had permitted to share those images among them. This was what the children of Israel must break away from. And this, first and foremost, was why Yahweh had brought them out of the "iron's forge" that was Egypt. Not so that they could go to win themselves a little kingdom already occupied by others. As training it was tough, but it was the only way the children of Israel could become "a people who were an inheritance for him." Piece by piece, Yahweh had created nature only so that one day some people might detach themselves from it. But it was a process that began anew every day, time without end.

While all the other commandments have to do with routine day-by-day behavior, the ban on images is metaphysical, offering a means for understanding the peculiarities of the one God. He was not the first of the gods to seek to impose himself at the expense of all others, as anyone coming from Egypt and harboring memories of Akhenaten would have been aware. Yahweh had created man, a being who lived and breathed images in the unceasing activity of his mind, and now he was supposed to renounce them, against the grain of his own makeup.

To sever one's connection with images meant to sever one's connection with the cosmos, since the gods were woven into the cosmos. Images made it possible to move, as though from branch to branch, from one element to another of the cosmos, until one reached the gods, and to come back from the gods. This is why Yahweh put the ban on images before every other prohibition.

Nothing could signal a more radical separation, not just from the gods, but from nature in all its forms. The children of Israel, however, were not so subtly metaphysical. It was enough for Yahweh to tell them to destroy every simulacrum they found, large or small, whether of metal, stone, or wood. He didn't waste his energy offering any but the most basic explanations. He let word get about that those simulacra had eyes that didn't see, ears that didn't hear, mouths that didn't speak. Learned pagans who heard such accusations would be hard put not to break out in smirks of commiseration.

But the real contrast went far deeper. Yahweh had introduced a law that, like his name, was sufficient unto itself. In the face of this, the chain of necessity would at most be a chain of sins. Nothing could suffice to bridge the gap between the law and the cosmos. So "the least numerous among the peoples" found itself possessed with the most powerful of weapons. And it made sense that this separation should take place in a tiny part of the whole, because it was precisely the whole that was to be rejected.

The Ark—Yahweh said to Moses during those forty days on the mountain—must be topped with a "cover," *kapporeth*, which in turn was to be protected by Cherubim with outspread wings. Composite, theriomorphic, protective beings, the Cherubim were related to those winged bulls with human heads that watched over the doors of Mesopotamian temples and palaces. And now, in the Tent of Meeting, they were to be forged "in solid gold on each side of the Cover." And they must be placed face-to-face. Gazing at each other, as if nothing else existed. In Solomon's temple, too, the two Cherubim would continue to loom, their wings spanning ten meters, each one being about five meters high: "The wing of one Cherub touched the wall and the wing of the other Cherub touched the other wall, while at the center of the House their wings touched, wing to wing." The bodies of the Cherubim were carved from the wood of olive trees, then clad in gold. And in bas-relief on all the walls of the House were other Cherubim, amid "palms and flower garlands inside and out."

What was the difference between the solid gold Cherubim that, at Yahweh's request, were to watch over the Ark and a calf forged from the earrings of the sons and daughters of Israel? Both were images copied from things that existed. Yet Yahweh had only just ordered, at the beginning of the Ten Commandments, "You shall not make any idols, nor any image of anything that is in the heavens above, or on the earth beneath, or in the waters under the earth."

The Cherubim were unequivocally an image of something that "is in the heavens above," something one couldn't do without on earth, since they would have to protect not only the Ark but, one day, the Holy of Holies in Solomon's Temple. And they were the ultimate intermediary between Yahweh and Moses: "When Moses entered the Tent of Meeting to speak with Him, he heard the voice that spoke to him from the Cover that was over the Ark of the Covenant, between the two Cherubim, and he would speak to him." Before their appearance in the Tent of Meeting, the Cherubim had been Yahweh's warhorses, as David would one day celebrate in song: "He tipped the heavens and came down, / with a thick cloud beneath his feet / he mounted a Cherub and flew, / he appeared on the wings of the wind."

The ban on images was a central precept that was bound to be violated. First of all by Yahweh himself, who had made man "in our own image, like unto us." Yahweh had wanted to create a being in his own image—and to that being was transmitted the propensity to create things in his own image, or in the image of other things.

That the imposing presence of the Cherubim in both the Tent of Meeting and Solomon's Temple was hardly in line with the ban on images is something any number of commentators have chosen not to mention. But Cassuto, fearlessly honest as he was, felt he had to say something: "Why did the Torah, on the one hand, enjoin that Cherubim be set up in the tabernacle and, on the other, account the making of the calf as a grave iniquity?" A question that threatens to undermine the entire Bible, and that has never found a satisfactory answer. Certainly not the one Cassuto offers, which only makes the incompatibility all the more glaring: the Cherubim were "products of the imagination," hence anyone "will readily understand that they are only images, and is unlikely, therefore, to make the mistake of attributing to them actual divinity; but one who looks at a bovine statue, since he knows that there are many bulls in the world and that they are creatures of such tremendous strength and such enormous fertility that the heathen peoples considered them to possess divine attributes (the Canaanites gave the father of their gods the designation 'Bull'), is liable to err and ascribe to that likeness, and even to living oxen, a divine character and to worship them as deities."

Adam and Eve would not easily have thought of those Cherubim they saw with a "flaming, whirling sword to watch over the way to the tree of life" as "products of the imagination."

God of the invisible, averse to every image of the invisible, Yahweh spoke to Moses only of what happened on earth, in people's lives, before their deaths. Death was the ultimate barrier, beyond which nothing certain was told. Rewards and punishments were things of this earth, things that might be protracted for generations. There was no limit to the detail Yahweh was ready to go into when it came to the accountancy, the liturgy, the rules of everyday life. But with death all details stopped, aside, that is, from the place of burial. Where, if possible, families and generations were to be united. What was excluded was the continuous back-and-forth between the visible and the invisible that, in Egypt, passed through apparent doors. Also excluded was that care for the dead that manifested itself in all kinds of offerings. The dead were impure, and that was that. The Egyptians might well have been defined as those who constantly *fed* their dead. For the Jews the one important thing was to free oneself from their impurity. The gates that led to the invisible were barred and barred they must remain.

There was a "Gate of Heaven," but only Jacob had been allowed to see it. In this, too, the children of Israel sought a radical separation from everything around them. And practiced a willful, determined disavowal of what had gone on for thousands of years before them.

"The cloud covered the Tent of the Meeting and the Glory of Yahweh filled the Dwelling." It was the sign that the children of Israel could at last resume their travels: "When the cloud rose above the Dwelling, the children of Israel would journey on in all their journeyings. But if the cloud did not rise up, they did not move, until the day when it did rise. For Yahweh's cloud was over the Dwelling during the day and a fire was inside it all night, before the eyes of all the house of Israel, in all their journeyings."

The cloud did not observe a constant rhythm, as do day and night, or the seasons. One had to adapt to *its* rhythm. This, too, was something that made the children of Israel different, and their lives more unpredictable: sometimes the cloud stayed down for "two days, a month, a year," and until it rose again the children of Israel would not break camp and resume their journey. So their march was always being interrupted and certainly had nothing of the rhythm of a conquest. Once again this would become part of their physiology, and their education. They had to work hard at the idea that it was not they who decided: "They obeyed Yahweh's command, following Yahweh's instructions, through Moses." It wasn't soldiers who gave the signal to march, but priests, Aaron's sons, blowing on two trumpets of solid silver.

For a people whose only experience was nomadic herding or slavery, the question of the Dwelling was not something that could quickly or easily be solved. They had no models, they had no temples. To find a perfect construction, they would have had to go way back, to the ship that had wandered long on the waters of the Flood. Then, too, Yahweh had given instructions as to materials and dimensions. In that case the wood had been cypress; now he was prescribing acacia. In both cases they were to be mobile constructions, they would have to slide over something, be it water or land. The two long shafts inserted in metal rings would be like the two hulls of a catamaran. That way the Ark could be carried, to a destination as yet unknown. The materials were different, lots of metals this time, and plenty of drapery. The Ark was called *aron*, "chest," "trunk," while Noah's ark had been called *tevah*. In the Vulgate, Jerome uses the same word for both: *arca*. In fact they had similar shapes. They were ships for survivors.

In the Ark, the two shafts had to stay in place in their metal rings: "The shafts will stay in the rings of the Ark, they will never be taken out." Why not? It was as if the Ark had to be ready to move, at a moment's notice, always. It was a place on which everything else rested. But it was also constantly prepared to move. This corresponded to the entire history of the children of Israel and their ever-rejected, ever-resurgent nomadism.

The Ark alternated between maximum mobility and maximum stability. At the beginning it was always ready to be on the move, indeed it prompted movement. At the end it was to be fixed and rooted in a single place, Jerusalem. When Nebuchadnezzar destroyed the Temple, the Ark was hidden in the woodshed and no one knew where to find it.

But there had always been two Arks. One with the second Tablets of the Law, which Moses had written; the other with the broken Tablets that Yahweh had written. In the event of war, this latter Ark followed behind the column of the children of Israel, while the other led them, up front.

To consecrate the Tent of Meeting, every part of it had to be anointed with anointing oil: "You will take the anointing oil and anoint the Dwelling and everything that belongs to it, you will consecrate it, together with all its parts, and it will be holy." Not only

the priests but every single object, even the support beneath the
bowl where the priests washed their hands, had to be anointed so
as to be holy. Every surface must be wiped and made damp. This in
memory of the waters, from which all things originated and from
which they had moved away. A king is *mashiah*, "anointed," and
the Messiah is "the Anointed," one in whom the anointment required to consecrate any object, hence the entire world, is concen-
trated. Anointment is the sign of election, and it must be Yahweh
himself who grants it, as in Isaiah: "The spirit of Adonai Yahweh is
within me, / because Yahweh has anointed me."

Anointment was a common rite in the most disparate civiliza-
tions; it would be used to consecrate both the Vedic kings and the
kings of France. But Jewish doctrine brought in an additional element: consecration could not be achieved with oil alone; blood was
required: "Then Moses took the anointing oil and the blood that
was on the altar, and he sprinkled it on Aaron and on his clothes,
and on his sons and his sons' clothes, and in this way he consecrated Aaron and his clothes, his sons and his sons' clothes." Two
dense, heavy liquids came together in the act of consecration. Blood
brought something extra to consecration, as we discover when Moses, having killed the ram of investiture, "took a little of its blood
and spread it on the lobe of Aaron's right ear, on the thumb of his
right hand, and on the great toe of his right foot." Then he did
the same for Aaron's sons. What did this add to consecration with
anointing oil? We're not told. But it's clear that blood—and the
thought of blood—was all-pervasive.

"You will take the bullock's blood and you will smear it on the
horns of the altar with your finger, then you will pour all the blood
around the base of the altar." With four horns on its sides, the altar
recalled an animal, and those horns had to be smeared with the
animal's own blood. So the blood belonged to the altar—and was
refreshed at every ceremony. At the same time the blood had to
be got rid of. When the Temple was built in Jerusalem a complex
system of drainage channels and basins was devised so that the
blood would disappear from view. There was an insurmountable

duplicity in this relationship with blood: it was not to mix with parts that would be eaten, but must congeal at the four extremities of the altar where offerings were made. Forbidden to men, blood was indispensable for Yahweh.

Everywhere blood marked a dividing line. It brought together the person sacrificing and the animal sacrificed—a meeting that would allow the priest to eat the "meat of desire" without suffering the irremediable condemnation due to one who ate flesh without first offering it in the Tent of Meeting. "Because the life of the flesh is in the blood and I have placed it on the altar for you, to redeem your lives, because blood insofar as it is life redeems. Therefore have I said to the children of Israel: none of you shall eat the blood, nor shall the guest who is staying with you eat blood."

If blood was "the life of the flesh" and must be smeared on the altar, this meant that life itself was being offered on the altar. Every sacrifice was a self-sacrifice. And if it wasn't to be a suicide, it would have to be a killing. What the doctrine never explains is why life wasn't conceivable without redemption, or propitiation. And why propitiation wasn't conceivable without killing. Life alone, however devout, however obedient to Yahweh's laws, was not enough. One had to have that blood smeared on a stone with four horns at its corners. Always, without exception, blood. *Sine sanguinis effusione non fit remissio*, "Without bloodshed there is no redemption": this was the formula as it would one day be set down in the Letter to the Hebrews.

There were twelve tribes, but some rules applied to only one of them, the Levites: "You shall separate the Levites from the children of Israel and the Levites will be mine . . . Because they are given to me, yes, given, from among the children of Israel. I took them for my own in place of all those who open the womb, which is to say in place of every firstborn from among the children of Israel; because every firstborn from among the children of Israel, whether man or beast, belongs to me: the day I struck down every firstborn in the land of Egypt I consecrated them to myself and I took the Levites in place of every firstborn from among the children of Israel. I give the Levites as a gift to Aaron and his sons, from among the children of Israel, that they might carry out the service of the children of Israel in the Tent of Meeting and to redeem the children of Israel, so that there might be no scourge among the children of Israel, when they approach the Sanctuary."

Yahweh wasn't sparing himself any repetitions on this occasion. The revolution he was announcing was a major one. As the children of Israel came closer to Canaan, where their firstborn might still be burned on the altars of the *tophet*, Yahweh announced that the firstborn from among the children of Israel were to be redeemed by other firstborn, *his* firstborn: a tribe of priests. Each of the Levites would be the ransom for each of the firstborn of the other tribes of Israel.

This was an absolutely new and deeply disturbing way of applying the principle of *substitution*. And this time it wasn't a trick thought up by humans. It was Yahweh himself who demanded it. And everything had been decided that night they left Egypt. Only on this basis had it been possible for Yahweh to choose the Levites *in place of* all the other firstborn of Israel. Before substitution, with its powerful unstoppable mechanism, could be set in motion, a primordial substitution had first to be carried out, one where what substituted was also killed. Substitution was the most rapid, flexible procedure for allowing people to press ahead in the things of life, but it couldn't happen if there hadn't first been a killing. This was why, alongside all the various ways in which Yahweh was worshipped, animals continued to be sacrificed on the altar of the Dwelling.

"The concept of 'consecration' is so wide-ranging that we must attempt to define it more precisely," observed Friedrich Schwally in his study on "the holy war in ancient Israel." Common to all understandings of *consecration* is the idea that a living creature or an object is removed from ordinary use and common life, and *invested by the invisible.* At its furthest extreme, consecration implies destruction or killing, acts that absorb creature or object entirely into the invisible. At the other extreme, consecration is an imperceptible film stretched over the creature or object, separating it from its surroundings. Whichever is the case, creature or object no longer belong to themselves and lose any claim to self-sufficiency. This is the exact opposite of what happens in the secular world, where nothing can be consecrated because the invisible is not recognized.

The Levites liberated the firstborn among the children of Israel from the obligation of *consecration* to Yahweh. An obligation that implied being chosen as privileged ones, but also as victims. Now that obligation was transferred to the Levites. They would not possess a land of their own and would be obliged to celebrate the rites. They were *detached*, once and for all, removed from ordinary life. It was as if they had already been sacrificed.

Anyone counted in the census would have to pay half a shekel, Yahweh told Moses. Why? For each person this would be "their ransom, when they are counted, so as not to be struck by a scourge." Whoever you were, the moment your existence was recorded, you became a kind of hostage, waiting to be redeemed. But the payment was the same for both rich and poor: "The rich man shall not pay more, the poor man shall not pay less than a half shekel as Yahweh's levy."

The instructions Moses received for the census were the premise for all relations between Yahweh and the children of Israel. And everything turned on the notion of the *ransom*. One day, among Christians, it would be known as redemption. *Redemptor* is the technical term for a person who pays a ransom.

With the Law of Moses the ransom became a tribe: the Levites. It was only thanks to the existence of the Levites that the firstborn of the other tribes could be ransomed. To each Levite head counted corresponded the head of a ransomed firstborn. Except there were more firstborn than Levites, two hundred and seventy-three, to be precise. What was to be done about them? Inexorable as it was, the principle of substitution was applied once again. Every head would be substituted with a certain sum of money: "You will take five shekels a head . . . You will give the money to Aaron and to his sons as a ransom for those in excess." Those one thousand, three hundred and sixty-five shekels acquired as a ransom formed the basis for the fortune of the priests "who guarded the Sanctuary."

Twice, in Exodus, Yahweh orders: "You shall not come before me with empty hands!" On the second occasion the words come directly after these: "You shall ransom every firstborn among your children." Human life, it seemed, was always *in debt* to Yahweh, a debt that had to be repaid immediately, on the first possible occasion, offering the first fruits, or the surplus, or the firstborn, without delay ("you shall not delay [the offering] of the surplus and of your liquors"). The firstborn were an exception, insofar as they could be *ransomed*, one by one, by the same number of Levites, since the Levites did not belong to men, but to Yahweh.

Unlike the other tribes of Israel, the Levites did not own land. "I am their property," said Yahweh to Ezekiel. Every distinction between *auctoritas* and *potestas*, something that would become urgent when Israel finally had a king, was preceded by this even more fundamental distinction, separating the priests from all the rest of Israel. It was a way of removing them from the land and at the same time imprisoning them in a place separate from every other: the Sanctuary. Like the renouncer in Vedic India, the Levite was the first man who could and must live at once outside and inside society.

But once isolated from the other tribes and given the task of "service in the Tent of Meeting," the Levites presented an accounting conundrum. With no land to cultivate, what could they offer?

Yahweh wanted this sorted out immediately: "When you take from
the children of Israel the tithe that I grant to you from them as your
inheritance, you will take from it a levy for Yahweh amounting to
the tenth part of the tithe." This was the mechanism on which cal-
culations of compound interest would be based. And once again
it was a question of asserting the need for a levy. The Levites were
themselves a levy out of the whole of the tribes of Israel, but this
did not exempt them from the duty of raising their own levy for
Yahweh. Which this time would be a *levy on a levy*. The rest of the
offering would be "a salary for you, in exchange for your service in
the Tent of Meeting." The Levites could do whatever they wanted
with the part that was to be considered their salary: "You can eat
it wherever you choose, you and your household." This was a work
contract, set out in the clearest possible terms. In this way, Yahweh
added, "you will not profane the holy things of the children of Israel, lest you die."

When they reached Kadesh, the children of Israel were en-
raged, because there was no water. They spoke scathingly: "Why
didn't we die when our brothers died before Yahweh! Why did you
lead the community of Yahweh into this desert to have us die, us
and our herds? And why did you bring us up out of Egypt into this
miserable place? It is not a place where we can sow crops, there are
neither figs, nor vines, nor pomegranates, nor even any water to
drink!"

Moses didn't know what to say. Together with Aaron, he fled
the crowd that had surrounded them and took refuge in the Tent
of Meeting. "Then the Glory of Yahweh appeared." And Yahweh's
voice told Moses to pick up his stick once again, the stick that had
been so useful in the past, and strike the rock. Where he struck,
water would well up. That would calm the "rebels" down.

As when he was dealing with the Pharaoh and Egypt's wise
men, or with Pharaoh's soldiers, Moses didn't rely on words, but
on magic. He used the power of a piece of wood that he kept in his
hand to lean on. Now it was to make water flow from rock.

But this was not the last of his magic tricks. Moses was alone and knew he had escaped a lynching. His sister Miriam was dead and had been buried in Kadesh. Aaron, the one who did the talking, had died on the top of Mount Hor and "all the people of the house of Israel had mourned him for thirty days." The children of Israel hadn't done complaining. They hated the manna. They said, "Our spirit is disgusted by this bread, it's too light." This was an insult not to Moses but to Yahweh himself, who had made the manna grow "like frost on the ground."

It was time for a new and mysterious punishment: "Then Yahweh sent fiery snakes against the people, and they bit the people: many died among the people of Israel." This time, rather than rebelling against him, they turned to Moses for help: "We have sinned, because we spoke against Yahweh and against you. Pray to Yahweh for us that he might take these snakes away!"

Once again the solution didn't require words. Yahweh said to Moses, "Make a bronze snake and place it on a pole: whoever is bitten and sees it will live." Stick and snake had been the first magical instruments Moses used many years before. They had given him a crushing victory against Egypt's wise men, who claimed to know more magic than anyone else. Now he would have to use them again, in a way that was quite perplexing. Rather than throwing his stick in front of Pharaoh and turning it into a snake, he was to forge a fiery snake, in bronze—in short, a perfect idol—then he was to place it on a hooked stick, like his crook. And the miracle wouldn't be the transformation of the one into the other, but the mere fact of looking at them both. What's more: the miracle would occur only for those who had already been infected by the evil: "whoever is bitten and sees it will live." The decisive fact in their survival would be *seeing* an idol, something apparently entirely contrary to the doctrine of Yahweh. Or one might suppose that in these extreme and exasperated circumstances, with the children of Israel dropping down one after another in the desert and Moses now speechless, Yahweh had resorted to an extreme doctrine, something he had never spoken of before. Which now manifested itself in a healing flash, only to disappear immediately afterward.

Many years after that day in the desert—how many years exactly no one knows—the children of Israel were under siege in Jerusalem and Hezekiah, one of their kings, coming a century after another king, Joash, was the first who "got rid of the high places and broke the stelae, cut the Asherah and smashed to pieces the bronze snake that Moses had made, because the children of Israel had been offering incense to it: they called it Nehushtan." The destruction of the Asherah was something long expected. But what about the bronze snake? The miraculous object that Moses had forged suddenly reappears. Up to this point no one had said that the snake was still there, in Jerusalem, in Solomon's Temple, as a cult object to which people offered incense. Was it a sacred object, worthy of worship, or an idol like any other? Hezekiah "smashed it to pieces" with the same fury he had shown in pulverizing the stelae on the heights. But this created a theological puzzle that the second book of Kings ignores. Can one be saved by an image and at the same time condemn that image? And how had it come about that this bronze snake had been a cult object, since the times of Moses, while other metal animals were abhorred? Wasn't smashing the bronze snake to pieces an insult to Moses? Yet the Bible quickly asserts that "there would never again be a king like him [Hezekiah] from among all the kings of the Jews," and explains that "he observed all the commandments that Yahweh had given Moses." So Moses was always on his mind. But the question of the bronze snake went much further than Hezekiah, embracing the entire history of the Jews. Until one day Jesus, speaking to Nicodemus, said these words, that only John set down for us: "And just as Moses raised the serpent in the desert, so the Son of Man must be raised, so that whoever believes in him may not perish, but have everlasting life." This was a new, albeit transposed, assertion of *salvation through an image*. But if the bronze snake was smashed to pieces like any other of the "dirty idols," there was nothing left that one might look to as a sign of salvation.

So long as the children of Israel lived in the desert, they had been able to evoke the gods they left behind in Egypt and even to seek to fashion new idols. But they were all phantoms. Now, between leaving the desert and entering Canaan, they came across different peoples who worshipped their gods in these same places, celebrating them in sanctuaries. Above all there was the danger of the women devoted to the worship of these gods.

This emerged in the land of Moab, named after the firstborn son whom Lot had had with his daughter. These people were relatives, but impure relatives, born from incest. Yahweh had said, "Don't torment Moab, don't make war on him"; all the same, the children of Israel and the Moabites lived in a state of reciprocal suspicion. In Moab people worshipped Chemosh, "a black stone in the form of a woman." And in Shittim, or the Acacias, where the children of Israel camped, there was a place called the "Well of Lewdness."

Then it so happened that "the people began to fornicate with the daughters of Moab. They invited the people to attend sacrifices to their gods, the people ate and bowed down before their gods. Israel cleaved to Baal Peor and Yahweh's anger was kindled against Israel." To placate that anger it wasn't enough to hang "all the leaders of the people . . . before the sun," as Yahweh ordered Moses to do. Something else would have to happen: a Midianite—a woman from the land where Moses had lived for forty years—slipped in among the children of Israel "while they were weeping at the entrance to the Tent of Meeting." It was a cover for an amorous encounter. But Phinehas, Aaron's grandson, caught on, surprised the Midianite in bed with a son of Israel, and "transfixed them both, the man of Israel and the woman, through the belly. Then the scourge ceased to afflict the children of Israel." Some would claim that Phinehas, filled with a sudden, prodigious strength, was able to raise up the two joined and transfixed bodies on the point of his spear. Everyone was to see them. Then Yahweh said that Phinehas had saved the children of Israel, "by being jealous on my behalf in the midst of them, so that I did not destroy the children of Israel despite my jealousy."

All this can be read in Numbers 25:1–11. But Ernst Sellin, severe and audacious biblical scholar as he was, was not convinced. He felt sure there was an omission, an enormous omission. And he thought he had found a hint of it in some verses in Hosea. A whole tradition had been buried in the sand and needed digging up. According to that tradition, "Moses in the Acacias, Shittim, in the sanctuary of his God and his people, after this cleaving [of the people] to Baal Peor, as a result of which the people had been called to repent and had made amends, had been treacherously killed." A labored, tortuous sentence announcing the horrible truth erased from Numbers, but resurfacing not only in Hosea, but also in Nehemiah and in the Deutero-Isaiah. If Moses had been the first of the prophets, the man who had taught the children of Israel what a prophet was, and if the destiny of prophets, as would be seen time and again, right up to Stephen's grand retelling of the Jewish story before the Sanhedrin, was to be killed, then Moses himself must have been killed. If Hosea said, "They have dug a deep grave in the Acacias, Shittim," that must have been the isolated and soon-to-be-forgotten tomb of Moses in the land of Moab, facing Beth Peor. And Sellin noted: "In the founder of a religion, this is a trait that inevitably calls attention to itself."

After Sellin published his book, other biblical scholars contrived, in universal accord, to turn their gaze elsewhere. Only Freud chose to base his *Moses* on Sellin's hypothesis, as if it were proven and accepted. When a friend told him that Sellin had later retracted his theory (which wasn't exactly the case), Freud answered, "It could be true anyway."

Isaac lived all his life in Canaan; Abraham had spent part of his life there. Likewise Jacob. After that the children of Israel had passed more than four hundred years in Egypt. They had had nothing more to do with Canaan and by now knew almost nothing about the place. Canaan was just a name that turned up in stories about their three ancestors. Centuries later, the Jews who headed for Palestine after the diaspora would find themselves in a similar situation. Palestine was a place they knew from a book: the Bible.

The children of Israel knew that Canaan was the land Yahweh had promised them and that other people were already living there, but not much else. They did not know if "the population that lives there is strong or weak, whether there are many people or few; or even what the land they live in is like, whether good or bad; or what kind of towns they live in, if they are camps or fortresses; if the grass is rich or sparse, if there are trees or not." They had left the vast kingdom that was Egypt and gone hungry for years on their way to a land that might well prove harsh and bleak. A land where perhaps they wouldn't find so much as the shade of a tree. Those sent ahead to scout would have to push on as far as the torrent of Eshkol before finding a bunch of grapes. They brought it back, after forty days, along with some pomegranates and figs. They were the proof that there were things growing in the Promised Land.

They added that milk and honey really did flow in the land, even though they hadn't actually seen it. But they confirmed that there were big, fortified cities, where the Amalekites lived, their number one enemy. There were also Hittites, Jebusites, Amorites, and Canaanites. Compared with them, the men of Israel felt "like grasshoppers."

Shortly before he died, Moses once again stood before the waters: the Jordan. He had set out from the Red Sea and now he halted beside this great river. It was then that Yahweh told him to give some last instructions to the children of Israel. These orders would be clearer than ever, explaining what the people must do, when no longer under his guidance, on the other side of the waters: "When you have crossed the Jordan into the land of Canaan, when you have put to flight all the inhabitants of the country, you will destroy their images, destroy all their forged metal statues, and demolish their high places. You will possess the land and live there, because I have given you the land to possess it. You will cast lots to share out the land among your families; to the more numerous families you will give a larger inheritance and to the less numerous a smaller; each will get what comes to them by lot. You will share out the land according to the tribes of your fathers. If you do not put the inhabitants of the country to flight, those you leave will be pricks in your eyes and thorns in your sides, they will attack you in the land you inhabit. And then what I planned to do to them, I shall do to you."

It was time to say goodbye. Moses was a hundred and twenty years old and complained he could no longer "go out and come back," although "his eye was not dimmed, nor had his freshness faded." There was little doubt that he could have gone with his people across the Jordan into the Promised Land. But Yahweh had told him, "You will not pass this Jordan." Then Yahweh had gone on talking, without further mention of Moses, except with regard to the transfer of power: "Yahweh, your God, it is he who shall pass before you, he who will destroy these nations before you, and you will take their land. It will be Joshua who passes before you, as Yahweh has spoken."

Then Moses decided to write down the Law: "Moses wrote this Law, gave it to the priests, the sons of Levi, who carried the Ark of the Covenant of Yahweh, and to all the elders of Israel." And Moses commanded that seven years later, "in the year of release from debts and for the feast of Tabernacles," they should *read this Law* "before all Israel": men, women, children, guests. The forty harrowing years in the desert were over, only a memory now. Now they would have to concentrate on a long public reading, so that everyone, without exception, could "work hard to practice all the words of this Law." It was the beginning of the canon, modern scholars observe, although "the idea of reading the whole of

Deuteronomy in the presence of a large festive community does create a few difficulties."

But it wasn't over yet: "Then Moses took the blood and sprinkled it on the people. He said, 'This is the blood of the Covenant that Yahweh has made with you in accordance with all these words!'" Apparently the book on its own wasn't enough. But neither was the blood, on its own. Maybe in the past it would have been, but not now. Now the book was required. But the book couldn't be separated from the blood. The blood had to come before it, and to follow after it. A substance was needed, a substance that was *life itself.* Fluid, continuous, that the word could immerse itself in, and emerge from. Yet at the same time blood was contamination. It was the blood of slaughtered animals. It was life itself, but also something that can be seen only after killing. Blood was the invisible made manifest through killing. To reach the invisible, one must pass through killing, whether inflicted on another or suffered yourself.

Right afterward, "Yahweh said to Moses, 'So, your last days are at hand. Call Joshua, stay with him in the Tent of Meeting so I can give him his orders.'" Once again, a decision had to be taken as to who would be in command; and at once there was talk of something that must be read: a song. "Moses wrote this song that day and taught it to the children of Israel." It wasn't a song of glory, but a testimony against the people of Israel themselves, because, Moses said, "after I die you will grow corrupt and stray from the path I have prescribed for you."

The moment had come to recount the most obscure and unfathomable event of all: the election of Israel. To do so one must return to the origins: "When the Most High divided the peoples, / when he scattered the children of Adam, / then he set boundaries between the peoples /according to the number of the children of Israel; / since Yahweh's portion was his people, / Jacob his portion of inheritance."

Yahweh had given his Angels the task of overseeing the peoples, to each angel a people. With one exception, the children of Jacob, whom Yahweh kept for his own portion. But where was Jacob to be found? "He finds him in a desert place, / in a howling whirlwind; / he girdles him about, takes care of him, / protects him like the apple of his eye. / Like an eagle that stirs her nest / and glides over her young, / spreads her wings and gathers them up / carries them away in her feathers." Such was the first appearance of Israel. Yahweh would deal with all other peoples through the mediation of his Angels. Only with Israel would the relationship be unmediated. So much so, Job would one day observe, as not to leave even the "time to swallow my spit."

This was what had happened, for those who were interested. But why it had happened, and above all why it had happened in that way and in those places, was not explained. Why did Yahweh's "portion" have to turn up in a howling desert? Cautiously, in a whisper as it were, Gerhard von Rad observed, "the strange idea that Yahweh 'found' Israel in the desert cannot simply be ascribed to poetic license." On the contrary, it could be the most ancient tradition with regard to election, something that reemerges in Hosea: "Like grapes in the desert / I had found Israel."

Before going into Canaan, the children of Israel had been given instructions regarding the Law and certain future events: among the latter the fact that one day—how far off they did not know— "you will be able to set a king over you, a king chosen by Yahweh." It had been expected, then, that Israel would ask for this out of a spirit of imitation, wishing to have a king "like all the nations round about." But even here certain limitations must be established: the king must not be a foreigner; he must not have too many horses, lest he go back to Egypt to acquire even more; he must not have too many wives, lest they cause his heart to stray; he must not have too much gold or too much silver. Above all, though, he must always—"all the days of his life"—read a book, a copy of the Law that he would get from the Levites. A king who reads just one book, every day, "so that his heart might not set itself up above his brothers," was the ideal king, and one day, in the rather distant future, such a king would turn up for the children of Israel.

The children of Israel must also be aware—and Yahweh warned them through Moses—that a new figure would emerge: the prophet: "Yahweh, your God, will stir up for you and among you, among your brothers, a prophet like me: it is to him you must listen!" So Moses was not unique, but the first of a new dynasty. And they would no longer be called magicians or wise men, as Moses might still have been considered, but they would lay claim to this new name: prophet. How were they to be recognized? The answer was clear: "If the prophet speaks in Yahweh's name and what he says does not take place, does not happen, then his word is not Yahweh's word and the prophet has spoken from presumption and you shall not be afraid of him!" With the prophets one entered—and would nevermore leave—the realm of fact, of verifiable events.

Shortly before announcing the Ten Commandments, Yahweh said to Moses, "I am a jealous God, who punishes the children for the sins of their fathers, as far as the third and fourth generation." When, after Aaron's death, Yahweh began to lay down all the precepts that the children of Israel must observe, at one point he said, "Fathers will not be put to death for their children, nor will children be put to death for their fathers: each will be put to death for his own crimes." This last phrase was shocking. Jeremiah and Ezekiel would both repeat it. And the same principle forms the basis for the *ius*, from Justinian to the Napoleonic Code.

Men would no longer be able to punish children in place of their fathers, but Yahweh would go on punishing generations of descendants of anyone who had violated his laws. In their eagerness to arrive at the majestic Commandments, many scholars have passed hastily over these words, which nevertheless have a biting precision: that Yahweh's punishments extend "to the third and fourth generation" of the guilty man's descendants is repeated in Exodus

34:7, Numbers 14:18, and Deuteronomy 5:9. So how could Yahweh's words be reconciled? Once again everything turned on the nature of guilt. Was it circumscribed, precisely located? Or was it diffuse, shifting, hard to contain? Once again, as with all Yahweh's pronouncements, there was no question of choice: one had to accept them all, simultaneously. Such was the duty of those who observed the precepts, carrying them on their foreheads in the form of phylacteries and keeping them constantly in mind. But what mattered most was not the observance of the single precepts. Rather it was the recognition of the Law as a sovereign, all-encompassing entity, forever hovering over everything. Other peoples would also produce detailed codes and obsessive rules. The children of Israel were to have the Law: "These words that I prescribe for you today you shall hold in your heart, you shall teach them persistently to your children and you will speak of them, when you are sitting at home and when you are in the street, when you lie down to sleep and when you rise, you will attach them as a sign on your hand and they will serve as phylacteries between your eyes, you will write them on the doorposts of your houses and on your doors." More important than the single precepts of the Law was the fact that the Law was the supreme, ever-present entity, outside of which nothing was acceptable. This was the irreducible difference between the Law of Moses and every other code. But the day would come when someone would speak of "those prevarications that belonged to the previous covenant." All at once the idea was floated that within the Law itself lurked an abuse of power.

It was important to Yahweh not just that the children of Israel obey all his precepts, but that they should not add any of their own: "Everything I order you, you must be careful to do: you shall not add anything to it or take anything from it." Yahweh's Law was *all* the law there was. Men were not to be allowed to add so much as a postscript. And the Law must be systematically implemented. This was a major development and Yahweh made no attempt to hide the fact. On the contrary, he established a starting point after which the Law must be implemented in its entirety: "When you have crossed the Jordan and are living in the country that Yahweh, your God, has given you to possess, when he has achieved peace for you with respect to your enemies and you are living in safety." From that moment on, there would be no alternative but to implement the Law. Then life would no longer be as it had been during the years in the desert: "You will no longer behave as we do here, today, each person acting as seems right in his own eyes, because thus far you have not arrived at the place of peace and the inheritance that Yahweh, your God, is giving to you."

When it came to war, Moses was quick to establish two very different sets of rules. The first, applicable to "all towns that are quite distant from you," was no different from the codes of behavior followed by other peoples of the Middle East. One began by offering peace in return for a town's surrender. If the enemy did not accept, one laid siege to the town and attacked it. At that point every man must be put to the sword. "But the women, the children, the animals, and everything in the town, all its spoils, you shall take as plunder and you will eat the spoils of your enemies that Yahweh, your God, has given you."

But for the "towns of those peoples that Yahweh, your God, gives to you as your inheritance," Moses laid down quite different laws. These peoples were to be cut off from all others and condemned to *herem*, which is to say, exterminated. But what crime exactly had these peoples committed? First and foremost the crime of living in the places that Yahweh had promised to the children of Israel. Places where no trace of any past, inevitably reprehensible, must remain.

There was the danger that "they may teach you to imitate all the disgusting things they do for their gods, which would lead you to sin against Yahweh, your God." This was the really serious problem: imitation. The religions of these peoples that they were going to root out were hardly different from those of other Semitic peoples, as far off as Mesopotamia. But they were a threat, because the children of Israel would be in contact with them. And this would be enough to provoke that first of all crimes: imitation. Whatever form it takes, imitation is always a *departure from oneself*, a momentary, temporary betrayal, perhaps, but nevertheless such as to allow a glimpse of the possibility of a total and definitive betrayal. This is what Moses had understood when he came down from Sinai, amid the smoke and cries of the people dancing around a golden animal. The fact that imitation was the first of all evils was one of the most covert departures in the doctrine that Moses was laying down. It was not to be explicitly declared, yet it galvanized all the precepts. And this established the singularity of the doctrine. All other doctrines, starting with the most revered, Egypt's, could be *translated* the one into the other, with the help of a few tricks and contrivances. Moses not only rejected translatability, but made it the origin of all evil.

The *herem* was not just a wartime measure. In tones of irrefutable authority, Exodus warns: "Whoever sacrifices to gods other than Yahweh alone will be condemned to the *herem*." No other part of the Middle East had such a rule. The coexistence of many gods had always been precarious and turbulent, but reciprocal extermination was never an option. And it wasn't just a question of killing anyone who sacrificed to other gods. One might be distracted and seduced by a "prophet" of these gods, "even if he makes the sign or performs the miracle he predicted to you." Or danger might come from others who were not prophets: among whom "your brother, your mother's son, your own son or daughter, the woman you embrace, the friend who is your second self." If one of these were to whisper, "Let us go and serve other gods," there was nothing for it: "You will have to kill him." And it will be "your hand" that kills him, a violation of the Commandments. But not even this was enough. After that "the hand of all the people" would be involved and "you shall stone him with stones and he will die."

Any number of biblical scholars have sought to explain that the entry of the children of Israel into the land flowing with milk and honey was a mainly peaceful process of gradual filtration, during which the new arrivals tended to settle in the "mountain regions of Palestine, which for the most part were still uncultivated"; only in a later period, driven by the need to find grazing for their livestock, would they begin to move down into the plain among the many city-states of the Canaanites. Of the military campaigns of the children of Israel no verifiable evidence has come down to us. The ruins of Ai and Jericho date back to a time centuries before the conquest recounted in the book of Joshua. As Von Rad would have it, all this suggests that "the real battles with the Canaanites were minor affairs." And Caspari has no hesitation in claiming that the Israelites were drawn into the war against their will, and subjected to "a painful military initiation at the hands of foreign instructors." Whose fault was it? The foreigners', always. And that sometimes meant foreign women.

Yet Yahweh had spoken in quite other terms, even when the children of Israel were still in the desert with Moses at their head: "You will devour all the peoples that Yahweh, your god, delivers up to you, your eye will show no pity for them and thus you will not serve their gods, since that would be a trap for you." And to make it absolutely clear what peoples he was talking about, right after announcing the Ten Commandments, Moses added, "When Yahweh, your God, has brought you into the country where you will go, and has driven out numerous peoples before you, the Hittites, the Girgashites, the Amorites, the Canaanites, the Perizzites, the Hivvites, and the Jebusites, seven peoples stronger and more numerous than yourselves, when Yahweh, your God, has delivered them over to you and you have defeated them, you will commit them to anathema, *herem*, you will not form alliances with them, and you will not have pity on them, you will form no marriage alliances with them, you will not give your daughter to one of their sons and you will not take one of their daughters for your son, because that would turn your son away from following me and he would serve other gods, and the wrath of Yahweh would be kindled against you and he would soon destroy you."

When the children of Israel were about to cross the Jordan, Yahweh told Moses he must climb Mount Nebo and die there, just as earlier his brother, Aaron, had gone to die on another mountain. In this way, Yahweh said to Moses, "you will only see the land from afar, you will not enter there, into the land I am giving to the children of Israel." This death on the brink of completing his mission was a punishment for something that had happened years before, "because you and Aaron were not true to me in the midst of the children of Israel, at the waters of Meribah in the desert of Zin." That day the people's "quarrel" with Yahweh had been settled, as so often, with a miracle: the water that flowed from the rock. But the miracle was a sign of weakness. It had been a day of profound doubt: not as to whether Yahweh was to be preferred to other gods, but as to whether he existed at all. Moses was punished because, obliged to mediate, he had found himself being maltreated by both the quarreling parties. Questioning Yahweh's existence unleashed immediate consequences: "Then came Amalek and fought against Israel at Rephidim." The Amalekites were to be Israel's perennial shadow. They, too, could have been found and chosen by Yahweh in the midst of the howling desert. Instead they would follow in Israel's footsteps, like its antitype, always ready to strike hard then melt away. Their aim was not just to defeat Israel, but to destroy it, have it cease to exist, as Israel had doubted whether Yahweh existed.

The Amalekites did not appear in the list of the seven peoples dwelling in Canaan. Yet that was where they lived, in the southernmost part. They were nomads. They did not have any land they could claim as their own. It was another condition they shared

with the children of Israel after their flight from Egypt. The Amalekites did not want to accept them, because it would have meant
having other nomads in Canaan. Hence the Jews' suspicion that
the Amalekites would prove a lethal enemy. And hence the Amalekites' decision to attack them, starting with the stragglers behind
the main caravan, exhausted from their desert march, barely capable now of resisting anything that wasn't the desert itself.

For the first time, Israel had encountered a people determined
to eliminate Israel as such. That memory would be set apart forever. It was not just another war. Israel waited for the moment
when some semblance of calm had been established, when the
previous inhabitants of the Promised Land had been pacified. It
seemed there was nothing left to do but offer first fruits and tithes
to Yahweh. And observe his precepts. But no. The Amalekites were
still there—and they were a different story. They alone had won
themselves an inextinguishable execration, renewed from generation to generation, for something they did *on a particular day* in
Rephidim. Deuteronomy gives the details: "Remember what Amalek did, along the way, when you were coming out of Egypt, how
they came toward you, on the way, and cut off the retreat of all
your stragglers, at the back, while you were worn out, exhausted."
It wouldn't be enough, with Amalek, to defeat and enslave them.
This project would be more unusual, more difficult. Once again
Deuteronomy is determined to clarify: "As soon as Yahweh,
your God, has granted you respite from the enemies around you
in the land that Yahweh, your God, has given you to possess as
your inheritance, you will cancel the memory of Amalek from
beneath the heavens: do not forget it!" Memory was to serve to
erase a memory.

Moses had reached the end of a very long speech during which
he had taken care to sum everything up, knowing it would be his
last opportunity. And he said, "So! Today I have put before you
life and goodness, death and evil. What I am ordering you today
is to love Yahweh, your God, and to walk in his ways, to observe

his commandments, his precepts, his judgments. Do that and you will live and multiply." Moses did not say that he had put before his audience *life and death*, as was all too obvious, but "life and goodness," as opposed to "death and evil." Death continued to be something you could only remove, expel, annul. Yet whose presence had to be recognized in every detail by anyone intending to carry out the first of Moses's orders, to "love Yahweh."

The same day Moses presented his song to all the people, Yahweh asked him to climb Mount Nebo. And added, "Look out over the land of Canaan which I am giving to the children of Israel to possess; then die on the mountain where you have climbed and be reunited with your ancestors, just as your brother Aaron died in Hor, on the mountain, and was reunited with his ancestors." So Moses pronounced words of blessing for each of the twelve tribes and climbed up Nebo, to die.

Moses was mourned for thirty days, just as his brother, Aaron, had been mourned for thirty days. It would be said of him, "Never again, in Israel, would there be a prophet like Moses, whom Yahweh knew face-to-face."

Unlike the patriarchs, Moses went to his death alone. Miriam and Aaron had gone before. Zipporah and his son Gershom had gone back to Midian. Even his tomb was a lonely one, near Canaan, but not in it, "in the valley that is in the land of Moab, facing Beth Peor." But where exactly we don't know: "No one has known his tomb to this day."

The Bible does not say it, but a number of traditions make the claim: that Moses did not accept Yahweh's decision that he was not to set foot in the Promised Land. He even asked if he could go there, not as head of the people, but as an ordinary person. And this, too, was denied him. "Thou shalt not go from this bank of the Jordan to the other," was Yahweh's reply. Then Moses asked that at least his bones, like Joseph's, might eventually be buried in the Promised Land. "Nay, not even thy bones shall cross the Jordan."

This was even more unbearable, and incomprehensible. So Moses asked why. Yahweh answered that when Jethro's daughters had introduced him to their father, they had said, "An Egyptian freed us from the hands of the shepherds." And Moses had not corrected them, had not pointed out that he was not an Egyptian but a Jew. Only he who acknowledged his origins could be received into the land of Israel. Once again, Egypt proved an obstacle, a barrier, above all for the man who had liberated the children of Israel from Egypt.

Israel's first enemy was not men but water. Just as the Red Sea had parted so that they could cross with dry feet, so, too, must the Jordan. This hostility to water, together with the longing for a land where everything would flow and even overflow, marked Israel out from the beginning, from the time when it was no more than a "wandering Aramean" crossing desert and empty plain in search of some place of liquid abundance. *To pass across the waters* was something Israel did not feel able to do, unless with divine help. And this was a scar cutting across everything Israel thought and felt. But it could hardly have been otherwise. Thus "the priests who carried the Ark of the Covenant of Yahweh would stop, with dry feet, in the middle of the Jordan, while all of Israel passed by, with dry feet, until all the nation had finished crossing the Jordan."

Those who crossed the Jordan had all been born in the desert and none of them had been circumcised. Rough-hewn folk who needed polishing up. They had never seen Egypt and knew nothing at all about Canaan. Something essential was lacking before these young people could enter the settled world: the *cut*, separation, hence circumcision. The peoples of Canaan were already in alarm over the imminent invasion of these tribes marching toward them from the desert and "felt breathless in the presence of the children of Israel." But Joshua knew that one could not yet really call these people the children of Israel. John Chrysostom would make the situation perfectly clear: the Jews could not pass off circumcision as "a single commandment," when "on the contrary it is the commandment that imposes on you the entire yoke of the Law." Just as Yahweh had given the law of circumcision to Abraham long before dictating the Tablets of the Law to Moses, so now circumcision must be seen as the precondition of every other rule. Nothing can be used and accepted *as it is*, whether among the fruits of the earth or among men. Everything requires a cut, a separation. "When you plant a fruit tree, you will treat its fruit as its foreskin: for three years the fruit will be like foreskins to you, you must not eat it. The fourth year, all the fruit will be consecrated in a feast to Yahweh. The fifth year, you will eat the fruit." With male children it was the same, except that the foreskin was to be cut the eighth day after birth.

Uncircumcised, one could not enter the fullness of life. Those born in the desert preparing to enter the Promised Land were to stop on a flinty hill. Joshua ordered that they all be circumcised. From then on the place was called the Hill of Foreskins. It was also the last place where the children of Israel ate manna. Henceforth that food would be no more than a memory, mixed with relief and disgust. Then "they ate the produce of the land of Canaan," which did not flow with milk and honey, but had fruit in abundance.

Sour and spiteful, the words of John Chrysostom found confirmation eight centuries later, in the supreme scholar of Judaism, Maimonides. Toward the end of his *Guide for the Perplexed* one reads that Moses chose to reintroduce circumcision, which had been abandoned for more than four hundred years, the very night the people left Egypt, so that the blood of the circumcision was mixed with the blood of the lambs that was smeared on the doorposts. Quite undaunted, Maimonides simply ignores the fact that the book of Exodus makes no mention of this.

It is true, though, that immediately after the description of what happened the night they left Egypt, Yahweh told Moses and

Aaron that henceforth the Passover rite should be celebrated only by the circumcised: "No foreigner shall eat thereof." Maimonides is shrewdly superimposing two separate moments. Since he was eager to establish that circumcision was the prerequisite of every Law, it had to be established right away, on the edge of the desert, while the Tablets of the Law would be shown to Moses only later, in the middle of the desert.

The story of that fatal night is thus presented as follows: "When God ordered the Passover lamb and the condition was established that no one would slaughter it unless they had first practised circumcision on themselves, on their sons and on whoever else made up their households, and that only then 'could they come close to do it,' they had everyone circumcised. The multitude of the circumcised, say [the Sages] was such that the blood of the circumcision mixed with the blood of the Passover lamb, and it is to this that the prophet alludes when he says, 'wallowing in your blood' (Ezekiel 16:6), that is the blood of the Passover lamb and the blood of the circumcision."

But what was the real reason for circumcision? Maimonides replies thus: "I believe that one of the reasons for circumcision is to diminish copulation and weaken the member, to limit its action and leave it at rest as much as possible." Eminent rationalist as he was, Maimonides did not, however, believe that this was a sufficient explanation and added, "This precept does not have the purpose of making good a physical imperfection. On the contrary, it is a remedy for a moral imperfection. The real purpose is to inflict physical pain on the member without in any way disturbing those functions necessary for the survival of the individual or impeding procreation, but diminishing passion and excessive concupiscence."

But this still didn't exhaust the reasons for circumcision. The physical pain of circumcision had another purpose, and Maimonides goes on: "To my mind there is another very important reason for circumcision: it guarantees that those who profess the idea of the unity of God can be distinguished by the same physical sign, impressed on them all. So he who does not have that sign, being a foreigner, cannot pretend to belong to them; otherwise some people might act in such a way as to exploit or trick those who profess this religion. No one would ever practice this act on themselves or on their sons if not out of real conviction; because it is not like a wound on the leg or a burn on the arm, but something extremely tough." And Abraham's conviction when he concluded his "covenant for faith in the unity of God" had been equally *tough*. And here Maimonides comments, "This is another important reason for circumcision, and perhaps more important than the earlier reason."

At first the children of Israel said they were only asking to cross the territories of Canaan: "We will not pass over any fields or vineyards, we will not drink the water from any wells, we will stay on the main road." That was what they said to the king of Edom, referring to themselves as "your brother Israel," since the Edomites were descendants of Esau. But the king of Edom threatened to fight to defend his territory. So the children of Israel took a different route.

Of the many Canaanite peoples, the king of Arad launched an immediate attack on the children of Israel and took a number of prisoners. "So Israel made a vow to Yahweh and said, 'If you consent to deliver this people into our hands, we will consecrate their city to anathema.' Yahweh heard Israel's cry and handed over the Canaanites. They were consecrated to extermination, they and their cities." It was the first time that the children of Israel had consecrated one of the peoples of Canaan to the *herem*. Yahweh approved. All was in order. But they did not put their plan into action at once. They kept it in reserve.

The first king the children of Israel fought was Sihon, king of the Amorites: "They defeated him and his sons and all his people and left not a single survivor and conquered the land." From that point on the children of Israel instilled terror wherever they moved. Balak, king of Moab, said to his elders, "Now this mob will go and graze all over the land, the way an ox eats up everything green in the country."

The Promised Land was not virgin country, untrodden and un-explored, where everything grew just as it should. Quite the contrary: this was a ready-made world that others had built, then fled from. Everything was abundant, everything was to hand, but the country was empty, empty as the desert where the children of Israel had spent forty years. More than any milk and honey, this was the miracle. Entering the country, all the children of Israel would have to do was to introduce certain rules. To the eye, nothing would have changed, since rules are invisible. And the new inhabitants of the place would feel safe. They would say, "Our justification shall be to take care that all these commandments are observed before Yahweh, our God, just as he ordered us."

The move to the "good land," the Promised Land, was a move from the dry to the damp, from the separate grains of sand to the continuous flow of running water, from the desert to "the country of streams and wells and deep springs gushing from mountain to valley." Dried up and shriveled after forty years of divine indoctrination of the severest kind, "amid fiery snakes and scorpions," the children of Israel longed for those waters, for whatever flows and has substance, like bread rather than manna, that "bread that is too light."

The practice of exterminating one's enemies was applied again and again by Joshua in the first battles beyond the Jordan. Jericho, Makkedah, Eglon, Hebron, and Debir were all given over to the *herem*. With regard to Libnah, it was said that "he let no one escape," and the same was true of Lachish. The book of Joshua offers these details here and there, but at the end, commenting on the military campaign as a whole, it confirms: "He consecrated every living being to the *herem*, as Yahweh, God of Israel, had ordered." Then Joshua "went back to the camp in Gilgal." He had defeated all the kings surrounding them "in a single campaign," but the children of Israel hadn't yet decided where to settle. They were still looking at everything from their tents.

The prescription of the *herem* for certain enemies found its counterpart in what Israel could expect when attacked by a powerful enemy they had been warned of: "A nation from afar, from the ends of the earth, like a gliding eagle, a nation whose tongue you will not understand, a nation with hard faces, that has no respect for the old and no pity for the young." Then Israel would be reduced to feeding on itself. "The most delicate and tender of your women, she who would never dare place the sole of her foot on the ground, so delicate and tender she is, will look spitefully on the man in her arms, likewise on her son and her daughter, and on the placenta that issues forth from her, and on the children she has generated; for she will eat them in secret, having nothing else, in the anguish and desolation to which your enemy will reduce you, in your own homes."

From the one side as from the other, the most ferocious cruelty was foreseen, with no survivors. But with this difference: for Israel destruction would never be total. Some "remainder of Israel" would always be left, even if "but few of you will remain (where once you were numerous as the stars in the sky)." At the other end of time, this *remainder of Israel* corresponded to the grace once reserved for the three Patriarchs; it guaranteed that Israel would continue to exist.

Yahweh wanted to be very clear about this: "So it will come to pass that, just as Yahweh was pleased to help you and to multiply you, so Yahweh will be pleased to have you die and wipe you out; so you will be torn away from the land that you are entering to possess. Then Yahweh will disperse you among all the peoples, from one end of the earth to the other end of the earth, and there you will serve other gods of wood and stone, that you did not know, neither you nor your fathers. You will have no peace among these nations and there will be no place where you can rest the sole of your foot. There Yahweh will give you a heart that trembles, listlessness in your eyes, and anxiety in your soul. Your life will be suspended before you and you will be frightened night and day, not believing in your own life anymore." And yet the *remainder of Israel* would continue to exist.

These words of Yahweh's were spoken immediately after Moses had announced that new figures would appear among the people and that they would be called *prophets*. Yahweh was offering himself as a model.

Joshua had not been long in the land of Canaan when a crime occurred that would be repeated over and over by the children of Israel: the crime of sparing something from the *herem*, "concealing it, hiding it among the baggage." Not to destroy some object or some person of a defeated city meant contaminating the children of Israel's camp. A crime with fatal consequences, Yahweh said: if Israel were to preserve so much as a crumb of what has been consecrated to anathema, it would never be able resist its enemies.

Achan, from the tribe of Judah, finally confessed: "I saw a fine cloak from Shinar amid the plunder, two hundred silver shekels, and a gold ingot weighing five hundred shekels; I wanted them and took them; they are buried in the middle of my tent with the money beneath." Joshua had his story checked: Then "Joshua took Achan, son of Zerah, and the money, the cloak, the gold ingot, his sons and his daughters, his oxen and his asses and all his small animals, his tent and everything that was his. All Israel was with him. They were taken to the valley of Achor. And Joshua said, 'What devastation you have caused us! And today it is Yahweh who shall devastate you.' Then all Israel pelted him with stones. Some were burned, some were killed with stones. They piled a big heap of stones over him, which is still there today."

Other kings joined forces against Joshua and other kings fell, even when leading "a people numerous as sand on the seashore." Only the Hivvites from Gibeon agreed to make peace. The other towns "were all taken after war. Because Yahweh had decided to stiffen their hearts to fight against Israel, so they could be consecrated to anathema, and not find mercy, and be exterminated, in accordance with Yahweh's instructions to Moses." Applying the *herem* was a deliberate strategy on Yahweh's part, something Moses was aware of. Even the resistance of the various kings was a divine stratagem that would make it easier for Israel to destroy them. So in the end "Joshua took the whole country, in accordance with all that Yahweh had told Moses, and Joshua gave it as an inheritance to Israel, sharing it out among the tribes. And the country rested from war."

Sharing out the conquered lands and cities among the tribes of Israel was a painstaking, time-consuming affair. Joshua drew lots, "following the instructions Yahweh had given to Moses." One case remained unresolved: Jerusalem, because, "with regard to the Jebusites living in Jerusalem, the children of Judah could not dispossess them and the Jebusites have lived in Jerusalem alongside the children of Judah, onto this day."

One day, in his old age, Joshua felt the need to assemble all the tribes of Israel in Shechem and remind them how their story had unfolded, starting with the places beyond the Euphrates where their fathers had lived when they "served other gods." He spoke of Abraham, Isaac, Jacob, of Moses and Aaron, of Egypt, and the time when they "lived in the desert for long days." Then he remembered how, in more recent times, they had fought the Amorites, the Perizzites, the Canaanites, the Hittites, the Girgashites, the Hivvites, and the Jebusites, winning every time.

Joshua was not convinced that the tribes had kept their memories fresh, sharp, and incontrovertible, now that they had achieved "peace in relation to all the enemies around them." He wasn't convinced they really understood that, just as none of the "good words" Yahweh had spoken in their regard had been left "unfulfilled," so the same could happen in the future with regard to the

"bad words, to the point of wiping you off the face of the earth."
Then Yahweh might say, "You will fast disappear from the good
land I have given you." And Joshua wanted to remind them of
something else Yahweh had said about the "good land" they had
just conquered: "Then I gave you a land on which you had not labored, cities you did not build and in which you live, vineyards
and olives you did not plant, with which you feed yourselves." It
was as if the children of Israel had fallen straight out of the sky
into this land where nothing was the fruit of their labor. They must
always remember that. With these words, Joshua ended his speech.
But it wasn't enough for him that those listening agreed with what
he said. He decided to set up a big stone "under the oak tree in
Yahweh's sanctuary." He said the stone was to serve "as a witness
against us, because it has heard all the words Yahweh has spoken
to us." Joshua was sure that stone would have plenty of opportuni-
ties to testify.

Once in the Promised Land, the children of Israel were not always fighting and conquering. Sometimes they turned their minds
to the past. The figure of Moses, who had ruled over them, reappeared. And they said to themselves, "Woe to the son of Amram
that ran before us like a horse, but whose bones remained in the
desert."

Not only had Moses not been buried in the Promised Land, not
only was his tomb unknown, somewhere out in the empty plain of
Moab, enemy territory, but it was in the valley facing Beth Peor, the
place where Haron, one of the five Angels of Destruction, was imprisoned. The powers of salvation and ruin were right next to each
other, and couldn't be found. Some said things had been arranged
thus so that the Angel of Destruction would be paralyzed, when he
tried to "rise out of the depths [and] open wide his mouth."

VIII

AN UNREDEEMED

GHOST

No one exemplifies Freud's theories better than Freud himself. Rather than science, psychoanalysis is autobiography. This is not the irreparable limitation it might seem, since Freud's psyche was vast enough to host many others, albeit not all. And no book of Freud's exemplifies psychoanalysis better than *Moses and Monotheism*. No other work was characterized by so many misgivings, hesitations, interruptions, justifications, and procrastinations. Nor cloaked in such a cloud of fear: the fear of revealing a secret—a dangerous, perhaps damaging secret. At the same time, no book of Freud's, not even *The Interpretation of Dreams*, parades so much pride in its central discovery. This is the work of Freud's *late style*, "that will never be sufficiently admired," thought Walter Benjamin, the style of "one who has little or nothing to lose," as Freud himself claimed, a reckless man willing to take an unprecedented risk.

The first reason Freud gives for his misgivings is unconvincing, and the reader immediately appreciates it is a red herring: he was concerned, he claimed, that the book might "reawaken the enmity of the Catholic Church," dominant in Austria. But Freud had been feeding the Church's appetite for scandal for more than thirty years without batting an eyelid. And the Catholic Church has never been overly sensitive to questions relating to the Bible. Freud's anxieties lay elsewhere. He feared he would wound and offend the Jews, and this at a time—the book's outline was laid down in 1934 and it would be published in 1939—when they were being mortally wounded every day. Hence he swings back and forth between recklessness and reticence, but when he is reckless, he is so with the terseness and toughness that is the hallmark of his greatest discoveries. So the book opens with a daring statement that gives away its core trauma at once: "To deprive a people of the man they celebrate as the greatest of their sons is not something one undertakes willingly or lightly, especially when one belongs to that people oneself." Freud could hardly have been clearer, or more drastic: the aim of the book is to deprive the Jews of the greatest of their sons. And this trauma will be aggravated by another: in the course of the argument the Jews are also to be deprived of the greatest of their ideas, monotheism, whose discovery Freud will attribute to the Pharaoh Akhenaten. So Moses was not Jewish but a foreigner, and his doctrine was an imitation of a foreign doctrine. Nothing was *peculiar* to the Jews except their capacity to follow a foreigner and his foreign doctrine. All this could easily be seized on as an authoritative confirmation of quite other theories, rampant at the time, regarding the supposed *secondary status* of the Jews, their inability to create anything, compounded with a treacherous vocation for following others, imitating them, blending in among them. And ultimately, beating them at their own game, hence exploiting them. Such an idea had opened the way to the image of the hook-nosed Jewish banker, so frequent in the cartoons of the late nineteenth century. It lay behind the notion of a Jewish conspiracy to dupe the entire world. And now Freud, the Jew par excellence, disrupter of every order, comes along in his old age to offer the most eagerly awaited of confirmations: that of the victim who speaks in favor of his death sentence.

At this point one is bound to acknowledge that Freud's hesitations and fears were amply justified. His book would be inflicting a double trauma. But the first person to have suffered that trauma was Freud himself. As a result he developed a specific pathology to which the text is testimony. If religion, as Freud here affirms for the last time, is a "neurosis of humanity"—or, to be precise, a vigorous variety of the obsessional neurosis—then any discussion of religion (and in particular Freud's discussions of religion) will be tainted by the same obsessional neurosis. Of which the first and most eloquent symptom is compulsive repetition. The trauma Freud inflicts on his readers consists first and foremost in this claim: *Moses was an Egyptian*. But let's go to the text: the first part is made up (in the *Studienausgabe*) of nine pages entitled "Moses, an Egyptian." The second part (of thirty-four pages) bears the title "If Moses was an Egyptian . . ." As if this wasn't enough, in the first two pages of the second part, the expression "Moses, an Egyptian" is repeated six times. Freud is behaving like the traumatized person who insists on repeating the traumatizing words, hoping they can be reduced to mere phonetic husks.

Equally striking is the sequence of phrases at the beginning and end of those passages where Freud tells us he has decided not to pursue his research or at least to circumscribe its scope. In the first part:

"Our research ought to accept this unsatisfying, what's more uncertain result and in so doing fall short of its goal of answering the question as to whether Moses was an Egyptian."

At the end of the first part:

"It would have been sufficient to have some objective proof of the dates of the exodus from Egypt and of Moses's life. But no such proof is forthcoming, hence it would be better not to go on with our exposition of all the other conclusions that would follow from the theory that Moses was an Egyptian."

In the second part:

"For the second time the thread we had hoped to weave around the hypothesis that Moses was an Egyptian has been broken. And this time, it would seem, without any prospect of our mending it."

At the end of the second part:

"Further development of my work would tie up with certain considerations I elaborated twenty-five years ago in *Totem and Taboo*. But I'm not sure I have the energy to pursue all this to the end."

At the beginning of the third part (*first* premise, written shortly after the *Anschluss*):

"Very likely the authorities would not care at all what I wish to write about Moses and the origin of monotheistic religion. But I'm not sure I'm right about this. For on the other hand it seems quite plausible that malevolence and the lust for sensationalism could

stand in for what weight I might lack in the regard of my contemporaries. So I will not make this work public, though that must not
deter me from writing it."

   This passage is quickly contradicted in the following and *second* premise to the third part. By this time Freud is in London,
and tells us so: "Certain that now I would be persecuted not just
for my way of thinking but also for my 'race,' I and many of my
friends left the city that was my home from earliest childhood and
for seventy-eight years." And the decision is taken: *Moses* will be
published. But this doesn't put an end to his doubts and fears; on
the contrary, they grow more intense, and are brought out in the
open. For the first time, albeit indirectly, Freud hints at possible
reactions to his book *among the Jews*, writing, with painful irony,
that in London "many have been concerning themselves with the
health of my soul, pointing me to the way of Christ or enlighten-
ing me as to the future of Israel." And he adds: "The good people
who have written to me in this manner clearly don't know much
about me; all the same I expect that when this work on Moses is
published in translation for my new compatriots to read, a good
number of them will not be feeling the same sympathy toward
me that they do now." And there's more. Aside from his understandable fears with regard to the powers in the world around
him, Freud realizes that his doubts have to do with himself, and
he allows us a precious glimpse into his own self-analysis: "In-
ner difficulties have not budged an inch with political upheavals
and changes of address. Now as before I feel uneasy with regard
to the work itself and find I lack that awareness of the unity and
togetherness that should prevail between an author and his writing." This sentence demands further attention: *never* before had
Freud acknowledged an internal division in the relationship between himself as author and his writing. And mightn't this be
traced back to the same Jewish misfortune that Freud had so recently identified in the preceding pages of Moses, the misfortune
of a people obsessed by the *one* but constantly forced to produce

the *two*? Going back five pages in *Moses* we read: "To the well-known dualities of that story—*two* groups of people who come together to form the nation, *two* kingdoms, into which the nation divides, *two* names of God in the biblical sources—we can add two more: *two* foundations of the religion, the first repressed by the second before returning victoriously onto the scene, *two* founders of the religion, both bearing the same name, Moses, whose personalities we must distinguish from each other." But what was the cause of all those dualities, Freud goes on to ask. A trauma, the *same* trauma that *Moses* was reenacting in book form: "All these dualities are necessary consequences of the first, of the fact, that is, that one part of the people had undergone an experience that we shall have to consider traumatic, while another part had not." Now, in a London milling with refugees, the seventy-eight-year-old, cancer-ridden Freud acknowledged that he, too, was one of those traumatized Jews who had lived beside a foreigner called Moses the Egyptian. Once he had spoken openly of a division between himself and his work, Freud had no choice but to set down, yet again, as though scrupulously observing some prescribed ritual, all his doubts and misgivings: "To my critical faculties, this book, which takes the man Moses as its starting point, seems like a ballerina balancing on the toe of one foot." All the same, heedless of her precarious position, that ballerina was about to throw herself into the dizzying *chassé-croisé* that is the third part of Freud's *Moses*.

The further one proceeds with *Moses*, the more obsessively Freud repeats and justifies himself. At the beginning of the *second* section of the *third* part, he offers, with all appropriate apologies, an "often literal" repetition of the *first* section, albeit with abbreviations here and additions there. Rather like a gag by Karl Valentin. And what are the additions about? "How the peculiar character of the Jewish people was formed." But Freud doesn't want us to suppose he isn't aware how labored this all is. And he leaps at the chance for some self-criticism: "I know this kind of presentation is neither functional nor artistically satisfying. I disapprove of it without reserve."

From self-condemnation it's a short step to confession. And here, with surprising candor, Freud admits that there can be only one explanation for his clumsy approach, one that "it is not easy to admit": "I was not able to hide the traces of the rather unusual way in which this work began." Only a page earlier he had been speaking of the "memory traces" that humanity inevitably drags after itself, and immediately, in a crucial statement, had specified what memory he was talking about: "Men have always known . . . that they had a primordial father and that they killed him." The case histories of the individual who answered to the name of Sigmund Freud and the collective that is humanity had never been so close to coinciding.

At this point all Freud can do is go on staging this duplication. At once he admits: "The fact is that this book has been written twice over." And he adds that in the *third* part, whose *second* section contains these words, we will find "the really offensive and dangerous" part of the work, something that had long tormented him "like an unlaid ghost" (*unerlöst* also means "unredeemed"). Proceeding with his confession, Freud now finds a new justification, which would also be the best justification an obsessional neurotic could ever come up with to explain his compulsive repetitions: "There are things that have to be said more than once and that can never be said often enough." This sudden flare of pride is immediately followed by more self-criticism and the final admission: "The work comes out as best it can and often presents itself to the author as independent from him, alien even." But this is exactly—and Freud had just shown as much—how something that has been repressed does in fact present itself. And the proximity of these remarks suggests that his *Moses*, or rather "The Man Moses," as the German edition is entitled, could well be Freud's own repressed memory, something that for many years and with enormous effort he had been attempting to bring to the surface, just as the Jewish people, for many centuries and with enormous effort, had sought to recover their memory of Moses, the father they had killed.

Since there is no evidence at all for Moses's life outside of what we read in the Bible, which offers more gaps than anything else, any detailed reconstruction of that life must inevitably be spun from a core of delirium. But Freud was well aware that "the delirious idea conceals a part of the forgotten truth"—what, after all, had he spent his whole life looking for, if not the *forgotten truth*? So when in the summer of 1934 "having time on my hands and not knowing what to do" (the best possible circumstance for the emergence of forbidden metaphors), he began to string together some thoughts about the "man Moses," and confided what was happening to him not to an analyst, but to a novelist, Arnold Zweig. "I quickly found the formula: Moses created the Jew, and my book would have the title: *The Man Moses, a historical novel.*" Behind it all was a question that Freud poses in the same letter in the tersest possible fashion (while in the book it would be carefully hidden behind endless convolutions): "Faced with these new persecutions, one asks oneself once again what is it the Jew has become, and why has he drawn upon himself this perennial hatred?"

Freud, then, had meant to answer that tremendous question with a "historical novel." And his genius encouraged him to proceed quite literally. At this point he was struck by the conviction that he had discovered *who* Moses was. A few months later he wrote to Zweig again: "In some correspondence about Tell el-Amarna, where excavations are not even half finished, I have found an observation regarding a certain Prince Thutmose, about whom nothing else is known. If I had millions of pounds I would finance further excavations myself. This Thutmose could be my Moses, and I could boast of having guessed as much." The unknown Thutmose might well have proved a momentary fancy, soon to be forgotten. But four years later, when *Moses* was finally published, he reemerged. Freud described him as a "disciple of the religion of Aton, except—in contrast to the pensive king—he was energetic and impassioned." What's more, "perhaps as governor of an outlying province he had come into contact with a Semitic tribe that had settled there generations before." Thus Thutmose had become Moses. And Moses turned out to be the prince "about whom nothing is known." So the boldest of Freud's reconstructions of religious history was based on a name casually surfacing in an excavation. Thutmose, pure name and nothing else, was the point of the ballerina's foot on which the whole of *Moses* must balance. More, as Freud conscientiously acknowledged in a note, he wasn't even the only Thutmose. There was at least one *other*, since this was also the name of "the sculptor whose workshop had been found at Tell el-Amarna." Even insofar as he was Thutmose, Moses was two.

These were the last months of his life and Freud knew that a murderous wind was blowing across Europe. Clear-sightedness had always been his greatest gift. What should he do? What he'd always done: follow his vocation. At this point it would have seemed natural to lay Germany down on his kilim-covered couch like any other patient. His theory certainly put him in a position to do that. And his theory would also have allowed him to interpret certain gestures as symptoms of a delirium of omnipotence. But Freud wasn't interested. He had something more "offensive and dangerous" in mind: to lay the Jews on his sofa, analyze them. How? By, once again, lying on the sofa himself, just as he did forty years before, when writing *The Interpretation of Dreams*, a book that teems with *his* dreams. A last effort of self-analysis was required. And now as never before Freud was afraid. So he covers his back; time and again he returns to square one, starts over, repeatedly acknowledging his shortcomings. Yet, inch by inch, he pushes the argument forward, weaves together what he himself described as a "historical novel," the family saga of a people, which is also the story of a single man: Moses. And Moses is Freud himself. How many patients had he seen presenting obsessions that, in the end, were no less plausible . . . But now, once again it is a matter of facing up to a vaster obsession, an obsession that is also a knowledge, and a knowledge that could all too easily, were he not to finish this book, or fail to lay to rest that "unredeemed ghost" (*unerlöster Geist*) that is his *Moses*, disappear along with him.

Freud distinguished himself from his contemporaries not for his ability to destroy or neutralize myths, but as one of the very few to bring new variations to them. His Oedipus does not explain the myth of Oedipus and hence drain it of meaning, but rather offers the most recent, effective variant of this myth in modern times. The same is true of *Moses*. Here, if anything, Freud found himself on even more intractable ground, having set out to mythologize the founding of exclusivist monotheism, the kind that is not satisfied with proclaiming a god sovereign but insists that all other gods are *false and mendacious* and as such must be banned. Thus the myth, a supremely polytheistic force, must serve as the basis of its own death sentence. A process not unlike that which has a democracy voting into power someone intent on destroying it: Hitler was the obvious example in those years, the same years in which *Moses* was written.

Blindly faithful to his mythopoeic inspiration, what Freud feared more than anything else was that he would wound the people of whom he himself was a son. And would do so retelling the story of the man who had been that people's father. Much twisting and turning. Freud himself, following the logic of myth, would take on the roles of both Moses *and* Moses's murderer. A *double* role.

As things stand, *Moses* is built on a single affirmation: "Moses created the Jew," a claim we first find in the 1934 letter to Arnold Zweig and now again restated more or less word for word at the end of *Moses*: "It was the man Moses who created the Jews." But if, as the first two parts of the book would obsessively repeat, Moses was *not* a Jew and exclusivist monotheism was not a creation of the

Jews, but of the Pharaoh Akhenaten, then the Jews were stripped of their most noble attributes. Hence Freud felt he ought to compensate them in some way. And only one was available to him: the tormented history of the Jews had marked a "progress in spirituality." So he devotes the last part of Moses, by far the weakest, to this idea. In fact no one has ever convincingly shown why the biblical prophets should be spiritually superior to Plato. Certainly Freud fails to do so in *Moses*. On the contrary, with the bluntness that was one of his most precious intellectual qualities, he couldn't help observing that while it was true that the Jews had achieved "ethical heights that remained beyond the reach of other peoples of the ancient world," nevertheless, their ethics betrayed "the same unfinished and unfinishable nature typical of compulsive neurotic reaction formations."

As for that celebrated "progress in spirituality," it was hard to see what the first step might have been. When Freud identifies it, he does so with an astonishing move that has repercussions for his entire vision of Moses. Delving into prehistory, a territory where Freud proceeds with the somnambulant assurance of the tourist guide, the decisive moment that supposedly set in motion the Jews' "progress in spirituality" is located in the passage from matriarchy to patriarchy. But on what might such an audacious claim be based? Imperturbably, Freud answers, "This shift from mother to father marks a victory of spirituality over sensuality, hence a progress in civilization, since motherhood is established by the testimony of the senses, while fatherhood is an assumption, based on judgment and presupposition." The irresolvable incertitude acknowledged in the maxim *Pater semper incertus* is made to correspond to the victorious "stance that raised the process of thought above the perception of the senses." For sure, no one before Freud had ever come to such an improbable conclusion, one that smacks of vaudeville, and reflects on the story of Moses himself, who was an exemplary case of progress in spirituality but also of *pater incertus*. There will always be some uncertainty as to whether Moses was Jewish or Egyptian, the advocate of the exclusivist monotheism of Akhenaten or the Midianite Moses who worshipped Yahweh, a vulcan god hardly different from other Middle Eastern deities; in short, if Moses was a poor Jewish newborn saved by the Pharaoh's daughter or the Egyptian prince Thutmose whose name had so recently reemerged in the excavations of Tell el-Amarna. That uncertainty, Freud seems to insinuate, would remain forever unresolved, and continue, in the shadow, to haunt every "progress in spirituality."

The whole story of Moses, as Freud retells it, is a story of repression, latency, and resurfacing of what was repressed. But the most glaring repression is Freud's own with regard to the Bible. It is so glaring that his many contemporary commentators seem unable to see it: throughout his *Moses* Freud simply ignores the preceding history of the Jews, from Noah to Abraham to Joseph. As though that business of a tribe of seminomadic shepherds could be of no interest for him. Perhaps it felt like a family saga with which he was all too familiar.

In *Moses*, Abraham is mentioned just once, with some sarcasm, in relation to the biblical claim that it was he who introduced circumcision. An awkward and belated attempt to invent a past for oneself, Freud comments ("a remarkably clumsy invention"). How could they have introduced this of all signs to distinguish themselves in a country, Egypt, where circumcision had been practiced from time immemorial? The sarcasm doesn't let up: "A Jew going to Egypt would have been obliged to recognize all Egyptians as his relatives, all brothers in Yahweh." Freud's impatience with the patriarch Abraham explodes. All those stories of him and Yahweh were too intimate, stories of a small tribe lost among a thousand others.

To understand monotheism as Freud saw it, one has to shift one's attention to a far larger stage, that of Egypt when, with Thutmose III, it "became a universal power." This claim is followed by a revealing phrase that names three powers together, apparently united in an indissoluble pact: "This imperialism was reflected in

their religion as universalism and monotheism." Real monotheism, then, is connected to absolute power and an absolute principle
that repudiates all the gods. It thus becomes clear why, up to that
moment, the Jews did not exist as a people.

But if Moses did "create the Jew," what were the Jews before
Moses? A shapeless, pliant mass without a past? Where was the
memory of the God of Abraham, Isaac, and Jacob? Freud neglects
the Bible of the patriarchs the same way Yahweh neglected the
Jews in the long interval between the death of Joseph and the birth
of Moses. Perhaps his gaze strayed elsewhere. The omnipotence
of the author replicates the capricious omnipotence of Yahweh,
whose interest in the Jews reawakens only when Moses appears on
the scene.

Freud's profoundly irreligious sentiment—the most dramatic of
his instincts—demanded that the gods be dissolved by a power that
had to be absolute: an empire. The unique and exclusive god was an
imperialist god. Who, with an enormous expense of effort, would
then involve himself in the vicissitudes of a people to whom empire
and even mere independence were doggedly denied. Thus it was
that the Jews eventually withdrew and took refuge in the domains
of the mind. But a subtle thread connected Moses the Egyptian to
another Moses, Moses Ben Maimon, a man who would approve of
Jewish rites only if they were the exact opposite of pagan rites. If
other peoples worshipped certain animals, Maimonides would order those animals to be killed.

Freud's internal psychic drama, prime object of a self-analysis
that had been going on for more than forty years, had its roots
in his wilfully irreligious stance. By vocation and out of personal
fascination, he had spent his life working with the same powers
that over the centuries had taken shape in myths and rituals. Almost nothing else interested him and he applied himself to almost
nothing else. But from the start he had been determined not to
succumb to those powers. *Wo Es war, soll Ich werden*, "Where the
Id was, the Ego shall be": that proclamation, lying at the core of

a personal program that owed nothing to the past, could be read on the hallucinatory banner he carried into war. Raising *Moses* as his banner, Freud threw himself into the final battle. With many a hesitation and much reluctance, indeed an ill-disguised terror, while nevertheless surrendering himself to the same allure that once led him to the stuff of dreams.

In showing that Moses was an Egyptian and that his monotheism had been an Egyptian invention, while at the same time ignoring everything the Bible said about the Jews up to the death of Joseph, and finally concentrating on just one man, Moses, and insisting that he had "created the Jew," Freud had inflicted on the Jews what he, in his terminology, would have called a deep narcissistic wound.

But this was not the ultimate hidden and specific objective of Freud's *Moses*. If the Jews were to be deprived of their patriarchs and even Moses had been a foreigner, and a murdered foreigner to boot, what was left that was specifically and irreducibly Jewish? That "progress in spirituality," that wilful, ongoing dogged project based on two principal points: the rejection of images and the rejection of the gods. And this achievement, which Freud presents in a somewhat soft version, of the variety you might safely include in some high-school graduation speech, was supposed to be the supreme achievement of humanity.

Why? The crucial move was to reduce the Jews' relationship with religion to their relationship with "the man Moses." All external powers were dismissed so that everything could be traced back to a tension within the community. Not only could one do without the gods, but even without the one God: the Yahweh whom Moses the Midianite worshipped was the merest vulcan deity, and the God of Moses the Egyptian no more than a synonym for "truth and justice," categories that apply to the sphere of society. Maat, the Egyptian goddess of order in the world, always associated with the hoof and the feather, was replaced by a voice that said, "I am who I am." Freud himself had never heard that voice and wasn't overly concerned to know its thinking. For that "progress in spirituality" all that was required were two injunctions that Moses relayed to the people: the condemnation of all gods and the ban on images. Only in this way could one finally establish a safe distance from, even a *cordon sanitaire* around, the sacred. Which, precisely in *Moses*, Freud defines figuratively, thus: "The sacred, originally, was nothing other than the protracted will of the primordial father." A will severed by a murder.

What *Moses* performs is a total annulment of all relations with religion. Once Moses has been killed, religion falls away from the Jewish people like a dry scale. The patriarchs were erased; Moses was a foreigner. All that was left of him was a memory and the laborious recovery, over the centuries, of repressed material, but that would be enough to feed the Jews' "progress in spirituality." So *Moses* became a founding story about a founding story: which was as close to a new myth as a period unable to produce myths was likely to get. And this time it would be a myth telling of the final separation of humanity from religion. The Jews had been the small destructive band of commandos that history sent ahead to stage—or in psychoanalytic terms enact—that change.

But what, meantime, had happened to the other peoples in the wide world? For Freud those others were first and foremost the Greeks, to whom he was drawn by a fascination he was eager to punish. The *others* were the excavated statuettes that stared at him across his desk: Egyptian and Greek statuettes, obviously. They were his *teraphim*, like the ones Rachel had hidden and saved from her father, as Genesis recounts. Now, approaching the end of his *Moses*, Freud found himself obliged to compare the Jews with the Greeks. It was a comparison he had always both feared and hankered after. He needed to establish, measuring it against the Greeks, how far that "progress in spirituality" had surpassed them. His judgment is eventually couched in a paragraph that can't be read without embarrassment, and might even be funny, were one not aware of the long, lacerating, and inflexible quarrel with religion that had dominated Freud's life, allowing him to achieve an unprecedented level of clarity within a willful incomprehension:

"The priority that for two thousand years [*lapsus*: why *two thousand*, as though the Jews hadn't devoted themselves to "progress in spirituality" before the birth of Christ?] the Jewish people afforded to spiritual endeavors has naturally had its effect: it has helped to stem that coarseness and inclination to violence that usually prevail there where the nurture of muscular strength is the people's ideal. The balance that the Greeks achieved between physical and spiritual activities was denied to the Jews. But in splitting the two, they nevertheless opted for the higher value."

One is struck, at this crucial point in the work, by the poverty of the argument, in sharp contrast to the determined, subtle, and penetrating investigation that preceded it. As if Freud were seeking to *save Judaism's face*, reaffirming its primacy only pages after having taken apart, piece by piece, the basis of that primacy. There was a "higher value" and it had to be asserted, even if that meant putting out one's own eyes, as though Freud were punishing himself for an excess of clear-sightedness. It was his way of experiencing Oedipus's fate, substituting Jocasta with the Jews.

Even in Freud's own terms the "higher value" he ascribes to Judaism could be considered such only if one accepted the woeful proposition that "the nurture of muscular strength" was "the people's ideal": the people in question being the ancient Greeks. This was the same Freud who had felt faint on the Acropolis when faced with the evidence that *the Acropolis existed*. Describing that feeling he had written: "As if someone, in Scotland, walking on the shores of Loch Ness were suddenly to see, stranded on the bank, the body of the famous monster and were obliged to admit, So, the water snake we never believed in really does exist!" However intensely venerated, Greece, for Freud, would always be a *water snake*.

Freud's dilemma was not so different from the predicament that tormented many assimilated Jews of his time, most of them far less lucid than he was: the impossibility of religious belief went hand in hand with the impossibility of renouncing the notion of being chosen, long ago, by a God in whom they didn't believe. Yahweh was a legend like everything else that had to do with religion, but the Jewish way was still the best, the most enlightened, the most progressive, the most intellectual. Freud eliminated Yahweh as just another symptom of obsessional neurosis, but in return he attributed the greatest possible reality to a man, "the man Moses." He recognized in Moses the reincarnation of the primordial father, whom the brothers of the primal horde had killed. Moses, too, had been killed, and once again by his own people. But this had happened on the threshold of history, in a time period that could be established, in places that were well known, between Egypt and Palestine. This time the father did not belong to an indeterminate prehistory, equally remote from everyone. This time he was much closer and belonged to one unique story. The advantage the Jews enjoyed over all other peoples lay in this: the consequences of Moses's death affected them directly. It was a twofold privilege: that of being closer to the sacred and that of having killed it. They knew the sacred better than anyone else and had disposed of it before anyone else.

In a letter to Gretel Adorno, Walter Benjamin observed that in Freud's late style the "greatest thoughts" were presented "in passing." Which is exactly how one might read a passage in *Moses* that Freud himself considered rash. Lamarckian in the extreme, reckless as it is extravagant, it can nevertheless claim the merit of placing in doubt the entire, universally accepted framework of relationships between men and animals: "To accept the ongoing existence of these memory traces in our archaic inheritance is to throw a bridge over the abyss that separates individual and collective psychologies, making it possible to treat whole peoples as single neurotics. Even granting that to date we have no stronger proof for the presence of memory traces in archaic inheritance than those residual phenomena of analytic work that require a derivation from phylogenesis, nevertheless this evidence seems good enough to posit such a state of affairs. If this is not the case, we shall make no further progress along the path we have been following, whether in analysis or collective psychology. Ours is an unavoidable temerity.

"Doing this, we also achieve something else. We reduce the gap that past ages of human arrogance have excessively enlarged between man and animal. If an animal's so-called instincts, that allow it to behave from the start in what is a new living environment as if it were old and long familiar, if this instinctive life of animals has an explanation it can only be this: that animals bring with them into their new existence the experiences of their species, that is to say, they have preserved in themselves memories of what their ancestors experienced. In the man-animal, at bottom, it would be the same. His archaic inheritance, albeit of a different scope and content, corresponds to the animal's instinct."

What follows from this is that the confidence and precision of movements in the animal world must be seen as a highly formalized way of reacting to any new situation that presents itself. Not only do animals possess a memory but they know how to use it more efficiently than the "man-animal," who is invariably awkward in his movements when adapting to a new situation. This is a profoundly disturbing prospect: we are to see all living creatures as dominated by their past—remote past included—which determines all their actions, actions that could thus become as rigid and unalterable as animal instincts (here in fact Freud uses the word *Instinkt*, which he generally avoids). Or alternatively be subject to alternating phases of repression, latency, and reemergence, as happens with the "man-animal."

But what would this past be exactly? At this point Freud starts a new paragraph with a short sentence that could stand as a summary of the whole book: "After all this discussion I have no hesitation in claiming that men have always known—in the particular manner described above—that they had a primordial father and that they killed him."

Moses's first achievement, then, was to have forced men to *remember*, that one foundational event in their lives: the murder of their primordial father. And here Freud royally ignored the fact that, in Deuteronomy, Moses dies *alone*, he is not murdered. Freud's source was a slim, dense book, published in 1922 by the scholar Ernst Sellin, who put forward, on the basis of some verses in Hosea and with unflinching self-assurance, the theory that Moses was murdered, thus reconstructing a lost tradition that "Goethe, curiously, had posited without any evidence at all"—and here Freud was referring to Goethe's essay *Israel in the Desert*, included in the *West-östlicher Divan*, where Goethe claims that Moses was killed by Joshua and Caleb, who had lost all patience with his inept, despotic behavior.

These were exceedingly precarious footholds, though it's true that for anyone writing in German, Goethe is their Homer. Sellin's hypothesis, on the other hand, had been rejected, albeit respectfully, by all biblical scholars (and Buber, in his *Moses*, published in 1946, would refuse even to discuss it). But for Freud those footholds were vital. Throughout his book he assumes it is generally agreed, even though he never dwells on the point, that Moses was murdered. The Law implies the killing, as the killing implies the Law. Eliminate one term of the equation and the whole framework collapses. The entire history of the Jews was woven between those two extremes.

Jung spoke of the "collective unconscious," Freud of "archaic inheritance" and "memory traces." But where in our neural networks were these traces to be located? Jung, shrewdly, avoided any historical or neurological explanation; Freud extended distant memory to include the entire animal kingdom and, in the "man-animal," had it focus on a single action: the murder of the primordial father. Animals had used their "archaic inheritance" to shape their instincts and shut themselves in their paddock. Men, on the other hand, constantly repressed that single act in their past, preserved it in a state of latency, then allowed it to reemerge. The Jews were different from all other races in that they had not buried that event in remote prehistory but had placed it at the beginning of their known history. As a result they had a closer, more intimate relationship with their divinity, something that provoked embarrassment and occasionally repulsion in other peoples, because the Jews brought into the here and now something everyone found painful to remember.

One might ask why Freud placed the sentence reasserting his theory about the murder of the primordial father at this point in *Moses*. Is it a straightforward repetition of the claim made in *Totem and Taboo*? Not exactly: here the murder of the primordial father appears in a context where *Homo sapiens* is collocated in the zoological continuum (a *step forward* that Freud felt deserved recognition). Within that continuum, the terror instilled by the primordial father is to be attributed to those species that dominated man, pursued him, and sometimes killed him: the predators. So if the totemic animal was, to Freud's thinking, a substitute for the primordial father, the father is necessarily a substitute for the primordial predator. In whose regard *H. sapiens* had elaborated two objectives: to replace it (hence escaping its dominance, by killing it if necessary) and to imitate it, so as to appropriate its powers: exactly what happened, in Freud's account, during the solemn totemic sacrifice.

Yerushalmi wrote that Freud's theory in *Totem and Taboo* is "to put it bluntly, *kaputt*," and in fact no anthropologist studying totemic mythology takes any account of it these days. But the theory itself became the basis of another mythology: Freud's. A single sentence will do to establish the primal scene: "This then is the clan, which on a solemn occasion viciously kills its totemic animal and devours it raw, flesh, blood, and bones; every member of the clan is present, all dressed up to imitate the totem, imitating its sounds and movements as if they wanted to stress their identification with it." This scene was still very much in Freud's mind when, in *Moses*, he wrote that men have always known that they had a primordial father and, above all, that they had killed him. "After all this discussion" (meaning: after *all* Freud's writings) it can finally be said that the whole of humanity does not remember but *knows*, in fact has *always* known, that it had a single primordial father. This, Freud claimed in *Totem and Taboo*, was the real sin of Adam and Eve: "The crime that must be expiated can be nothing other than the killing of the father." This was the only version of events that could make sense of the passion of Jesus. And it was this sin that was repeated with the murder of Moses. The *one* God preceded all the other gods simply because he was that God that men, in the beginning, had killed, before inventing other gods for themselves. And this was the basis of the privileged truth (or rather "the truth content," as Freud puts it) of Judaism, and what set it apart from every other religion. And that "truth" had reemerged with the murder of Moses, who was Yahweh's voice and stand-in. This alone was enough to justify the "perennial hatred" that the Jews continued to bring upon themselves. And also to explain why that murder is not explicitly narrated in the Bible. But if in Numbers we read, "The entire community began to talk of stoning Moses and Aaron," and in Exodus Moses says, "I barely escaped being stoned," this means, according to Freud's reasoning in *Totem and Taboo*, that this stoning did occur. The children of Israel who followed Moses into the desert were "primitives," and primitives "have in effect done what, all evidence suggests, they intended to do." In primitives as in neurotics, Freud believes, there is no clear distinction between intention and completed action.

The Jews had had to find a euphemism to speak of what had happened to Moses, transforming it into the prohibition to enter the Promised Land. But traces of the crime remained. And what was Freud's self-proclaimed *science* if not the determined search for traces?

The killing of the primordial father was the basis of Freud's personal mythology, but the basis of that basis was killing itself. And the overbearing father was the predator to whom his children, by killing him, became assimilated. Decisive as it was for the fate of the species, this event reemerged only when the Jews remembered and renewed it, placing it at the origins of their own history, in the figure of Moses. They thus took on themselves the task of representing, in a single detailed and localized moment in their history, something all humanity had passed through.

The novelty of *Moses* lay first and foremost in establishing a necessary connection between killing and the Law. Otherwise the doctrine would never have won the "privilege of freeing itself from the compulsion of logical thinking." Because of this "privilege" the Jews were exposed to "perennial hatred" in that they drew attention to something everyone had done but had no intention of remembering. It was a bold gambit on Freud's part to have all this, *none of which* the Bible actually says, appear as the basis for the Bible itself.

Writing about Moses, Freud was daring and consistent right up to the penultimate paragraph. Then he sealed the whole thing— which might be likened to a "never-ending analysis"—with a surprisingly banal conclusion in sharp contrast to all that had gone before.

This was the only way to avoid pushing things to the point where his vision could have been turned upside down. All the reflections on the Jews brought together over the course of the book and constituting a series of injuries and wounds at the expense of their self-image could easily have become so many interlocking reasons for admiring them, or at least for granting them irreducible specialness of a new variety. These people who had nothing that was truly their own, who imitated foreign ways, adapting to them and eventually transforming them, these people forever split in two, because at bottom undetermined in themselves, were the closest one could come to the ancestor of us all, to *H. sapiens*. Who like the Jews had distinguished himself first and foremost for appropriating segments of the zoological continuum that had not always belonged to him, but rather to the big cats or to the insects.

To become a predator and then again to elaborate a superorganism called society, set up as a self-sufficient and aggressive body, were huge, overreaching achievements, when one considers the behavioral heritage with which *H. sapiens* was initially equipped. Something that might be compared with the discovery and consequent practice, thanks to the Egyptian Moses, of a law that set itself apart from all previous laws. To the same extent that the Jews were the only ones who could lay claim to the murder of the primordial father, not in that time out of time that is myth, but on the threshold of their documented history, so they became the race most immediately associated with the achievement of *H. sapiens* in setting himself apart from all other species. And this was particularly true of certain characteristics that *H. sapiens* usually sought to deny. All of which made the Jews by definition a source of disturbance in whatever society they found themselves.

Assuming Freud wrote *Moses*, as he claims in the 1934 letter to Arnold Zweig, to establish the causes that had made the Jew what "he has become," the object, that is, of a "perennial hatred," he could hardly go on to use his discovery of the Egyptian origin of Moses, however scandalous this might or might not have been, as an argument for his central thesis. Such a discovery could only be, in his own terms, a narcissistic wound inflicted on the Jews. But for non-Jews, including anti-Semites? It was the merest curiosity. They would go on detesting the Jews, even if the first Jewish legislator turned out to be an Egyptian. Indeed, it might even confirm their conviction that the Jews always needed to lean on someone else.

Nor could he rely on the discovery that the God of Moses was split in two, with the pure, severe Egyptian God on the one hand, and the rude, arrogant, vengeful, vulcan, Midianite God on the other. That, too, the non-Jew would simply see as a curiosity. Gods in general were anyway accused of a whole range of bad behavior.

So what argument could Freud adduce? Only one that everybody understood had to do with themselves, something they wanted to put behind them but that the Jews insisted on bringing to the fore, thus drawing upon themselves inexhaustible reserves of rancor and intolerance. The fact, in short, as Freud, but also the biblical scholar Sellin, would have it, that Moses was killed by the children of Israel. And that this killing brought to the surface another killing, that of the primordial father, which is to say of *everyone's* father, not just the father of the Jews. No one could accept that this drama be part of the daily life and religion of a people, who thus kept it constantly alive and active. At most, in recent times, it might be part of the audacious scholarly theories of a Charles Darwin or a Sigmund Freud, who had put forward the idea in a book in 1913, *Totem and Taboo*. What was not acceptable was that it reemerge as the memory of a primal sin, or rather *the* primal sin, and among a people who claimed *exclusive* possession of that sin, as though it didn't, in all its ferocious brutality, belong to everybody. Thus one was back with the Jews as chosen people, not, this time, chosen as an act of grace, but as grounds for condemnation. A condemnation that had been operative for centuries and could yet grow harsher still, when in 1939 Freud revealed once and for all the origins of the tale.

Ingenuous scholar that he was, Freud acknowledged that *Totem and Taboo* came out of the mingling in his mind of three other books: W. Robertson Smith's *Lectures on the Religion of the Semites*, J. J. Atkinson's *Primal Law*, and Darwin's *The Descent of Man*. All three works converged around the "hypothesis of a primordial crime, an original sin," which, as Freud saw it, "must have been a murder." But it was the connection with Darwin he was most eager to stress, recognizing as he did, in Darwin as in himself, the "great progress of truth," due to someone who had been rejected and opposed "for decades" (a killing and period of latency in Freud's terms) before finally being honored with burial in Westminster Abbey. The origin of the "primordial horde," on which *Totem and Taboo* is based, was to be traced back to Darwin, its one possible pedigree.

There was, however, an obstacle: Darwin never mentions any *primordial horde* in *The Descent of Man*. On the contrary, the

passage that comes closest to the scenario Freud imagined di-
verges from it radically in both content and tone, the latter being
cautious throughout: "Therefore, looking far enough back in the
stream of time, and judging from the social habits of man as he
now exists, the most probable view is that he aboriginally lived in
small communities, each with a single wife, or if powerful with
several, whom he jealously guarded against all other men."

The first difference one notes is between singular and plural.
Freud speaks of an *Urhorde*, a compact, threatening mass (chapter
10 of his *Massenpsychologie* is entitled "The Mass and the Primordial Horde"), while Darwin speaks of "small communities" more
like families than tribes. Above all the behavior of the head of the
community is reconstructed "judging from the social habits of
man as he now exists," the habits, that is, of the head of the Vic-
torian family. The argument proceeds in the opposite direction to
Freud's. For Freud, man "as he now exists" can be understood only
by acknowledging that he *knows* (and *knowing* is far stronger than
remembering) that the tyrannical father of the primordial horde
was killed by his children; for Darwin, on the other hand, we can
infer the behavior of the primal father from the habits of the Euro-
peans (or rather, the English) in the second half of the nineteenth
century.

Freud faced a tough choice: either he gave up on Darwin as
his precursor, which would mean stepping back from what he
had already written about the progress toward truth; or, bouncing one ball off another, billiard fashion, he could use an intermediary to foist onto Darwin something that did not actually
belong to him. The intermediary was Atkinson, an ethnographer
who had spent years in New Caledonia, and wrote at a time when
Darwin had already been raised onto his pedestal. Two sentences
would do it, sentences that Freud cited as "the direct consequence of relationships in Darwin's primordial horde," the horde
Darwin had never mentioned, and certainly not in the singular:
"a youthful band of brothers living together in forced celibacy, or

at most in polyandrous relation with some single female captive. A horde as yet weak in their impubescence, they are, but they would, when strength was gained with time, inevitably wrench by combined attacks, renewed again and again, both wife and life from the paternal tyrant." Here at last were the two words Freud had been looking for, in vain, in the writings of Darwin: "paternal tyrant." At this point the argument was clinched: Robertson Smith had introduced the totemic (and cannibalistic) meal while the primordial horde and the murder of the father could be attributed to Darwin, via devious recourse to Atkinson. The only thing he needed to show now, Freud thought, was how it came about that an ordinary man of the early twentieth century *knew* all this, in the depths of his unconscious, his behavior being influenced accordingly. This was the next and indispensable "progress of the truth" that would be achieved in *Totem and Taboo* and confirmed, with ramifications, twenty-six years later in *Moses*.

"In the course of these negotiations, Moses himself disappeared, just as Aaron had disappeared, and it would be ingenuous not to see that Joshua and Caleb had felt it right to put an end to the rule of a limited man they had tolerated for so many years, dispatching him to the same place as the many unfortunates who had preceded him; thus resolving the problem once and for all and taking determined possession of the entire west bank of the Jordan and the land to be had there."

Dogged and blunt, this text tells how Moses was killed just before the children of Israel crossed the Jordan. But the author is not Darwin, who never wrote about Moses and never made any reference of any kind to the killing of the primordial father; nor is it Freud, who on the contrary had based his whole theory on the killing of the primordial father, and hence of Moses. It is Goethe. And the sentence turns up hidden away among the prose fragments that form the second part of the *West-östlicher Divan*, a territory few readers would ever penetrate. A century after its publication copies of the first edition were still on sale.

Written in 1797 and published in 1819, this passage may well be the first in which a writer talks about the children of Israel killing Moses. But even here there is some evasion: the word *kill* is never used. Instead we hear that Moses *disappears*, though Goethe makes it quite clear who wanted to be rid of him and why. The primordial memory can only present itself *veiled*.

As Freud saw it, even if one accepted that Moses caused the memory of the primordial father to resurface, thus conquering the children of Israel, who yearned to be reconciled with that remote and ominous figure, this would still not have been enough. At most it would have founded a tradition, passed on in texts and sacred rites, but without the power to develop the "compulsive characteristics typical of religious phenomena." For that to happen Moses himself would have to be killed. Then the memory of the killing would have to disappear for a long period of latency. Finally reappearing to be fixed forever in the Pentateuch. At which point *Jewishness* would crystallize, once and for all. And other peoples would look on the Jews with bewilderment or hostility. Or both. How could this people put on flagrant display something that no one wished to remember? Claiming, what's more, that they had been chosen precisely for this purpose.

It was essential that killing and the Law be brought together in a single person. All the same, the connection between this obscure mingling and "progress in spirituality" (a section title that Freud chose as a catchphrase for *Moses*) was not altogether clear. And his claim that the Greeks had not achieved that "progress" having focused their attention on muscular strength sounded simply preposterous. Hence *Moses*, too, like so many other episodes in the history of Judaism, appeared irremediably split. There was an obscure story, going back to the primal horde dreamed up by Freud himself (not Darwin, who never used the expression); and there was a story that was all too explicit and culminated in this self-proclaimed "progress in spirituality." In the middle: a "perennial hatred" that was running riot.

If Lamarckism is finally unacceptable, because it has no verifiable basis, we are still faced with the question as to how someone might remember something that others did and that he did not witness. How *cultural memory*, as it is called, is possible. Freud wanted to be rid of that most irksome of obstacles, Jung, the despised defector, as soon as possible: "I do not believe," he observes right away "that anything is to be gained by introducing the concept of a 'collective' unconscious." At the same time Freud sensed that mere *cultural* transmission could not alone explain how certain phenomena asserted themselves. "A tradition based exclusively on communication would not be able to produce the compulsive character typical of religious phenomena. It would be listened to, assessed, and perhaps rejected like any other message from without, never attaining the privilege of freedom from the compulsion of logical thought. Rather, it must first have undergone the fate of repression, the condition of confinement in the unconscious, before it could then, on resurfacing, produce such powerful effects, casting its spell on the masses, as religious traditions do, something that has left us amazed and, in the past, unable to offer an explanation."

How can one explain, after all, that the past is *active now*? And how apply the complex mechanism of repression, latency, and resurfacing to *all* of the past, rather than just those areas characteristic of religion? Freud was unerringly loyal to what Yerushalmi called his "psycho-Lamarckism." But it could hardly suffice. No sooner had he dismissed Jung's collective unconscious as unhelpful than he offered a remark that seems equally unhelpful: "The content of the unconscious is in any case already collective, a universal human heritage." It's a clumsy remark that has us thinking more of UNESCO than of the remote past of the human race. A *heritage* is something that by definition one can draw on at will. But how can one draw on the unconscious at will when its defining characteristic is precisely that it eludes the will? Unable to place his "memory traces" in man's neurological tissues and forced to resort to some generic collective presence of the unconscious, Freud's only alternative was to recognize the *impossibility* of accessing any past that an individual himself had not experienced. Yet the past of *all* does continue to act, albeit sporadically and indirectly, in each of us. An insoluble dilemma. Unless, that is, one accepts the idea of a total *simultaneity* (hence timelessness) of the past and consequently that the psyche is something whose boundaries "you will never, in your going, discover, not even if you travel every road." Thus Heraclitus, via Diogenes Laërtius. But this was never going to be Freud's way, Freud who could claim to have reasserted the Jewish privilege, based on *memory*, exactly as he came close to demonstrating the impossibility of such a thing. A maze no one has yet found their way out of.

We gain access to the past through scholarship, studying *sources*, which is to say the traces the past has left behind; not memory traces, but tangible objects (bones, simulacra, scriptures). Or alternatively—and it's the only other way—through mythical narratives, stories that cannot be placed in chronological time. Darwin, in *The Descent of Man*, and Freud, in *Totem and Taboo*, invented a hybrid form, crossbreeding these two ways. Their anthropological theories, like the narratives that accompanied them, were soon taken apart and dismissed. But the hybrid form remained intact, indeed flourished throughout the twentieth century, assuming numerous other forms. This circumstance has been largely responsible for obscuring the vexed question of how access to the past is even *possible*. If the past loses its otherness, or if that otherness is attenuated, it more easily appears as a mere duplication of the present or thereabouts. At that point the past will tend to resemble, very closely, the things we already know and can control. But it will have lost its distinctive element, absence. At this point it will be evident that the oceans of speculation regarding *cultural memory* often have the function of euphemizing this state of affairs, which is dramatic and affords no simple solution. The past exists and acts in the here and now, sometimes violently. No one can doubt this. But nor can anyone explain how this happens. And we may sometimes suspect that the most useful knowledge is to be had right where the mind runs up against this irreducible impossibility.

What Darwin and Freud had most in common was a deep, even superstitious faith in their "irreligiousness." Everything that happened to men must come from men. Every invisible or divine power was to be attributed to a visible and human power. This meant tracing back the many deliriums to which the human race had succumbed over thousands of years to a chain of cause and effect within man himself. Darwin, who was more relaxed and perfunctory in this regard than Freud, explained the invisible with reference to "a little fact which I once noticed: my dog, a full-grown and very sensible animal, was lying on the lawn during a hot and still day; but at a little distance a slight breeze occasionally moved an open parasol, which would have been wholly disregarded by the dog, had anyone stood near it. As it was, every time that the parasol slightly moved, the dog growled fiercely and barked. He must, I think, have reasoned to himself in a rapid and unconscious manner that movement without any apparent cause indicated the presence of some strange living agent, and no stranger had a right to be on his territory." From this brief impression gathered on a sultry day Darwin went on to claim, in the following sentence, "The belief in spiritual agencies would easily pass into the belief in the existence of one or more gods." And with this, strictly speaking, the whole question of the origin of the divine could be considered settled, for Darwin.

Freud's case was more tormented and troubled. For him the "collective psyche" could keep "alive for thousands of years the guilt caused by a single action" so that it "continued to act in generations who could not have the slightest idea of that action." And again, as ever, he meant an action performed by *humans*.

But one way or the other both the curiosity and alarm of Darwin's dog that summer's day and humanity's millennia-long guilt for actions that remained entirely obscure to them each served to demonstrate the same point: that religion had nothing whatsoever to do with what usually passed for *divine*, and in particular with any reverence for the invisible.

The reaction of Darwin's sensible dog to the parasol stirring in the breeze seems no more convincing than the fact of protracting over millennia "an emotional process such as might arise in generations of children mistreated by their fathers, into later generations that, precisely as a result of the father's murder, had been spared such a treatment." Darwin and Freud were clearly worlds apart, when it came to psychology. But both were bent on tracing back everything to what they saw as *the facts of life*, even though, in Freud's case, those *facts* might be "psychic realities," not "realities of fact."

But how did this turnaround come about, and in whom? In neurotics, Freud answered, since "it is the hallmark of neurosis that it places psychic realities above realities of fact, reacting to thoughts with the same seriousness that normal people reserve for reactions to real facts." And here Freud added a question that was also a provocation: "Could not something analogous have occurred among primitive peoples?"

These words appear in the closing lines of *Totem and Taboo* and amount to the last missiles launched from the obscurity of a work that both anthropologists and even psychoanalysts would read with some embarrassment. But Freud did not waver and quickly warns, "We must be careful not to transfer the contempt for what is merely thought and wished for, typical of our sober world, dense as it is with material values, to the world of the primitive man and the neurotic, rich only in interior events."

This was as far as Freud felt he could take the argument in 1913, and a few lines later the book ends. But in 1939, when he had nothing more to lose, he wanted to clarify the ultimate aim of his entire oeuvre: to treat all subjects of *whatever* kind—patients first and foremost, but also primitive peoples, groups, the masses, nations, and finally entire species—as obsessive neurotics. The premise was that neurosis was the norm, not just the human norm but the zoological norm. Whatever the circumstances, the neurotic reacts with a *surplus* of thoughts, emotions, and intentions that he then needs to channel into a single reaction. Only he can't. This applies not just to humans, but to living creatures in general. Compared with men, animals have simply had longer to formalize their reactions in what we have come to call *instincts*. While men are still in thrall to the chaos of impulses that push them in different directions, tearing them apart. Hence they are still dependant on an action that someone, long ago, may have committed, or perhaps only had *the intention* of committing: the killing of the primordial father.

"Which of the prophets did your fathers not persecute?" These forthright, scathing words were spoken by Stephen during his vehement recapitulation of the history of the children of Israel before the Sanhedrin. If *all* the prophets had been persecuted, the same must go for the first of all prophets, Moses. And Stephen was alluding to the words of another persecuted prophet, Jesus, who had said, "You are the children of those who killed the prophets."

More than the lines from Hosea that Sellin studied and amended—a corrupt text that admits of various interpretations— the words of Stephen and of Jesus clearly state that getting killed is a prophet's fate. But Freud chose not to mention those words. To do so would mean venturing into the vast world outside the Old Testament. Everything must be cleared up within the book's terms.

Freud's concern that the Jews might see his *Moses* as a hostile act, committed at a time they were living in the greatest of dangers, was entirely justified. This, too, goes some way to explaining the caution, backtracking, and superfluous summarizing that one finds everywhere in *Moses*.

Most of all, to assert that the Jew was the creation of a single man, and that this man, Moses, was a "foreigner," might well be taken as mockery with regard to a people who had made such efforts to distinguish themselves from foreigners of every kind. But even more scornful, perhaps, were the passages on circumcision. What had been the mark, the one mark of *separation* that Yahweh imposed on the patriarch Abraham, turned out to be a custom "inseparably connected with Egypt," something Moses had introduced as a "connection" to his people when he decided to join the tribe of the children of Israel. Circumcision thus became a memory and testimony of all Egypt stood for. And the man who had established the institution was himself an Egyptian.

As for the Levites, the tribe supposedly made responsible for rituals in the Temple, they were simply Moses's ceremonial entourage: "It is unthinkable that a great lord like the Egyptian Moses would join a foreign people without bringing his own retinue." In just a few short preparatory passages of his "historical novel," Freud had taken apart the foundations of Judaism. What was left might well celebrate a "development toward a superior spirituality," but it no longer had anything at all to do with that mysterious being who had appeared to the Egyptian Moses as he stood before the burning bush and introduced himself with the words "I am the God of Abraham, the God of Isaac, and the God of Jacob." That being, like Moses himself, was now long buried in some place no one knew. Which was what Freud had always wanted.

"Perennial hatred" for the Jews has always had two targets: the Orthodox Jew and the assimilated Jew. The Orthodox Jew because he remains stubbornly *separate* from everyone else, out of obedience to his traditions, in dress, diet, and rituals. The assimilated Jew because when it comes to certain activities—the legal profession, banking, business, science, scholarship, trade—he *imitates* non-Jews all too well. And these activities are all exemplary of what separates *H. sapiens* from the animal world. *Separation* and *imitation* are the two mortal sins. In the Jew they left all-too-visible traces that no one wanted to be reminded of: our separation from the animal world and our imitation of a part of that world: the predators. In moments of tension—and any moment is potentially such—hatred would flare up toward those who called unpleasant memories into being. Best chase them away, or eliminate them.

Back in Egypt, Joseph had been the first assimilated Jew; Moses the first separated Jew. But that meant that assimilation came *before* separation, and that separation had been introduced by an Egyptian, hence the Jew had no real nature of his own. This was the deepest wound, one Freud hesitated to inflict on the Jews.

The assimilated and enlightened Jew is the dry Jew, who avoids all contact with the waters above and the waters below. He considers himself alien to all religiosity and is proud to be so. Yet he takes the condition of being elect as an indisputable fact. After all, it is the one remaining distinction that prevents him from confusing himself with the countless multitudes of the *goyim*.

Romain Rolland was enthusiastic about *The Future of an Illusion* and wrote as much in a letter to Freud. However there was something missing in the book, he thought. There was no reference to what Rolland saw as "the authentic source of religiosity," which could be defined as *oceanic feeling*. It was an expression Rolland had taken from Ramakrishna: "A salt doll went to measure the depth of the ocean, but before it had gone far into the water it melted away. It became entirely one with the water of the ocean. Then who was to come back and tell the ocean's depth?"

Like a woodworm, this oceanic feeling ate into Freud. And emerged two years later in the opening page of *Civilization and Its Discontents*. But in a letter to Rolland Freud quickly played down this use: "Don't expect an appreciation of the 'oceanic' feeling,

I am simply trying to deduce it by analysis, so as to have it out of the way, as it were." Was that feeling really such an obstacle, even to Freud, who considered himself immune from all mysticism ("Mysticism, like music, is something unavailable to me")? Why then make it the departure point of a book that would set out to explain that civilization is of necessity unhappy? Whatever the case, wishing to be quite clear on the matter, Freud offered a personal observation as a premise: "I find no trace of this 'oceanic' feeling in myself." And at once he sets the machinery of analysis in motion: "The following line of thought is thus available to us: normally nothing is more certain than the sense of ourselves, of our Ego. This Ego seems autonomous, unitary, clearly distinct from everything else. That this apparent state of affairs is fictitious, that the Ego finds, internally and without any clear boundary, its continuation in an unconscious psychic entity which we refer to as the Id, for which it functions as a front, so to speak, we discovered for the first time thanks to psychoanalytic research, from which we hope to learn much else about the relationship between Ego and Id. But externally at least it seems the Ego sustains clear and sharp lines of demarcation." This was all Freud was ready to admit. And it excluded access to any sort of oceanic feeling. The boundary had been set.

Freud belonged to those, and there are many, who remain aloof from the blessing of the waters, the final and supreme blessing that Jacob bestowed on Joseph. But the oceanic feeling, which he claimed to know nothing about, would not leave him be, as emerges from the countless hints scattered through the writings of this ideal *patient*, so prodigal of symptoms. The last of these hints comes in the last sentence on the last page of the last volume of the *Gesammelte Werke*, a posthumous, isolated fragment: "Mysticism: the obscure self-perception of the realm outside of the Ego, the Id." What is the subject who does the perceiving here, or rather, which perceives itself? Apparently the Id, hence the territory that the Ego was supposed to have conquered, drained, and reclaimed, much as civilized man had drained the Zuiderzee. But clearly this hadn't happened, if the Id was still able not only to perceive, but to perceive itself.

As Levenson saw it, "The blunt term 'Jew-hatred' is, in some contexts, preferable to the genteel euphemism 'anti-Semitism,'" especially when one considered that so many Semites were anti-Semites, the most obvious example being the Mufti of Jerusalem, an enthusiastic supporter of Hitler. And in fact throughout his *Moses* Freud avoids the term *anti-Semitism*, even though the main purpose of the book, as he had written to Arnold Zweig, was to discover the origins of the "perennial hatred" that the Jews had drawn upon themselves and to which they had been subjected. For all its hesitations and glitches, the book did eventually arrive at that goal: compared with all other nations, the Jews had *less successfully repressed*, and even allowed to emerge in their founding figure, Moses, the greatest event in the history of *H. sapiens*, the killing of the primordial father, which is to say the Great Predator whose place *H. sapiens* was to take. For many, the Jews were simply bound to be intolerable; they were *too close* to the origins of us all, too similar to a disturbing memory. Actually, the most disturbing memory of all. Far more than inflicting new narcissistic wounds on the Jews—something he had been doing all his life—it was this discovery Freud was eager to arrive at in his last work. Now the "unredeemed ghost" would be exposed to universal view.

IX

THE FIRST
GENERATIONS

"The breath, *ruah*, of Elohim hovered over *Tehom*, the Waters."
Tehom was a proper noun, used without an article, any adjectives
taking feminine inflections. It meant "Sea" or "Waters." Elohim
"hovered"—here the Hebrew has the same word used to describe
the gliding of an eagle. *Tehom* came before light, before time. It was
not an element of nature, but the entity that came before any kind
of life.

There had been a Prince of the Waters, who had rebelled against
Yahweh. He was called Rahab. "Was it not you who cut Rahab to
pieces, / who pierced the dragon through?": thus Isaiah speaking
to Yahweh. The only witness of the struggle was Wisdom: "I was
there when he marked his boundary on the waters."

A trace of this primal conflict turns up in Elohim's first act in
Genesis, the separation of the upper and lower waters: "Then Elohim made the firmament and separated the waters that are below
the firmament from the waters that are above the firmament. So it
was." This is the only time that Genesis confirms "so it was."

Nothing is more mysterious than the cosmogonic waters. They
are the only element at once outside the world and inside the world.
Elohim places the firmament "in the midst of the waters," so that it
"separates the waters from the waters," like a lid of purest crystal,
two inches thick, that through countless cracks allows a light to
filter in from outside. And where from, if not the waters above?

That double mass, closing the universe in an invisible grip, is
the indispensable precondition of every distinction, including the
first distinction of all, light. And it offers Elohim his first opportunity to say that something is "good." In the cosmos, the waters are
irreducibly female. The "abyss," *tehom*, that Genesis speaks of in its
opening verses, is akin to the Accadic *tiam-at*, "sea," which in turn
appears as a feminine figure in Tiamat, the monster whom Marduk fights, as Indra must slay Vritra, another monster, another

inexhaustible reserve of waters. For life to manifest itself, in whatever form, something boundless, unbroken, and liquid is required. And life's relation to those waters never ends, emerging in thought and gesture.

Rather than hovering or gliding, as the verb in Genesis 1:2 suggests, the breath of Elohim was to divide the waters. It was not a question of "creating" them, and certainly not *ex nihilo*, as scholars have been claiming since the second century C.E. Rather, of "separating," *bara*, something that preceded the light. And the waters, above and beneath, were furrowed by a "breath," *ruah*. Insofar as they were everything, dark and indefinite, the waters inevitably included the mind within themselves. They were the closest you could get to a mental material.

The second day of creation, when Elohim decreed the separation of the waters above and below, the waters rebelled and "embraced each other all the more closely," as if wishing to remain in eternal coitus. The act of separation Elohim imposed "was the only act of the sort done by God in connection with the work of creation. All other acts were unifying" (a sharp observation of Louis Ginzberg's). It was also the only moment when the primordial mass opposed him. At which Elohim decided to destroy the world he was just beginning to create. He summoned the Angel of the Face and ordered him to return everything to chaos. The Angel shot fire from his eyes and at once quoted Isaiah: "He who divided the waters [of the Red Sea] before them." Terrified, the waters recognized the words of the yet unborn Isaiah and relented. Only of what happened on the second day does Genesis not say, "Elohim saw that it was good."

The most insidious of the Mesopotamian gods as far as Yahweh was concerned was Ea. He had detached himself from the other gods, choosing to live not in the sky, but in Apsu, the boundless expanse of the waters below. His very nature was fluid: he was depicted with two streams of water spouting from his shoulders or from the vase he held in his hand. But Ea was also the shaper, who gave things their form, who marked out borders, placed stones on boundaries. But he did not impose his will because "the ways of water are devious." Shrewdly, he chose rather to send the other gods where he wanted. Ea established order starting from the waters, not separating himself from the waters. He was not so imperious as Yahweh, was subject to illness, sometimes deceived, most of all by his granddaughter Inanna. Rather than fighting the gods, he shared out powers among them. The Bible never names him, never disapproves of him.

The primal vision of the continuous and the discrete was available to all in the night sky. The numberless scattered pinpoints of the stars were the discrete, the Milky Way the continuous. And the Milky Way contained other stars, because the continuous contains the discrete. That vision was man's lingua franca. Whatever the latitude, they saw it, and pondered it.

The Milky Way was the celestial river that flows on, down to the earth, and also the body of a goddess, Ganga, running through Shiva's hair. Corresponding to Malkuth, the Kingdom, the tenth *sephirah* that descends from the "river that is on high" of the celestial waters. And René Guénon observed that "the reservoir of the celestial waters is naturally identical to the spiritual center of our world: it is from here that the four rivers of the *Pardes* branch off and flow toward the four points of the compass."

In an article published in 1926, Guénon remarked that "the symbols or myths were never intended to represent the movements of the celestial bodies, but the truth is that one often finds among them figures inspired by that movement and destined to express by analogy quite other things, because the laws of that movement translate physically the metaphysical principles on which they depend." This applies, beyond the planets, to the constellations of the Zodiac and as far as the Milky Way. And beyond that? The Milky Way is the last object visible to the naked eye. Everything else, the

boundless expanses opened up to us through microscopes, tele-
scopes, and particle accelerators, could never be seen by the eye
alone. Spaces where we no longer find the correspondences that lay
the basis for analogy. Which thus withdraws from the scene, as if
its job were now done. Symbolism can exist only in what we can
see with the naked eye. Confirming its character of preordained
harmony.

Symbols are figures that contain their meanings—multiple
meanings, sometimes opposite, but always agreeing in some "order of existence"—as a cup contains its liquid. Which might be
the water and blood that issued from the side of Christ, pierced
by the spear of the centurion Longinus. Or the *soma* that induces
euphoria. The cup is the heart. So the tarot cups became hearts in
French playing cards.

As Guénon has it, "every true symbol bears its multiple meanings in itself, and this has always been the case, since symbols are
not made as they are in line with human convention, but following
the 'law of correspondence,' which connects all worlds together."
Hence one can claim that "symbolism is an exact science," and
that the different meanings of symbols may reveal themselves to
whoever observes them attentively. We can also posit a primordial period when this did indeed happen, both as a discovery of
knowledge and a revelation of "'non-human' origin." So the world
and its order appeared as covered by a web of meanings. And the
threads of this web were what the Vedic seers called *bandhu*, "connections."

No order is complete; no order dominates; no order holds.
Yet everything happens *as if* order held. Simulation is an indispensable element of every order. Rituals are unlike other events
to the extent that they are the most perfect and most approximate
simulations. That is why they have always been intrinsic to order.
Where ritual is absent the precepts of the law step in. But these are
for the most part negative: they no longer tell us what we need to
do, as ritual does, but what we mustn't do. At which point order is

supposed to hold *all by itself.* And it is exactly then that it reveals its incompleteness and fragility. In rushes punishment, which takes everything back to its initial, undetermined state. Such was the back-and-forth of the history of the children of Israel, as narrated in the Bible.

Every attempt to establish an order in whatever area of life, however small or large, is always insufficient, impermanent. Every order is opposed to the normal state of things, where entropy is ever at work, ever invincible. Yet every attempt to establish an order invites us, forces us, to posit something on which all else depends. We should hardly be surprised, then, looking back to the origins of human thought, if we invariably run into words that point to a cosmic and mental order: *ṛta, asha, maʾat, me, díkē, śimāti, dao, torah.* Each of these words is a well too deep for any plumb line. From the beginning, observing the sky and its overwhelming multiplicity of forms, human thought sought to pick out a *kosmos,* a *small* order of forms, with respect to the whole range of those other possibilities that it did not contain, usually exemplified by the Milky Way, that part of the sky whose single constituent elements cannot be separated out. There can be no gods, no God, unless connected to those words that indicate an order. Divinity itself is inseparable from those words. What much later came to be understood with the term *science* is just our most recent attempt to articulate an order that had already been spoken of with many other names. All endlessly open, provisional, unsettled. All indispensable if some form of life was to keep going. The figure of the Messiah is the shadow one glimpses behind the perennial breaches in order.

"Yahweh Elohim planted a garden in Eden, to the East, and placed there the man he had fashioned." The male creature and the female creature, as yet unnamed, were put in a place that Yahweh Elohim had "planted" and tended. And man was put in the garden "to till it and watch over it." It was a place that required care and protection, carrying on the work of the first gardener. Among the many plants, Yahweh Elohim pointed out two: the tree of life, in the center, and the tree of the knowledge of good and evil, whose exact location is not given. All the other trees were "pleasant to see and good to eat." Whichever way you turned, there were attractions for eye and palate. Only the fruit of the tree of the knowledge of good and evil was to be forbidden. And this after Yahweh Elohim had just told the man, "You can eat from every tree in the garden."

Whoever ate the fruits of the two trees that Yahweh Elohim had spoken of would assimilate two qualities of Yahweh Elohim: knowledge—not all knowledge, but "the knowledge of good and evil"—and eternal life. If the man and woman had gone to the center of the garden, looked at the tree of life, and eaten its fruit, apparently nothing would have changed. Life would have gone on exactly as before. But the man and woman would have possessed, once and for all, eternal life. It didn't happen. Their attention didn't gravitate to life, but to knowledge. Or rather, the woman was distracted from every other object of attention, thanks to an animal, the cunning serpent. It was a diversion that would have immediate and perceptible consequences. Man, Yahweh Elohim said, speaking to we know not whom, had "become like one of us." This was unacceptable. The important thing now was to "stop him reaching his hand to take from the tree of life as well, eat the fruit from that and live forever." What would have been feasible just moments before, since no one had forbidden it, now had to be prevented with all haste as the worst possible calamity. It wasn't acceptable that knowledge and eternal life be brought together. Had the man and woman not fixed their attention on that particular tree, had they eaten from every other tree, more or less at random, including the tree of life, which was easy to recognize since it grew in the center of the garden at the point where the four rivers divided, everything would have remained, to all appearances, as it already was. And everything would have changed, because man would have been able to live forever. Would Yahweh Elohim have allowed it? Only one thing is clear: Yahweh Elohim would not allow simultaneous possession of both knowledge and eternal life. Which was what Adam and Eve were on the brink of achieving. They would have to be driven out of Paradise at once. And never so much as see the tree of life again.

Paradise was enhanced nature. Of nature one says that it was created. Of Paradise that it was planted. Nature was exposed to the raw clash of the elements. Paradise was the first order. Not distinguished from the rest of creation for the elements that made it up, but for the fact that it was surrounded by a wall. Adam and Eve would remember that order, where they had lived for a while. And pass on the memory to their descendants. Who would keep it alive, even as they became mixed up in many genealogies. Again and again they would try to bring the memory to visible life. But something prevented them. They might be good gardeners. But only when they imitated this *other* garden. For mankind order was always something superimposed on another order—now remote and inaccessible.

The first appearance of beauty occurred with the tree of good and evil. Eve saw at once that the tree was "good to eat," but at the same time that it was "pleasant to the eye and the tree was beautiful to contemplate," *pulchrum oculis*, as the Vulgate has it, *oraîon toû katanoêsai* in the Septuagint. This is the first time we have *pulchrum* in the Bible. From the very beginning beauty, for men, was associated with something forbidden. Even if it was not beauty as such that was forbidden. Eve could have gone on contemplating the tree's beauty without ever giving in to the urge to eat its fruit. Adam was beside her and said nothing. When Eve handed him the fruit and Adam ate it, their attention turned to something they had right in front of them. Instead of contemplating the beauty of the tree, Adam and Eve felt as though scales had fallen from the image they had of themselves: "They knew that they were naked." For the first time they used their hands to make something: "They sewed together fig leaves and covered their loins."

Nakedness didn't have to do with sex so much as with incompleteness. They realized their bodies would always be lacking something. For the moment it was just leafy loincloths, but one day it would be knapped flint. Or in the more distant future, a bow. The prosthesis came as an overcompensation for incompleteness. And was the first knowledge to come down from the forbidden tree. They looked around and saw that none of the animals felt the need to add anything to themselves. They were all complete. And complete they would remain.

To create the world Elohim had had to invent necessity. It was necessity that made the world what it was. It knew nothing of good and evil, fell like rain on the just and unjust alike. Elohim invented it, then was the first to violate it, because he wished to make choices, to isolate something or someone, rather than another. He made man "in his image," while no other creature was like him. And again a little later when he chose to find man "a helper similar to him," he couldn't find one, because man was the only creature who enjoyed the privilege of resembling his Creator. So he created the woman, pulling her out of the man, and Adam didn't reject her as too different from himself, but said, "This time, this is bone of my bones and flesh of my flesh."

Elohim's first violation led to all the others. When Adam and Eve chose to eat the fruit of the tree of knowledge they were simply repeating a previous choice. Original sin was a copy. If Yahweh then stayed so doggedly beside his chosen creatures, it was out of loyalty to that first choice, dense as it was with consequence. Which was one reason he afforded so much importance to loyalty on man's part.

Adam and Eve could have tasted the fruit of the tree of life, the same way they could eat so many other fruits in Paradise. They could even have done it by accident, the way a goat grazes the grass in one place then in another. There was no need to choose. Only when it came to the fruit of the tree of knowledge did they have to choose, because in that case they would be doing something forbidden. The only thing forbidden up to that point. Hence the only opportunity they had to exercise the power of choice. And choice implies consciousness. Even if choice is, as many suppose, illusory, nevertheless the impression of choosing is not illusory. And it is in that impression that consciousness, which might otherwise be absent, emerges. What was new when they made their choice was this emerging consciousness.

Necessity, which Elohim had chosen as an order for the world, does not admit of exceptions or intervention from without. It operates alone. But on the sixth day Elohim created a being in his own image, hence one able to intervene in necessity by exercising choice. It was the first violation of the order of the world, one Elohim himself had caused. Original sin was a repetition, an echo, with a hint of imitation of that other intervention, Elohim's. Condemning Adam, Elohim was condemning himself, and the tormented story of the world had begun, a story no longer entrusted entirely to necessity. There can be no stories with necessity. Only a succession of states. But the Bible is a story.

Elohim was the first to fashion an idol, when he created Adam and said: "Let us make a man in our image and our likeness." Imitating himself, he set an unstoppable mechanism in motion, since a creature created as an imitation would in turn try to imitate the one who had made him. It was one of his powers, that derived from his artificer.

To create something in his own image is the most dangerous thing a god can do, because the living image can always imitate the one who made him, the one who was the first master of imitation, in that he had imitated himself. And imitation might eventually culminate in substitution. Which is what the serpent said to Eve,

Eritis sicut dii, "You will be like gods," because before anything else knowledge is the practice of imitation. To eat the fruit of the tree of knowledge was to gain access to imitation. And one can set no limits on imitation, except by putting oneself on a level with the gods. The Seventy acknowledged the serpent's intelligence as more characteristic even than his cunning, calling him *phronimótatos,* "the one most able to reason" of all living creatures. Making man in his own image, Elohim had got too close to his creation. While the Greeks would make do with a formula such as anthropomorphism, which in the end is fairly innocuous, Elohim introduced something far more dangerous: theomorphism. This is another reason Yahweh was so ferocious when it came to opposing idols. He did not want man to see himself as what he was: the first idol of all idols. But even the Olympians, who never troubled themselves to ban images, were never so ruthless as when someone excelled in imitating them. Marsyas, Niobe, and Arachne would pay the price.

In the dialogues set down by the author of the Psalms, one arrives, on occasion, at quite extreme levels of intimacy between the worshipper and his God. An ambiguous, painful intimacy: "Do you perhaps imagine that I am really like you?" Elohim once said. If man was made in Elohim's image it was inevitable he would be drawn to count on that likeness. And so condemn himself. Man was *made* of imitation, but imitation was also his first sin.

Biblical scholars of every school and inclination have always enjoyed putting together lists of aspects of Genesis that can be found in previous or parallel cosmogonies around the Mediterranean. The flood, the tree of life, Paradise, the Leviathan, the Sabbath: the more one decoded stone tables and papyrus scrolls, the less there seemed to be anything new. Above all, one gradually became aware of an epic literature that preceded the Bible but sank without a trace, of which we know nothing save what appears in the Bible as direct quotation, for example, the songs of Lamech and

Deborah, or allusions of the kind that occur in the prophets and the Psalms. And in this literature, the similarities seemed all the more evident.

So what remains that is peculiar to the first three chapters of Genesis, uncontaminated by precedents? Umberto Cassuto, who, like Adolphe Lods and a handful of others, had worked hard to reconstruct the epic, prebiblical literature in all its ramifications and affinities, nevertheless insisted on one aspect that was quite unique to Genesis: guilt, original sin, in all its enigmatic nature. Neighboring texts might have arrived first at everything else: "In the eastern environment it is possible to find analogies also to other features of our section, for example, to the tree of life, the serpent, the cherubs, and so forth . . . But to the heart of the story, that is, man's transgression and punishment, there appears, according to our present knowledge, to be no parallel among the other oriental peoples."

The uniqueness and specificity of the Bible lay in sin, the claim that the founding act behind the history of the world was a sin. This centrality of sin, as the cornerstone not just of Genesis but the entire Pentateuch, Cassuto links to another essential characteristic: "The Torah, which uses a simple prose style as the vehicle of its teachings, without undue embellishment of poetic metaphors and figures of speech, not only meticulously avoided making any use whatsoever of this legendary poetic material, which, if embodied in a book of prose, might have been understood literally by the reader, but it even voiced a kind of *protest* against these myths whose pagan origin was still discernible, and more particularly against the concepts of the heathens themselves."

They are words where the great scholar betrays his own pursuance, without veering to one side or another, of the same approach that he attributes to Genesis: a willful determination to *separate*. At the same time, and contrarily, Cassuto meant to recognize the fundamental unity and cohesion of the stuff of myth. There's no doubt that right from its very first verses Genesis strikes a new note, a manner of speaking that has no precedent in any other story of the world's origins. It is not only the focus on sin that distinguishes these first three chapters of Genesis. It is a way of telling the story, something that marks it out from every other cosmogony, even when made up of the same elements.

Adam gave a name to "all the beasts of the field and all the birds of the heavens." Yahweh Elohim had them file by before him "to see what he would call them." Meantime the creature deciding the names still had no name of his own. Even when Adam gave a name to his woman, we learn only that "the man called his woman with the name Eve because she was the mother of every living thing." And their sons, Cain and Abel, got their names in the same way. Then Cain begat Enoch. And Genesis lists the names of the descendants of Enoch and of his women. But thus far the name Adam had never been used as the name of a single man. Adam meant "man" and indicated the whole species, male and female. It is only when Seth is born that Adam is used as the name of a single man: "Adam knew his wife once more and she bore a son whom she called Seth." In the creation story, the first man is the last to be called by his name, and this at the moment when he renounces his paternal right to name his son. The being who had decided the names must remain in the shadows, already indistinguishable in the multitude of his descendants.

Adam fell ill when he was nine hundred and thirty-three years old. Around him, all the family members were amazed. They had no experience of illness. Seth thought his father was feeling bad because nostalgic for Paradise. He proposed to go there and bring him back some fruit. He wasn't aware that the Cherubim with the sword of circling flames would forbid him from entering.

All Adam and Eve took from Paradise were a few sweet smells. Soon enough they were hungry and couldn't find anything to eat. Eve said to Adam, "Kill me. Perhaps Elohim will let you back into Paradise." Adam said, "Let's not upset the Lord any more. You are flesh of my flesh, I can't kill you." So they decided to do a great penance. Eve immersed herself in the Tigris for thirty-seven days, without saying a word. Adam did the same in the Jordan. In the end all the fish in the Jordan gathered around Adam and the water ceased to flow.

There was a moment, after they were banished from Paradise, when Eve left Adam. She set off westward, aimlessly. She was pregnant, but by whom she wasn't sure. Adam, or the serpent? She wasn't sure she had lain with the serpent, but she suspected she might have. Desperate, she wept. Then twelve Angels came to her side. Michael passed a hand from her face down to her belly. And at once she gave birth to a baby boy with a shining face. Then Eve cried, "I have gotten a man through an angel of the Lord." It was Cain.

Giving birth to her firstborn, Eve made a pun: "I have acquired, *qaniti*, a male, thanks to Yahweh." And his name was Cain, Qayn. The firstborn is the center of attention shortly afterward, when we hear that the second son, Abel, "offered the firstborn of his flock, with their fat." And won Yahweh's approval. Election is already there in the very first episode of man's history.

The first of all firstborns was Cain. He was also the first human being to be born from sexual intercourse. Nothing is said of him except that "after a while, he offered the fruits of the earth to Yahweh as an offering." And Yahweh did not approve. Whatever happened before that does not get told. One can only suppose that for a certain period of his life it hadn't occurred to Cain to offer Yahweh anything, or perhaps he hadn't dared. It was not something anyone had done before. We never hear of his mother or father making offerings.

The gift was rejected. The offerings remained what they were, fruits of the earth, pulled from the ground, inert. Abel, the younger brother, made the same gesture, with a different gift: he killed "the firstborn of his flock, with their fat." The Bible doesn't say he killed them, but "he offered them." The clarification "with their fat" suggests animals killed to be eaten. And Abel's offer was approved.

We don't know how Cain realized that Yahweh had not approved of his offering. But immediately he "felt a great wrath and his face darkened." These are the first feelings described after the flight from Paradise. So Yahweh spoke to him, as if he were standing in front of him. Cain was also the first person Yahweh talked to about good and evil, with an allusive and ominous warning, in verse. A puzzler for the philologists, who have never convincingly established how the syntax works.

Cain was grim; his offering hadn't been accepted. But he still hadn't invited his brother to the fields to kill him. Then Yahweh said, "Why are you grim and why has your face fallen? For sure, if you do what is right, you will raise yourself up. But if you don't do what is right, sin is lurking behind the door; it desires you, but you can master it." The Vulgate, as ever, is illuminating: *Cur concidit facies tua?*—"Why has your face fallen?"—*statim in foribus peccatum aderit*—"sin will soon be at the door"—*sub te erit appetitus ejus, et tu dominaberis illius*—"sin will desire you and you will master it."

It was the first moral lesson, where we learned that evil desired man. The expression was very close to the one Yahweh Elohim had used talking to Eve: "Your desire will be for your man, and he will master you." The desire that woman and evil have for man is to be an indelible aspect of life, Yahweh Elohim was announcing. And in both cases it was up to man to prove himself master. After which, nothing more is said, if not that "Cain said to Abel, his brother, 'Let us go into the fields' and, when they were in the fields, Cain rose up against Abel, his brother, and killed him."

Before Abel no one had ever spoken of killing animals. Though there must have been dead animals, otherwise how could Yahweh have given Adam and Eve tunics of skin to cover themselves? Two choices were then made. Abel chose "the firstborn of his flock, with their fat." And Yahweh preferred his offering to Cain's. It was the first example of election: from earth to heaven, and from heaven to earth.

When Abel offered his sacrifice, men were still frugivores, by divine prescription. Their flocks provided only milk and pelts. There was no question of killing the animals. Hence this bloody sacrifice was *the first killing*. Abel's offering pleased Yahweh, Cain's did not. Soon afterward, Cain killed Abel. That election was at once a privilege and a death sentence could hardly have been made more clear, right from the start. And the whole of history up to Kafka and beyond would simply confirm this.

Why did Abel, "in the course of time" and after his older brother, Cain, had offered Yahweh the fruits of the earth, choose to kill "the firstborn of his flock" to offer them "with their fat" to Yahweh? And why did Noah, as soon as he set foot on dry land, choose to take some of "every clean animal and every clean bird," kill them, and offer them to Yahweh?

The word *offering* or "oblation" appears for the first time in the Bible in reference to Cain. In his case the "fruits of the earth" could be understood as an homage, as when a host offers a guest the first fruits of his land. At the time Yahweh was allowing man to eat only of the fruits of the earth and nothing else. To offer those fruits was to do something both reverent and allusive, *as if* Yahweh wished to share them with man.

Abel's case was quite different. So far the Bible had never mentioned the act of killing. And Yahweh had not yet allowed man to eat meat. We do not know why Abel felt the need to kill some of his animals and offer them to Yahweh. If his action is to be seen as an imitation of his brother's, it was *as if* Abel were inviting Yahweh to share the meat of the animals, with its fat.

Once man had entered the realm of guilt, there was only one ritual that could remind him of his preceding state. It was understood that killing was inevitable, but at the same time it was expected that life remain unharmed, hence that the victim's blood not be consumed. It was a way of denying, or at least glossing over the fact, that a killing had taken place, that mankind was no longer in Paradise, his origin, but in a decadent world, which could easily have disappeared forever, had not Elohim one day *remembered* Noah.

Every sacrifice presupposes a bloody sacrifice. Which is why Abel's offering pleased Yahweh, and Cain's did not. Blood is the only incontrovertible manifestation of life. The first fruits of the earth alone are not enough. Which brings us to the crucial question about sacrifice: why must a living being be killed in order to approach the invisible? It's a question that has never been answered, or you might say that all of history has been an attempt to answer it. A failed attempt.

Simone Weil poses the most daunting of questions: "The Lamb is somehow slain in heaven before being slain on earth. Who does the slaying?"

Guénon: "The animal sacrifice proves fatal to Abel, while Cain's vegetable sacrifice was rejected; he who is blessed dies, he who lives is cursed."

The Bible has no rivals when it comes to the art of omission, of not saying what everyone would like to know. Why didn't Cain's offering please Yahweh? What happened in the first seventy-five years of Abraham's life, before Yahweh said to him, "Go away!"? Why did Samuel choose Saul, whom he had never met nor heard of, as first king of Israel?

If the abundance of legends and commentaries that have grown up around the Bible is so vast it is partly because its omissions are so difficult to accept. How was it possible to deal with the story of Cain and Abel in the way Genesis tells it, without knowing a little more, without at least getting some reassurance as to the malice of Cain and the innocence of Abel? But the peculiarity of the Bible is all here: it will not reassure us. Hermann Gunkel thought that Cain had offered the first fruits of his fields. Rabbinical exegesis, on the other hand, claimed he had offered "produce of the poorest quality (*Bereshith Rabba* XXII, 5)." The Bible says neither the one nor the other.

Many consult the Bible, few read it from beginning to end, verse after verse. Northrop Frye thought most readers gave up about halfway through Leviticus, which is the third of the Old Testament's thirty-nine books. Only by reading the Bible through can one weigh the omissions against the repetitions, which are equally glaring. And only by summing omissions and repetitions can one grasp that unique phenomenon, so unlike any other, which is the Bible.

Cain said to Yahweh, "My guilt is too great for me to bear." But Yahweh would not allow Cain to be killed at once. His guilt meanwhile endured—and overflowed into the world. How could it ever be contained? With another crime. A killing was required, one that would defer every other killing. Life would be the constant deferment of a death sentence. One would have to sacrifice, *in a certain way.*

Everyone could see that Cain was a killer, thanks to the "mark" that Yahweh had placed on him "lest anyone who came across him should kill him." But long afterward, people would ask what one was supposed to do if one came across someone like Abel killed in the fields and did not find the person who had killed him. Then the elders in the nearest village would choose a heifer "that has never labored and does not know the yoke" and lead it to a gorge with a stream that never ran dry at the bottom. "They will break the heifer's neck in the stream." At that point the Levites stepped up as witnesses. "Then all the elders of that town, the closest to the victim, will wash their hands over the heifer whose neck has been broken in the stream. They will speak up and say, 'Our hands have not spilled this blood and our eyes have not seen anything. Pardon your people Israel that you, Yahweh, have redeemed and do not put innocent blood in the midst of your people Israel!' So shall the blood be forgiven them and you shall have put the innocent blood away from you, because you will have done what is just in the eyes of Yahweh."

Guilt is contagious and diffuse. To escape one crime, another is required. This is the basis of sacrifice. But only here, in this prescription in Deuteronomy, did someone dare to say that the victim of the second crime—the sacrificial crime—was "innocent blood": a young animal that had never labored or known the yoke. And for the first time we hear what would one day become Jesus of Nazareth's watchword: "If you had known what this means: *I desire mercy, not sacrifice*, you would never have condemned the innocent." It is hardly a coincidence that the action was connected with the *washing of hands* on the part of the killers. Another man would do the same thing one day, though then it would be a Roman. It was as if, in a corner of the Bible, the writer prefigures what must necessarily happen in the future.

What was the killing of the heifer? Many scholars thought it a sacrifice. Others objected that there was no altar, only flowing water. There was talk of "innocent blood," but the heifer was killed by breaking its neck. There was no need to spill its blood. Yet it died so that "innocent blood" might be taken from the midst of the children of Israel. But was killing a heifer really enough, if a murderer remained on the loose, unidentified, undisturbed, in the community, spreading the contagion of his guilt? Apparently it was, but then those who had killed the heifer had to deny that they had done so, and even that they had seen it done. There was an occult economy of guilt from which no one was exempt. On the contrary, everyone inevitably contributed to it. What could stop it, then, at least for a while? Only the water of a stream that never ran dry.

The killing of the heifer did not follow any of the sacrificial canons. But it did require the presence of priests and it did include a prayer. As in the case of the scapegoat, the setting was not a place of worship, but empty territory outside the community. And the motive behind the rite was the same: to free the community from guilt.

So why could it not be included among the regular sacrifices? Because sacrifices take place inside the community, while this rite was an admission regarding the impossibility of fully understanding how the world was constituted. An act was performed and denied at the same time. The sign that something had to be done, but could not be acknowledged. The prayer that accompanied the act was harrowing: "Our hands have not spilled this blood"—and so on.

There were ten generations between Adam and Noah. An obscure period of which we know little: a sequence of names, no account of what they did. The earth was new, fresh. Men lived for hundreds of years, without growing tired. Conceiving evil in their hearts from the day they were born. The first poetic interlude in Genesis was sung by Lamech to his two wives, Adah and Zillah. It extolled revenge, as celebrated by a descendant of Cain who claimed to have surpassed his ancestor in wickedness. Lamech sang, "I killed a man for my wound / and a child for my bruise," without offering any details as to what the "wound" and the "bruise" might be. Unlike Cain, Lamech had repeated the act of killing. Hence "Cain would be revenged seven times / and Lamech seventy plus seven." The double killing made Lamech even more untouchable than Cain. Nothing else is said of him; all we know is that he boasted of his exploits, and was father to Noah.

Only a few generations had passed when, looking down to earth, the "sons of Elohim realized that the daughters of men were beautiful." Of the "sons of Elohim" we know only that they resided in heaven. And between heaven and earth an erotic attraction seemed inevitable. But Zeus, Apollo, and Hermes all had their profiles and stories and of course names, as did the "daughters of men" who attracted them, whereas the "sons of Elohim" coupled with women of whom we know only that they were beautiful and that they gave birth to beings who were quite extraordinary, the *gibborim*, who were like the heroes; and the powerful *nephilim*.

These celestial interferences were risky and could not last. Otherwise they would have brought about a chronic imbalance in the order of the world. Zeus decided that the age of the heroes must be brief and stormy. The Trojan War followed the divine plan to be rid of them all. Yahweh, too, would not tolerate the growing numbers of *gibborim* for long. Prodigious as they were, such creatures would soon have tried to escape death. And ordinary men would perhaps have copied them. This was unacceptable. Life on earth must be based on the acceptance of death. There were not many *nephilim*, who would be scattered throughout the world and would become the stuff of legend. But what of men? Their lives would have to be shortened, so that they grasped the basis of their existence. "Then Yahweh said, 'My spirit will not dwell always in man, because he is just flesh. His days will be one hundred and twenty years." The reduction would take place gradually. At the time men were living more than seven hundred years.

The age of the "children of Elohim" would remain a mysterious, fleeting interval in the history of mankind. Around the names of the Greek heroes a wealth of stories would be woven that would enrich all ages to come. Of the "sons of Elohim" neither stories nor names would remain—nor anything of the "daughters of men" whom "they chose for themselves."

In his commentary on Genesis, Umberto Cassuto describes the paragraph about the "sons of Elohim" as "one of the obscurest in the Pentateuch." There are many disputed elements: most of all, who were the "sons of Elohim," *one Elohim*. In other biblical passages the expression refers unequivocally to the *Angels*, but they are usually defined as *malakhe Elohim*, "messengers of god." The population of the Angels was mixed. Aside from "the angel congregation standing before the Lord to serve Him," there were also the "demons" and the "destroying angels." One Talmudic tract that Cassuto cites claims that the Angels who serve the Lord have no offspring, while "the demons do procreate." And this is what happened with the "daughters of men." But there is no suggestion of violence. On the contrary, the expression used—"and they took them as wives"—was "the usual expression for legal marriage."

Genesis says nothing about the reaction of ordinary men to this erotic descent from the heavens that was to populate the earth with semidivine beings. If there was guilt involved, men were mere spectators. Yet it was at this time that Yahweh saw "the wickedness of man." Or to be more precise, he saw that men in their *cogitatio cordis*, as the Vulgate puts it, thought only of evil from the day they were born. So that "Yahweh repented of having created man and was vexed in his heart." Still, aside from Cain's earlier crime, we are given no examples of this wickedness. All we have is a sequence of names and the fact that Lamech boasted of having committed two murders. An ominous silence weighs on those first generations. The world was still young, but already Yahweh regretted having created it. The earth was degenerating, had grown corrupt. And the expression used—"all flesh had corrupted its ways," *corruperat omnis caro viam suam*—only added to the obscurity.

As for the evil perpetrated among men, the Seventy speak of *adikía* and the Vulgate of *iniquitas*: the most generic of terms including every possible kind of *evil*. So Cassuto had good reasons for his perplexity: Yahweh's troubled heart and his first regret, which prompted him to command the flood, were provoked by events about which absolutely nothing is said. This is quite different from the Greek and Mesopotamian stories of the flood, which give specific and explicit reasons for what happened.

The Anunnaki commanded the flood because men were making too much noise. Enlil had told the assembled gods, "Sleep eludes me, with all this din." The living would have to be wiped out. From his palace of subterranean fresh waters, Ea, the god of order, sent a dream to Utnapishtim the Far Distant, with whom he loved to converse. He must build a cube-shaped ship, if he was to survive.

Yahweh Elohim commanded the flood because men thought of nothing but doing evil. But he alerted Noah, a "just man and perfect," and ordered him to build "an ark of cypress wood." One day Utnapishtim would tell Gilgamesh what had happened after his boat had crossed the wilderness of waters: "I set out an offering upon the mountain peak." Then the gods "smelled the pleasant fragrance, / The gods like flies gathered over the sacrifice."

When his Ark finally found solid ground, Noah, too, first "built an altar to Yahweh, took of every clean animal and of every clean bird, and caused holocausts to rise up from the altar." The fire completely consumed the victims. Noah had been planning that holocaust even before he boarded the Ark, in the event that they survived. That was why he had chosen seven couples of clean animals and one of unclean animals. Some of the couples of clean animals were already destined for the sacrifice. Yahweh "smelled the soothing fragrance and said in his heart, 'I shall not curse the ground again because of man, for the aim of man's heart is evil, from youth on.'"

Once settled on the mountain, as the waters began to withdraw, Utnapishtim had offered a sacrifice that the gods had rushed to savor. Noah offered a sacrifice of animals that were completely burned up.

Both these men who were chosen to survive did exactly the same thing: killed animals and sacrificed them. Shortly afterward, both were blessed. Then Elohim spoke to Noah and his sons to tell them what they would be eating from now on: "Everything that moves and lives shall be your food, as the green grass, I have given you all this. But you shall not eat flesh with its life, which is its blood."

If the first form of sacrifice is the holocaust, as Noah's offering, celebrated immediately after setting foot on dry ground, would lead us to suppose, and if a holocaust is, as de Vaux observes, "primarily an act of homage, expressed with a gift," one is bound to wonder why this gift had to be the killing of a perfect male quadruped, small or large, and its successive complete destruction by fire. Was that the only possible form of *gift*? Or in any event the most correct? Following what criterion? A gift is meant to give pleasure. Why would an animal with its throat cut, its blood spilling onto the edges of a stone block and smeared on the four points of its corners, amount to a pleasing ever-repeated and ever-to-be-repeated gift for Yahweh? Taking care all the while that the flame never went out?

When Moses, standing outside the Tent of Meeting, explained the doctrine of the holocaust, he did not speak of a "gift"—the term was too human—but an "offering." And he repeated the word over and again: "When one among you offers an offering to Yahweh, if it's a herd animal, it shall be from the large or small herd animals that you will offer your offering. If his offering is a holocaust of a large animal, he will offer a perfect male, he will offer it at the entrance of the Tent of Meeting, so that it be pleasing in Yahweh's eyes."

As in Cain's times, what mattered was to do something that would please Yahweh. But this presupposed a previous state when one was not yet pleasing to Yahweh. If his approval had to be won, this could only mean that in the beginning man—any man—was at fault. A fault that might also be seen as a *debt*. Debts are settled through an adequate, usually precious, exchange. The quadrupeds who lived together with man were no doubt precious to them. But other kinds of offering would have been equally precious. What made quadrupeds the only regular object of these offerings was a specific quality they had. They were *alive*. If the debt man owed was life, it could only be settled with other life. Which would always be insufficient, of course. Hence the holocausts had to be repeated.

Moses chose not to explain the premise behind the actions he prescribed. Perhaps those listening already knew, or perhaps they wouldn't have understood. But if those who followed him were to go on living, they would have to perform those actions—and not perform other actions.

Life does not belong to the living. Like the blood and the fat, it belongs to Yahweh ("All the fat is Yahweh's"). This is the real reason for the destruction in the holocaust. The victim's blood must be spilled on the edges and corner points of the altar. But in no circumstances can it be eaten. Otherwise men might think they could extend their lives with other life. But life belongs exclusively to Yahweh and is entirely at his discretion.

Here we are getting very close to the specific difference between Yahweh and the gods of the surrounding peoples, the Egyptians, the Mesopotamians, the Phoenicians. All these gods required sacrifices, because only sacrifice allows the divine to circulate, but none of them were as uncompromising as Yahweh in claiming the totality of life for themselves, and in forbidding men to dispose of it freely.

Leviticus reasserted the rule, already set out in Genesis, that one must not eat meat with blood, but then added another: every animal must be killed before the Tent of Meeting and its blood spilled on the altar. Why this clarification? Because otherwise the blood would spill on the earth, and the earth itself would take Yahweh's place. The *genius loci* could accept blood, and approve of it. It could be as powerful as a god.

Enlil's flood was a rash thing to do, out of all proportion; Ea, "who knows everything," told him as much. It would have been more prudent to punish men with decimation, sending ferocious beasts among them. Lions or wolves would have done it. Or perhaps a famine or two. Or a plague. The flood was to be reckoned a divine mistake.

Ea's reflections convinced Enlil, instigator of the flood. He took Utnapishtim by the hand, had him board his ship again, and said to him, "Until today Utnapishtim was no more than a human. /

Henceforth, he and his wife / shall be like unto us, to the gods! / But they will dwell far away, at the confluence of the rivers." Which is why Utnapishtim was called "the Far Distant," because he lived a life without end, but in a place beyond reach, where fresh waters and seawaters mingle: a place that came before the world and on which the world still floated, without knowing it. Who but Gilgamesh could ever have got there? And with what result?

The peculiar voice of Qohelet can already be heard in Siduri, the hostess "on the edge of the sea," who pours a drink for Gilgamesh and guides him over the waters. Like Qohelet, Siduri spoke with great sobriety of the last things: "When the gods created mankind / They appointed death for mankind, / Kept eternal life in their own hands." It was her way of speaking of the *vanitas*. At once, using similar words, Qohelet and Siduri offered their advice. Siduri: "Wear fresh clothes. / Keep your head washed." Qohelet: "Let your clothes be always white / and always have oil on your head." One must never forget to keep one's head in contact with something liquid.

"I who came from Uruk," said Gilgamesh. Uruk, a city with huge walls of baked brick, nicknamed "the sheepfold," a mile long, with orchards a mile long, founded by the Seven Sages, "city of prostitutes, courtesans, and hierodules," city of the temple of Ishtar, who wanted Gilgamesh for her lover, and whom Gilgamesh rejected. There had been too many other lovers before him.

Gilgamesh wanted the advice of Utnapishtim the Far Distant, who had been granted a life that would never run out. "But now," Utnapishtim told him "who can gather the gods on your behalf / That you, too, may find eternal life which you seek? For a start, you must not sleep for six days and seven nights." Even as he spoke drowsiness descended on Gilgamesh like a whirlpool and a mist.

He slept for seven days. Waking up he claimed he had only slept a moment. But you couldn't fool Utnapishtim. The game was up. So Gilgamesh said, "Death is waiting in my bedroom, / And wherever I set my foot, Death is there, too." Gilgamesh was dirty, his skin plastered in filth. Utnapishtim ordered that he be washed, go back to being the splendid young man he was, and set off toward his home city, at the end of his journey. But what would be a suitable parting gift for him?

Then Utnapishtim revealed to Gilgamesh "the secret of the gods" : there was a plant, a prickly plant, at the bottom of the waters. Gilgamesh dived down and picked the plant. He thought he had conquered "the breath of life." He said, "I shall take it back to Uruk." On the voyage home with his ferryman Ur-shanabi, he stopped by a freshwater well. And dived in. While he was still underwater "A snake smelled the fragrance of the plant. / It came up silently and carried off the plant." When Gilgamesh got out of the water, he "sat down and wept. / His tears flowed over his cheeks." Then he looked at Ur-shanabi and said, "I did not gain an advantage for myself." What he had found would just be a treat for the snake. They resumed their journey. Then Gilgamesh sent the ferryman ahead to see if Uruk still existed, with its huge walls, its orchards, and the temple of Ishtar. If Uruk still existed, then Gilgamesh existed too. But the life he had sought, eternal life, belonged only to Utnapishtim the Far Distant, even though, on meeting him, Gilgamesh had said, "I look at you, Utnapishtim / And your limbs are no different—you are just like me." Utnapishtim was lying down, quietly.

The first part of world history, up to the flood, might be thought of as an experiment that didn't meet the expectations of the experimenter. And ended with the observation, on Yahweh's part, that as far as man was concerned "the thoughts of his heart had always been directed toward evil."

But when, after the flood, Yahweh said, "I shall not curse the ground again because of man," it wasn't because he had seen any change in man's nature. On the contrary, he used almost the same words he had before the flood: "the aim of man's heart is evil, from youth on." But this had now become the reason for holding back from destroying man. He wasn't to be saved because he'd suddenly grown good and obedient, but because it was now acknowledged that his heart had been evil from the start. All the same, nature must not be corrupted by man's wickedness. It would follow its course as before, unrelenting. Suddenly Yahweh spoke in verse: "Summer and winter, day and night / shall never cease." Individual men could still be maltreated and suffer for the crimes of their fathers, but nature would preserve its sovereign indifference. Then "Elohim remembered Noah," and caused a breeze to blow across the boundless waters. Something similar had happened before the earth was created.

Before creation, fresh waters and seawaters had flowed together, Apsu with Tiamat. The flood was a temporary return to that state. It wasn't just an enormous calamity. It was the reconstitution of things as they had been before everything began. Hence it was said, "the wellsprings of the great deep burst, and the windows of heaven were opened." There had always been a two before any one.

As in the cosmos the first separation had been between upper and lower waters, so on earth it was between the *pure* and the *impure*. But it was only in Noah's time that the distinction appeared. According to the Elohists, Noah was ordered to enter the Ark thus: "From all the animals, of every flesh, you will bring two of every species, to keep them alive with you: they will be male and female." According to the Yahwists, thus: "Enter in the ark, you and all your household . . . Of all clean animals you shall take for yourself seven and seven, the male with his female, and of all beasts that are not clean, two, the male with the female."

The Yahwist presumes that Noah already knew which animals were pure and which impure, clean and unclean, even though no mention had been made of this as yet. That distinction must have been implicit in the structure of the world, like the separation of the waters. You couldn't not know about it. So Noah had no hesitation when it came to choosing pure and impure animals. *Pure* and *impure* was a distinction you understood before it had been established. Why were there to be different numbers of pure and impure animal pairs? Because some of the *pure* would be sacrificed.

The Babylonians were the great masters of the sky, those who had recognized in it the arrangement of a *kósmos*, and remnants of their learning would be passed on through the *Timaeus* and the Vedas as well as the Pyramid Texts. The framework of the *kósmos* that Plato talked about had been established in all its details by the wise men of Babylon.

It was precisely this that the children of Israel would have to put behind them, to unlearn. But one could hardly wipe away such an immense past without some sign to mark the break. When after the flood Elohim for the first time made a covenant with men, he said to Noah, "I have set my bow in the cloud, and it shall be a token of the covenant between me and you." What was this bow? For centuries, countless interpreters, believers and not, Jews and Christians, supposed that this meant the *rainbow*. But Ellen van Wolde has convincingly shown that this is a misleading euphemism. On seventy-two of the seventy-six occasions when this word appears in Genesis it denotes a powerful weapon of war or of the hunt. It is the one weapon that allows Marduk to inflict a mortal wound on Tiamat. In the *Enuma Elish* the description of Marduk's bow suggests further meanings, encoded in the cosmic order. A bow is also drawn by the arms of the most daunting and beautiful of goddesses: Ishtar. And the arrow always corresponded to a secret region of the heavens, teeming with stories: between Sirius and Orion, the region of the Celestial Hunter. At odds over almost everything, the Egyptians and Mesopotamians came together in the sky, in Sirius. Both agreed that this was the axis around which everything turned. It was the bow of the Celestial Hunter, celebrated by Anu before the gods: "Anu raised it and began to speak in the assembly of the gods, / after clasping the Bow, he said: 'It is my daughter.'" And now Elohim set his bow in the clouds. No sign could more eloquently have served notice that, from this moment on, the history of Noah and his descendants would diverge ever more radically from everything that had come before. What Elohim set in the sky, hanging there between himself and men, was the sign of sovereignty, *his* bow, to which he would now allow men access, as a token of their pact. From now on men could consider themselves masters of "all the animals of the earth and all the birds of the heavens." Even if it proved an illusory sovereignty.

Obeying Elohim, Noah came out of the Ark. Followed by all the creatures, one by one, countless pairs of animals of every species. Long processions, particularly the insects. As many as had gone into the Ark, so many came out. None had mated during the voyage. In times of calamity mating was prohibited. And, during the long months of the Ark's drifting, death too had been suspended, had not struck down even the most ephemeral of lives. Noah had no idea what Elohim's intentions were now. His last manifestation had been the tremendous disaster that had wiped out the earth. Now his voice was inviting him to set foot on the earth once again, barely dry as it was. And what if Noah were to put that foot wrong, from the start, make the sort of mistake that would arouse Elohim's anger, as had happened to all the other men of his generation? Noah decided to do something that had never been done before. He built an altar. Nothing more than a square stone block. But no one in the past had thought of it. Then he took "of every clean animal and of every clean bird" and killed them, one by one, beside the altar. Then he arranged the many pieces of flesh on the altar in such a way that they would be completely burned. Or so we must suppose, because the Chronicler writes that he "caused holocausts to rise up from the altar."

It was a strange, systematic slaughter of single animals. And their bodies were laid side by side on the same stone. Yahweh approved. The smell of the burned flesh, horrible to men, was pleasing to his nostrils. Then Yahweh said to himself, "I shall not curse the ground again because of man." Had his assessment of man changed? No, man remained exactly as he was. But it was no reason to destroy him or the earth, as had almost happened just a short while before. All the same, man would have to follow a few rules. And his life would have to submit to a few changes. First and foremost it would come to pass that from now on men would inspire "dread and fear" in all creatures. This was a major departure, since Elohim, immediately before creating Adam, had thought of giving him and his descendants nothing more than "authority" over all the creatures of the earth. Between "authority" and "dread and fear" there was quite a stretch. But apparently this was what the times required. And right afterward Elohim announced another change: men would be able to eat meat as if it were "green grass," whereas before they had been eating only the fruits of the earth. The concession was qualified by just one rule: "You shall not eat meat with its life, which is its blood." There followed some words about killing. Whoever killed a man—whether the killer were an animal or another man—would in turn be killed. It wasn't clear by whom, which meant that it was not necessarily a question of revenge. The only thing that was clear was that the killer would be killed, even when it was an animal that had killed a man. The killing of a man was a circle you couldn't escape. And Elohim added, "For in the image of Elohim, Elohim made man." They were the same words Elohim had said to himself just before creating man, though he hadn't said them to man as yet. But now he did say them to Noah, right after thinking that "the aim of man's heart is evil, from youth on." So this creature who had been made in Elohim's image nursed in his heart a desire for evil. So it was and so it must ever be, Yahweh thought. It was one of the divine thoughts that men found most elusive.

Drawing up a first "pact" with men, Elohim focused on just two actions: eating and killing. He wasn't offering men guidance. He didn't talk about idols, adultery, stealing, or respect for parents; apparently only the acts of eating and killing could lead to a sin so serious as to violate the pact. And eating had to do with killing, since Elohim was now allowing man to eat meat. Or more exactly the meat of animals he had killed. But if the blood, which is life, were removed from the meat, then the killing would not be a real killing, Elohim implied, using an argument very close to those some Vedic ritualists used when talking about sacrifice.

Finally Elohim decided that *his* bow would be the seal of the covenant. It was a pact made up of the fewest possible terms. When one day Elohim felt the need to renew the pact, everything would get more complicated. But right now, with Noah, he didn't want anything else, as if those few simple prescriptions actually included everything that would be added in the future. Above all man was granted dominion over nature. It was accepted that he had an advantage, in terms of sheer force, over all other creatures. At the same time Elohim kept life for himself. This way man would never be self-sufficient. He could kill animals, but he couldn't eat their blood. And he would have to sacrifice, because only after he had sacrificed had he once again been pleasing to Elohim. These precepts presented an obvious problem, in that man, both to sacrifice and to eat, would have to take the life of other creatures. But Elohim thought this glitch could be overcome: before eating the meat of animals man would simply have to drain away the blood. And sacrifice? Noah had celebrated a holocaust, where the animal was totally burned up. Rather than being suppressed, life vanished from the terrestrial scene and passed in its entirety into the realm of Elohim. It was on this basis that the life of men could go on.

Theophrastus, who considered the Jews a "race of philosophers"—a rare opinion, not unlike that of Megasthenes, who thought the Jews close to the "brahmans of India"—declared his repugnance for their sacrifices: "They still sacrifice animals following primitive customs. If they wished to impose the same kind of sacrifices on us, we would reject them." He found their ceremonies repugnant because still too close to their origins: "They were the first to immolate animals and even men from necessity, rather than because they wanted to." Their holocausts were proof of this, in that they were entirely separate from any alimentary use of ceremonies: "They did not in fact eat the meat of their victims. They threw the animal in the fire whole, at night, having poured honey and wine over it, and performed their sacrifices quickly, so that he who sees all should not witness the horror of it." After which, "during the day, they do nothing but talk about the divine and at night they contemplate the stars, raising their eyes to the sky and invoking them in their prayers." Many scholars have objected that the *tamid* did not take this form, that the victims were not drenched in honey and wine. Yet Leviticus says: "The whole burnt offering is to remain on its coals on the altar through the night, till morning, and the fire must be kept burning on the altar." As Theophrastus had pointed out, this focus on the holocaust, sacrifice as pure destruction, constituted the most eloquent mark of the singularity of the Jews.

Olah, the holocaust, was the first and most important of sacrifices. Not just because, when first performed, by Noah, Yahweh said, "I shall not curse the ground again because of man," but because it was the one sacrifice described as *tamid,* which is to say, "perpetual," "continual," "nonstop," something to be performed every morning and every evening. On the Sabbath, when everything was to rest, the number of holocaust victims actually doubled. Over the eight days of the Feast of the Tabernacles one hundred and ninety-one animals would be sacrificed, the number shrinking each day until, on the last, the day of the Meeting—when, it was written, "you shall do no servile work"—only "one bull, one ram, and seven unblemished yearling lambs" would be killed. For all the time life went on and however it went on, the holocaust was being performed, the one constant event, precondition for every other. All rules regarding behavior were based on this assumption. It was the circulation of the blood of the Law. Animal blood spilled on the altar. Leviticus 1–8 and Numbers 28–29 laid down meticulous, often identical instructions regarding the

holocaust and the communion sacrifices. With this solemn conclusion: "An everlasting rite for your generations wherever you
shall dwell."

During World War II the Nazis put into effect a systematic plan
to exterminate the Jews. They were gathered in camps, concentration camps, extermination camps. Sometimes they were moved
from one to the other to be killed. Most of the corpses were burned.
These are the basic facts, set down in plain words.

One day someone thought of referring to that plan and its im-
plementation with the world *holocaust*. Via paths no one will ever
entirely explain, as is always the way with the history of words, the
term spread widely and rapidly, until it became *the* specific term to
describe those events. And was even granted, on occasion, a capital
letter. But where the Nazi plan was something wholly new, *holocaust* was not a new word. On the contrary, it was an ancient word,
in the terminology of sacrifice. Genesis speaks of "holocaust," *olah*,
the first time it speaks of an altar. And the first holocaust of all was
offered by Noah, who built the first of all altars. What the holocaust
was, Yahweh would explain to Moses: "And Yahweh spoke to Moses, saying: 'Give this order to Aaron and his sons and tell them,
This is the law of the holocaust: the holocaust will be on the coals,
on the altar, all night until morning, and the fire of the altar will
go on burning there. Then the priest will put on his linen garment
and his linen breeches on his flesh, he will raise the flesh of the holocaust that the altar fire will have devoured and put it on the side
on the altar. Then he will remove his garments and put on other
garments, and he will take the ashes outside to a clean place."

So it was that the systematic extermination of one people by
another came to be given the name of a religious ceremony instituted in ancient times in the words of the God of the exterminated
people. This was a tremendous mistake, indeed an atrocity. But
more than the mistake itself, it was atrocious that it was not seen as
a mistake. On the contrary, people insisted on it. Other terms were
criticized so that they could be substituted with it. In this way the

Nazis were granted an immense, quite underserved honor: it was acknowledged that for years they had been performing a ceaseless religious ceremony, while actually they were engaged in systematic killing. What's more, that religious ceremony belonged to the most ancient tradition of the people they were aiming to exterminate. The growing collective sensibility with regard to the extermination of the Jews developed hand in hand with the more and more widespread use of the word *holocaust*. But that greater attention—and even the growing awareness of what happened—was not enough to make obvious what a tremendous mistake was being made, day by day, every time the extermination of the Jews was spoken of. And all the while people were talking of memory, often celebrating memory. Some believed that memory in itself was the most effective antidote to a certain kind of horror. But how could this be true of the memory that describes its object with a word that is not only mistaken, but misleading, laden with meanings unknown to the person pronouncing it. Can we really remember if we are using a word whose meaning we have forgotten?

Evil does not reach its perfect state simply by being committed. It is at least equally important that it be wrongly named, since this guarantees that the mind cannot come to see it clear and whole. So long as this state of affairs persists, the evil can safely elude a judgment that sees it for what it was.

Hosea lived in the reign of Jeroboam II, in the eighth century B.C.E. Some of his words are obscure and elusive. Others possess a conclusive clarity: "I want mercy, not sacrifice / knowledge of God, not holocausts." As a condemnation of sacrifice this is as terse and resolute as it gets. Jesus quoted the opening words the day he chose Matthew as one of his disciples. Matthew was busy with his job, collecting taxes. "*Misericordiam volo et non sacrificium*," Jesus replied to those who scolded him for sitting at table with "tax collectors and sinners." Clearly anyone who could put together those two categories, as if they amounted to a sum of worldly behavior, was no fool. The reference Jesus made to sacrifice here was hardly clear, but the following sentence simply dazzles for its clarity: "In truth I haven't come to call the righteous, but sinners."

For Jesus that passage in Hosea must have constituted a key—one of the most powerful in the Bible—so much so that he would soon be quoting it again: "If you knew what was meant by: *I want mercy, not sacrifice*, you would never have condemned the innocent." What strikes us this time is the connection between sacrifice and guilt. Jesus was suggesting that the practice of sacrifice was strictly connected to the condemnation of innocents. And this time the claim, based on Hosea, was deeply disturbing. No one had ever dared to bring those two words together: *innocents* and *sacrifice*. One could deplore sacrifices when they were made to Baal or Anath, or any of the other endless gods. But here Jesus was talking about sacrifices made to Yahweh, in observance of the rules in force since the day Noah came out of the Ark and presided over the first holocaust. Actions that had always been considered holy. But now Jesus was talking of *innocents condemned*, as if sacrifices were to be thought of as so many long-drawn-out and much-repeated miscarriages of justice. It had taken eight centuries for someone to pronounce those words, and sacrifices were still being celebrated in the temple, following the detailed prescriptions Yahweh had laid down on various occasions. And now someone came along who, just before quoting Hosea, had spoken words that might have been understood as evil: "Here there is something greater than the Temple."

Jesus quoted Hosea's words on sacrifice in two very different situations. The first time had to do with *election*, his calling of Matthew; the second had to do with *condemnation*, the violation of the law of the Sabbath, which could be punishable by death, as in the case of the man whose name we don't know who had gathered firewood on the Sabbath. Even the sense of the quotation was different. In the first case Jesus was asserting that being well-disposed toward everyone—"tax collectors and sinners" implied everyone following the ordinary ways of the world—together with the ability to help these people was more important than observing religious rites. Here *sacrificium* meant any ritual action. In the second case Jesus slipped Hosea's verse into the middle of an extremely tough admonition: "If you knew what was meant by: *I want mercy, not sacrifice,* you would never have condemned the innocent." The immediate import of this sentence was that sacrifice could imply the *condemnation* of the innocent. Because sacrifice always implies the choice—the *election*—of a victim. But even if one took *sacrificium* to mean all the actions involved in observing the law, it could easily happen that a harmless collector of firewood found himself being condemned to death. In just a few words Jesus had undermined the very foundations of the Law.

Then there was a hidden connection between these two occasions when Jesus quoted that verse from Hosea: both cases turned around the verb *to eat.* The first time Jesus was accused because he was eating with tax collectors and sinners; the second time because one day, while he was walking in the fields, his disciples, "being hungry, began to pluck the ears of corn and to eat," *vellere spicas et manducare.* At once the Pharisees objected: "Look, your disciples are doing something that is not lawful on the Sabbath." Jesus replied by challenging them to remember a moment in the life of David: "When he and his men were hungry, didn't they go into the House of God and eat the consecrated bread, which neither he nor his men had the right to eat, only the priests? Or haven't you read in the Law that on the Sabbath the priests in the Temple break the Sabbath and commit no crime?" Words he followed up with a phrase that on its own was enough to demonstrate what a dangerous subversive Jesus was: "Yet I say to you that here there is something greater than the Temple." That "here," *hic,* is the thorniest part of the sentence. It didn't just mean "here on earth," but "in this story," a story that had to do with people who are hungry and *eat.* The act of eating was evidently and indissolubly connected with sin, regardless of whether those eating were "tax collectors and sinners" or disciples walking in the field, plucking ears of corn because they were hungry. To trace sin back to its origins one had to go via the act of *eating*. An action that could not be contained by the Law, implying that the Law was not *everything*. *Eating* signifies, before anything else, our ineluctable dependence on the world, which we must draw on at every moment, for every breath, if our lives are to continue. This is the *hic* that is "greater than the Temple," the ground on which every Temple must stand.

After the flood, and even after Elohim made his first pact with the men who had survived it, there was still something missing on earth, something indispensable: intoxication. Noah discovered it when he went back to being a "man of the earth" and the first cultivator of vines. The more unsettling the discovery, the sparer the words that announce it and the more far-reaching their consequences.

Noah got drunk and fell asleep in his tent, naked. "And Ham, the father of Canaan, saw his father's nudity and told his two brothers, who were outside." Out of this briefest of scenes, with its two moments inside and outside the tent, would come the malediction of Canaan and his people, who would fight the Jews for centuries, with varying success, occupying the Promised Land before they did. But if Noah's fault seems obvious, Ham's is not. In Michelangelo's version of the scene, painted in the Sistine Chapel, Noah's three sons wear fluttering loincloths that leave their sexual organs quite exposed. So what was Ham's crime? To have *pointed to* the sexual organs, as Michelangelo showed. An excessive, inadmissible intimacy. To stare at another's sex recalls certain popular cults that would one day descend from Ham's son. Hence the account in Genesis, packed into the fewest possible words, immediately clarifies: "Ham, father of Canaan."

Noah woke up and "learned what his youngest son had done to him." "What he had done to him" is the expression one uses for the worst offenses. Like water snakes, rumors went around, in the tradition, about *other* terrible acts Ham had committed: he must have castrated, or even sodomized, his father.

But, as ever, the biblical test is hardly interested in the storms it provokes. For Noah to learn that Ham had discovered his nudity and pointed it out to others was reason enough to curse him instantly—him and all his descendants: "Cursed be Canaan [son of Ham]! The slave of slaves will he be to his brothers!" The gong that set the history of the Jews in motion had been struck.

As was the case when Yahweh chose between Cain and Abel, Noah's choice between his sons was not based on merit. Shem had done nothing that set him apart from Japheth. Both had gone into Noah's tent, walking backward, holding a cloak. They had both *respected the proper distance*. They had taken care not to see their father naked. But barely had he woken from his drunken sleep than Noah was saying that Yahweh was "the God of Shem" and not of Japheth. Who, however, should be allowed to "enlarge himself." But far away. The sons of Japheth were the Goyim, the peoples of the coast, who would join forces with the sons of Shem against the Canaanites. Being allies they would be welcomed "in the tents of Shem" as well-loved guests. But foreigners nevertheless.

Some generations after the flood, humanity as a whole provoked an intense aversion in Yahweh, when he saw them come together with enormous enthusiasm to tackle one great project: the building of the Tower of Babel. Prior to that, all they had done was multiply their numbers and dominate the earth. Yahweh decreed that never again would there be a single community, but many tribes, each unable to understand the words of the others. Finally, years later, he would decide to isolate and guide not the humans as a race but a single man, seventy-five years old: Abraham who lived

in the city of Ur. And to him, for the first time, Yahweh promised
something that would come to pass in the future.

Yahweh *had to* clash with the most powerful gods, the neighboring gods. In the case of Egypt the struggle lasted for the whole
of the Old Testament, from Abraham to Zachariah. A ferocious,
willful, repetitive, never-ending struggle. In the case of Babylon it
was the opposite; a huge omission, leaving just a few fragmentary
traces: the figure of Nimrod, who appears like a flash, and twenty
lines from Genesis on the Tower of Babel.

They were both strategies of destruction, and perhaps omission
would prove the more effective of the two. If the Tower of Babel
gets less space than the genealogy of Shem it was precisely because
it presented such an immense obstacle, which would have to be
wiped out as soon as possible: a *single language*, the possibility that
men might name a god with fifty different names, as was the case
with Marduk, and nevertheless understand one another: "All the
earth had but one language and one speech." What was urgently
required was a word that was *separate* from every other, as, with
Abraham, there would be a family separate from every other. Between Noah and Abraham there were ten generations, of which
nothing is said, aside from a sequence of names. Just one event
sufficed to account for the period: the failed building of the Tower
of Babel. The first diaspora, which affected all men alike, and the
fading memory of that one language spoken from Adam on, were
simultaneous events. Several centuries would pass before the dis-
persal of the children of Israel in the direction of Babylon, after
destruction of the Temple in Jerusalem at the hands of Nebuchadnezzar's troops. The children of Israel then attributed to themselves, as if it were their unique destiny, what had already been the
destiny of all.

Unlike the creation story and the flood, the story of the Tower
of Babel has no Akkadian parallels, though it takes place in the

heart of Mesopotamia and refers to the most celebrated architectural structure of the area: the ziggurat. As for Babylon, the *Enuma Elish*, the Akkadian Genesis, recounts that it was built initially in the heavens, brick by brick, by the gods themselves, the Anunnaki, to celebrate the victory of Marduk over Tiamat. The tower of the Esagila, "the House pointing upward," also rose into the heavens. After which Marduk came down to earth and built himself a sanctuary modeled on the celestial Esagila. Travelers who visited Babylon spoke of its magnificence.

Genesis says nothing of all this, as if the project for the Tower of Babel had been exclusively a human initiative. Driven by two conflicting motives: "Let us make a name for ourselves, so as not to be scattered across the face of all the earth." It wasn't clear why the desire for glory should be strictly connected with the fear of being scattered. And to whom could this glory be broadcast, when the whole of humanity was still gathered together in Babylon? As for being scattered, it was a fear that implied a previous threat, as though Yahweh had already indicated his disapproval of this excessive concentration of men in one place. For the rest, the resolve to reach the sky need not necessarily be considered a manifestation of hostility. On the contrary, it might have been a sign of supreme devotion.

Both Yahweh and the men working hard to build the tower, brick on brick (the higher the bricks were placed, the more they were precious, more precious even than the lives of the men who placed them there), knew perfectly well what drove them. Yahweh would never have allowed men to dedicate a temple to him that imitated a temple built by *other* gods, and in the sky to boot. And long before the celestial Jerusalem. Men had a presentiment that their frenetic building work, during which women "gave birth molding bricks, tying the baby to their body in a sheet while they went on molding bricks," would be their last shared project. Otherwise, why were they so afraid of being dispersed? This way they would at least leave one tangible and glorious memory.

But a supernatural wind began to blow when the Tower was

already so high you couldn't see the top. It was a wind like no other, a wind that meant only destruction. When the bricks, which the builders had signed, one by one, with their names, began to fall, the men realized they could no longer understand one another. Like animals of different species. The thing they had feared was happening. They were scattered, from that moment until the end of time, when—as Zephaniah's prophetic voice would have it—Yahweh will transform the many languages into one "pure lip" (*Quia tunc reddam populis labium electrum*). Then the scattered peoples will come from "beyond the rivers of Ethiopia," to serve Yahweh "with one shoulder," *humero uno*. United as they had been only once before, in that remote past when they built the Tower of Babel.

The diaspora was a punishment, and presupposed a sin. The first was the dispersion that occurred after the collapse of the Tower of Babel. A dispersion that involved all men. But how had they arrived in Babel? "When men journeyed from the east they found a plain in the land of Shinar and settled there." Until the Tower collapsed. Every successive dispersion would repeat that first division of the descendants of Noah's three sons. And would be the privilege and calamity of a single family, the children of Israel, a family descended from Shem.

It may well be that the builders of the Tower of Babel did not have evil intentions. Nor does Genesis say they did. They wanted something people had always sought: a way to the heavens, a safe, reliable way. And they wanted it to be visible. That was their sin. Or at least their enormous mistake. But even mistakes can bring about the desired result. Nothing was more odious to Yahweh than men's presumption that it was they doing whatever they did, as if they were autonomous. And never had Yahweh made this clearer than when they started to build the Tower of Babel: "If they begin doing this, they will be able to do everything they decide to." There was a danger that the relationship would be turned upside down:

rather than men serving Yahweh, Yahweh might become a power at the service of men. Who, after all, still desired a Tower with its "head in the heavens"? It was a way of getting close to Yahweh, to imitate him better.

Genesis mentions Nimrod in three sentences, one of which is immediately repeated, as if it were a proverb. "Kush begat Nimrod. He was the first man to be powerful on earth (*Ipse coepit esse potens in terra*). He was a mighty hunter before Yahweh. So it is said, 'Like Nimrod, a mighty hunter before Yahweh.'" Out of this extreme compression with its refusal to offer any detail would spring a myriad of stories and details as one scholar after another had his say. Putting together the various fragments of information, one does learn a little about Nimrod's life.

First, Nimrod was born when his father, Kush, was already aging. And was all the dearer to his father for it. His father gave him a precious heirloom: the garments of animal skins that Yahweh had given Adam and Eve and that Kush himself had had from Ham. Those garments represented something that would dominate Nimrod's life: the hunt. They weren't the skins of dead animals, but animals killed as prey. When an animal saw those skins, it would remember and crouch down before the hunter. Men, too, would submit to him. In Rabbi Eliezer's *Chapters* it is said that Yahweh was the first sovereign and Nimrod the second. The ninth and last would be the Messiah. Nimrod is declared the first of human sovereigns because the hunt is the beginning of all power. But his life wasn't spent entirely out in the wild. Nimrod founded a city. "He built Nineveh." And Resen, "the great city." Then Nimrod traveled as far as Iran, where he taught the Persians to worship fire. This doctrine went back to his grandfather Ham, who in Iran was called "living star," Zarathustra. A name passed on to Nimrod.

Although most commentators present Nimrod, simply on the basis of his name, as "he who caused man to revolt against God," others suggest a quite different story. Many claim that it was Nimrod who started building the Tower of Babel. But according to *Targum Yerushalmi* 10:11, Nimrod left Babylon precisely because he was opposed to the project of the Tower. He migrated to Assyria where Yahweh gave him four cities as a reward. In the Jasher, the *Book of the Just*, published in Venice in 1625, it is said that Nimrod went looking for animals to sacrifice on an altar he had built for Yahweh. The link between hunting and sacrifice, which would reemerge three centuries later with Karl Meuli, was affirmed here with peremptory dispatch. Confirming this and more, one *haggadah* claims that Nimrod was the first man to eat meat.

There were four Great Hunters, whose stories would be scratched out, omitted, disguised: Orion, Zagreus, Rudra, Nimrod. Even the Bible, with its special vocation for omission, is obliged to acknowledge that the exploits of Nimrod, about whom it has no intention of telling us anything, were universally celebrated: "This is why it is said: 'Like Nimrod, a mighty hunter before Yahweh.'"

In the Bible, Nimrod is one aside, a few lines long, in a list of names, the descendants of Ham. But look behind that name and an abyss opens up. Something similar was true for Orion, Zagreus, and Rudra. All hunters—and for each there was a further story embedded behind the story actually told. And the story told allowed you to avoid the other story, which mustn't be told.

In the words of James Darmesteter, "the *Book of the Just*, a compilation of Jewish legends surrounding the scriptures, from the creation to the beginning of the Judges, apparently written in the twelfth century, tells how, when Nimrod was building the Tower of Babel, the men at the top of the tower would shoot off arrows against the heavens; they fell back stained with blood and the men said to themselves: 'Oh, we have killed everything there is in the heavens.'" This was Nimrod's secret, never told, always frightening. But he wasn't the only one to do this. The legendary Wu Yi, a king of the Shang dynasty, did something similar, as Se-Ma

Ts'ien recounts in his terse prose: "Emperor Wu Yi was behaving crazily: he made an image with a human form and called it Spirit of the Sky; he played with it (at tiles) and ordered a man to arrange (the tiles) on the Spirit's side; since the Spirit of the Sky lost, the emperor offended and insulted him. He made a bag of skin and filled it with blood; he hung it in the air and shot arrows at it, saying he was shooting them against the sky. Wu Yi went hunting in the land between the stream and the river Wei, there was a tremendous thunderclap, and Wu Yi was struck by lightning and died." Both Nimrod and Wu Yi were hunters. They had to be.

There were two great stories that Abraham would have heard time and again: the flood and the Tower of Babel. But in his city, Ur, there were plenty of other stories going around. The world had been struck by a sudden paralysis on another occasion, when Anzu, the eagle with the lion's head, tall as the gods when he stood up on his two paws, had stolen the Tablet of Destinies from the god Enlil, king of the Anunnaki. Then, too, nature had stopped still, as if nothing could happen or grow ever again. But the Bible has nothing to say about this.

Enlil had built himself a perfect room that no one knew about where he would immerse himself in a "holy water." And he wanted to find a guardian whose strength he could rely on. He chose Anzu, who seemed to have been "born from mountain rocks," with a beak like "a saw" and a body clad in a metal mesh. Enlil thought no one would dare to fight him.

Anzu was the only one who watched Enlil when he undressed to immerse himself naked in the pool in the perfect room. One by one Enlil removed the tokens of his power: his crown, the band around his head, his cloak of divinity, and last of all the Tablet of Destinies, a clay tablet he always had with him, hung on his breast. That was what Anzu wanted more than anything else: "I shall take the gods' Tablet of Destinies for myself / And control the orders for all the gods." While Enlil was naked, immersed in the water, Anzu grabbed the Tablet, "flew off and went into hiding." At once "rites were abandoned . . . radiance faded, silence reigned." Without radiance order was no more, because order cannot sustain itself alone. The gods were bewildered, paralyzed. They tried to think who might be able to find Anzu and kill him. Adad, son of Anu, refused the task. Likewise Gerra, son of Anunitu, and Shara, son of Ishtar.

But there was a more intelligent god, farther away, a god who lives in the subterranean sea, the Apsu: Ea. At moments of periodic cosmic crisis, such as the flood, it was thanks to Ea and Ea alone that the world was brought back to life. Ea knew the Anunnaki couldn't solve the problem themselves, because they were only gods. They would need the help of Mami, "Mistress of All Gods." And Mami chose Ninurta, the "superb beloved," her son, and told him to "fix the hour" for attacking Anzu, deploying all the marvels of metamorphosis. He would have to "seize him by the throat" and have his feathers fly in the wind "as good news."

Everyone thought Anzu would be hiding in the most remote mountain places, and so he was. But when Ninurta found him, "his mantel of radiance covered the mountain." No one had ever encountered such a sight. When Ninurta let fly an arrow, Anzu held tight to the Tablet of Destinies and the arrow flew back to the cane thicket whence it came. The same was true for many more arrows. "Deadly silence came over the battle, and conflict ceased."

Ninurta was daunted, convinced he was beaten. He asked Sharur to go as a messenger to the clairvoyant Ea and report on the situation. Ea listened and made no comment, but offered Ninurta some new advice. He should tire Anzu, then try to clip his wings, left and right. If Anzu let out a groan, turning to his wings, Ninurta should seize the chance to aim an arrow at his heart. So it was. Ninurta won back the Tablet of Destinies, while Anzu's feathers were scattered in the wind.

Enlil, Ninurta's father, immediately sent a messenger to his son, to praise and glorify him, but above all to recover the Tablet of Destinies, which he wanted safely back in his own hands. Ninurta looked at the messenger and asked, "Why have you come here / So aggressively?" He didn't trust him. Then the vizier Birdu began to list all the new glories that would be heaped on Ninurta, the new names he would be invoked by, the new cities and temples where he would be worshipped. We are not told what Ninurta answered.

Terah, Abraham's father, took his family and "had them leave Ur of the Chaldees to go to the land of Canaan." So says Genesis, and leaves it at that. The Chaldees were the most recent arrivals in Ur, which was located at the tip of a narrow triangle whose other points were the towns of Uruk and Eridu. The history of the area began in Eridu, about fifteen kilometers from Ur and believed by the Sumerians to be the oldest city in the world. Genesis calls it Irad, the same name given to one of Cain's grandsons. And the Cainites were the first to build cities.

To leave Ur was to leave a city that was all cities. Of Terah we know only that he served "other gods." Whose names are not mentioned. And would never be mentioned, unlike the gods of Canaan, who were to be constantly evoked and condemned. To abandon Ur meant to flee from the Tablet of Destinies that the Mesopotamian gods kept hanging on their chests as the supreme guarantee of their power. It was this that Yahweh could not under any circumstances accept. There must be no necessity, no reckoning, no measure that excluded his lightning-fast forays on earth—devastating or liberating as they might be. There must be no stories, or rather, there must be just one story: history. That was why, though he couldn't have known it, Terah had to leave Ur. That was why Yahweh ordered his son Abraham to *go away*, when his father stopped in Harran.

X

EZEKIEL SEES

Ezekiel found himself "among the exiles" from Jerusalem, on the banks of the Kebar. They were on the road to Babylon. "The heavens opened." Four beings appeared in a fiery cloud. "They were human in form," each with four wings and metallic calf's hooves. Human hands. But only one had a human head. The others: a lion's head, a bull's, an eagle's. They walked upright, like "coals of fire." Four wheels, their "rims filled with eyes," followed them. Wherever the four beings moved, the wheels went with them. When the four beings came close, Ezekiel "heard the noise of their wings advancing, as of the noise of great waters, as of the voice of Shaddai: the noise of a crowd, like the noise of an armed camp." Where were they going? "They went where the spirit was to go. Nor did they turn as they walked." Between them were glowing coals that moved together with them.

Ezekiel went facedown on the ground. He recognized the glory of Yahweh. And at once heard his voice. It told him to oppose that "rebellious house" that Israel had become. But he need not fear them, even though he was "seated on scorpions." There was but one order Ezekiel must obey: "Open your mouth," Yahweh said, "and eat what I give you." It was a scroll, written on front and back. "Then I opened my mouth and he made me eat this scroll." It tasted of honey.

After the fall of Jerusalem and the first deportation, after being imprisoned, then thrown into a pit and finally rescued by an Ethiopian eunuch, Jeremiah found himself subjected to something he would loathe more than anything else: they dragged him off to Egypt, where a colony of mercenary Jews had settled and were now in the service of the Pharaoh, at Elephantine. For Jeremiah those Jews were utterly despicable. The mere idea of returning to Egypt was bad enough—the only proper reaction to Egypt being to *leave* it once and for all—but these mercenaries had done worse: they had got permission from the Pharaoh to build a temple to Yahweh. This in violation of the rule that there must be only one temple, in Jerusalem. They celebrated holocausts and communion sacrifices and observed the Sabbath and the Passover. But there was also the suspicion—confirmed twenty-six centuries later, when the first Elephantine papyruses came to light—that they tolerated the presence of other gods. And what Jeremiah feared most of all was the looming figure of the Queen of the Heavens, Yahweh's sacred consort. Rightly it seemed, at least if we accept the evidence of one papyrus, which has a Jew swearing by Anath-Yahu, which is to say by the Canaanite goddess Anath, Yahweh's consort.

The Elephantine Jews were the first assimilated Jews, faithful to the customs of their fathers but also open to those of the people around them. In that garrison city, rising from the Nile at the border with Nubia, mixing with Egyptians, Persians, Arameans, and Caspians, these mercenary Jews were living in an early cosmopolitan community, enjoying a life of "happy banality," "with no martyrs, no sages, no philosophical torment." Which is exactly what disgusted Jeremiah. As he saw it, these people were even worse than those who had gone to "praise / and serve foreign gods." Jerusalem had already been destroyed, but the devastation must now strike farther afield: "I will take the remnant of Judah, / those who turned their faces / to enter the land of Egypt, to dwell there, / and they will all perish: / in the land of Egypt they will fall, / they will perish by the sword and from famine, / from the least to the greatest, they will die by sword and famine, / they shall be an execration and a desolation, / a curse and a disgrace. / I will punish those that live in the land of Egypt / as I have punished Jerusalem, / with the sword, famine, and plague." This, according to Jeremiah, was Yahweh's plan.

The Jews of Egypt gave Jeremiah a spirited response, insisting that their practices were neither new nor exotic, but had always been around, even in the Kingdom of Judah: "The word you have spoken to us in the name of Yahweh is not something we intend to listen to, because we mean to carry out everything that has come from our mouths, which is to say: offer incense to the Queen of the Heavens and pour libations, as we always have, we and our fathers, our kings and our princes, in the city of Judah and in the streets of Jerusalem, when we had all the bread we could eat, when we were happy and knew nothing of calamity."

The evil Jeremiah claimed to have uncovered in Egypt had flourished long ago in the kingdom of Judah. "When we were happy," the Jewish mercenaries had the effrontery to claim. At which point Jeremiah felt obliged to resort to the most serious condemnation of all. Yes, Yahweh would let them go on offering incense and libations to the Queen of the Heavens, but there would be consequences: "I have sworn by my great name, / Yahweh has said, / that my name shall no longer be invoked / by the mouth of any man of Judah / who says, Adonai Yahweh lives! / in all the land of Egypt." There would be no *return to Egypt*, ever, nor ever again would Yahweh dwell together with other gods, or be joined together with the Queen of the Heavens. Yahweh's very name must be obliterated, in Egypt.

More than a century and a half passed, until one day, in 410 B.C.E. the priests of Khnum, the god with the ram's head, protector of Elephantine, where the mummies of the sacred animals dwelled in the mausoleum dedicated to him, decided to take revenge on the Jewish mercenaries who lived alongside them. They conspired with the army of nearby Swen, sacked the Temple of Yahweh and reduced it to rubble. They could no longer bear those endless sacrifices of lambs and goats, all that blood flowing so close to the mausoleum of Khnum. Their neighbors, as they saw it, were a band of deicides.

Nebuchadnezzar was not to be seen simply as the enemy who would besiege and devastate Jerusalem. Before all else he was the executor of Yahweh's plan, his instrument on earth. In return for which he was to receive a reward. He conquered Tyre, but "received no payment, for him or his army, for the war he waged against Tyre." So Yahweh decided to offer him something far more attractive: Egypt. A move that was also a pretext for striking yet another blow against that most abominable of places: "Behold, I shall give Nebuchadnezzar, king of Babel, the land of Egypt: he will carry off its riches, seize its spoils, sack the land and use it as a payment for his armies. As a reward for his efforts I shall give him the land of Egypt, because his armies did it on my behalf." So a faithful executor of orders was to be rewarded while at the same time Egypt would once again be punished for its everlasting sins and for having provoked anew in the house of Israel "the crime that consists in turning toward it." That Nebuchadnezzar might be allowed to plunder Egypt as a reward for having destroyed Jerusalem was an adroit piece of foreign policy. It was thanks to him, after all, that the children of Israel had been thrown out of Jerusalem, as Yahweh wished.

Captivity in Babylon was always tied to the destruction of Egypt. To wrest the children of Israel from Jerusalem was to take them back to earlier times, when they did not have a land of their own. And to defeat Egypt meant to annihilate the power that gathered in itself all that was incompatible with Israel. Thus at last, thanks to the stratagem of two ferocious wars, everything was taken back to the point of departure. The history of Israel could start over. Every diaspora was a return to the origins.

It wasn't only Egypt's power that was disturbing. Even more grievous was its beauty. And, even more grievous than that, the suspicion that Egypt, with its obsessive, meticulous rites, had found a way of eluding death. All this would have to be punished and destroyed. No one said it with greater lyrical flourish than Ezekiel: "Who shall I compare you to in your greatness?" To a cedar of Lebanon that towers over every other tree, its topmost leaves in the clouds: "Amid its branches nested / all the birds of the sky; / under its boughs / all the beasts of the field gave birth. /

In its shade dwelled numerous nations." So what was the problem? It was too beautiful. "No tree in God's garden / could match it for beauty." So much so that "all the trees of Eden envied it / which are in God's garden." Far more than the Promised Land, supposedly flowing with milk and honey, Egypt was truly paradisiacal. Which was simply too much. Precisely because "its topmost leaves have climbed into the clouds and its heart has swollen with its height," Yahweh delivered Egypt "into the hands of the ruler of nations"—meaning Nebuchadnezzar—who "will treat it viciously." The great tree was to crash down to earth. And now "among its splinters dwell / all the birds of the sky / and among its branches / all the beasts of the field are to be found." Even after it had fallen, living creatures continued to find refuge there, as if among ruins.

Then it became clear why the cedar couldn't go on as it was: "Because all are given up to death / to the region of the Underworld, / in the midst of the children of men / toward those who go down in the pit." Obviously someone must have imagined that the cedar might last *forever*. And that was unacceptable.

When the cedar was cut down, Yahweh added, "I caused people to mourn; I filled in the pit over it," while the nations shivered, hearing the crash of its fall. All the Egyptians who had lived in the shade of the cedar came out one by one and were swallowed up in Sheol, in the region of the Underworld. And there, finally, even what remained of the tree disappeared. In that moment all the trees already lying there since the beginning of time, "all those who had drunk water, were consoled," because at last they had their sovereign beside them. "Who could compare with you, in your glory and greatness, from among the trees of Eden? And yet you had to go down with the trees of Eden into the region of the Underworld; lying among the uncircumcised, with those slain by the sword."

For years the house of Israel had been tormented by certain secret thoughts. Especially unsettling was the suspicion that the

Egyptians too might be *chosen*—or at least might think of themselves as such. After all, they, too, were circumcised. Finally, Ezekiel said it, with his usual furious sarcasm, imagining the descent of Egypt into Sheol, after the devastation inflicted by Nebuchadnezzar.

"Are you then more fair than the others?" It was with these mocking words that the *gibborim*, the "heroes" of the distant past, supposedly greeted Egypt in the kingdom of the dead. They had gone down into Sheol "with all their battle gear; they put their swords under their heads and laid their shields on their bones, for the terror of the heroes had reigned over the land of the living." Now Egypt, with its Pharaoh, would be welcomed among those armour-clad bones. Egypt, too, Ezekiel insisted, had "spread terror over the land of the living." But it was all over now. They would be shut up in Sheol, mixed up with the "princes of the North and all the Sidonites." No longer could they enjoy the illusion of being *favorites*. Death embraced all, aloof and impartial.

Moses had clashed with the Pharaoh as the spokesman of an enslaved people facing the leader of an ancient kingdom. At the same time Yahweh was fighting it out with Raab, Prince of the Waters, Dragon of the Waters, who had always been his first enemy and who always came back to strike again. All human attempts were destined to fail, said Isaiah, unless upheld by "Yahweh's arm." The first—perhaps only—function of men was to reawaken divine strength: "Awake, awake, clothe yourself in strength, arm of Yahweh, / awake, as in the days past, of generations gone by! / Was it not you who cut Raab to pieces, / who speared the dragon? / Was it not you that dried out the sea, / the waters of the great deep, / who transformed the depths of the sea into a road / so that those who had been redeemed might pass there?" What had happened in Egypt would go on happening, in the same land of Egypt, but elsewhere as well, and forever.

Hatred for Egypt derived from hatred for the waters. Egypt was "a great dragon crouching / in the midst of its rivers, / saying: 'These rivers are mine, / it was me who made them.'" But one day, said Ezekiel, "I will put hooks in your jaws / and I will have the fish of your rivers stick to your scales." Egypt will be forcibly dragged out of its life-giving waters and left for dead as a carcass in the desert, waiting to end up "as a meal / for the wild animals and the birds of the sky."

More than for its idol worship, or its endless gods, or its powerful magic, which after all was more or less endemic at this point, it was Egypt's waters that had brought upon it an inexhaustible hatred: "Because he said, 'The Nile is mine, it was me who made it,' because of this, behold I am against you and against your rivers." To fight Egypt was not like fighting any other kingdom, teeming with idols and given over to wickedness. Egypt was something more remote. In a class of its own. To fight Egypt meant first and foremost to *subdue the waters.*

Yahweh, a god with no family, established over time two family relations with the children of Israel. First of all Israel was his firstborn, as Moses was told to announce to Pharaoh. And Israel was also Yahweh's bride, as would emerge later, with the prophets. But a willfully adulterous bride. "By the roadside you sat waiting for them / like an Arab in the desert," said Jeremiah. While storm clouds gathered over Israel and the empires of the world queued up to grab its territories, while a stream of prisoners flowed from Jerusalem to Babylon, for years and years Hosea, Ezekiel, and Jeremiah went on and on repeating that it hardly mattered which evil kingdom came to devastate Israel, these armies were no more than the chance executors of a punishment Israel had brought upon itself, prostrating itself before "filthy idols"—thus Ezekiel in particular described any and every simulacrum of other deities—and offering its body to countless lovers, Assyrians or Egyptians, foreigners always. On the heights, in the pleasant shade of the terebinth trees, Israel went on regardless, celebrating without cease the rites of idol worship and prostitution.

As Jeremiah saw it, idol worship was like a "wild she-ass of the desert" that "sniffs the wind in the heat of her desire," seeking a mate. And finding him among foreigners: "I love foreigners / and go after them." Yahweh wondered, "Why do my people say, / We are wanderers, / we will no longer come to you?" And he asked another question: "You who prostituted yourself to so many lovers, / could you come back to me," like a bride already repudiated? Deuteronomy forbade it. Then one need only raise one's eyes to the heights: "On which of these hills / have you not been ravished?" It was there that Israel "prostituted herself / under every green tree." There "she committed adultery with stone and wood." How could the lost bride be found again, if not by canceling out the past and going back to the beginning?

One day Yahweh spoke to Ezekiel to tell him the story of Jerusalem as if it were the story of a woman. He presented her as the daughter of an Amorite and a Hittite—hence not one belonging entirely to the house of Israel. At birth they had not wrapped her in swaddling clothes and rubbed her with salt. On the contrary, they had "exposed her to the earth of the land." Yahweh saw her, passing by, smeared in her blood. He gathered her up and told her "in the midst of her blood: 'Live! Grow!'"

Telling his story, Yahweh spoke to Jerusalem as if she were there before him: "You have grown and are tall, you have entered your puberty, your breasts have grown firm and your hair has thickened, but you were naked and exposed. I passed by and saw you were of an age for love, spread a fold of my garment over you, I covered your nakedness, I swore an oath, made a covenant with you, says the Lord Yahweh, and you were mine. I washed you with water, I cleaned your blood and anointed you with oil. I dressed you again with embroidered cloth, put dolphin skin shoes on your feet, wrapped you in fine linen and covered you with silk. I bedecked you with jewels, put bracelets on your wrists and a necklace around your neck. I put a ring in your nose, earrings in your ears, and a splendid diadem on your head. I clothed you in gold and silver; your garment was fine linen, silk, embroidered cloth; you ate fine flour, honey, and oil, you grew most beautiful and worthy to rule. News of your beauty spread among the nations, because it was perfect, thanks to the splendor I covered you with."

And what happened then? "You trusted in your beauty and, relying on your fame, you prostituted yourself and gave yourself to every passing stranger, and became his." Those sumptuous clothes were used to decorate the heights, because those were the places the woman called Jerusalem liked best. Everything was used for depravation: "You made yourself statues of men and prostituted yourself with them." All that Yahweh had given her now became a gift to offer to her idols. Even her children—"you offered them up, laid them bare to your lovers." And while this was happening, "you did not remember the days of your youth, when you were naked and exposed: when you crawled in your blood."

Nor were the betrayals limited to the immediate vicinity: "you prostituted yourself with the sons of Egypt, with their big members, whoring more and more to vex me." Egypt, for Yahweh, was always the pinnacle of abomination. But the young woman, insatiable as she was beautiful, wouldn't stop. After Egypt, she chose to whore with "the sons of Assur," but they couldn't satisfy her. So she went on and whored "in a land of merchants, in Chaldea," but wasn't sated there either. She was a "perfect whore," but unlike a common prostitute, instead of receiving gifts, she offered them to all her lovers: "You bribed them to come to you from all around and whored with them."

How to punish her? Yahweh said: "Since you have shown off your sex and your nakedness has been unveiled," the many lovers would be gathered together and "they will strip you of your clothes, seize the things that made you splendid, and leave you naked and vulnerable. They will stir up a mob against you, stone you, and cut you up with their swords."

At that point, Yahweh added, "my jealousy will turn away from you, I will be calm, and no longer grow vexed." All the same he would go on recalling Jerusalem's crimes, comparing them with those of Sodom and Samaria and concluding that Jerusalem's were far worse. Jerusalem would be forced to suffer and remember.

Then comes a reversal nothing has prepared us for. Yahweh said, "But I shall remember my covenant with you in the days of your youth and I shall establish an everlasting covenant in your favor." Why? "Then you will know that I am Yahweh, so you may remember, so you may feel shame, so you may fall silent, in your disgrace, when I shall pardon you for everything you have done." It was a provisional seal on the enthralling story of love and punishment between Yahweh and Jerusalem.

Hegel wrote that the whole of human history was set in motion by the *struggle for recognition*, on which basis the dialectic between servant and master emerged. But that struggle was preceded by another, between Yahweh and his people. And the issue was always recognition. The one and omnipresent God had to struggle to have a tiny community, that he himself had singled out, recognize him for what he was. The struggle proceeded in a back-and-forth that gives the biblical account its rhythm. And like the war between servant and master it was a struggle to the death. Man was a servant who had been granted an illusory sovereignty, allowing him to behave as if he were an independent entity. This was unacceptable to Yahweh. The radical prophet Ezekiel made this clear to the children of Israel: "And you shall know that I am Yahweh when their corpses are strewn among their filthy idols, around their altars, on all the heights, all the mountaintops, under every green tree and every leafy oak, where they offered fragrant odors to all their filthy idols." Only then "you shall know that I am Yahweh," a formula Ezekiel repeats obsessively, and adds, "You shall know that I am Yahweh who smiteth."

It was 591 B.C.E., the sixth year after the deportation. Ezekiel was sitting in his house in exile, with "the elders of Judah sitting before him." At a certain point Ezekiel said, "the hand of the Lord Yahweh fell upon me." He had the likeness of a sudden flame: "From the waist down, fire; from the waist up, a glow like shiny metal." From out of the glow came a hand that took Ezekiel by a lock of his hair. The elders saw him lifted off the ground.

Ezekiel found himself back in Jerusalem with the glory of the god of Israel before him. It wasn't a new vision. More like a continuation of the one he had had on the banks of the Kebar when he found himself in the middle of the captives being taken into exile and "the sky opened." A voice guided him. At the door of the Temple there was the statue of a winged bull, as in Babylon. Then the voice ordered Ezekiel to make a hole in the wall of the temple courtyard. Ezekiel looked through the hole and saw "images of every kind of reptile and horrible beast and all the filthy idols of the house of Israel drawn on the wall, all around." There were many elders, too, with censers in their hands. Beyond them, near the door on the north side of the Temple, you could see women weeping for Tammuz. The voice went on guiding Ezekiel. Who now saw this: "At the entrance to the Temple of Yahweh, between the porch and the altar, there were about twenty-five men, their backs to the Temple, faces to the east. They were bowing toward the east, toward the sun."

Then the destruction began. Six men appeared, each with a "weapon of slaughter." One was dressed in linen and held a scribe's writing kit attached to his belt. Yahweh's voice spoke to this man, telling him to mark a cross on the foreheads of the "men who groan and wail for all the abominations committed there." To the other five men the voice said, "Old people, young men and young women, women and children, kill them till they are exterminated, but do not touch any who have the cross." The five began by killing "the elders who were in front of the House." Then they went into the city. While they were about the massacre, Ezekiel was left alone and fell to the ground, asking Yahweh if he meant "to wipe out all the rest of Israel, unleashing his fury against Jerusalem." Soon afterward the man dressed in linen with the writing kit at his belt came back and said, "I have done as you ordered." Then Ezekiel told him to go between the wheels of the Cherubim and collect the glowing coals. Which he must scatter over the city.

"The glory of Yahweh moved from the threshold of the House and stood over the Cherubim," whose wings were teeming with eyes. Each had four faces, four wings, and on the wings the "shapes of human hands." Even the wheels beneath the Cherubim were full of eyes. The wings of the Cherubim made a roar "like the voice of Shaddai, when he speaks." Ezekiel looked up and saw the Cherubim stretching their wings and leaving the earth, followed by their wheels. He remarked, "As for the shapes of their faces: they were the faces I had seen on the banks of the Kebar." Sometime later he told "those in captivity all the things that Yahweh had shown me."

Deportation to Babylon was devised because the "house of Israel" had become a "house of rebellion," which must be subdued with the toughest measures. Thus Yahweh needed a prophet with a forehead "as hard as diamond, harder than stone." Even his modus operandi would be quite unusual: an acting-out first, words later.

So Ezekiel changed himself into a gloomy child at play: he picked up a brick and scratched a shape on it, which was supposed to be Jerusalem. Then he put his brick under siege, digging a furrow to represent the trenches of the besieging army. Then Yahweh told Ezekiel, "Get an iron pan; place it like an iron wall between yourself and the town, then turn your face that way and the city will be besieged and you will besiege it." While Ezekiel was busy with this pantomime, those watching him were supposed to understand.

But there was more: Ezekiel was now to lie down on his left side and take upon himself the sins of Israel, for as many days as the years of those sins had been. One hundred and ninety. Then Ezekiel must turn on his right side and stay there for another forty days. Only then, Yahweh said, "will you turn your face and your bare arm to the siege of Jerusalem and prophesy against her." To spare any mistakes, Yahweh tied Ezekiel down with ropes so that, he said, "you won't be able to turn from one side to the other until you have completed your days of stillness." But how was Ezekiel to live in the meantime? Eating a bread of wheat and barley, beans and lentils, and measuring out a small amount of water to drink each day: "You will eat a barley bread; you will bake it on mounds of human excrement, in the sight of the people." This to show "how the children of Israel will eat their unclean bread among the nations where I will banish them." Ezekiel balked at this. He had never allowed anything unclean to pass his lips, he said, never polluted himself. Yahweh was understanding and said, "I'll grant you ox manure instead of human excrement, so you can bake your bread on that." In any event the house of Israel would not have enough bread and water, but would all be "oppressed and rot in their guilt."

When he wasn't having visions, Ezekiel spent long periods in obstinate silence. Once for seven days. And again throughout the siege of Jerusalem until the city fell. The world around must be rejected, totally, in every detail. The white heat of the words that then erupted from his mouth were in proportion to the silence that preceded them and with which they alternated.

Yahweh warned Ezekiel that something sudden and terrible was about to happen to him. "Son of man, I am about to take away the delight of your eyes, but you will not complain, nor weep, and no tears shall come to your eyes. Sigh and keep silent! Do not wear mourning; put on your turban and put your sandals on your feet, do not cover your mustache, and do not eat the bread that people bring you." Then the voice changed. It became Ezekiel's voice and said, "I spoke to the people in the morning and my wife died in the evening." Beginning next morning, Ezekiel carried out Yahweh's prescriptions to the letter: he did none of the things custom demanded of the bereaved, forbade himself to weep or to complain. Above all he didn't speak. But why? Once again, in order to be "a premonition" for anyone who might understand. Even at the cost of seeing his own life devastated, he must show, as in a pantomime, what would happen to everyone all too soon, when Jerusalem was destroyed.

This, too, was part of a prophet's job. And by no means the easiest. It meant that from one moment to the next he must turn himself into the most insignificant of actors who crosses the stage performing a few prescribed gestures. Then disappears. And once offstage he would find himself in a landscape of ruins.

"Thus said Yahweh" was a formula used by the prophets and false prophets alike, and the false prophetesses: "They say, 'thus said Yahweh,' when Yahweh hasn't sent them; and they expect that he confirm their word." Like "foxes among the ruins," they misled the people, "saying 'Peace!' when there is not peace." They were Ezekiel's greatest torment. And Yahweh had told him, "Prophesy against the prophets of Israel who prophesy." But how to guarantee that the real prophet be recognized, and through him Yahweh?

Then Ezekiel decided not to speak anymore, only *show*. His mime would signal what very soon would be the fate of all. It was Yahweh who gave him the idea: "As for you, son of man, pack your bags for exile and set out, in the daylight, before their eyes; from the place where you are, set out in exile toward another place, before their eyes; perhaps they will see that they are a rebellious house. Take your bags, bags as if for exile, in the daytime, before their eyes, and go out in the evening, before their eyes, as if leaving for exile. Before their eyes you will break through the wall and go out from there. Before their eyes you will hoist your bag on your back and go out in the dark, you will cover your face, you will not look at the land, because I have made you a portent for the house of Israel." Ezekiel obeyed his orders to the letter. "I went out into the darkness, before their eyes, my bag on my back." The people of Jerusalem saw him and said, "What are you doing." Nothing that you won't be doing soon enough, Ezekiel told them. And so it was, not long afterward. But many had said, "This vision refers to days far hence, he is prophesying for times far in the future." Ezekiel demurred: "Adonai Yahweh spoke thus: There will be no more delay as far as my words are concerned." The only true prophets would be prophets of the present. They would show what was already happening.

The house of Israel didn't need a commander, but a lookout: "If I bring the sword against a country, the people of the country choose a man to be their lookout. He sees the sword coming against the people, sounds a ram's horn and warns them." Once again Ezekiel was saying something that had previously been left implicit, or suppressed. For all it boasted of its military achievements, the house of Israel hardly distinguished itself for its conquests, but rather because it chose someone *who was able to see evil*. People supposed that evil lay at the origin of things, and that the noblest of all tasks was to see it in time and sound the horn.

The prophet was nothing more, nothing less, than a kind of lookout. Yahweh said to Ezekiel, "As for you, son of man, I have set you as a lookout for the house of Israel. You will hear my word from my mouth and you will warn them for me." But a lookout could at least point to the dust clouds the enemy was kicking up as he advanced. The prophet had nothing but words, and people took him for "a singer of love songs, blessed with a good voice, playing nice music: they listen to what you say, but do not act accordingly." So what to do? Wait for "this to happen." What matters is the *this*—and there is always a *this*: "And look, this is happening!" Only then "will they know that there was a prophet among them." But by then the *this* will already be upon them. Compared with the lookout, of whom he is a less effective version, the prophet is condemned to speaking too soon and in such a way that the *this* is recognized too late.

If in the ancient world the Jews were accused of having instituted a "life hostile to humankind"—Hecataeus was already saying as much—many of the children of Israel felt the same way about their prophets. These men shared a certain spitefulness, spoke with great vehemence, and as a matter of principle deployed only two registers: condemnation and consolation, vast deserts of condemnation, that is, relieved by rare oases of inconceivable sweetness. There was no question of modulation. Those who listened to them, on the other hand, shifted constantly from one register to another, taking care, whether by instinct or design, to avoid the extremes.

The prophets had something of the priest and something of the king. Yet were neither priest nor king. This was their weakness. They launched into exhortations and got themselves killed. Looking back over the entire history of Israel from Abraham on, Ezra sums up the fate reserved for the prophets thus: "The people killed the prophets who urged them to go back to you."

Actually, the Bible describes the violent death of only one prophet, Zachariah, who was stoned in the Temple. But the apocryphal *Vitae prophetarum* claims that six prophets died violent deaths. So we must add Amos, clubbed to death; Micah, tossed in a pit; Isaiah, sawn in half; Jeremiah, stoned; and Ezekiel, killed by men of the tribes of Dan and Gad.

All the writings of the prophets, from Isaiah to Zachariah, followed the same trajectory. No variants were allowed. Mostly it was condemnation and consequent punishment, often with scrupulously detailed lists of who would be struck down, where, and how. This took up the greater part of the texts. Then, at the end the reversal, the *restauratio messianica* and a celebration of the new, whole life—salvation. Whether a text was written in the eighth century B.C.E. or the sixth made no difference, and this because, as Édouard Dhorme observed, "prophecy could not close on a tragic vision." Still, there were different levels: every catastrophe was at once a memory and an announcement of future catastrophe. Until one arrived at "the day of Yahweh," when the sacrificial victim would be the entire world. The Vulgate is terse, remarking that on that day *"praeparavit Dominus hostiam."* At the end of the ceremony there would be nothing left but desert, without Noah and his Ark this time.

Yet even this, in Zephaniah, is followed by a *restauratio*: "those who will remain of Israel"—the irrepressible *remnant*. But hadn't they perished too, along with "all the inhabitants of the earth"? Not at all, the *remnant* survived, and would no longer perpetrate injustices or propagate falsehoods. "They shall graze and lie down and none will dismay them." That will be the time, Yahweh announced, when "I will rescue the lame sheep / and lead home the scattered" in a land at once happy and, at this point, empty.

When he moved away from extremes, Ezekiel was capable of a sobriety no prophet before him had achieved. None of his predecessors had said with such clarity that the children need not pay for the sins of their fathers, nor their fathers for those of their children: "It will be the one who sins that dies. The son shall not be responsible for the sin of the father and the father shall not be responsible for the sin of the son. The justice of the just will come down on the sinner himself and the wickedness of the wicked will fall on the wicked man himself." This was nothing less than the basis of every *ius*. Without that separation of sins there could be no law.

This was a huge step and undermined the conviction that Adam's sin must have repercussions for everyone born after him. What we have then is two forms of accountancy, one juridical, the other theological. The principle Ezekiel announces doesn't cancel out the other, but makes communal life possible, since community can flourish only when upheld by the *ius*. At the same time one had to be careful not to deny theological wisdom, since, together with the transmission of sin, that wisdom implied the transmission of goodness. If it is true that the sins of the fathers are visited on the children generation after generation—and this was already, Joseph de Maistre would write, an "inconceivable mystery"—it was also true, thanks to an even more inconceivable mystery, that "often what was done with ill intent, by operation of some spiritual mechanics, turns out for the good." And this time the reflection is Baudelaire's. Proceeding even farther along the road of "inconceivable mystery," one arrived at the revelation of "the reversibility of the suffering of the innocent in favour of the guilty." Without that obscure "reversibility" the Christ figure would not have been able to do as he did, in the sense foreshadowed in the Deutero-Isaiah: "My righteous servant will justify the multitudes, / and it is he who will take on their iniquities."

Those who heard Ezekiel were right when they said, "Yahweh's way is not balanced!" In the Vulgate: *Non est aequa via Domini!* (an even more severe formulation, since *aequitas* is superior to *iustitia*). They had heard any number of times how Yahweh would punish this or that crime for generations and generations, down to the grandchildren of the grandchildren, and now this toughest of prophets, Ezekiel, was claiming that guilt was entirely circumscribed in the person who committed the crime. And likewise, as a consequence, the punishment. Yet the very same Ezekiel went around promising ruin for everyone, to the point of extermination almost, for crimes that only some, or perhaps many, but certainly not all had committed. How could these two equally electrifying assertions coexist? There was no answer, if not the Old Testament taken as a whole, and even then, for some, only if read together with its sequel, the New Testament.

Ezekiel was the only prophet to attribute to Yahweh words from which we can infer that, at a certain point in history, Yahweh himself gave Israel laws that were *unjust*. The formulation in question amounted to the exact opposite of one that Yahweh had used shortly before: "So I brought them out of the land of Egypt and led them into the desert. I gave them my statutes and showed them my laws that a man may live by if he follows them." But Israel had rebelled. And Yahweh had been on the point of destroying them. "But my eye had pity for them, so that I did not destroy them; I did not make an end of them in the desert." Soon afterward, he had gone back to saying, "Behave according to my statutes, observe my laws and follow them." But Israel again rebelled.

This time Yahweh made a decision not corroborated by any other text: "And I, for my part, gave them statutes that were not good and laws they could not live by." Which wasn't all: Yahweh specified which of the new statutes were "not good": "I caused them to be polluted with their offerings, which consisted in passing [through the fire] every creature that opens the womb." This was a way of referring to the sacrifices of the peoples of Canaan, including, once again, the sacrifice of the firstborn. And before anyone could ask for an explanation, Yahweh went on: "The aim was to fill them with horror, so that they would know that I am Yahweh." It was enough to leave one dumbstruck. Yahweh, then, was capable of proposing horrifying statutes, for the sole purpose of once again shaking up Israel, now in exile. And then, Yahweh said, "I will bring you out of the places where you are in the midst of other peoples and I will gather you from all the countries where you have been scattered, with a strong hand, an outstretched arm, and outpourings of rage. I will lead you into the desert of other peoples and there I will mete out justice to you, face-to-face." What had happened showed how indirect and inscrutable Yahweh's ways could be. And now Ezekiel was going to be so bold as to offer an astounding example.

One day Ezekiel found himself in the midst of a valley thickly strewn with bones. Dry, white bones, stripped of flesh. Yahweh asked Ezekiel, "Can these bones live?" A scandalous question, because it was well known that once down in Sheol the dead assumed a larval, bloodless, fleshless existence. But Ezekiel did not claim to know. He said, "Adonai Yahweh! You know that." Then Yahweh told Ezekiel to prophesy to the bones and what to prophesy. He did not say that bones in general could one day live again. He just pointed to the bones of these dead, or rather these people "killed." Ezekiel obeyed and "prophesied as he had been in-structed."

"There was a noise and then a tumult." The bones came close and clattered together. There were so many, they made a din. And on the bones grew flesh and nerves. In the end, when an invisible breath entered their reassembled bodies, "they got to their feet, a very great army."

This wasn't an announcement of what would happen one day to men in general, the dead scattered across the valleys of the world. It was the announcement of what would happen to the house of Israel. But something more was required. Before the ranks of men who had taken the place of the bones, Ezekiel was to perform a single, appar-ently incomprehensible act. Yahweh told him to take a small piece of wood and write on it, "Judah and the children of Israel joined to him." Then he should take another piece of wood and write, "Joseph and all the house of Israel that is joined to him." At this point, in the general silence, Ezekiel should take the two pieces of wood and try to line up their edges, so that they seemed a single piece, held tight in his hands. No one grasped what was going on—the birth of the symbol. But when they asked him to explain, Ezekiel, like all the prophets, chose a narrower perspective. He said these two small pieces of wood were reuniting the two kingdoms of Israel in one: "I will make them one people in the land, on the mountains of Israel, and a single king shall be king of all."

"When Israel was a boy, I loved him." Yahweh was speaking, in Hosea, like a rejected admirer. The rivals who stole Israel from Yahweh had but one aim: to sacrifice to the Baals, burn incense before idols. So Yahweh was forced to reveal that he had loved the children of Israel even before that, when they were not yet even boys but toddlers. "It was I taught Ephraim to walk, / leading them by the arm, / but they did not know I was taking care of them. / With human strings I held them up, / with ties of love." It was a bold confession on Yahweh's part: the recognition that the elect may well not even know they are elect. Yahweh had taught them to walk, like a loving wet nurse, but perhaps the memory of those moments had been lost to infant amnesia. Election wasn't only a risk for the elect, but for Yahweh, who had chosen. A sort of haze might leave Israel's youngsters at the mercy of those others, the new arrivals, who would lure them away. And Yahweh ended up in the situation of the jilted lover: "My heart is turned upside down, / and my guts boiled within me."

It was rare for Yahweh to show his feelings so openly. But how could one speak of physiology with regard to Yahweh? There is a sort of twitch in the text here, as if Yahweh felt obliged to drop his all-too-human mask. "I will not give vent to the heat of my anger, / I will not destroy Ephraim again, / because I am God and not a man, / the holy inside you / and I do not wish to devastate"—the city, that is. *Und will nicht kommen zu verheeren*, reads Luther's magnificent version—"And I shall not come to devastate." On the one hand, then, the need for human drama, in all its registers and backs-and-forth, physical and psychic, in which Yahweh was willing to play a part; on the other, an unbridgeable distance: "because I am God and not a man," and then—the most mysterious point of all—"the holy inside you," *hágios* in the Septuagint. So inside anyone speaking to Yahweh there was an area that was "holy" and incompatible with all other human reactions. Only thanks to that *hágios* would Yahweh say, "I shall not come to devastate."

There were two kingdoms, Samaria and Jerusalem. There were two parties, the Egyptian and the Assyrian. And if one was not to be crushed there was no choice but to ally oneself either with Egypt or with Assyria. Ezekiel loved to speak in parables, as Jesus one day would. Many supposed that those parables referred to a distant future, and hence could safely be ignored. But for the most part they referred to the feverish present, as in the case of the parable of the two depraved sisters.

There were, Ezekiel began, two sisters, Oholah and Oholibah. Oholah was Samaria, Oholibah was Jerusalem. It all began in Egypt—but where else could it have begun? Even in their teens the two sisters were already fornicating in Egypt, "*in adolescen-tia sua fornicatae sunt.*" "Their breasts were squeezed and their young nipples pinched." And with regard to the sisters, Yahweh added, "They were mine and bore me sons and daughters" (in the Vulgate: *Et habuieas, et peperunt filios et filias*; in Luther: "I took them as wives and they bore me sons and daughters"). Then Oholah began to hanker after Assyrians: those warriors "dressed in hyacinth," *vestitos hyacintho*, governors and prefects, solemn and imposing on their primped-up horses, all "desirable young men," *iuvenes cupidinis*, she lost her head for them. Oholah forni-cated with the finest sons of Assyria. But she didn't forget Egypt. She had fond memories of those first lovers. And the Assyrians caught her in flagrante, dragged off her children, and put her to the sword. She became "a byword among women: she had been punished."

Oholibah saw all this and decided to outdo her sister. Even more than Oholah she was *insanivit libidine*, "crazed with lust." Initially, though, she just followed in Oholah's footsteps. She, too, was attracted to the Assyrians, but was even more excited when she saw them painted in vermilion on the walls of Babylon, "thighs tightly sashed, heads turbaned." She couldn't help herself. "As soon as she set eyes on them she craved for them and sent messengers to Chaldea. And the Babylonians came to her, to the bed of love [*cubile mamarum*, "bed of tits," in the Vulgate], and they defiled her with their whoring, and when she was defiled her soul drew away from them."

"*Saturata est anima ejus ab illis*," says the Vulgate: Oholibah re-alized she'd had enough of the Assyrians. She went on fornicating with them, but meantime "remembered the days of her youth when she fornicated in the land of Egypt. She was hot for sex with men who had flesh like the flesh of donkeys and a member like the mem-bers of horses." She remembered the men who had first caressed her breasts. Egypt always had a quality that was not only more ancient but also more intense and enticing than anywhere else.

Then Yahweh decided to bring together Oholibah's old lovers

and set them against her: "Look, now I will stir up against you the lovers from whom you turned your heart away, I will have them come against you from all over, the sons of Babylon, all the Chaldeans, Pekod, Shoa, and Koa, and with them all the sons of the Assyrians, all attractive young men, governors and prefects, captains and nobles, all on horseback." This "coalition of peoples" would lay siege against Oholibah. And in the end would "tear off your ears and nose and put the rest to the sword." She could count on it: "No longer will you lift your eyes to them and no more will you remember Egypt." Such was Yahweh's ploy: the depraved men would cut to pieces the depraved woman who had grown tired of them. And Yahweh would hand Oholibah her sister's cup, a "wide and deep cup," a cup of "devastation and dismay," and she must drink it to the dregs. Then Oholibah would smash it to pieces and gnaw on the shards.

Around Oholibah's sumptuous bed "the din of a crowd" was heard. Men she didn't know were plundering her perfumes and jewels. They kept entering and leaving the room. They came "from every part of the desert, put bracelets on their wrists and sparkling crowns on their heads." It still wasn't enough: Yahweh demanded that the two depraved sisters submit to the judgment of "righteous men." An assembly was called. And they decided to stone them and cut them to pieces with the sword. "So you will know that I am Adonai Yahweh."

In the parable of Oholah and Oholibah, Yahweh presented himself as a man who marries two sisters—which went against one of the precepts of Leviticus—only to be quickly abandoned by both, each actually vying with the other to betray him more. Neither sister has so much as an instant of regret, neither tries to turn back. Even as adolescents they ignore their husband. Yet only when Oholah had already been punished and Oholibah had out-done her in depravation did Yahweh say, "I will move my jealousy against you and they shall treat you with fury." Implying that thus far, despite their antics, he had still been thinking of the sisters as *his*, and as the mothers of his children. Who were now to be wiped out together with them: "May they kill their sons and their daughters, and may their houses be consumed with fire."

Oholah means "His tent"; *Oholibah*, "My tent is in her." Names from nomadic tribal life. The Tent of Meeting was the place where Yahweh chose to show himself to Moses: "It is there that I shall meet you and speak with you." Oholah and Oholibah contained within themselves the presence of Yahweh.

But Ezekiel wasn't the only one to tell the tale of Yahweh and his faithless brides, though he is the most brutal when it comes to detail. Hosea had spoken of it too. The premise was that the children of Israel were children of Yahweh and had betrayed him, as one reads in the opening lines of Isaiah: "I brought up children, raised them / and they were unfaithful to me."

And who was the mother of those children? In Hosea, Yahweh chose to deny that Oholah and Oholibah were his wives: "Accuse your mother, accuse her, / (because she is not my wife / and I am not her man)." But this repudiated mother had behaved very much as Ezekiel described. She, too, had been on the lookout for lovers, though Yahweh put thornbushes in her path to confuse her: "She will go after her lovers / and not reach them, / see them and not find them. / Then she will say: / I must go away and go back to my first man, / because I was better off then than now!" Yahweh was her "first man," soon abandoned, to whom, however, she went back, disappointed with her affairs. But this "first man" was hardly accommodating: "I will put an end to all her merriment, / her parties for the new moon, her Sabbaths / and all her ceremonies." After which there would be punishment: "I will devastate her vines and her fig trees, / of which she used to say, 'They are mine, a present / from my lovers!' / I will turn them into a forest / and the wild beasts will devour them." But once having punished her, this "first man" would take her into the desert to seduce her all over again, as if nothing had happened. The desert was the only proper place for Yahweh and his beloved to start seeing each other again. "That day it will so happen, / says Yahweh, / that she will call me, 'My man,' / and you will no longer call me, 'My *baal.*'" And this because the word *baal*, "husband," had become forever loathsome, pronounced as it was exactly like the name of the god Baal, who would no longer ensnare the bride. Everything started anew and Yahweh said, "And I will betroth me to you forever . . . And I will betroth me to you in faithfulness, / so that you may know Yahweh."

The return to Jerusalem from captivity in Babylon was recorded in great detail. Not only the members of the various families, but the number of horses, camels, asses, servants, and even singers, male and female. "Those who looked for the records of their family lineage and couldn't find them were excluded from the priesthood." Before being a territory, Israel was a progeny, a past you could reconstruct, step by step. As soon as they were back in Jerusalem "they rebuilt the altar on its base," and "there they offered holocausts to Yahweh, morning holocausts and evening holocausts."

Then they began rebuild the Temple. "When the builders laid the foundations of the Temple of Yahweh, the priests were present, in their ceremonial vestments, with trumpets, and the Levites, sons of Asaph, with cymbals." A crowd stood around. "And many of the priests, the Levites and the older heads of the households, who had seen the first House, wept and groaned while they watched the men laying the foundations of this house. And others raised cries of joy and happiness, and the people couldn't make out the difference between the noise of cries of joy and happiness and the noise of the laments and the weeping."

Ezra, priest and scribe, arrived in Jerusalem from Babylon decades after the return of the children of Israel, when the Temple had already been rebuilt. He led a caravan and brought with him a letter from King Artaxerxes that granted those Jews who had remained in his kingdom the right to return to Jerusalem with "all the gold and silver that you will find in the province of Babylon and the voluntary offerings that the people and the priests bring for the House of their God in Jerusalem."

It was a long walk, but Ezra did not want to ask for help: "I felt ashamed to ask the king for soldiers or horsemen to protect us against our enemies during the journey; in fact we said to the king: the hand of God is upon all those who seek him, for the good, but his strength and wrath are with those who turn away from him."

At last they reached Jerusalem and rested for three days. On the fourth day they began to weigh "the gold and silver and the objects in the House of our God . . . All counted and weighed and the total weight written down." Then they offered holocausts: twelve bulls, ninety-seven lambs, twelve goats. Still there was no respite. As soon as the ceremonies were over, the elders came to Ezra to tell him what had happened shortly after the return from captivity: "The people of Israel, the priests and the Levites, did not keep themselves separate from the peoples of the land . . . They took their daughters for themselves and for their sons, and the holy seed was mingled with the peoples of the land."

Then Ezra was furious and despaired and tore his clothes. He waited until the evening offering, then spoke. How could it be, he said, that exactly when the grace of Yahweh showed itself, "allowing a remnant of refugees to survive and giving us a tent peg in his holy place," we immediately started scorning his commandments again and "tying ourselves in marriage to these abominable peoples?" Wouldn't this be the occasion for Yahweh, Ezra insisted, to "destroy us without leaving any remnant?"

Ezra spoke and wept. And the people around him wept as well. Then Shechaniah, son of Jehiel, spoke up and said that there was a way out of this: "Let us at once make a covenant with our God and repudiate all the women and their children." Ezra stood up and had "the chief priests, the Levites, and all Israel swear to do what had been said." And he ordered them to do it at once.

It was the rainy season, and someone pointed out that this was hardly something you could do "in a day or two." Others were against the idea. "But the children of captivity did as had been agreed." Ezra presided over the operation. He drew up a long list of those who must obey: "All these men had taken foreign wives, and they repudiated them and sent their wives and children far away." The people who once *went away* became the people who sent away. Whom? Their women and children.

When the "children of captivity" came back to Jerusalem and the decision was taken to expel all foreign wives and their children (the Moabites being the first to be mentioned), Nehemiah realized that there were many in the city who could no longer speak the language of the Jews: "He rebuked them and cursed them; he flogged them and pulled their hair; and made them swear in the name of God: "Do not give your daughters to their sons and do not take their daughters for your sons or for yourselves." But Nehemiah also insisted that they remember a famous precedent: "Wasn't this how Solomon, king of Israel, sinned? No people ever had a king the like of him. He was beloved of God and God made him king over Israel. Yet even he was induced to sin by foreign women."

Solomon, who built the Temple that the "children of captivity" had just finished rebuilding, was—and this, too, ought to be remembered—the son of David, and David was the descendant of a Moabite, Ruth. And it's quite plausible that the story of Ruth was written in times not so distant from those when Nehemiah wrote of his return to Jerusalem from the court of Artaxerxes, where he had been one of the king's cupbearers, a powerful man whose word was respected. Ruth was a Moabite, widow of a Jew whose mother, Naomi, she had chosen to follow, out of pure affection, into the land of the Jews. Ruth had said to her, "Your people will be my people and your god will be my god."

When the two women were back in Bethlehem, one hot night, in the season of the barley harvest, it so happened that Ruth, who was working in the fields as a foreign laborer, had stretched out in the barn at the feet of a rich property owner, Boaz, who was asleep at the time. And that night she conceived a child with him. Boaz then did all he could to make Ruth his wife, despite the custom of the levirate that obliged a widow to marry one of her dead husband's brothers.

The book of Nehemiah tells how the inhabitants of Jerusalem were duty bound to expel their children and wives because contaminated by the blood of foreign women; the book of Ruth tells how a foreign woman servant, with the aid of some shrewd maneuvering, was accepted among the children of Israel and became an ancestor of David, and hence of the Messiah.

Both books were received into the biblical canon. They were among the most recent, where the stories told, rather than being those of an entire people, as in earlier books, recounted the lives of single persons, like Esther or Jonah or Daniel or Ezra. As one nears the end, the canon splits into streams and rivulets, unrelated and contrasting, sometimes incompatible. But those streams all flowed from one river, which rises in Genesis. The important thing was to recover the taste of those now remote waters.

No one forgot that Ezra was first and foremost a scribe. The people of Jerusalem gathered together by the Water Gate. They told Ezra to bring the book of the Law of Moses. Ezra climbed on a wooden dais. He had six men to his right and seven to his left. He read from the book of the Law "from dawn until midday before the men, the women, and those who could understand. The ears of all the people listened to the book of the Law." When Ezra opened the book all the people got to their feet. After the reading, thirteen Levites commented on "the Law of God, explaining it, giving sense to the words so that people could understand what had been read."

Ezra told the people they mustn't weep, because that day had been consecrated to Yahweh and "in fact, all the people were weeping as they listened to the words of the Law." Ezra insisted: they must eat "rich dishes, drink sweet drinks, and take food to those who had none ready." It must be a day of "great joy, because they had understood the words that had been made known to them."

Another thing they rediscovered was the feast of the Tabernacles, which hadn't been celebrated since the times of Joshua. They had forgotten it. "The children of Israel will live in huts during the feast of the seventh month." They found this rule written in the Law. So they went off toward the mountains and came back with "branches of olive and wild olive, myrtles and palms and other leafy trees, to make huts for themselves." The courtyards, the roofs, the Temple, the open spaces by the city gates all sprouted various shades of green. Everything was covered in thick foliage. The inhabitants of Jerusalem lived under leaves for seven days. And "they read from the book of the Law of God, day by day, from the first day to the last."

XI

AROUND
THE RUINED
TEMPLE

So long as the children of Israel were traveling in the desert, they formed a single caravan, settling in a single camp. And they had but one place of worship: the Tent of Meeting. But when they entered the Promised Land and took possession of their inheritance, the tribes would parcel out the land among them. So where were they to worship now?

At this point a novelty came along that carved a rift between past and future. Moses said, "Take care not to offer your holocausts in any place you see, but offer them only in the place that Yahweh chooses among one of your tribes and it is there that you will do everything I tell you to do." There could no longer be multiple places of worship, as there had been at the time of the patriarchs.

What Moses now described was something quite different: a single place, chosen by Yahweh—and only in that one place were all the ceremonies to converge. The Tent of Meeting would be replaced by the Temple of Jerusalem. This injunction that all sacrifices of whatever kind be celebrated in a single place marked a sharp break with everything that had come before. One God meant one place of worship. It was a principle that would separate the Jews not only from all other peoples but even from themselves. To tie worship to a single place meant to accept the vicissitudes of history. A liturgy must go on perpetually, regardless of turbulence of whatever kind, while cities are entities that rise and fall. The landscape was full of tells covering the ruins of ancient cities. This was the moment when the children of Israel were ordered to conform to history, everyone's history. And this was supposed to occur in their "place of rest," where at last Yahweh would put them beyond the incursions of those who did not possess anything of the kind. Yet one day even the Temple that had been rebuilt after exile in Babylon would be destroyed. Ushering in another diaspora.

Only in the Alexandrian age would Athens and Jerusalem, having always ignored each other, have occasion to clash and reveal their insuperable enmity. Antiochus Epiphanes was not just a conqueror but a mortal theological enemy: "He sent an elderly Athenian to force the Jews to abandon the laws of their fathers and no longer to live according to the laws of God, and again to defile the Temple of Jerusalem, dedicating it to Olympian Zeus, and the temple in Gerizim to Zeus the Host." The second book of the Maccabees tells us nothing else about this elderly Athenian, and of all the characters in the Bible one could hardly say that he has received a great deal of attention from the scholars. Yet that old man finally revealed that Athens could not accept Jewish *untranslatability*. And certainly he would never have written, as did Areus, king of Sparta, that "the Spartans and Jews were brothers descended from the progeny of Abraham." In all lands and all empires Zeus had imposed his name on the names of other gods. So why not in Jerusalem? It wasn't just a question of taming and devastating a province of what had been Alexander's empire. It was a theological war finally emerging as such. And too late, for by now it was a war between epigones, on both sides. But it would go on forever.

Even when Antiochus Epiphanes took the bold step of building a gymnasium in Jerusalem "according to the custom of the Gentiles"—a tremendous affront, since this meant having young men walking around nude, the circumcised openly mixing with the uncircumcised—the deeper struggle was always between sacrifices and sacrifices. "He built the abomination of desolation on the altar of the sacrifices," one reads in the first book of the Maccabees. What are we to understand by this? The evil Antiochus Epiphanes had ordered that a second altar be built on top of the altar of the Temple in order to perform other, incompatible sacrifices: "The twenty-fifth of the month they offered sacrifices on the altar that was above the altar of the sacrifices." Sacrifice was the ultimate way of asserting sovereignty. No one, whether Jew or Gentile, would have dared to imagine that one could live without sacrifices.

To profane the Temple of Jerusalem, as did Antiochus Epiphanes, "fierce of face and skilled in intrigue," meant above all to interrupt the "perpetual sacrifice." As Exodus prescribed, every day without exception the children of Israel were to celebrate the holocaust of a lamb in the morning and a second lamb at dusk. Two small animals had to be entirely burned up every day "at the entrance to the Tent of Meeting." Otherwise Yahweh would not be present, Yahweh who had said, "It is there I will meet the children of Israel and the place shall be consecrated by my glory." Sacrifice wasn't something special reserved for certain days, occasions or festivals. It must be continuous, "perpetual," *tamid*. A barrier of smoke rose endlessly between the worshippers and the Tent of Meeting. If that smoke should cease to rise, the place would be defiled, as in the time of Antiochus Epiphanes.

"What use is the abundance of your sacrifices to me? / asks Yahweh / I am sated with the holocausts of rams / and the fat of fatted animals; / the blood of bulls, lambs / and goats, I do not desire." These words, to be found in the opening lines of the book of Isaiah, offer reason enough, you would suppose, to announce the abolition of the practice of sacrifice. Yet right up to its second destruction in 70 C.E., nine centuries after Isaiah and three after the wickedness committed by Antiochus Epiphanes, the Temple of Jerusalem continued to be wrapped in the smoke of daily holocausts. Maimonides claims that "inasmuch as many beasts were slaughtered daily in that holy place, the flesh cut into pieces, and the intestines burned and washed, there is no doubt that if it had been left in that state its smell would have been like that of a slaughterhouse." Hence, every morning and afternoon there were fumigations with incense, of which Isaiah had said, "Incense is an abomination for me." Even when Ezra's caravan arrived, loaded with precious objects returning to Jerusalem, the first concern was to celebrate holocausts.

But no one among the children of Israel was so foolish as to suppose that holocausts were celebrated to please the senses of the invisible God. Rather than the sacrifice itself, what Isaiah was attacking was the visible aspect of sacrifice: the blood soaking the altar and getting sprinkled on those present. Finally someone was saying that this moment, thought to be sacred and indispensable, could also be deplored. But the real response to Isaiah would come much later, in the Letter to the Hebrews: "He entered the sanctuary once and for all and not with the blood of goats and bulls but with his own blood, to gain for us an eternal redemption." The enigma of the sacrifice was contained in those words: all men needed to be redeemed and, in order to redeem them, living beings had to be ceremonially killed. For redemption to work, blood was required. Even if that meant the blood of a single divine being.

Along with sacrifices, Isaiah also condemned trees, and with equal vehemence: "They shall be ashamed of the terebinths / that you have taken delight in / and you will perish thanks to the gardens / that you loved! / You will be like a terebinth / whose leaves wither away / and like a garden / that has no water." Unlike the words on sacrifice, no reason was offered for this diatribe. Isaiah didn't say that Yahweh loathed trees and gardens. Yet the condemnation is no less severe. Scholars assume that behind the terebinths and the gardens we are to glimpse the shadow of the idols they might be sheltering, even though Isaiah makes no mention of idols here. But confirmation comes in another passage of Isaiah: "This people is forever provoking me: / they sacrifice in gardens / and burn incense on bricks." What Isaiah was suggesting was that nature itself, with its cycle of growth and dissolution, was an idol. Indeed, the first idol, a beloved idol.

Jeremiah reported Yahweh's words thus: "The children of Judah have done evil in my sight . . . They have built the high places of Topheth in the Valley of Ben-Hinnom / to burn their sons and their daughters in the fire, / something I did not order and that did not enter my heart." Ben-Hinnom, or, in Hebrew, Ge-Hinnom became *géenna* in Greek—and via the Greek the word would penetrate many other languages, becoming Gehenna, another word for hell.

The valley of Ge-Hinnom was just a few miles south of Jerusalem. Thus the city of the one Temple bordered on hell, almost. Only in the reign of Josiah was Topheth condemned once and for all. Eventually it would become a rubbish dump, where carcasses and rubble were heaped. Jeremiah had foreseen it: "When that time comes, said Yahweh, / they shall take the bones of the kings of Judah from their tombs / and the bones of its princes / and the bones of its priests / and the bones of its prophets / and the bones of the people of Jerusalem. / They will be exposed to the Sun and the Moon, / and all the Army of the Heavens, / that they loved, that they served, / and behind which they marched, / that they consulted and before which they bowed down / Since they will not be gathered and buried, / they will be trash on the surface of the soil." And that day "one will no more say Topheth, nor Valley of Ben-Hinnom, / but Valley of Slaughter, / and the dead will be buried in Topheth until there is no room."

Diodorus Siculus told how, in 308 B.C.E., under attack from the king of Syracuse, the Carthaginians felt their gods had deserted them: "They also believed that Cronus had turned against them because in times past they had sacrificed the most vigorous of their sons to him, whereas more recently they had been buying and raising children to offer in sacrifice. And when they looked into the matter they found that some of the sacrificial victims were fictitious. Reflecting on all this and seeing the enemy camped outside the city walls, they were overcome by a superstitious dread for having neglected to honor the gods of their fathers. In their zeal to make up for their omissions, they chose two hundred of the noblest children and sacrificed them publicly. Others who might have been included sacrificed themselves voluntarily, no fewer than three hundred of them. There was a bronze statue of Cronus in the city, hands reaching out with open palms inclining downward to the ground, so that each of the children placed there slithered down and fell into an opening full of flames."

Halfway between the commercial and military ports of Carthage was an extensive, securely fenced area of around six thousand square meters. It was a cemetery for children and animals—lambs, kid goats—ritually burned as offerings to Baal Hammon and his celestial consort, Tanit. Between the eighth and the second centuries B.C.E. their funeral urns were buried here, in nine layers sunk in rectangular ditches marked out by pebbles and covered with stone slabs, on which were placed stelae often in the form of urns and often decorated with drawings. These include Baal Hammon's disk and crescent moon and Tanit's triangle topped with a circle. In some bas-reliefs the goddess appears with a tambourine at the door of the temple.

When, from 1921 onward, archaeologists began to dig up the area, they found thousands of funeral urns, which were most numerous in the Punic city's period of maximum expansion. The inhabitants were Phoenicians who had come from Canaan moving westward, led—as Timaeus tells us—by a princess of Tyre: Dido.

Some of the stelae were impressive, rising above a small urn at the base, which might contain the remains only of a single lamb or goat. Some stelae were decorated with figures of sheep. In the oldest layers, one urn in three contained animal remains. But only one in ten between the fourth and third centuries, as if the sacrifices of children had become more frequent. "*Vita pro vita, sanguine pro sanguine, agnum pro vicario [?],*" was a common expression, etched on the stelae. Together with the bones and ashes one often found amulets, beads, small jewels. The archaeologist who first dug the site called it *tophet,* a biblical word one finds in Jeremiah.

For centuries rabbis tried to sidestep and euphemize the bloody sacrifices. But it was hard to get around the Torah. For example, where it says, "Abel offered the firstborn of his flock, with their fat." If despite the Bible's vocation for concision *fat* gets a mention it can only mean that its role in the sacrifice was central. But Rav Sheshet tried to compare the fat of Abel's lambs to the fat "burned during fasting, fasting that is equivalent to sacrifice because of its power to cancel out the burden of sin." So at last the fat became invisible. This was written in the Babylonian Talmud. Centuries later, in the 1930s, Jacob Gordin, unimpressed by the biblical evidence, offered a similar dodge: "Abel is a shepherd, but his sacrifice is not a bloody one: he sheared his sheep and offered their wool; he is the forefather of the Jewish people." So the soft *wool* took the place of irksome *fat*.

When the Temple of Jerusalem was destroyed by order of Emperor Titus the Jews were forced to stop all their bloody sacrifices since these were admissible only in the Temple. From one moment to the next the priests found themselves deprived of their functions. And the rabbis set themselves up in place of the *kohanim*. The rabbis were not priests, rather they expounded the Torah. The bloody sacrifices could no longer be celebrated, but only remembered and commented in the numerous passages in which they were mentioned in the Torah. Mostly in Leviticus and Deuteronomy as far as the ritual prescriptions were concerned, but everywhere, from Genesis on, when it came to actual occurrences. This process would allow the Jews, wrote Guy Stroumsa, to "transform their religion radically, 'modernizing' it, we might say, but without this being evident, pretending (and sometimes believing) they hadn't changed anything essential." Stroumsa must have been fond of the idea of "modernization" since he immediately repeats it: "In fact, it really was a modernization of their religion, with a new emphasis on the internalization of worship, making it something private." But if this development is seen as positive—in line with the current connotations of the word *modernization*, which Stroumsa does not quiz—it follows that the Jews should have thought of Titus as a benefactor, not a persecutor. Without him "the slow, all-too-slow transformation of religion could not have been set in motion, a transformation to which we owe, among other things, our European culture." Here he first assumes that without the trauma that was the destruction of the Temple the transformation of the Jewish religion would have been "too slow"; and second, that this transformation, aside from other consequences (which?), would bring about the birth of "European culture," an idea open to a huge range of interpretations, many of them contradictory. Yet Stroumsa, abandoning his usual caution here for rashness, takes its meaning as given. And most of all he sees it as a consequence of the process that shaped rabbinic Judaism between the first and the fourth century C.E., a process that came under threat only when Emperor Julian sought to rebuild the Temple of Jerusalem many years after its destruction. Had Julian succeeded, Stroumsa implies, we could have said goodbye to the "modernization" of Judaism and with it "European culture." Once again the blood of sacrificed animals would have trickled down the altar of the Temple of Jerusalem.

During the days of its destruction, the air of Jerusalem was thick with the dust of rubble. But this did not mingle with the smoke of the "perpetual" sacrifice of the lambs, goats, and other animals that were entirely burned up on the altar every morning and evening. That smoke had ceased to rise. Nor would it ever again be seen or smelled. When could those sacrifices be resumed if they were only to be celebrated in that one place? Many said that at this point the Temple could be rebuilt only with the advent of the Messiah. But would the Messiah be needing those sacrifices?

Almost three centuries after its destruction, Emperor Julian invited the Jews to rebuild the Temple and ordered work to begin. Gregory of Nazianzus had scornfully referred to Julian as "the Apostate" because he had been raised as a Christian and now wanted to restore the pagan religion of the empire, which by this time—from the reign of his uncle Constantine on—had embraced and professed the cross. But Julian had understood that everything revolved around sacrifice. He was impatient with the pagans, with their apathy and carelessness, their unwillingness to perform sacrifices, the rituals for which they had very likely forgotten; he abhorred the Christians, sullied by the "stain of atheism," because they were forever talking of sacrifice while refusing actually to kill any animals; and he was irritated with the Jews, who aside from a few obsessions, such as the Sabbath and the oneness of god, were religious people, yet claimed they could no longer celebrate sacrifices because the Temple of Jerusalem had been destroyed.

The empire was a huge machine and Julian was preparing to set it in motion against another empire, the Sassanians, yet was unable to revive or impose the ancient and venerable sacrificial ceremonies. There were those who wanted to reduce religion entirely to prayer. But "prayers without sacrifices are just words, prayers with sacrifices are living words"; so wrote Julian's friend and teacher the Neoplatonist Salutius.

Nothing stirred Christian loathing of Emperor Julian so much as his plan to rebuild the Temple of Jerusalem. As John Chrysostom saw it, the decision raised Julian to the very summit of wickedness. And if building work was eventually interrupted it was because fire from heaven had flared up among the stones and the laborers. The ordinary earthquake that the chronicles record was not enough. Appeased and exultant, John Chrysostom tells the story thus: "Emperor Julian was madly determined to get the work done. But when he was told what had happened he feared that if work went on it might draw down fire on his own head. So together with the entire Jewish people, he retired, beaten.

"Even today, if you go to Jerusalem, you can see the bare foundations and, if you ask for an explanation, you will hear none other than the one I have given. We are all witnesses to this, because it did not happen in remote times, but in our own days. Just think how magnificent is this victory of ours. This did not happen in the times of the benevolent emperors; no one can say that Christians came along and prevented the work from being carried out. This happened at a time when our religion was being persecuted, when all our lives were in danger, when we were all afraid to speak, when the pagans were flourishing. Some of the faithful hid away in their houses, others fled the city and took refuge in the deserts. This was the state of things when these events took place. So the Jews have no excuse for their effrontery."

At times pagans and Christians would vie with each other in turning the chosen people, the Jews, into the rejected people, a sort of historical nemesis that intensified in the three centuries following the destruction of the Temple. Emperor Hadrian decided to rebuild Jerusalem, but as a pagan city from which Jews would be banned. He called it Aelia Capitolina. John Chrysostom suggested "stopping the Jews' mouths," and never tired of reminding the ailing exiles of the reason for their condition: "Isn't it clear that [Yahweh] hated you and has turned his back on you once and for all?"

Under Emperor Constantine, Christianity at last moved from being a persecuted minority religion to a religion of state, a process countless scholars would enquire into, from Budé to Gibbon and beyond, "without reaching a convincing conclusion." Still today people talk of the "mystery of the ancient world's conversion," as John Scheid put it.

Tangled with that mystery there's another, something that occurred in the same period of time, that is between the destruction of the Temple in Jerusalem in 70 C.E. and the law of Constance II as implemented in the Codex Theodosianus in 341 C.E.: *Cesset superstitio, sacrificiorum aboleatur insania*, "Superstition must end, the folly of sacrifices shall be abolished." A sentence that seals the definitive condemnation of blood sacrifices, henceforth to be considered illegal. From that date on, a practice that had been widespread for thousands of years, even among religions that were hostile to each other, became an act punishable by law.

Yet the idea of sacrifice would continue to animate Judaism and Christianity, which even today can be defined as "sacrificial religions without blood sacrifices." As for paganism, despite suffering

similar stern attacks on the practice of blood sacrifice in the same
period, it would remain a sacrificial religion right to its final agony,
the destruction of Eleusis in 396, when anyone carrying out blood
sacrifices risked the death penalty.

What had now become a serious crime had for centuries been
the common basis of religious practices throughout the Mediterranean and Near East. Emperor Julian was well aware of this. As
he saw it, Jews and pagans were alike precisely in their practice of
blood sacrifices: "Abraham sacrificed as we do, always and constantly." This alone was enough to guarantee an easy coexistence
with the Jews, who "agree with the nations in everything except
their belief in one god. That is their peculiarity, alien to us, since
as far as everything else is concerned, in their temples, sanctuaries, altars, purifications, and certain precepts, they are like us."
The Jews had always celebrated and drawn up detailed rules for
blood sacrifices, like all the "nations." Compared with the Greeks,
in fact, who did not have liturgical texts, Leviticus and Deuteronomy offered monumental accounts. And if they now insisted
on not celebrating these sacrifices merely because Emperor Titus
had had the Temple in Jerusalem destroyed, very well, another
emperor—Julian himself—would arrange to have it rebuilt so that
then everyone could go back to the proper way of celebrating their
religions, each sacrificing to his own gods, whether one or many.
What mattered was to sacrifice. But to get back to that situation
one irksome obstacle must be overcome: the Christians. As Julian
saw it they were heretical twice over: toward pagans and Jews because "they have abandoned the ever living gods for the cadaver of
the Jew." At the same time they departed from Jewish traditions
by fielding childish gimmicks, such as the "circumcision of the
heart," in preference to—and hence substituting—that of the flesh,
the only kind prescribed to Abraham. As for sacrifices, either they
hid hypocritically behind the Jewish position, that they could no
longer be celebrated following the destruction of the Temple; or
they went so far as to speak of a "new sacrifice." But in that case,
Julian objected, "why not make sacrifices yourselves, given that

you have invented your own new sacrifice and have no need of Jerusalem?" On this point, the crux of it all, Julian's contemporary
John Chrysostom would answer his question with vehement elo-
quence, claiming that Christian sacrifice was "inexhaustible" and
"daily" because "we offer the same person, not one sheep today
and another tomorrow." The unbridgeable gap was between the
blood of animals, spilled day by day on the altar, and the blood
of God spilled just once on the cross. As Julian saw it, this was
sophistry. To John Chrysostom it was the irreversible transition
from what is accomplished with an act to what is "accomplished
in the memory (*anámnēsis*) of what was accomplished then." This
passage to *anámnēsis*, the perennial memory, marked the end of
the long era of animals killed on altars. Now they would be killed
just the same, but in the absence of precepts and prayers, without ritual gestures or witnesses, save the killers themselves. Julian
wasn't convinced. It was another invention of Jesus and Paul, who,
he wrote, "outdid all the wizards and charlatans of every time and
place."

This passage from act to "memory" was the Christians' unbeat-
able weapon—and John Chrysostom focused on the gesture with
vivid confidence. It was to be a twofold memory: of a single, dat-
able fact—the killing of Jesus on the cross—and of a proclaimed
metamorphosis: the bread and the wine that became the body and
blood of Christ and were eaten and drunk. One had to remember
two acts, then, at once inevitable and inextricably connected: the
killing and the consuming. But the consuming depended on a single transforming phrase, without which it would be no more than
something one did anyway every day. The two fundamental acts
of sacrifice—killing and communion—split off in opposite directions. The killing no longer took place on an altar, but in the place
prescribed for executions. The communion did not imply that one
ate the body of the victim, but another substance that *substituted*
for that body and into which that body had been *transformed*. The
divine being was killed and eaten, but following a procedure that

was quite unprecedented. And it was that procedure, and that alone, that was to be rehearsed, forever. Equally shocking and new was the fact that the victim was to be eaten *with his blood* in breach of the law Elohim proclaimed to Noah.

In the twenty-one months he was emperor, Julian realized that all around him a gesture, or series of gestures, that had been performed for centuries—one couldn't even say since when, exactly— were becoming impossible, impracticable, unacceptable: blood sacrifices. To kill an animal—small as a lamb or big as a bull— offering it to an invisible entity, whom one declared divine, was an entirely familiar act wherever Julian chose to look. There was no region of the Roman Empire where it was not known and practiced. But now this act was meeting, constantly—for quite different and sometimes contrasting reasons—a resistance, an obstacle. Yet even two peoples like the Greeks and the Jews, who had little or nothing in common—something that the Greek Julian was proud of—had for hundred of years gone on burning animals whole on altars. The Greeks called it *holókauston*, the Jews called it *olah*. For both, these ceremonies were absolutely essential. Yet now, in a surprising convergence, and always for reasons that seemed to have nothing to do with each other, pagans, Christians, and Jews were all united in circumventing these rites.

We shouldn't suppose that the Mediterranean peoples suddenly felt squeamish about killing animals, small or large, in the course of a religious ritual, as if blood sacrifice had become an embarrassment to be rid of. In the very years of the first extraordinary expansion of Christianity, Europe teemed with crypts and caves dedicated to the worship of Mithras where the practice of blood sacrifice was more intense than ever. There were portrayals of the indomitable god performing the *tauroctony*, thrusting a sword into the throat of a bull. We know of more than five hundred variations, scattered as far afield as Arabia and Britain, the Sahara and Bulgaria, but with the greatest concentration around Rome.

The devotees of the god who issued from the rock were mainly imperial soldiers and administrators, legionaries, and centurions defending the empire's borders, particularly in the north and the Balkans, men used to moving on to new destinations. The religion they followed had no devotional texts; rather its dogmas were expressed in images. The liturgy focused around the blood that flowed from a large animal and the consequent ceremonial meal.

The young god Mithras hunts on horseback, with the aid of a snake and a lion. His arrows never miss. A bull is chased until it falls, still fighting. Mithras leaps onto its back and pulls up its head with his left hand while the right plunges a short Persian sword into the beast's jugular. The wind lifts the cloak behind the god, who looks away from the bull even as he kills it. A scorpion clasps the bull's testicles. A crow observes the scene with the stern air of the priest. Blood streams from the wound.

We will never know for certain what went on in the Mithraic ceremonies. What is clear, though, is that in the second and third centuries in particular—but also, as with all pagan rites, for part of the fourth—endless obscure devotees entrusted their salvation to this one image: the slaughter of a bull draped with the *dorsuale*, the cloth spread on an animal that was to be sacrificed. The killer was a god. *Et nos servasti aeternali sanguine fuso*, "You have saved us, too, by shedding the eternal blood." These words can be read on the painted inscription in the Mithraeum in Santa Prisca on the Aventine Hill. Once again one has to ask the central, never satisfactorily answered question about sacrifice: why did salvation always have to be preceded by killing?

There are invisible lines—albeit not many—that divide history into a before and an after: one was the moment when pagans, Jews, and Christians alike imposed a repudiation of blood sacrifices, making them a thing of the past. It was an upheaval that, in Europe, lasted the entire fourth century, the first tremors of which, however, had been felt long before. The reasons given for it were many and contradictory.

For the devotees of Mithras, as for others, the fourth century proved fatal. From the moment when Constantine on the Milvian Bridge decided to follow the cross it was clear that the days when Diocletian had recognized the bull-slaying god as protector of the empire were over. For some decades the Mithraic inscriptions disappeared, then reappeared in a last brief blaze, and for good reasons, in the years of Emperor Julian. But as early as 377 a letter of Jerome's mentions the destruction of a Mithraeum. The last Mithraic inscription appeared just a few years later, in 385.

For the Jews the second destruction of the Temple of Jerusalem offered the magnificent and unarguable pretext for ridding themselves of the encumbrance of blood sacrifices. An overwhelming amnesia gradually occulted vast tracts of the past. Leaving as its only trace—though nevertheless a deep trace—the requirement to eat kosher. No other community was as careful to avoid blood, having for so long and so urgently demanded blood as an element of worship. Thus what had once been the basis of the act of eating meat was now canceled out: eating meat, for the children of Israel, had been admissible only if preceded by a blood sacrifice, in which the blood soaked the altar and drained off it onto the feet of the officiating priest. The prohibition against eating meat with its blood did not pass from the Jews to the Christians. On the contrary, succulent meat, meat full of blood, was ever more in demand. Until this vast and implacable process of shrouding the past in euphemism would leave only Friday fasting.

With the Temple gone it was no longer possible to celebrate the rites in observance of all the Torah's precepts. Yet the Torah remained. And there would be a place of meeting: the synagogue. Dura-Europos, a half-Semitic, half-Greek name, outpost of the Roman Empire on the Euphrates, was a painted city: both public and private buildings were painted all over from top to bottom. And written over, too: "there were hundreds if not thousands of inscriptions of a religious character scratched or painted on the walls of temples, public buildings, and private houses." With plenty of horoscopes and magical symbols. All the temples were decorated with frescoes representing "gods and goddesses, mythological scenes, and scenes of sacrifices performed by their donors." And, "alongside the temples, the private houses shone with gay colors." The merchant Nebuchelos kept his business diary on the walls of his house, to save on precious papyrus. Bethel, Mamre, Hebron, Machpelah were remote, unapproachable names now. But the figures of the holy story were always close by. And some reappeared on the walls of the synagogue, to be seen there for a little more than ten years, before the Persian conquest.

The synagogue in Dura-Europos was a converted house in a tight row of houses. It had a room for around a hundred people, with benches on each side. Every inch of the high walls was frescoed with episodes from the Bible, as if the law forbidding images had never been pronounced. There was also a naked young woman, seen from the thighs up, standing in the waters of the Nile with a child in her arms: it was Pharaoh's daughter's handmaid, who had rescued Moses. A long lock of black hair fell slantwise down her back. Another episode showed Esther, wearing the clothes of the royal house of Iran. The biblical stories were synoptic and simultaneous. The rescue of Moses was juxtaposed with scenes from the life of Ezekiel. The throne of Ahasuerus was almost the same as Solomon's. The exodus, Jacob's dream, and Solomon between two women are all right next to one another. Elijah had a whole wall to himself. He was fed by crows and raised the son of the widow of Zarephath from the dead by stretching out on the boy's body. The bull he sacrificed on Mount Carmel burst into flames while the priests of Baal waited in vain for the same to happen to their sacrificial victims and King Hiel hid under the altar and was bitten by a snake. But why were Elijah's stories shown side by side with the vision of Esther on the throne?

Michael Rostovtzeff, eminent historian of the ancient world who himself discovered the synagogue in Dura-Europos, observed,

"We cannot detect any governing idea, of a symbolical character, behind the distribution of the pictures. At least I have failed to find one." Other scholars failed too. In this first and last depiction of the biblical stories in a synagogue it is implicit that they are to be read as a single body, where each part represents the whole and proceeds from the whole. And where every detail has equal relevance. It was a guide, all too often ignored, for future readers.

No figure in the paintings of the ancient world has the force of the officiating priest, clad in a long robe of white linen, wearing a conical hat, likewise white, in the fresco of the temple of the Palmyrene gods in Dura-Europos. If ever eyes could petrify, they are his eyes. Beside him, and decidedly beneath, is Conone, the donor. "May Conone son of Nicostratus be remembered," reads the inscription above his head.

Far more than the commissioning patron, the figure you cannot forget is the officiating priest. Franz Cumont observes that "his ethnic traits are so carefully drawn one has the impression one is looking at the portrait of a Bedouin sheikh. The face is gaunt and bony, with a hooked nose: thin mustaches turn downward at the corners of the mouth and a sparse beard ends in two sharp points. Beneath his markedly arched eyebrows, the eyes, sharply outlined with black, open into almond shapes, while the iris is partially hidden under the upper lids, so that beneath this dark pool the cornea is white, giving his upward-turned gaze an expression of ecstasy." It's an accurate description, but to claim that the priest has "an expression of ecstasy" is the merest conjecture. All one can say is that the look in those eyes, which seems to come from some remote place, has a peremptory gravitas that runs right through the spectator as might the points of the blue blades, gleaming with white reflections, of the two sacrificial knives laid on a metal plate that the priest holds with his left hand. His right hand is dipping the stem of a reed into a three-legged vase. Beside the priest "an inscription gave his name, though all one can decipher with any certainty is the word *hieréus*, 'priest.'" Conone chose to be painted beside him, together with his daughter Bithnannaia, smothered in jewels—around her neck, on her breast, her head, her wrists—as well as three adolescent sons and a grandson.

It's a family portrait. But more than a single family this is the final farewell of an innumerable host of devotees who for centuries celebrated sacrifices to a multitude of gods. Who might be called Zeus or Artemis, or, as here, Yarhibol or Aglibol. The animal about to be sacrificed has been lost. What remains are the two blue knives. And the solemnity of the moment.

Dura-Europos lasted six centuries, under the Seleucid, Arsacid, and Roman empires. Then in the second half of the third century it was abandoned. Slowly the sand drifted over it, until, in 1921, while digging trenches, Captain Murphy of the British Army happened upon its ruins. It had been the place where the Olympian gods, the Palmyrene gods, Mithras, and Yahweh, were all equally painted. And, in the synagogue, with only a "slight modification of the style of the pagan paintings and sculptures of Dura." In that caravan city things divine were inevitably represented in the same idiom, like the lingua franca in the mouths of itinerant merchants.

Between the young bearded man holding a scroll of the Torah in the synagogue and the high priest with piercing eyes and the hat tapering at the top there was an evident affinity, as though between close relatives. The temples that appear here and there in the frescoes were of Greco-Syrian design. No one remembered the Temple of Jerusalem.

Ammianus Marcellinus tells how, during his calamitous expedition to Persia, from which he would not return, Emperor Julian hunted lions among the ruins of Dura-Europos.

XII

THE MESSIAH

Nothing could be added to the Torah, nothing taken away. To speak of a new Torah, as did the boldest devotees of the Messiah, rang of blasphemy. But the new precepts to which they had so often looked forward never materialized. Only in the Leviticus Rabbah could one read that "all sacrifices and prayers will be abolished in the Messianic days, except for the thanks offerings and thanksgiving prayers, because, as Isaac ben Judah Abrabanel . . . explains, in those happy days people will have no Evil Inclination and thus no sin, so that no offerings or prayers to atone for transgressions will be needed." Thus the destruction of the Temple of Jerusalem, which made sacrifices impossible, could be seen as the harbinger of messianic days.

But the wildest insinuation came from later cabalists. The Torah, they claimed, was indeed fixed forever, but only in the totality of its letters. Which could now be reordered in new ways. Ways that would be revealed in the messianic yeshiva. The house of study would thus take the place of the ruined Temple.

John the Baptist marked an irreversible break in time. "Before John there was the Law and the prophets; afterward the kingdom of God is announced and everyone does it violence." Here something is said that had never been said before. First and foremost, that the Law can come to an end and be replaced. Second, that an indefinite, mysterious entity—"the kingdom of God"—is approaching and "everyone does it violence." But who is this "everyone," an anonymous subject possessed of enormous power, since it can do "violence" to something no one can define?

From words such as these a reader might get the impression that a quite unprecedented event was about to unfold. It wasn't a question of a new god, or a new law, but of a sovereign order—a "realm"—that nevertheless was subject to violence from "everyone."

On the last day, says Isaiah, "the wolf and the lamb will graze together, / the lion will eat hay like the cattle. / As for the snake, it will live on dust." This was the ultimate transformation: the end of predation. Even the snake, origin of all evil, would lose its bite. The earth would no longer soak up bloodshed. As Maimonides saw it, Isaiah's words were to be understood figuratively, because in the messianic era nothing would be forced to change its nature. The prophet, he added, "found it extremely difficult to admit that a nature may change after the Work of the Beginning or that another volition may supervene after such a nature has been established in a definite way."

Maimonides deplored all yearning for the End of Days. But he recognized that the Torah did point to the advent of the Messiah. That day would come, he wrote, but "do not think that the Messiah needs to perform signs and miracles, bring about a new state of things in the world, revive the dead, and such like." *Such like* might be fine, maybe, for the Christians. Rather, the people "will offer up sacrifices, and will observe the Sabbatical years and the jubilee years with regard to all the commandments stated in the Torah." Finally, all the ritual shortcomings accumulated over the centuries would be set right. But it was important to understand that no "innovation will be introduced into creation. Rather, the world will continue in its accustomed course." The biggest change would be seen at the level of the word, because the prophecy of Zephaniah would be fulfilled: "Then I shall give the peoples a pure language." And "only in the Days of the Messiah will everyone know what the metaphors mean and to what they refer." This would be the real miracle, without anything visible actually changing. And one must remember that "the sages and prophets longed for the days of the Messiah not in order to rule over the world and not to bring the heathens under their control, not to be exalted by the nations, or even to eat, drink and rejoice. All they wanted was to have time for the Torah and its wisdom, with no one to oppress or disturb them."

Simeon the Just said, "The world depends on three things. On the Torah. On the liturgy. On beneficence." An objection might be raised here with regard to the liturgy: "Yes, of course, if the Temple exists. But what will happen when it is destroyed?" And he had an answer. "The order of the sacrifices is now well-established. When they recite them, I will consider that they have been offered and I will pardon their sins." This was the main difference for Israel after the destruction of the Temple: that the sacrifices could just as well be *recited*. More than for any other people, for the Jews it would be acceptable to eliminate the *what* of the sacrifice: the victims, the fire, the blood. Or in the Christian liturgy: the bread and the wine. For the Jews there was only one place where the liturgy could be performed, the Temple. Once that was lost, everything *must* become pure mental gesture. Thus recitation took the place of action. But the need for the sacrifice and its correctness remained as before.

Even without the Temple, the sacrifices would still be there. Because someone has to intercede, the priests: "It is not just the Torah that is needed, but also a *request for forgiveness*: it is important that man have a feeling of unworthiness with regard to the world." Rabbi Obadiah Bartenura remarked: "It is well known that, because of the sacrifices Noah offered, the Holy One, bless him, swore never again to unleash a flood upon the earth. It is a good thing that the world keep the practice of sacrifice." Only if some beings were killed on an altar could other beings have the guarantee that they would not be killed by their god.

In the Talmudic vision, the "main thing," *asl*, is study, if possible uninterrupted study. The rule is: "Focus your mind in study."

Everything else is secondary. It's not that there is life and then study as well. There is study—and life is to become an emanation of study: "When you are tired of studying, you can dedicate yourself to chores. But chores mustn't be your main goal while you give your free time to your study." To substitute sacrifice with study: a bold enterprise that began, after the second destruction of the Temple, with rabbinic Judaism and developed over the centuries, culminating not in a new devotional practice, but in the far-seeing research of some assimilated and nonobservant Jews.

The heir of the Temple was not the synagogue, but the yeshiva, the house of study. The synagogue could never be anything more than the place where the community met together. It would always be lacking the smoke of burned animals and the blood smeared on the four horns of the altar. The yeshiva was an empty room, where nothing was lacking, so long as there was a scroll to read.

As Maimonides saw it, there was an opposition—and an occult complicity—between sexual excitement and the house of study, in that the one was the most effective antidote for the other: "If you feel sexual excitement and suffer because of it, go to the house of study, read, take part in discussions, put questions, and be asked in your turn, for then this suffering will indubitably pass away." But was the opposite also true? Maimonides doesn't consider the matter. Nevertheless, the implication remains that the only two forces able to compete with each other had to be *study* and *sex*.

The Messiah's house of study will be immense, a bare room, eighteen thousand parasangs long, claims a Yemenite midrash: "And even the slaves and the slave-women of Israel who were bought for money from the nations of the world, the Holy Spirit will rest upon them and they will expound on their own and each one of them will have a House of Study in his house, the House of the Shekhina, the Divine Presence."

The primal state of the Torah is disorder. It lay before the Lord in the form of six hundred thousand letters. Then Adam appeared and sinned. So the Lord arranged the letters in phrases like "When a man dies in his tent." And again in others that had to do with inheritance, the levirate, and such like—this according to the *Midrash Talpiyot*. In each of these phrases death was named or implied. But when Adam's guilt is canceled out and forgotten, the Torah will go back to its primal state and will rearrange itself in other words.

Rabbi Jeremiah was an Amorite born in Babylon in the third century. As a young man he moved to Palestine, to learn. His last wishes were: to be buried in a white garment, with pockets, and in a cloak with a hood, shoes on his feet, and a stick in his hand. He also asked that he be laid bent over on one side, so as to be ready to follow the Messiah, when he came.

Rabbi Nachman of Breslov lived in Napoleonic times. Some of his pupils asked him what he thought of the emperor's rapid rise to power. Nachman answered, "'Heaven knows what his soul is, for it may be he has been switched. Since in the depths of metamorphosis souls are sometimes switched.' And at once he started to tell the story of the king's son and the maid's son who were switched." Nachman thought that "his teachings 'have no clothes.' Hence stories must be the clothes of doctrine." Years later, writing *L'Âme de Napoléon*, Léon Bloy tried to respond to the question about the emperor: "Once, in the times of my youth, and later too, when I loved novels of adventure and melodramas, I saw that what most fascinated me was uncertainty about a person's identity." According to Martin Buber, Nachman wasn't just "the last Jewish mystic," as well as "the first and thus far the only real creator of fables among the Jews." The story of the king's son and the maid's son was the closest he came to the Messiah.

Much of the story of the king's son tells of his adventures from the moment he had to leave his own country. At first "he spent the evenings in taverns with other young men, squandering his money on dancing girls." Then a dream led him to become the herdsman of a fierce and severe merchant. One day two animals escaped from the flock and the merchant ordered him to find them. But there was a thick forest all around and the herdsman became lost.

The king's son climbed up a tree and soon realized that the forest was haunted by spirits. The two lost animals reappeared, lying under the tree. Only to disappear again. When the king's son started wandering around the forest, a being appeared before him, with red hair, a gray face, and eyes of malachite. He was the sovereign of the forest. The king's son followed him for a long time. But one day the sovereign of the forest sent him away, telling him he must find a country called "the foolish country with the wise king." As a farewell gift, the sovereign of the forest gave the king's son a stick that had the power, when it touched them, to make animals sing.

The king's son managed to reach the foolish country with the wise king only to find that the ministers of the kingdom were distraught because the king had died and his son had turned out to be foolish like his ministers. So the country was foolish and had a foolish king. But the king had left a will in which he said that the kingdom should be delivered up to whoever was able to make the country's old name true again.

The king's son was put to the test. They led him into a room with a high throne of carved wood. The king's son quickly realized it was made of the same wood as the stick he had in his hand. At the top of the throne a rosette was missing. The king's son found it on the floor and put it back in its place. But, looking carefully, he saw that the room's bed needed moving a little. Likewise the table. And the candlestick. And the carved animals. When he touched these with the stick that the sovereign of the forest had given him, they started to sing. Then the ministers delivered up the kingdom to the king's son who had been switched with the maid's son.

One sign of messianic times will be fluidity. This is what Joel foresaw: "It shall happen on that day / that the mountains will drip with grape juice / and the hills will flow with milk, / all the streams of Judah will run with water / and a fountain will spring up from the House of Yahweh, / and swell the stream of the Acacias, Shittim," there where the children of Israel had spent many terrible hours long ago, with Moses. Fluidity and happiness seemed to coincide. No other image of the perfect life was ever so powerful. The thing they had always fought and fled—the Waters—now gathered around them, fed them. And the rest of the world? "Egypt will be laid desolate / and Edom a desert of desolation."

The messianic state is one of the many states in which things can exist. No one can say much about it beyond its name. But everyone knows it does exist.

When the Messiah comes, he will very likely pass unobserved, because he will only change some small things. And no one knows which.

The strongest affirmation of the Messiah is not to be found in the Bible, but in a prayer called Gevurot, "Powers," which, according to the liturgy, was to be repeated three times every day and four times on the Sabbath: "You who revive the dead."

SOURCES

The first number refers to the page, the second to the line on which the quotation ends. In this book, by "Bible" we mean what is usually called the Hebrew Bible or the Old Testament. Translations of Bible passages follow the version of Édouard Dhorme (Bibliothèque de la Pléiade, Gallimard, 1956–1971), but keeping in mind the versions of Nahum M. Sarna (Jewish Publication Society, 1989–1996) and Robert Alter (W. W. Norton & Co., 2019).

3, 19	Proverbs 8:24.
3, 23	Ibid., 8:30.
3, 27	Loc. cit.
4, 30	Sirach 24:3.
4, 32	Ibid., 24:4.
5, 2	Exodus 33:7.
5, 4	Ibid., 33:11.
5, 11	Sirach 24:5–6.
5, 14	Ibid., 24:10.
5, 16	Luke 9:58.
9, 6	1 Samuel 9:5.
9, 14	Ibid., 9:8.
9, 17	Ibid., 9:9.
9, 23	Ibid., 9:11.
9, 27	Ibid., 9:13.
10, 1	Ibid., 9:18–20.
10, 6	Ibid., 9:24.
10, 28	Ibid., 9:26.
10, 32	Ibid., 10:1.
11, 8	Ibid., 10:7.
11, 11	Ibid., 10:6.
11, 16	Ibid., 10:11.
11, 27	Ibid., 10:16.
11, 31	Ibid., 10:19.

11, 32   Loc. cit.

12, 5   Ibid., 10:22.

12, 7   Ibid., 10:24.

12, 23   Ibid., 10:25.

12, 25   Loc. cit.

13, 1   Ibid., 3:4.

13, 1   Ibid., 3:5.

13, 4   Ibid., 3:1.

13, 7   Ibid., 3:9.

13, 11   Ibid., 3:10.

13, 16   Flavio Giuseppe, *Antiquities of the Jews*, V, 10, 1.

13, 17   1 Samuel 2:22.

13, 18   Flavio Giuseppe, *Antiquities of the Jews*, V, 10, 1.

14, 5   1 Samuel 8:9.

14, 7   Ibid., 8:7.

14, 9   Ibid., 8:9.

14, 13   Ibid., 8:13–14.

14, 18   Ibid., 8:20.

14, 20   Loc. cit.

14, 34   Ibid., 1:28.

15, 5   Ibid., 12:6.

15, 6   Ibid., 12:7.

15, 9   Ibid., 12, 17.

15, 28   Ibid., 12:21.

16, 12   Ibid., 8:5.

16, 13   Ibid., 15:35.

16, 18   Ibid., 13:4.

16, 20   Ibid., 13:6.

16, 25   Ibid., 13:12.

16, 30   Ibid., 13:13–14.

17, 1   Ibid., 13:22.

17, 5   Ibid., 14:11.

17, 13   Ibid., 14:21.

17, 14   Ibid., 14:52.

17, 19   Deuteronomy 25:17.

17, 20   Ibid., 25:18.

17, 30   1 Samuel 15:3.

18, 3   Ibid., 15:8.

18, 5   Ibid., 15:9.

18, 7   Ibid., 15:21.

18, 18   Ibid., 15:13.
18, 21   Ibid., 15:14.
18, 22   Ibid., 15:15.
18, 31   Ibid., 15:20–21.
19, 1   Ibid., 15:22.
19, 2   Ibid., 15:23.
19, 4   Ibid., 15:24.
19, 7   Ibid., 15:28.
19, 11   Ibid., 15:31.
19, 13   Ibid., 15:32.
19, 14   Loc. cit.
19, 18   Ibid., 15:33.
19, 23   Ibid., 15:35.
19, 25   Deuteronomy 25:17.
20, 2   Matthew 12:7.
20, 8   Hosea 6:6.
21, 21   Deuteronomy 7:16.
21, 22   J. Rudhardt, *Notions fondamentales de la pensée religieuse et actes constitutifs du culte dans la Grèce classique*, Droz, Genève, 1958, p. 218.
21, 27   Exodus 34:12.
21, 32   Isaiah 34:2.
22, 1   Ibid., 34:4.
22, 4   Ibid., 34:11.
22, 6   Jeremiah 8:1.
22, 12   Ibid., 8:2.
22, 22   Deuteronomy 13:17–18.
22, 27   1 Samuel 28:3.
22, 31   Ibid., 28:6.
22, 32   Ibid., 28:7.
23, 5   Ibid., 28:9.
23, 6   Loc. cit.
23, 9   Ibid., 28:11.
23, 14   Ibid., 28:14.
23, 18   Ibid., 28:15.
23, 19   Ibid., 28:18.
23, 27   Ibid., 28:16.
23, 30   Ibid., 28:20.
24, 1   Ibid., 28:22.
24, 5   Ibid., 28:24.

24, 13	Ibid., 16:14.
24, 21	Ibid., 18:11.
24, 21	Ibid., 26:17.
25, 4	2 Samuel 1:14.
25, 14	1 Samuel 18:17.
26, 4	Ibid., 18:1.
26, 8	2 Samuel 1:23.
26, 10	Ibid., 1:26.
26, 18	Ibid., 21:9.
29, 4	1 Samuel 16:1.
29, 9	Ibid., 16:12.
29, 10	Loc. cit.
29, 14	Ibid., 16:13.
29, 15	Ibid., 16:14.
29, 17	Ibid., 16:12.
29, 18	Ibid., 16:21.
29, 21	Ibid., 17:57.
29, 22	Ibid., 17:58.
29, 25	Ibid., 25:3.
30, 8	Ibid., 25:10.
30, 18	Ibid., 25:18.
30, 21	Ibid., 25:22.
30, 26	Ibid., 25:23.
30, 33	Ibid., 25:35.
30, 35	Ibid., 25:37.
31, 2	Ibid., 25:39.
31, 3	Ibid., 25:41.
31, 8	Ibid., 25:42–44.
31, 13	Ibid., 16:23.
31, 15	Ibid., 18:1.
31, 16	Ibid., 18:20.
31, 17	Ibid., 18:23.
31, 31	2 Samuel, 24:1.
31, 33	Loc. cit.
32, 33	1 Chronicles 21:1.
32, 34	2 Samuel 24:1.
33, 6	Ibid., 24:10.
33, 21	Exodus 30:14–15.
33, 32	2 Samuel 2:11.
34, 6	1 Samuel 18:20.

34, 9	2 Samuel 3:13.
34, 11	Ibid., 3:16.
35, 11	Ibid., 5:19.
35, 21	Ibid., 7:26.
35, 21	Ibid., 7:29.
36, 2	Ibid., 11:2.
36, 3	Ibid., 11:3.
36, 12	Ibid., 11:11.
36, 22	Ibid., 11:15.
36, 28	Ibid., 11:27.
37, 2	Matthew 1:6.
37, 14	1 Kings 14:8.
37, 29	Ibid., 15:5.
37, 30	Loc. cit.
38, 4	2 Samuel 12:3.
38, 9	Ibid., 12:7.
38, 17	Ibid., 12:11.
38, 24	Ibid., 12:19.
38, 32	Ibid., 12:23.
38, 35	Ibid., 12:24.
39, 4	Ibid., 23:8.
39, 13	Ibid., 16:7.
39, 17	1 Kings 3:3.
39, 28	Ibid., 6:7.
39, 32	1 Chronicles 22:3.
40, 2	Loc. cit.
40, 4	Ibid., 22:5.
40, 10	Ibid., 22:7–8.
40, 14	Ibid., 22:9.
40, 17	Ibid., 22:5.
40, 22	2 Samuel 6:5.
40, 32	Ibid., 6:16.
41, 4	Ibid., 6:20.
41, 6	Ibid., 6:21.
41, 10	Ibid., 6:23.
41, 12	Ibid., 7:27.
41, 18	Ibid., 7:6.
42, 18	Ibid., 15:30.
43, 2	1 Kings 1:1.
43, 12	2 Samuel 19:1.

43, 17	Ibid., 19:7.
43, 21	Ibid., 16:22.
43, 24	Ibid., 20:3.
44, 3	Ibid., 21:15.
44, 7	Ibid., 23:15.
44, 10	Ibid., 23:16.
44, 20	John 4:10.
44, 27	1 Kings 3:9.
44, 31	1 Chronicles 28:9.
45, 6	2 Samuel 16:9.
45, 11	Ibid., 16:13.
45, 15	1 Kings 2:8.
45, 19	Loc. cit.
45, 20	Ibid., 2:2.
45, 22	Ibid., 2:9.
45, 24	Ibid., 2:10.
45, 31	Ibid., 1:2.
45, 33	Ibid., 1:4.
46, 7	Ibid., 1:25.
46, 16	Ibid., 1:34.
46, 20	Ibid., 1:35.
46, 21	2 Samuel 23:1.
46, 24	Ibid., 23:4.
51, 16	1 Kings 2:33.
51, 18	Ibid., 2:46.
51, 22	Ibid., 1:4.
51, 26	Ibid., 2:17.
51, 28	Ibid., 2:20.
51, 29	Ibid., 2:21.
52, 3	Ibid., 2:22.
52, 16	Ibid., 2:24.
52, 18	Ibid., 2:25.
52, 24	Ibid., 3:7.
52, 25	Ibid., 3:5.
52, 28	Ibid., 3:8.
52, 33	Ibid., 3:9.
53, 9	Ibid., 3:13.
53, 14	Ibid., 5:9.
53, 22	Ibid., 5:10.
54, 2	Ibid., 5:12.

54, 4	Ibid., 5:13.
54, 6	Loc. cit.
54, 9	Ibid., 5:17.
54, 13	Ibid., 5:20.
54, 15	Loc. cit.
54, 19	2 Chronicles 1:15.
54, 20	1 Chronicles 22:5.
55, 1	2 Chronicles 2:6.
55, 9	Ibid., 2:13.
55, 10	Loc. cit.
55, 14	Ibid., 2:14.
55, 23	Ibid., 4:12–16.
56, 5	1 Kings 6:7.
56, 8	Ibid., 6:29.
56, 10	Ibid., 9:11.
56, 12	Ibid., 9:12.
56, 14	Ibid., 9:13.
56, 18	Ibid., 7:2.
56, 22	Ibid., 6:18.
56, 24	Ibid., 6:27.
56, 34	Ibid., 5:10.
57, 11	2 Chronicles 3:2.
57, 14	Ibid., 5:7.
57, 18	Ibid., 5:13.
57, 21	Ibid., 5:13–14.
57, 28	Ibid., 6:1–2.
58, 2	Ibid., 6:12.
58, 4	Ibid., 6:13.
58, 6	Ibid., 6:18.
58, 10	Ibid., 6:19.
58, 13	Ibid., 7:1.
58, 16	Ibid., 7:5.
58, 19	Ibid., 7:7.
59, 7	1 Kings 8:60.
59, 9	Ibid., 8:41.
59, 15	Ibid., 8:43.
59, 26	Ibid., 9:6.
59, 28	Ibid., 9:7.
59, 31	Loc. cit.
60, 4	Deuteronomy 28:37.

62, 7   1 Kings 10:2.

62, 11   Ibid., 10:4–5.

62, 13   Ibid., 10:5.

62, 25   Ibid., 10:7–8.

62, 27   2 Chronicles 9:7.

63, 11   1 Kings 10:2.

63, 17   Matthew 12:42; Luke 11:31.

63, 21   Matthew 12:38.

63, 22   Loc. cit.

63, 28   Matthew 12:42; Luke 11:31.

64, 6   1 Kings 10:8.

64, 15   Song of Songs 1:2.

65, 6   Ibid., 1:2, 8:14

65, 8   G. Ceronetti, *Le Rose del Cantico*, in *Il Cantico dei Cantici*, Adelphi, Milano, 1975, p. 55.

65, 12   Song of Songs 8:13

65, 14   Pausanias, I, 19, 2.

65, 19   Song of Songs 7:8.

65, 22   Ibid., 7:1.

65, 23   Ibid., 7:8.

65, 25   Ibid., 8:3.

65, 29   Ibid., 6:12.

66, 3   Ibid., 8:14.

66, 18   G. Foot Moore, *Judaism in the First Centuries of the Christian Era*, Harvard University Press, Cambridge, vol. I, 1927, p. 84.

66, 32   Ibid., pp. 86–87.

68, 2   Yadaim 3:5, in J. Barton, *A History of the Bible*, Penguin, London, 2019, p. 219.

68, 7   S. Weil, *Cahiers*, in *OEuvres complètes*, ed. A. A. Devaux and F. de Lussy, Gallimard, Paris, vol. VI, book iv, 2006, p. 296.

68, 9   Ibid., p. 134.

68, 24   J. W. Goethe, *Hegire*, in *West-östlicher Divan*, in *Gedenkausgabe der Werke, Briefe und Gespräche*, ed. E. Beutler, Artemis, Zürich-Stuttgart, 1949, p. 287.

68, 25   J. W. Goethe, *Hebräer*, ibid., p. 415.

69, 2   Loc. cit.

69, 12   Ibid., p. 416.

69, 18   Ruth 3:8.

69, 25   J. W. Goethe, *Hebräer*, cit., p. 416.

69, 26   Loc. cit.

69, 32   Loc. cit.

69, 34   Loc. cit.

70, 7   Loc. cit.

70, 16   Yadaim 3:5, in J. Barton, *A History of the Bible*, cit., p. 219.

70, 31   Ecclesiastes 1:13.

71, 3   1 Kings 11:4.

71, 10   Ecclesiastes 10:4.

71, 22   Ibid., 1:8.

71, 26   Ibid., 3:14.

71, 29   Ibid., 9:2.

72, 20   Wisdom of Solomon 7:21.

72, 23   Ibid., 8:2.

72, 30   Ibid., 7:22–24.

73, 1   Ibid., 7:25.

73, 4   Ibid., 8:9.

73, 6   Ibid., 7:18.

73, 9   Ibid., 8:20.

73, 14   Loc. cit.

73, 18   Ibid., 8:21.

73, 28   1 Kings 11:1–3.

73, 31   Ibid., 11:4.

74, 4   Ibid., 11:8.

74, 9   Ibid., 14:12.

74, 12   Ibid., 15:1.

74, 12   Ibid., 14:11.

74, 21   Proverbs 7:9.

74, 22   Ibid., 7:10.

74, 24   Ibid., 7:10–11.

74, 25   Ibid., 6:25.

74, 27   Ibid., 7:13.

74, 30   Ibid., 7:14–17.

74, 33   Ibid., 7:18.

75, 1   Ibid., 7:22.

75, 22   Exodus 34:13.

75, 25   Ibid., 34:14.

75, 28   Deuteronomy 16:22.

75, 31   Judges 2:13.

76, 4   2 Kings 23:13.

76, 6   1 Kings 11:4.

76, 17   Ibid., 11:5.

76, 31   2 Kings 23:6.

76, 33   Ibid., 23:7.

77, 11   R. du Mesnil du Buisson, *Nouvelles études sur les dieux et les mythes de Canaan*, Brill, Leiden, 1973, p. 39.

78, 4   Deuteronomy 16:21–22.

78, 5   1 Kings 3:9.

78, 7   Ibid., 11:4.

78, 12   Ibid., 11:12.

78, 14   Ibid., 11:26.

78, 16   Ibid., 11:40.

78, 17   Ibid., 11:43.

78, 25   2 Chronicles 9:22–27.

81, 4   1 Kings 15:32.

81, 9   Ibid., 15:29.

81, 14   Ibid., 16:4.

81, 18   Ibid., 16:33.

81, 20   Ibid., 22:39.

81, 23   Ibid., 16:31.

81, 24   Ibid., 21:25.

81, 25   Ibid., 21:26.

81, 30   Ibid., 18:17.

82, 10   Ibid., 18:24.

82, 16   Ibid., 18:27.

82, 19   Ibid., 18:29.

82, 23   Ibid., 18:30.

82, 32   Ibid., 18:38.

82, 35   Ibid., 18:40.

83, 22   Ibid., 18:37.

83, 31   Ibid., 18:45.

84, 11   Ibid., 18:19.

84, 12   Ibid., 18:22.

84, 19   2 Kings 5:8.

84, 22   Judges 5:21.

84, 27   1 Kings 19:2.

85, 23   Ibid., 19:12.

85, 27   Ibid., 19:13.

86, 10   Ibid., 21:6.

86, 11   Ibid., 21:7.

86, 13   Ibid., 21:9.

86, 15   Ibid., 21:10.

86, 18   Loc. cit.

86, 20   Ibid., 21:13.

86, 24   Ibid., 22:39.

87, 7   C. Virolleaud, *La Déesse 'Anat*, Geuthner, Paris, 1938, p. 25.

87, 11   Ibid., p. 18.

87, 17   1 Kings 21:19.

87, 22   Loc. cit.

87, 23   Ibid., 21:23.

87, 31   Revelation 2:20.

87, 34   2 Kings 1:8.

88, 14   L. Ginzberg, *The Legends of the Jews*, Jewish Publication Society of
          America, Philadelphia, vol. IV, 1982, p. 186.

88, 16   1 Kings 22:38.

89, 13   2 Kings 2:1.

89, 15   Ibid., 2:11.

89, 24   Ibid., 2:14.

89, 26   Ibid., 9:1, 6:1.

89, 33   Ibid., 6:1–2.

90, 6   Ibid., 2:21.

90, 9   Ibid., 2:23.

90, 11   Ibid., 2:24.

90, 22   Ibid., 4:33–35.

90, 27   Sirach 48:13.

90, 31   2 Kings 13:21.

90, 33   Loc. cit.

92, 1   2 Kings 9:2.

92, 5   Ibid., 9:3.

92, 12   Ibid., 9:11.

92, 14   Ibid., 9:12.

92, 17   Ibid., 9:13.

92, 20   1 Kings 21:21.

92, 31   2 Kings 10:8.

92, 34   Ibid., 10:11.

93, 9   Racine, *Athalie*, Act II, scene v.

93, 10   2 Kings 9:30.

93, 13   Ibid., 9:31.

93, 19   Ibid., 9:32.

93, 25   Ibid., 9:34.

93, 28   Ibid., 9:35.

93, 29   Ibid., 9:37.

93, 30   Loc. cit.

93, 33   Ibid., 10:8.

94, 1   Ibid., 10:14.

94, 3   Ibid., 10:18.

94, 5   Ibid., 10:19.

94, 10   Ibid., 10:23.

94, 14   Ibid., 10:27.

94, 16   Ibid., 10:28.

94, 17   Ibid., 10:29.

94, 19   Racine, Preface to *Athalie*, in *OEuvres complètes*, ed. R. Picard, Gallimard, Paris, vol. I, 1950, p. 872.

94, 22   2 Kings 10:32.

94, 26   Ibid., 11:11.

94, 34   Racine, *Athalie*, Act I, scene ii.

95, 4   2 Kings 11:3.

95, 8   Ibid., 8:19.

95, 18   Racine, *Athalie*, Act II, scene viii.

95, 20   Ibid., scene v.

95, 24   2 Kings 11:20.

95, 25   Racine, *Athalie*, Act I, scene i.

95, 26   2 Kings 12:1.

95, 31   Racine, *Athalie*, Act III, scene iii.

96, 7   Ibid., Act V, scene vi.

96, 10   2 Kings 12:3.

96, 22   Ibid., 12:19.

96, 26   Ibid., 13:5.

96, 29   Ibid., 13:6.

97, 4   Ibid., 13:17.

97, 6   Ibid., 13:18.

97, 10   Ibid., 13:19.

97, 14   Ibid., 13:25.

97, 18   Ibid., 12:4.

97, 21   Ibid., 14:4.

97, 24   Ibid., 15:4.

97, 26   Ibid., 12:3, 14:3, 15:3.

98, 2   Ibid., 21:3.

98, 7   Ibid., 21:7.

98, 12   Ibid., 23:7.

98, 15   Ibid., 23:6.

98, 30   Ibid., 23:11.

99, 5   Ibid., 22:8.

99, 10   Ibid., 22:10.

99, 12   Ibid., 22:11.

99, 17   Ibid., 21:21, 17:12.

99, 22   S. Schama, *The Story of the Jews*, Vintage Books, London, 2014, p. 41.

99, 27   2 Kings 22:13.

99, 31   Ibid., 22:14.

100, 2   Ibid., 22:18–19.

100, 4   Ibid., 22:20.

100, 9   Ibid., 23:2.

100, 14 Loc. cit.

100, 21 Genesis 32:33.

100, 28 Deuteronomy 4:37.

103, 6   Genesis 11:27–30.

103, 11 Joshua 24:2.

103, 13 Ibid., 24:3.

103, 20 É. Dhorme, *Abraham dans le cadre de l'histoire* (1928, 1931), in *Recueil Édouard Dhorme*, Imprimerie Nationale, Paris, 1951, p. 195.

103, 23 Ibid., p. 209.

104, 2   Ibid., p. 245.

104, 9   Genesis 15:1.

104, 15 Ibid., 11:6.

104, 23 Ibid., 12:1.

104, 31 Ibid., 11:31.

105, 9   Ibid., 12:2–3.

105, 15 U. Cassuto, *A Commentary on the Book of Genesis*, translated from the Hebrew by I. Abrahams, Magnes Press, Hebrew University, Jerusalem, vol. II, 1997, p. 310.

105, 25 Genesis 22:2.

106, 12 Ibid., 6:9.

106, 14 Ibid., 6:12.

107, 31 Deuteronomy 26:5–10.

108, 1   G. von Rad, *Das fünfte Buch Mose. Deuteronomium*, in *Das Alte Testament Deutsch*, ed. O. Kaiser and L. Perlitt, Vandenhoeck & Ruprecht, Göttingen, vol. VIII, 1983, p. 113.

108, 19 Deuteronomy 7:7.

108, 30 Genesis 12:5.

108, 32 Ibid., 12:6.

109, 1   Ibid., 12:7.

109, 28   Ibid., 12:15.

109, 33   Ibid., 12:16.

110, 3   Ibid., 12:17.

110, 9   Ibid., 12:18–20.

110, 11   Ibid., 12:20.

110, 12   S. Weil, *Cahiers*, in *OEuvres complètes*, vol. VI, book iv, cit., p. 288.

110, 17   Genesis 12:11.

110, 19   Ibid., 6:2.

110, 24   L. Ginzberg, *The Legends of the Jews*, cit., vol. I, 1968, p. 222.

111, 8   Ibid., p. 223.

111, 12   Genesis 16:4.

111, 28   U. Cassuto, *A Commentary on the Book of Genesis*, vol. II, cit., p. 337.

111, 32   Loc. cit.

112, 7   Ibid., p. 338.

112, 10   Ibid., p. 352.

113, 5   Genesis 14:13.

113, 9   G. von Rad, *Das erste Buch Mose. Genesis*, in *Das Alte Testament Deutsch*, cit., vols. II–IV, 1976, p. 301.

113, 15   Genesis 14:18.

114, 4   Letter to the Hebrews 7:3.

114, 6   Loc. cit.

114, 8   R. Guénon, *Le Roi du Monde*, Bosse, Paris, 1927, p. 66.

114, 14   Genesis 15:1.

114, 19   Loc. cit.

114, 20   Ibid., 15:3.

114, 22   Ibid., 15:18.

114, 29   Ibid., 15:13.

114, 31   Ibid., 15:17.

115, 2   Ibid., 15:18.

115, 3   L. Ginzberg, *The Legends of the Jews*, cit., vol. V, 1953, p. 229.

115, 6   Genesis 17:12.

115, 25   É. Dhorme, in *La Bible. Ancien Testament*, ed. É. Dhorme, Gallimard, Paris, 1959, vol. II, p. 361, note 18.

115, 31   Jeremiah 34:18.

116, 15   Genesis 22:2.

116, 24   Ibid., 17:12.

116, 28   Leviticus 22:27.

117, 16   Genesis 17:18.

117, 28   Ibid., 18:2.

118, 3   Ibid., 18:10.
118, 7   Ibid., 18:12.
118, 11   Ibid., 18:13.
118, 14   Ibid., 18:15.
118, 25   Ibid., 15:7.
118, 26   Ibid., 15:8.
118, 31   Ibid., 15:18.
119, 2   Ibid., 18:27.
119, 10   Ibid., 18:17.
119, 16   Ibid., 18:23.
119, 23   Ibid., 18:26.
120, 16   Ibid., 19:8.
120, 22   Ibid., 19:15.
120, 27   Ibid., 19:27.
120, 30   Ibid., 19:28.
121, 3   Judges 19:1.
121, 7   Ibid., 19:3.
121, 18   Ibid., 19:22.
121, 35   Ibid., 19:23–29.
122, 2   Ibid., 20:37.
122, 9   Genesis 16:8.
122, 13   Ibid., 16:9.
122, 15   Ibid., 16:11.
122, 19   Ibid., 16:13.
122, 25   Ibid., 21:10.
122, 27   Ibid., 21, 12.
122, 29   Ibid., 21:13.
122, 34   Ibid., 21:14.
123, 6   Ibid., 21:16.
123, 10   Ibid., 21:18.
123, 14   Ibid., 21:19.
123, 16   Ibid., 21:20–21.
123, 27   Code of Hammurabi, paragraphs 146–47.
123, 34   Genesis 16:6.
124, 2   Ibid., 22:2.
124, 3   Ibid., 21:13.
124, 5   Ibid., 16:2.
124, 11   Ibid., 21:14, 22:3.
124, 13   Ibid., 21:13.
124, 25   Ibid., 21:12–13.

124, 34   S. Kierkegaard, *Crainte et Tremblement* (1843), trans. P.-H. Tisseau and E.-M. Jacquet-Tisseau, in *OEuvres complètes*, Éditions de l'Orante, Paris, vol. V, 1972, p. 124.

125, 2   Genesis 22:6.

125, 4   Ibid., 22:7.

125, 21   Exodus 13:2.

125, 24   Genesis 22:2.

125, 29   Exodus 13:13.

126, 14   Genesis 22:13.

126, 16   Loc. cit.

126, 29   Ibid., 22:8.

127, 30   Ibid., 22:10.

128, 18   L. Ginzberg, *The Legends of the Jews*, vol. V, cit., p. 256.

128, 22   Genesis 21:17.

128, 23   Ibid., 31:42, 31:53.

128, 32   Letter from F. Kafka to R. Klopstock, June 1921, in *Briefe 1902–1924*, in *Gesammelte Werke*, ed. M. Brod, S. Fischer, Frankfurt a. M., p. 334.

129, 5   Loc. cit.

129, 20   Ibid., p. 333.

129, 26   Genesis 22:3.

129, 32   E. Pocar, in F. Kafka, *Lettere*, ed. F. Masini, Mondadori, Milano, 1988, p. 1091.

130, 3   Isaiah 38:1.

130, 7   Ibid., 38:5.

130, 9   Ibid., 38:8.

130, 15   Ibid., 38:18–19.

131, 12   Job 1:1.

131, 21   Ibid., 1:13.

131, 30   Ibid., 2:4.

131, 33   Ibid., 2:3.

132, 5   Ibid., 1:5.

132, 5   Ibid., 1:10.

132, 13   Loc. cit.

132, 17   Ibid., 1:6.

132, 30   S. Weil, *Cahiers*, in *OEuvres complètes*, cit., vol. VI, book iii, 2002, p. 341.

133, 19   Job 2:7.

133, 23   Ibid., 2:9.

133, 27   Ibid., 2:10.

134, 7   Ibid., 7:1.

134, 10   Ibid., 13:25.

134, 12   Ibid., 7:17.

134, 13   Ibid., 7:20.

134, 15   Ibid., 6:4.

134, 17   Ibid., 13:14.

134, 18   Ibid., 14:2.

134, 20   Ibid., 13:27.

134, 24   S. Weil, *Cahiers*, in *OEuvres complètes*, cit., vol. VI, book iii, cit., p. 341.

134, 31   Job 10:16.

135, 1   Ibid., 7:19.

135, 3   Ibid., 10:21.

135, 16   Ibid., 42:7.

135, 16   Ibid., 42:8.

135, 27   Ibid., 42:15.

136, 2   Genesis 23:4.

136, 5   Ibid., 23:5.

136, 17   Ibid., 23:15.

136, 34   Genesis Rabba 79:7, in Y. Zakovich, *Jacob*, trans. V. Zakovich, Yale University Press, New Haven and London, 2012, p. 119.

137, 7   Genesis 25:5.

137, 11   Ibid., 25:6.

137, 25   L. Ginzberg, *The Legends of the Jews*, vol. I, cit., p. 300.

138, 2   Ibid., p. 302.

138, 3   Loc. cit.

138, 6   Loc. cit.

138, 11   Ibid., p. 306.

138, 13   Loc. cit.

138, 16   Genesis 25:8.

138, 20   Ibid., 26:2.

138, 23   Ibid., 26:5.

139, 6   Proverbs 6:23.

139, 13   Genesis 21:4.

139, 17   Ibid., 22:1.

139, 32   Ibid., 31:53.

140, 3   Exodus 3:6.

140, 8   Genesis 24:56.

140, 10   Ibid., 24:58.

140, 13   Ibid., 24:64–65.

140, 15   Ibid., 24:65.

140, 20 Ibid., 24:66–67.

140, 24 Ibid., 35:11.

141, 6 Ibid., 30:1.

141, 7 Ibid., 30:23.

141, 28 Ibid., 25:33.

141, 31 Ibid., 25:32.

141, 33 Ibid., 25:34.

142, 14 Ibid., 28:12.

142, 20 Ibid., 28:16.

142, 23 Ibid., 28:17.

142, 34 G. von Rad, *Das erste Buch Mose. Genesis*, cit., p. 228.

143, 1 Ibid., p. 231.

143, 5 Loc. cit.

143, 10 Genesis 28:2.

143, 17 Ibid., 30:43.

143, 21 Ibid., 31:43.

143, 22 Ibid., 31:26.

143, 25 Ibid., 31:24.

144, 4 Ibid., 31:37.

144, 9 Ibid., 31:44.

144, 12 Ibid., 31:53.

144, 23 Ibid., 31:32.

145, 2 1 Samuel 19:13.

145, 15 Genesis 31:42, 31:53.

145, 21 Ibid., 31:42.

146, 7 Ibid., 31:53.

146, 8 Loc. cit.

146, 14 Loc. cit.

146, 26 Ibid., 34:1.

146, 28 Ibid., 34:2.

146, 30 Ibid., 34:3.

146, 31 Ibid., 34:4.

147, 13 Ibid., 34:15.

147, 13 Ibid., 34:16.

147, 26 Ibid., 34:25–26.

147, 28 Ibid., 34:29.

148, 10 Ibid., 35:2.

148, 21 Ibid., 35:4.

148, 27 Ibid., 35:5.

148, 34 Ibid., 32:8.

149, 2   Ibid., 27:41.
149, 7   Ibid., 32:23–25.
149, 11 Ibid., 32:25.
149, 14 Ibid., 32:28.
149, 17 Ibid., 32:29.
149, 18 Ibid., 32:30.
149, 19 Ibid., 32:31.
149, 20 Ibid., 32:33.
149, 34 Ibid., 35:5.
150, 13 Hosea 12:4–5.
150, 19 Genesis 32:29.
150, 23 Micah 6:2.
150, 25 Hosea 12:13.
151, 24 Genesis 37:19.
152, 3   Bereshith Rabba 84:11–12, in L. Ginzberg, *The Legends of the Jews*, cit., vol. II, 1983, p. 8.
152, 7   Genesis 39:6.
152, 9   Ibid., 39:23.
152, 19 Ibid., 41:40.
152, 21 Ibid., 37:19.
152, 27 Ibid., 44:15.
152, 33 Ibid., 44:18.
153, 6   Ibid., 41:38.
153, 11 Ibid., 47:11.
153, 13 Ibid., 46:35.
153, 21 Ibid., 50:26.
153, 25 J. D. Levenson, *The Death and Resurrection of the Beloved Son*, Yale University Press, New Haven and London, 1993, p. 154.
154, 6   Genesis 50:20.
154, 29 Daniel 1:4.
155, 5   Ibid., 1:17.
155, 9   Ibid., 1:20.
155, 18 Ibid., 2:5.
155, 22 Ibid., 2:10.
155, 26 Ibid., 2:11.
155, 28 Ibid., 2:12.
156, 3   Ibid., 2:23.
156, 21 Ibid., 2:46.
156, 25 Ibid., 2:48.
156, 28 Ibid., 2:24.

157, 2   Genesis 47:8–9.
157, 20   Ibid., 32:29.
157, 29   Ibid., 35:4.
158, 2   Ibid., 46:7.
158, 3   Ibid., 46:26.
158, 4   Ibid., 46:29.
158, 6   Ibid., 47:7.
158, 8   Ibid., 47:9.
158, 11   Ibid., 47:11.
158, 11   Ibid., 47:27.
158, 15   Ibid., 50:13.
158, 19   Ibid., 37:3.
158, 21   Ibid., 48:8.
158, 26   Ibid., 48:18.
159, 6   Ibid., 49:1.
159, 10   Ibid., 49:4.
159, 12   Ibid., 35:22.
159, 13   Ibid., 49:4.
159, 21   Ibid., 49:5–6.
159, 24   Ibid., 49:6.
159, 26   Ibid., 49:7.
159, 30   Ibid., 49:10.
159, 32   Ibid., 49:14.
159, 33   Ibid., 49:17.
159, 33   Ibid., 49:21.
159, 34   Ibid., 49:27.
160, 7   Ibid., 49:25.
160, 14   Ibid., 49:30.
160, 17   Ibid., 49:32.
160, 24   Ibid., 48:22.
160, 27   Joshua 24:32.
161, 1   Genesis 34:30.
161, 3   Ibid., 34:31.
161, 8   Ibid., 50:2.
161, 10   Ibid., 50:3.
161, 20   Ibid., 50:7–9.
161, 23   Ibid., 50:11.
161, 25   Ibid., 50:13.
161, 33   Ibid., 50:25.
162, 1   Ibid., 50:26.

162, 4   Exodus 1:8.

165, 7   Ibid., 1:9.

165, 14   Ibid., 1:22.

165, 23   Ibid., 2:10.

166, 2   Ibid., 2:12.

166, 10   Ibid., 2:13–15.

166, 22   Ibid., 2:17.

166, 23   Ibid., 2:19.

166, 27   Ibid., 2:21.

166, 28   Ibid., 2:23.

166, 32   Loc. cit.

166, 33   Ibid., 2:25.

167, 4   Ibid., 3:3.

167, 8   Ibid., 3:4.

167, 12   Ibid., 3:8.

167, 16   Ibid., 3:11.

167, 19   Ibid., 3:14.

167, 23   Ibid., 3:18.

167, 25   Ibid., 3:20.

167, 29   Ibid., 3:21–22.

167, 33   Genesis 12:4b.

168, 7   Exodus 3:2.

168, 10   Genesis 22:13.

168, 11   Ibid., 22:11.

168, 13   Exodus 3:3.

168, 22   Ibid., 3:6.

168, 24   Ibid., 3:7.

168, 26   Ibid., 3:10.

168, 32   Ibid., 4:24.

169, 2   Ibid., 4:25.

169, 2   Ibid., 4:26.

169, 22   U. Cassuto, *A Commentary on the Book of Exodus*, translation from the Hebrew by I. Abrahams, Magnes Press, Hebrew University, Jerusalem, 1997, p. 16.

170, 2   H. Gressmann, *Mose und seine Zeit*, Vandenhoeck & Ruprecht, Göttingen, 1913, p. 57.

170, 19   Exodus 4:22–23.

171, 12   R. Alter, in *The Hebrew Bible*, ed. R. Alter, W. W. Norton & Company, New York and London, 2019, p. 228, n. 24.

171, 31   Exodus 5:2.

172, 24   Ibid., 5:4.

172, 27   Ibid., 5:8.

173, 8   Ibid., 5:21.

173, 13   Ibid., 5:23.

174, 20   Ibid., 5:3.

174, 31   Letter to the Ephesians 6:12.

175, 2   Exodus 7:22.

175, 8   Ibid., 7:3.

175, 10   Ibid., 7:4.

175, 12   Ibid., 7:5.

176, 2   Ibid., 8:4.

176, 8   Ibid., 8:10.

176, 23   Ibid., 9:15–16.

177, 1   Ibid., 10:16.

177, 6   Ibid., 10:7.

177, 14   Ibid., 8:21.

177, 19   Ibid., 8:23.

177, 22   Ibid., 8:22.

177, 24   Ibid., 8:24.

178, 7   Ibid., 10:28–29.

178, 11   Ibid., 12:12.

178, 15   Ibid., 11:1.

178, 19   Ibid., 12:5.

178, 28   Ibid., 12:29–30.

178, 33   Ibid., 12:31–32.

179, 2   Genesis 12:19.

179, 21   Exodus 12:42.

179, 23   Ibid., 12:11.

179, 27   Ibid., 12:17.

180, 19   R. de Vaux, *Histoire ancienne d'Israël*, Lecoffre-Gabalda, Paris, 1971, p. 344.

180, 34   Ibid., p. 345.

181, 2   Ibid., p. 346.

181, 5   Exodus 12:13, 12:23, 12:27.

181, 10   R. de Vaux, *Histoire ancienne d'Israël*, cit., p. 346.

181, 23   Ibid., p. 347.

182, 3   Ibid., p. 348.

182, 16   Ibid., p. 346.

182, 22   Ibid., p. 348.

183, 1   Exodus 13:2.

183, 18   Ibid., 22:28.

184, 25   Ibid., 13:14–15.

185, 3   Ibid., 13:13.

185, 19   Numbers 33:3–4.

186, 2   H. Binder, *Kafka-Kommentar*, Winkler, München, 1976, 2nd am-
          plified ed., 1982, p. 113.

186, 21   Numbers 33:3.

186, 26   F. Kafka, *Der Verschollene*, ed. J. Schillemeit, in *Kritische Aus-
          gabe*, S. Fischer, Frankfurt a. M., 1983, p. 124.

186, 32   Ibid., p. 394.

187, 11   Ibid., pp. 415–16.

187, 14   F. Kafka, *Tagebücher*, ed. H.-G. Koch, M. Müller, and M. Pasley, in
          Kritische Ausgabe, cit., 1990, p. 792.

187, 20   U. Cassuto, *A Commentary on the Book of Exodus*, cit., p. 161.

187, 26   Exodus 14:8.

187, 28   Ibid., 14:10.

187, 32   Ibid., 14:10–11.

188, 6   Ibid., 14:12.

188, 18   Ibid., 14:22.

186, 25   Ibid., 15:18.

186, 27   Ibid., 15:5.

189, 23   Ibid., 17:8.

189, 33   Ibid., 17:11.

189, 34   Ibid., 17:12.

190, 6   Ibid., 17:14.

190, 8   Loc. cit.

190, 12   Ibid., 17:16.

190, 21   J. D. Levenson, "Is There a Counterpart in the Hebrew Bible to
          New Testament Antisemitism," *Journal of Ecumenical Studies*
          22:2, 1985, p. 249.

190, 31   Deuteronomy 23:8.

191, 6   E. Meyer, *Die Israeliten und ihre Nachbarstämme*, Wissenschaft-
          liche Buchgesellschaft, Darmstadt, 1906, p. 346.

191, 17   Exodus 17:16.

192, 4   Ibid., 4:25.

192, 8   Ibid., 18:12.

192, 10   Ibid., 18:13.

192, 13   Ibid., 18:14.

192, 14   Ibid., 18:17.

192, 24   Ibid., 18:24.

192, 27   Ibid., 18:27.
192, 32   Numbers 12:2.
193, 1   Ibid., 12:4.
193, 5   Ibid., 12:6.
193, 7   Ibid., 12:7–8.
193, 11   Ibid., 12:9.
194, 5   Flavio Giuseppe, *Antiquities of the Jews*, II, 10, 2.
194, 7   Loc. cit.
194, 9   Ibid., 11, 1.
194, 12   Loc. cit.
194, 26   Exodus 25:3–7.
194, 30   Ibid., 25:8.
194, 32   Ibid., 25:21.
195, 5   Ibid., 26:1, 26:31.
195, 17   Ibid., 31:17.
195, 21   Ibid., 31:18.
195, 29   Ibid., 32:1.
195, 33   Ibid., 32:5.
196, 3   Deuteronomy 4:13.
196, 5   Ibid., 5:22.
196, 6   Loc. cit.
196, 15   Loc. cit.
196, 20   Exodus 32:4.
196, 26   Ibid., 32:6.
197, 2   Deuteronomy 9:14.
197, 5   Ibid., 9:25.
197, 9   Ibid., 9:27.
197, 14   Ibid., 9:28.
197, 25   Exodus 32:21.
197, 27   Ibid., 32:22.
197, 31   Genesis 6:5.
197, 33   Exodus 32:25.
198, 2   Ibid., 32:27.
198, 2   Ibid., 32:28.
198, 5   Ibid., 32:29.
198, 17   Ibid., 33:6.
198, 21   Ibid., 36:5.
198, 24   Ibid., 36:6–7.
199, 13   Ibid., 28:43.
199, 18   Leviticus 9:23–24.

199, 27   Ibid., 10:1–3.

199, 33   Ibid., 10:4.

200, 1   Ibid., 10:6.

200, 5   Ibid., 10:9–10.

200, 7   Ibid., 16:1.

200, 21   Ibid., 16:21–22.

200, 23   Ibid., 16:32.

201, 4   Numbers 15:32.

201, 9   Ibid., 15:35.

201, 27   Exodus 3:18.

202, 7   Numbers 11:5.

202, 10   Ibid., 11:20.

202, 19   Deuteronomy 8:2.

202, 22   Ibid., 8:18.

202, 25   Ibid., 8:19.

202, 27   Ibid., 4:27.

202, 32   Ibid., 4:11.

202, 32   Ibid., 4:12.

203, 4   Ibid., 4:16–18.

203, 7   Ibid., 4:19.

203, 9   Loc. cit.

203, 12   Ibid., 4:20.

203, 16   Loc. cit.

204, 15   Ibid., 7:7.

204, 26   Exodus 25:18.

204, 32   1 Kings 6:27.

205, 2   Ibid., 6:29.

205, 9   Exodus 20:4.

205, 18   Numbers 7:89.

205, 22   2 Samuel 22:10–11.

205, 25   Genesis 1:26.

206, 2   U. Cassuto, *A Commentary on the Book of Exodus*, cit., p. 407.

206, 6   Ibid., p. 408.

206, 15   Loc. cit.

206, 18   Genesis 3:24.

207, 3   Ibid., 28:17.

207, 9   Exodus 40:34.

207, 15   Ibid., 40:36–38.

207, 20   Numbers 9:22.

207, 26   Ibid., 9:23.

208, 15 Exodus 25:15.

208, 34 Ibid., 40:9.

209, 10 Isaiah 61:1.

209, 18 Leviticus 8:30.

209, 23 Ibid., 8:24.

209, 29 Exodus 29:12.

210, 7   U. Cassuto, *Biblical and Oriental Studies*, translation from the Hebrew by I. Abrahams, Magnes Press, Hebrew University, Jerusalem, 1973, vol. I, p. 2.

210, 14 Leviticus 17:11–12.

210, 24 Letter to the Hebrews 9:22.

211, 7   Numbers 8:14–19.

211, 32 F. Schwally, *Semitische Kriegsaltertümer*, Dieterich, Leipzig, 1901, p. 37.

212, 19 Exodus 30:12.

212, 24 Ibid., 30:15.

213, 7   Ibid., 3:47–48.

213, 9   Ibid., 3:32.

213, 11 Ibid., 23:15, 34:20.

213, 13 Ibid., 34:20.

213, 17 Ibid., 22:28.

213, 21 Ezekiel 44:28.

213, 31 Numbers 18:21.

214, 4   Ibid., 18:26.

214, 11 Ibid., 18:31.

214, 13 Loc. cit.

214, 16 Ibid., 18:32.

214, 24 Ibid., 20:4.

214, 27 Ibid., 20:6.

214, 30 Ibid., 20:10.

215, 5   Ibid., 20:29.

215, 7   Ibid., 21:5.

215, 9   Exodus 16:14.

215, 12 Numbers 21:6.

215, 16 Ibid., 21:7.

215, 19 Ibid., 21:8.

216, 9   2 Kings 18:4.

216, 24 Ibid., 18:5.

216, 26 Ibid., 18:6.

216, 32 John 3:14–15.

217, 13   Deuteronomy 2:9.

217, 16   L. Ginzberg, *The Legends of the Jews*, cit., vol. III, 1939, p. 352.

217, 18   Ibid., p. 382.

217, 23   Numbers 25:1–3.

217, 24   Ibid., 25:4.

217, 28   Ibid., 25:6.

217, 32   Ibid., 25:8.

218, 4   Ibid., 25:11.

218, 13   E. Sellin, *Mose und seine Bedeutung für die israelitisch-jüdische Religionsgeschichte*, Deichert, Leipzig-Erlangen, 1922, pp. 49–50.

218, 22   Hosea 5:2.

218, 25   E. Sellin, *Mose und seine Bedeutung für die israelitisch-jüdische Religionsgeschichte*, cit., p. 52.

218, 31   J. Assmann, *Exodus*, Beck, München, 2015, p. 438.

219, 4   Numbers 13:18–20.

219, 27   Ibid., 13:33.

220, 12   Ibid., 33:51–56.

220, 15   Deuteronomy 31:2.

220, 16   Ibid., 34:7.

220, 19   Ibid., 31:2.

220, 24   Ibid., 31:3.

220, 27   Ibid., 31:9.

220, 29   Ibid., 31:10.

220, 30   Ibid., 31:11.

220, 34   Ibid., 31:12.

221, 2   G. von Rad, *Das fünfte Buch Mose. Deuteronomium*, cit., p. 134.

221, 6   Exodus 24:8.

221, 20   Deuteronomy 31:14.

221, 23   Ibid., 31:22.

221, 26   Ibid., 31:29.

221, 33   Ibid., 32:8–9.

222, 7   Ibid., 32:10–11.

222, 11   Job 7:19.

222, 18   G. von Rad, *Das fünfte Buch Mose. Deuteronomium*, cit., p. 141.

222, 20   Hosea 9:10.

222, 24   Deuteronomy 17:15.

222, 27   Ibid., 17:14.

222, 32   Ibid., 17:19.

223, 1   Ibid., 17:20.

223, 7   Ibid., 18:15.

223, 15 Ibid., 18:22.

223, 20 Exodus 20:5.

223, 25 Deuteronomy 24:16.

224, 19 Ibid., 6:6–9.

224, 25 Letter to the Hebrews 9:15.

224, 30 Deuteronomy 13:1.

225, 6 Ibid., 12:10.

225, 12 Ibid., 12:8–9.

225, 15 Ibid., 20:15.

225, 22 Ibid., 20:14.

225, 24 Ibid., 20:16.

225, 33 Ibid., 20:18.

226, 21 Exodus 22:19.

226, 26 Deuteronomy 13:2.

226, 27 Ibid., 13:3.

226, 30 Ibid., 13:7.

226, 32 Loc. cit.

226, 33 Ibid., 13:10.

227, 2 Ibid., 13:10–11.

227, 7 G. von Rad, *Der Heilige Krieg im alten Israel*, Vandenhoeck & Ruprecht, Göttingen, 1951, p. 16.

227, 15 Ibid., p. 17.

227, 18 W. Caspari, "Was stand in Buch der Kriege Jahwes?," *Zeitschrift für wissenschaftliche Theologie* 54, 1912, pp. 110–11.

227, 24 Deuteronomy 7:16.

228, 5 Ibid., 7:1–4.

228, 11 Ibid., 32:52.

228, 14 Ibid., 32:51.

228, 15 Exodus 17:7.

228, 23 Ibid., 17:8.

229, 21 Deuteronomy 25:17–18.

229, 28 Ibid., 25:19.

230, 2 Ibid., 30:15–16.

230, 13 Ibid., 32:49–50.

230, 19 Ibid., 34:10.

230, 24 Ibid., 34:6.

230, 25 Loc. cit.

230, 31 L. Ginzberg, *The Legends of the Jews*, vol. III, cit., p. 422.

230, 33 Loc. cit.

231, 4 Exodus 2:19.

231, 15 Deuteronomy 26:5.
231, 23 Joshua 3:17.
231, 32 Ibid., 5:1.
232, 4 John Crisostomo, *Homilies Against the Jews*, 2, 2, 4.
232, 12 Leviticus 19:23–24.
232, 22 Joshua 5:12.
233, 2 Exodus 12:43.
233, 18 Moïse Maïmonide, *Le Guide des égarés*, trans. S. Munk, Verdier, Paris, 1979, p. 581.
233, 22 Ibid., p. 606.
233, 30 Loc. cit.
234, 7 Ibid., pp. 606–607.
234, 8 Ibid., p. 607.
234, 11 Loc. cit.
234, 15 Numbers 20:17.
234, 16 Ibid., 20:14.
234, 26 Ibid., 21:2–3.
234, 32 Ibid., 21:35.
235, 2 Ibid., 22:4.
235, 14 Deuteronomy 6:25.
235, 15 Ibid., 8:7.
235, 19 Loc. cit.
235, 20 Ibid., 8:15.
235, 23 Numbers 21:5.
235, 28 Joshua 10:30.
235, 31 Ibid., 10:40.
235, 32 Ibid., 10:43.
235, 33 Ibid., 10:42.
236, 8 Deuteronomy 28:49–50.
236, 16 Ibid., 28:56–57.
236, 19 Isaiah 10:20.
236, 21 Deuteronomy 28:62.
237, 4 Ibid., 28:63–66.
237, 13 Joshua 7:11.
237, 23 Ibid., 7:21.
237, 31 Ibid., 7:24–26.
237, 33 Ibid., 11:4.
238, 4 Ibid., 11:19–20.
238, 11 Ibid., 11:23.
238, 14 Ibid., 14:2.

238, 18 Ibid., 15:63.

238, 22 Ibid., 24:2.

238, 24 Ibid., 24:7.

238, 30 Ibid., 23:1.

238, 33 Ibid., 23:14.

239, 1   Ibid., 23:15.

239, 3   Loc. cit.

239, 7   Ibid., 24:13.

239, 13 Ibid., 24:26.

239, 15 Ibid., 24:27.

239, 22 L. Ginzberg, *The Legends of the Jews*, vol. III, cit., p. 464.

239, 30 Ibid., p. 125.

243, 12 Letter from W. Benjamin to G. Adorno, October 9, 1935, in *Brief-wechsel* 1930–1940, ed. Ch. Gödde and H. Lonitz, Suhrkamp, Frankfurt a. M., 2005, p. 244.

243, 13 S. Freud, *Der Mann Moses und die monotheistische Religion*, in *Studienausgabe*, S. Fischer, Frankfurt a. M., Vol. IX, ed. A. Mitscherlich, A. Richards, and J. Strachey, 1974, p. 503.

243, 19 Ibid., p. 504.

244, 2   Ibid., p. 459.

244, 28 Ibid., p. 504.

245, 13 Ibid., p. 465.

245, 19 Ibid., p. 467.

245, 24 Ibid., pp. 485–86.

245, 29 Ibid., p. 502.

246, 3   Ibid., pp. 504–505.

246, 9   Ibid., p. 506.

246, 16 Ibid., p. 507.

246, 21 Loc. cit.

246, 29 Loc. cit.

247, 8   Ibid., p. 501.

247, 13 Loc. cit.

247, 22 Ibid., p. 507.

247, 29 Ibid., p. 550.

247, 32 Loc. cit.

248, 2   Loc. cit.

248, 7   Loc. cit.

248, 8   Ibid., p. 548.

248, 11 Ibid., pp. 547–48.

248, 17 Ibid., p. 550.

248, 19   Loc. cit.

248, 20   Loc. cit.

248, 25   Ibid., p. 551.

248, 28   Loc. cit.

249, 7   Ibid., p. 575.

249, 10   Letter from S. Freud to A. Zweig, September 30, 1934, in *Briefe 1873–1939*, ed. E. and L. Freud, S. Fischer, Frankfurt a. M., 1980, p. 436.

249, 15   Loc. cit.

249, 21   Loc. cit.

249, 31   Letter from S. Freud to A. Zweig, April 9, 1935, ibid., p. 439.

250, 2   S. Freud, *Der Mann Moses und die monotheistische Religion*, cit., p. 509.

250, 4   Loc. cit.

250, 13   Ibid., p. 509, n. 1.

250, 24   Ibid., p. 550.

250, 32   Letter from S. Freud to A. Zweig, September 30, 1934, in *Briefe 1873–1939*, cit., p. 436.

251, 5   S. Freud, *Der Mann Moses und die monotheistische Religion*, cit., p. 550.

251, 30   Letter from S. Freud to A. Zweig, September 30, 1934, in *Briefe 1873–1939*, cit., p. 436.

251, 32   S. Freud, *Der Mann Moses und die monotheistische Religion*, cit., p. 553.

252, 5   Ibid., p. 557.

252, 12   Ibid., p. 579.

252, 14   Loc. cit.

252, 27   Ibid., p. 560.

252, 30   Loc. cit.

253, 21   Ibid., p. 494.

253, 26   Loc. cit.

253, 32   Ibid., p. 472.

254, 1   Loc. cit.

255, 11   Letter from S. Freud to A. Zweig, September 30, 1934, in *Briefe 1873–1939*, cit., p. 436.

255, 18   S. Freud, *Der Mann Moses und die monotheistische Religion*, cit., p. 557.

255, 31   Ibid., p. 508.

255, 34   Exodus 3:14.

256, 6   S. Freud, *Der Mann Moses und die monotheistische Religion*, cit., p. 567.

257, 9   Ibid., p. 561.

257, 28   S. Freud, *Brief an Romain Rolland*, in *Gesammelte Werke*, ed. A. Freud, S. Fischer, Frankfurt a. M., vol. XVI, 1999, pp. 251–52.

258, 21   Letter from W. Benjamin to G. Adorno, October 9, 1935, in *Briefwechsel 1930–1940*, cit., p. 244.

259, 13   S. Freud, *Der Mann Moses und die monotheistische Religion*, cit., p. 547.

259, 32   Ibid., pp. 547–48.

260, 6   Ibid., p. 537.

261, 21   Y. H. Yerushalmi, *Freud's Moses*, Yale University Press, New Haven and London, 1991, p. 82.

261, 29   S. Freud, *Totem und Tabu*, in *Studienausgabe*, vol. IX, cit., p. 424.

261, 32   S. Freud, *Der Mann Moses und die monotheistische Religion*, cit., p. 548.

262, 4   S. Freud, *Totem und Tabu*, cit., p. 437.

262, 10   S. Freud, *Der Mann Moses und die monotheistische Religion*, cit., p. 568.

262, 14   Letter from S. Freud to A. Zweig, September 30, 1934, in *Briefe 1873–1939*, cit., p. 436.

262, 17   Numbers 14:10.

262, 18   Exodus 17:4.

262, 22   S. Freud, *Totem und Tabu*, cit., p. 443.

263, 8   S. Freud, *Der Mann Moses und die monotheistische Religion*, cit., p. 548.

263, 9   Letter from S. Freud to A. Zweig, September 30, 1934, in *Briefe 1873–1939*, cit., p. 436.

263, 16   Loc. cit.

264, 16   Loc. cit.

265, 25   S. Freud, *Zeitgemässes über Krieg und Tod*, in *Studienausgabe*, vol. IX, cit., p. 52.

265, 27   S. Freud, *Der Mann Moses und die monotheistische Religion*, cit., p. 515.

265, 28   Loc. cit.

265, 30   S. Freud, *Totem und Tabu*, cit., p. 426, n. 2.

266, 7   C. Darwin, *The Descent of Man, and Selection in Relation to Sex*, Penguin, London, 2004, p. 659.

266, 32   S. Freud, *Totem und Tabu*, cit., p. 426.

267, 5   J. J. Atkinson, *Primal Law*, in *Social Origins by A. Lang and Primal Law by J. J. Atkinson*, Longmans, Green, and Co., London, New York, and Bombay, 1903, pp. 220–21.

267, 25   J. W. Goethe, *Israel in der Wüste*, in *West-östlicher Divan*, cit., p. 514.

268, 15   S. Freud, *Der Mann Moses und die monotheistische Religion*, cit., p. 548.

268, 26   Ibid., p. 557.

269, 2   Letter from S. Freud to A. Zweig, September 30, 1934, in *Briefe 1873–1939*, cit., p. 436.

269, 10   S. Freud, *Der Mann Moses und die monotheistische Religion*, cit., p. 577.

269, 22   Ibid., p. 548.

269, 27   Y. H. Yerushalmi, *Freud's Moses*, cit., p. 30.

269, 31   S. Freud, *Der Mann Moses und die monotheistische Religion*, cit., p. 577.

270, 10   Heraclitus 14[A 55] .

271, 25   C. Darwin, *The Descent of Man, and Selection in Relation to Sex*, cit., p. 118.

271, 28   Loc. cit.

271, 33   S. Freud, *Totem und Tabu*, cit., p. 440.

272, 1   Loc. cit.

272, 14   Loc. cit.

272, 18   Ibid., p. 442.

272, 25   Loc. cit.

272, 33   Ibid., p. 443.

273, 18   Acts of the Apostles 7:52.

273, 25   Matthew 23:31.

274, 4   S. Freud, *Der Mann Moses und die monotheistische Religion*, cit., p. 488.

274, 11   Ibid., p. 489.

274, 18   Ibid., p. 488.

274, 21   Ibid., p. 513.

274, 25   Exodus 3:6.

274, 28   Letter from S. Freud to A. Zweig, September 30, 1934, in *Briefe 1873–1939*, cit., p. 436.

275, 24   S. Freud, *Das Unbehagen in der Kultur*, in *Studienausgabe*, vol. IX, cit., p. 197.

275, 29   *The Gospel of Sri Ramakrishna*, ed. Swami Nikhilananda, Ramakrishna-Vivekananda Center, New York, 1952, p. 197.

276, 2   Letter from R. Rolland to S. Freud, July 20, 1929, in *Briefe 1873–1939*, cit., p. 406.

276, 4   Loc. cit.

276, 9 S. Freud, *Das Unbehagen in der Kultur*, cit., p. 198.

276, 20 Loc. cit.

276, 31 S. Freud, *Ergebnisse, Ideen, Probleme*, in *Gesammelte Werke*, cit., vol. XVII, 1999, p. 152.

277, 4 J. D. Levenson, *Is There a Counterpart in the Hebrew Bible to New Testament Antisemitism?*, cit., p. 248, n. 17.

277, 10 Letter from S. Freud to A. Zweig, September 30, 1934, in *Briefe 1873–1939*, cit., p. 436.

281, 1 Genesis 1:2.

281, 10 Isaiah 51:9.

281, 12 Proverbs 8:27.

281, 17 Genesis 1:7.

281, 20 Ibid., 1:6.

281, 21 Ibid., 1:7.

281, 27 Ibid., 1:3.

281, 28 Ibid., 1:2.

282, 16 L. Ginzberg, *The Legends of the Jews*, vol. I, cit., p. 14.

282, 19 Loc. cit.

282, 25 Isaiah 63:12.

282, 32 Genesis 1:12.

283, 5 T. Jacobsen, "Mesopotamia," in H. and H. A. Frankfort, J. A. Wilson, and T. Jacobsen, *Before Philosophy*, Penguin, Harmondsworth, UK, 1949, p. 159.

283, 25 R. Guénon, *Le Roi du Monde*, cit., p. 75.

283, 32 R. Guénon, *Symboles fondamentaux de la Science sacrée*, Gallimard, Paris, 1962, p. 36.

284, 10 Loc. cit.

284, 18 Ibid., p. 54.

284, 19 Loc. cit.

284, 23 Ibid., p. 35.

285, 30 Genesis 2:8.

285, 33 Ibid., 2:15.

286, 5 Ibid., 2:9.

286, 9 Ibid., 2:16.

286, 13 Ibid., 2:17.

286, 22 Ibid., 3:22.

286, 25 Loc. cit.

287, 23 Ibid., 3:6.

288, 1 Ibid., 3:7.

288, 3 Loc. cit.

288, 18 Ibid., 1:27.

288, 20 Ibid., 2:18.

288, 24 Ibid., 2:23.

289, 24 Ibid., 1:26.

290, 1 Ibid., 3:5.

290, 7 Ibid., 3:1.

290, 21 Psalms 50:21.

291, 16 U. Cassuto, *A Commentary on the Book of Genesis*, cit., vol. I, 1998, p. 83.

291, 28 Ibid., p. 39.

292, 6 Genesis 2:20.

292, 7 Ibid., 2:19.

292, 11 Ibid., 3:20.

292, 18 Ibid., 4:25.

293, 1 *Vita Adae et Evae*, 3.

293, 13 L. Ginzberg, *The Legends of the Jews*, vol. I, cit., p. 105.

293, 15 Genesis 4:1.

293, 18 Ibid., 4:4.

293, 23 Ibid., 4:3.

294, 1 Ibid., 4:4.

294, 6 Ibid., 4:5.

294, 17 Ibid., 4:6–7.

294, 25 Ibid., 3:16.

294, 30 Ibid., 4:8.

295, 1 Ibid., 4:4.

295, 12 Ibid., 4:3.

295, 15 Ibid., 4:4.

295, 16 Ibid., 8:20.

295, 19 Ibid., 4:3.

296, 16 S. Weil, *Cahiers*, in *OEuvres complètes*, vol. VI, book iv, cit., p. 350.

296, 19 R. Guénon, *Le Règne de la Quantité et les Signes des Temps*, Gallimard, Paris, 1945, p. 147.

296, 23 Genesis 12:1.

297, 3 U. Cassuto, *A Commentary on the Book of Genesis*, vol. I, cit., p. 205.

297, 13 Genesis 4:13.

297, 22 Ibid., 4:15.

297, 26 Deuteronomy 21:3.

297, 28 Ibid., 21:4.

298, 4 Ibid., 21:6–9.

298, 13 Matthew 12:7.

298, 20   Deuteronomy 21:8.

299, 11   Ibid., 21:7.

299, 21   Genesis 4:23.

299, 25   Ibid., 4:24.

299, 30   Ibid., 6:2.

300, 19   Ibid., 6:3.

300, 26   Ibid., 6:2.

300, 29   U. Cassuto, *A Commentary on the Book of Genesis*, vol. I, cit., p. 291.

300, 32   Ibid., p. 292.

300, 34   Ibid., p. 293.

300, 35   Ibid., p. 294.

301, 2   Loc. cit.

301, 5   Genesis 6:2.

301, 6   U. Cassuto, *A Commentary on the Book of Genesis*, vol. I, cit., p. 294.

301, 11   Genesis 6:5.

301, 14   Ibid., 6:6.

301, 21   Ibid., 6:12.

301, 33   *Le Poème d'Atrahasîs, ou du Supersage*, in J. Bottéro and S. N. Kramer, *Lorsque les dieux faisaient l'homme*, Gallimard, Paris, 1993, p. 555.

302, 6   Genesis 6:9.

302, 6   Ibid., 6:14.

302, 9   *Gilgamesh XI*, in *Myths from Mesopotamia*, ed. S. Dalley, Oxford University Press, Oxford, 2000, p. 114.

302, 10   Loc. cit.

302, 13   Genesis 8:20.

302, 21   Ibid., 8:21.

302, 32   Ibid., 9:3–4.

303, 2   R. de Vaux, *Les Sacrifices de l'Ancien Testament*, Gabalda, Paris, 1964, p. 36.

303, 19   Leviticus 1:2–3.

304, 4   Ibid., 3:16.

304, 24   *Enuma Elish*, in *Myths from Mesopotamia*, cit., p. 234.

305, 2   *Gilgamesh XI*, 193–94, in J. Bottéro and S. N. Kramer, *Lorsque les dieux faisaient l'homme*, cit., p. 575.

305, 9   *Gilgamesh X*, in *Myths from Mesopotamia*, cit., p. 150.

305, 13   Loc. cit.

305, 15   Loc. cit.

305, 16   Ecclesiastes 9:8.

305, 19   *Gilgamesh* X, in *Myths from Mesopotamia*, cit., p. 151.

305, 20   *Gilgamesh* XI, in *Myths from Mesopotamia*, cit., p. 119.

305, 22   *Erra* IV, in *Myths from Mesopotamia*, cit., p. 305.

305, 29   *Gilgamesh* XI, in *Myths from Mesopotamia*, cit., p. 116.

306, 2   Ibid., p. 117.

306, 7   Ibid., p. 118.

306, 10   Ibid., p. 119.

306, 14   Loc. cit.

306, 17   Loc. cit.

306, 24   Ibid., p. 109.

306, 30   Genesis 6:5.

306, 32   Ibid., 8:21.

307, 1   Loc. cit.

307, 7   Ibid., 8:22.

307, 10   Ibid., 8:1.

307, 18   Ibid., 7:11.

307, 25   Ibid., 6:19.

307, 29   Ibid., 7:1–2.

308, 17   Ibid., 9:13.

309, 1   *Enuma Elish* VI, 86–87, in E. van Wolde, "One Bow or Another?,"
          Vetus Testamentum 63:1, 2013, p. 136.

309, 9   Genesis 9:2.

309, 27   Ibid., 8:20.

309, 31   Loc. cit.

310, 2   Ibid., 8:21.

310, 8   Ibid., 9:v2.

310, 10   Ibid., 1:26.

310, 15   Ibid., 9:3.

310, 17   Ibid., 9:4.

310, 24   Ibid., 9:6.

310, 28   Ibid., 8:21.

310, 32   Ibid., 9:9.

311, 28   Theophrastus, in Porphyry, *De abstinentia*, II, 26, 3.

311, 29   Megasthenes, in Clement, *Stromateis*, I, 15, 72.

311, 32   Theophrastus, in Porphyry, *De abstinentia*, II, 26, 1.

312, 1   Ibid., 26, 4.

312, 6   Ibid., 26, 2.

312, 9   Ibid., 26, 3.

312, 13   Leviticus 6:2.

312, 19   Genesis 8:21.

312, 21   R. K. Yerkes, *Sacrifice*, Charles Scribner's Sons, New York, 1952, p. 140.

312, 27   Numbers 19:36.

312, 28   Ibid., 29:35.

313, 3   Leviticus 3:17.

313, 27   Ibid., 6:1–4.

314, 27   Hosea 6:6.

314, 31   Matthew 9:13.

314, 32   Ibid., 9:11.

315, 3   Ibid., 9:13.

315, 8   Ibid., 12:7.

315, 26   Ibid., 12:6.

315, 34   Ibid., 9:11.

316, 6   Ibid., 12:7.

316, 20   Ibid., 12:1.

316, 22   Ibid., 12:2.

316, 27   Ibid., 12:3–5.

316, 30   Ibid., 12:6.

317, 13   Genesis 9:20.

317, 19   Ibid., 9:22.

317, 33   Ibid., 9:24.

318, 8   Ibid., 9:25.

318, 17   Ibid., 9:26.

318, 19   Ibid., 9:27.

318, 22   Loc. cit.

319, 17   Ibid., 11:1.

320, 13   Ibid., 11:4.

320, 32   L. Ginzberg, *The Legends of the Jews*, vol. I, cit., p. 179.

321, 9   Zephaniah 3:9.

321, 11   Loc. cit.

321, 18   Genesis 11:2.

321, 32   Ibid., 11:6.

322, 3   Ibid., 11:4.

322, 9   Ibid., 10:8–9.

322, 27   Ibid., 10:11.

322, 27   Ibid., 10:12.

322, 33   L. Ginzberg, *The Legends of the Jews*, vol. V, cit., p. 198.

323, 17   Genesis 10:9.

323, 31   M. J. Darmesteter, "La Flèche de Nemrod en Perse et en Chine," *Journal Asiatique*, series VIII, 5, 1885, p. 220.

324, 9   Se-Ma Ts'ien, *Les Mémoires historiques*, ed. É. Chavannes, Adrien-Maisonneuve, Paris, vol. I, 1967, p. 198.

324, 21   *Anzu* I, in *Myths from Mesopotamia*, cit., p. 205.

324, 24   Ibid., p. 206.

324, 33   Ibid., p. 207.

325, 1   Loc. cit.

325, 2   Loc. cit.

325, 13   Ibid., p. 211.

325, 14   Loc. cit.

325, 15   *Anzu* II, in *Myths from Mesopotamia*, cit., p. 212.

325, 17   Loc. cit.

325, 20   Ibid., p. 213.

325, 24   Ibid., p. 215.

326, 2   Ibid., p. 219.

326, 8   Genesis 11:31.

328, 17   Joshua 24:2.

329, 1   Ezekiel 1:1.

329, 3   Loc. cit.

329, 4   Ibid., 1:5.

329, 6   Ibid., 1:13.

329, 7   Ibid., 1:19.

329, 11   Ibid., 1:24.

329, 13   Ibid., 1:12.

329, 17   Ibid., 2:6.

329, 18   Loc. cit.

329, 20   Ibid., 2:8.

329, 21   Ibid., 3:2.

330, 20   S. Schama, *The Story of the Jews*, cit., p. 23.

330, 22   Jeremiah 44:3.

330, 31   Ibid., 44:12–13.

331, 8   Ibid., 44:16–17.

331, 18   Ibid., 44:26.

332, 3   Ezekiel 29:18.

332, 9   Ibid., 29:19–20.

332, 13   Ibid., 29:16.

332, 31   Ibid., 31:2.

333, 1   Ibid., 31:6.

333, 3   Ibid., 31:8.

333, 4   Ibid., 31:9.

333, 8   Ibid., 31:10.

333, 10   Ibid., 31:11.

333, 12   Ibid., 31:13.

333, 18   Ibid., 31:14.

333, 21   Ibid., 31:15.

333, 27   Ibid., 31:16.

333, 32   Ibid., 31:18.

334, 5   Ibid., 32:19.

334, 10   Ibid., 32:27.

334, 12   Ibid., 32:32.

334, 14   Ibid., 32:30.

334, 29   Isaiah 51:9–10.

334, 34   Ezekiel 29:3.

335, 2   Ibid., 29:4.

335, 5   Ibid., 29:5.

335, 10   Ibid., 29:10.

335, 20   Jeremiah 3:2.

335, 27   Ezekiel 37:23, 6:13, 8:10.

335, 34   Jeremiah 2:24.

336, 2   Ibid., 2:25.

336, 3   Ibid., 2:31.

336, 5   Ibid., 3:1.

336, 7   Ibid., 3:2.

336, 8   Ibid., 3:6.

336, 9   Ibid., 3:9.

336, 17   Ezekiel 16:5.

336, 19   Ibid., 16:6–7.

337, 3   Ibid., 16:7–14.

337, 6   Ibid., 16:15.

337, 10   Ibid., 16:17.

337, 12   Ibid., 16:21.

337, 14   Ibid., 16:22.

337, 17   Ibid., 16:26.

337, 20   Ibid., 16:28.

337, 21   Ibid., 16:29.

337, 22   Ibid., 16:30.

337, 25   Ibid., 16:33.

337, 27   Ibid., 16:36.

337, 31   Ibid., 16:39–41.

337, 33   Ibid., 16:42.

338, 6   Ibid., 16:60.

338, 8   Ibid., 16:62–63.

338, 27   Ibid., 6:13.

338, 29   Ibid., 7:9.

338, 32   Ibid., 8:1.

338, 33   Loc. cit.

339, 2   Ibid., 8:2.

339, 9   Ibid., 1:1.

339, 14   Ibid., 8:10.

339, 21   Ibid., 8:16.

339, 23   Ibid., 9:1.

339, 27   Ibid., 9:4.

339, 29   Ibid., 9:6.

339, 30   Loc. cit.

339, 34   Ibid., 9:8.

340, 1   Ibid., 9:11.

340, 5   Ibid., 10:18.

340, 7   Ibid., 10:21.

340, 9   Ibid., 10:5.

340, 12   Ibid., 10:22.

340, 14   Ibid., 11:25.

340, 16   Ibid., 3:17.

340, 16   Ibid., 3:26.

340, 18   Ibid., 3:9.

340, 27   Ibid., 4:3.

341, 1   Ibid., 4:7.

341, 4   Ibid., 4:8.

341, 8   Ibid., 4:12.

341, 10   Ibid., 4:13.

341, 14   Ibid., 4:15.

341, 16   Ibid., 4:17.

341, 29   Ibid., 24:16–17.

341, 31   Ibid., 24:18.

342, 1   Ibid., 24:24.

342, 13   Ibid., 13:6.

342, 13   Ibid., 13:4.

342, 14   Ibid., 13:10.

342, 16   Ibid., 13:2.

342, 31   Ibid., 12:3–6.

342, 32   Ibid., 12:7.

342, 33   Ibid., 12:9.

343, 2   Ibid., 12:27.

343, 4   Ibid., 12:28.

343, 10   Ibid., 33:2–3.

343, 20   Ibid., 33:7.

343, 25   Ibid., 33:32.

343, 26   Ibid., 33:33.

343, 27   Loc. cit.

343, 33   Hecataeus, in Diodorus Siculus, XL, 3.

344, 14   Nehemiah 9:26.

344, 30   É. Dhorme, Introduction to *La Bible. Ancien Testament*, vol. II, cit., p. cvii.

344, 32   Zephaniah 1:7.

345, 5   Ibid., 3:13.

345, 6   Ibid., 1:18.

345, 9   Ibid., 3:13.

345, 11   Ibid., 3:19.

345, 20   Ezekiel 18:20.

345, 32   J. de Maistre, *Les Soirées de Saint-Pétersbourg*, Librairie Grecque, Latine et Française, Paris, 1821, vol. II, p. 220.

346, 2   Letter from C. Baudelaire to C. Asselineau, March 13, 1856, in *Correspondance*, ed. C. Pichois, with the collaboration of J. Ziegler, Gallimard, Paris, 1973, vol. I, p. 340.

346, 5   E. Cioran, *Exercices d'admiration*, Gallimard, Paris, 1986, p. 23.

346, 9   Isaiah 53:11.

346, 11   Ezekiel 18:25.

346, 31   Ibid., 20:10–11.

347, 1   Ibid., 20:17.

347, 3   Ibid., 20:19.

347, 6   Ibid., 20:25.

347, 9   Ibid., 20:26.

347, 14   Loc. cit.

347, 21   Ibid., 20:34–35.

347, 27   Ibid., 37:3.

347, 30   Loc. cit.

348, 1   Ibid., 37:9.

348, 2   Ibid., 37:7.

348, 3   Loc. cit.

348, 7   Ibid., 37:10.

348, 15   Ibid., 37:16.

348, 16   Loc. cit.

348, 24 Ibid., 37:22.

348, 25 Hosea 11:1.

348, 32 Ibid., 11:3–4.

349, 7 Ibid., 11:8.

349, 13 Ibid., 11:9.

350, 2 Ezekiel 23:3.

350, 3 Loc. cit.

350, 4 Ibid., 23:4.

350, 8 Ibid., 23:6.

350, 10 Loc. cit.

350, 15 Ibid., 23:10.

350, 17 Ibid., 23:11.

350, 21 Ibid., 23:15.

350, 26 Ibid., 23:16–17.

350, 32 Ibid., 23:19–20.

351, 6 Ibid., 23:22–23.

351, 6 Ibid., 23:24.

351, 8 Ibid., 23:25.

351, 10 Ibid., 23:27.

351, 13 Ibid., 23:32.

351, 13 Ibid., 23:33.

351, 16 Ibid., 23:42.

351, 20 Loc. cit.

351, 22 Ibid., 23:45.

351, 24 Ibid., 23:49.

351, 33 Ibid., 23:25.

352, 3 Ibid., 23:47.

352, 4 L. Gautier, *Introduction à l'Ancien Testament*, Bridel, Lausanne, 1914, vol. I, p. 435, note 1.

352, 7 Exodus 25:22.

352, 14 Isaiah 1:2.

352, 18 Hosea 2:4.

352, 23 Ibid., 2:9.

352, 28 Ibid., 2:13.

352, 31 Ibid., 2:14.

353, 2 Ibid., 2:18.

353, 8 Ibid., 2:21–22.

353, 14 Ezra 2:62.

353, 18 Ibid., 3:3.

353, 22 Ibid., 3:10.

353, 28 Ibid., 3:12–13.

354, 3 Ibid., 7:16.

354, 9 Ibid., 8:22.

354, 13 Ibid., 8:33–34.

354, 20 Ibid., 9:1–2.

354, 25 Ibid., 9:8.

354, 27 Ibid., 9:14.

354, 28 Loc. cit.

354, 32 Ibid., 10:3.

354, 34 Ibid., 10:5.

355, 2 Ibid., 10:13.

355, 4 Ibid., 10:16.

355, 6 Ibid., 10:44.

355, 9 Ibid., 4:1.

355, 16 Nehemiah 13:25.

355, 20 Ibid., 13:26–28.

355, 31 Ruth 1:16.

356, 26 Nehemiah 8:3.

356, 29 Ibid., 8:8.

356, 32 Ibid., 8:9.

357, 1 Ibid., 8:10.

357, 2 Ibid., 8:12.

357, 6 Ibid., 8:14.

357, 9 Ibid., 8:15.

357, 14 Ibid., 8:18.

361, 11 Deuteronomy 12:13–14.

361, 27 Ibid., 12:9.

362, 8 2 Maccabees 6, 1–2.

362, 15 1 Maccabees 12:21.

362, 24 Ibid., 1:14.

362, 28 Ibid., 1:54.

362, 33 Ibid., 1:59.

363, 4 Daniel 8:23.

363, 5 Ibid., 8:11.

363, 9 Exodus 29:42.

363, 11 Ibid., 29:43.

363, 19 Isaiah 1:11.

363, 29 Moses Maimonides, *The Guide of the Perplexed*, trans. S. Pines, University of Chicago Press, Chicago and London, vol. II, 1963, p. 579.

363, 31   Isaiah 1:13.

364, 10   Letter to the Hebrews 9:12.

364, 19   Isaiah 1:29–30.

364, 27   Ibid., 65:3.

364, 34   Jeremiah 7:30–31.

365, 17   Ibid., 8:1–2.

365, 19   Ibid., 7:32.

366, 2   Diodorus Siculus, XX, 14, 4–6.

366, 26   L. E. Stager and S. L. Wolff, "Child Sacrifice at Carthage: Religious Rite or Population Control?," *Biblical Archaeology Review*, January–February 1984, p. 41.

366, 33   Genesis 4:4.

367, 4   Berakhot 17a, in G. G. Stroumsa, *La Fin du sacrifice*, Odile Jacob, Paris, 2005, p. 122.

367, 9   J. Gordin, *Écrits*, Albin Michel, Paris, 1995, p. 167.

367, 25   G. G. Stroumsa, *La Fin du sacrifice*, cit., p. 114.

367, 28   Loc. cit.

368, 5   Ibid., p. 115.

368, 29   Gregorio di Nazianzo, *Orazioni*, 4, 1.

369, 3   G. W. Bowersock, *Julian the Apostate*, Harvard University Press, Cambridge, 1978, p. 83.

369, 14   Salutius, *On the Gods and the World*, 16, 1.

370, 5   John Chrysostom, *Homilies Against the Jews*, 5, 11, 9–10.

370, 12   Ibid., 7, 2, 3.

370, 15   Ibid., 6, 4, 4.

370, 19   J. Scheid, Preface to G. G. Stroumsa, *La Fin du sacrifice*, cit., p. 11.

370, 20   Loc. cit.

370, 27   *Codex Theodosianus* XVI, 10, 2.

370, 34   G. G. Stroumsa, *La Fin du sacrifice*, cit., p. 137.

371, 10   Julian, *Against the Galileans*, 356C.

371, 14   Ibid., 306B.

371, 28   Ibid., 194D.

371, 30   Deuteronomy 10:16, Letter to the Romans 2:29.

372, 2   Julian, *Against the Galileans*, 306A.

372, 6   John Chrysostom, *Homilies on the Letter to the Hebrews*, 17, 3.

372, 11   Loc. cit.

372, 18   Julian, *Against the Galileans*, 100A.

374, 23   Inscription in the Mithraeum in Santa Prisca on the Aventine Hill.

376, 2   M. Rostovtzeff, *Dura-Europos*, Clarendon Press, Oxford, 1938, p. 58.

376, 5   M. Rostovtzeff, *Caravan Cities*, Clarendon Press, Oxford, 1932, p. 213.

376, 7   Ibid., p. 214.

377, 3   M. Rostovtzeff, *Dura-Europos*, cit., p. 116.

377, 25   F. Cumont, *Fouilles de Doura-Europos*, Geuthner, Paris, 1926, p. 47.

377, 34   Loc. cit.

378, 16   M. Rostovtzeff, *Dura-Europos*, cit., p. 120.

381, 10   R. Patai, *The Messiah Texts*, Wayne State University Press, Detroit, 1988, pp. 247–48.

381, 24   Luke 16:16.

382, 5   Isaiah 65:25.

382, 13   Moses Maimonides, *The Guide of the Perplexed*, cit., p. 345.

382, 18   Maimonides, *Mishneh Torah* 14:5, 11–12, in G. Scholem, *The Messianic Idea in Judaism*, Schocken Books, New York, 1971, p. 28.

382, 22   R. Patai, *The Messiah Texts*, cit., p. 324.

382, 25   Maimonides, *Mishneh Torah* 14:5, 11–12, in G. Scholem, *The Messianic Idea in Judaism*, cit., pp. 28–29.

382, 27   Zephaniah 3:9.

382, 29   Maimonides, *Mishneh Torah* 14:5, 11–12, in G. Scholem, *The Messianic Idea in Judaism*, cit., p. 29.

383, 4   Loc. cit.

383, 6   *"Avot" et ses commentaires. Chapitre premier*, ed. R. Lévy, Verdier, Lagrasse, 2015, p. 41.

383, 8   Ibid., p. 46.

383, 11   Loc. cit.

383, 24   Loc. cit.

383, 28   Ibid., p. 47.

383, 32   Ibid., p. 148.

384, 5   Ibid., p. 150.

384, 24   Moses Maimonides, *The Guide of the Perplexed*, cit., p. 608.

385, 2   *Midrash yemenita*, in R. Patai, *The Messiah Texts*, cit., p. 257.

385, 6   Numbers 19:14.

385, 23   M. Buber, *Die Geschichten des Rabbi Nachman*, Fischer Bücherei, Frankfurt and Hamburg, 1955, p. 43.

385, 25   Ibid., p. 44.

385, 29   L. Bloy, *L'Âme de Napoléon*, in *OEuvres de Léon Bloy*, Mercure de France, Paris, vol. V, 1966, pp. 276–77.

385, 31   M. Buber, *Die Geschichten des Rabbi Nachman*, cit., p. 11.

386, 2   Ibid., p. 44.

386, 6   Ibid., p. 86.

387, 8   Joel 4:18.

387, 13   Ibid., 4:19.

INDEX OF NAMES, PLACES, AND WORKS

Uriah, 33, 36–37, 39, 42
Urim, 22
Ursa Major, 88
Ur-shanabi, 306
Uruk, 305, 306, 326
Utnapishtim, 302, 304–306
Uzza, 40

Valentin, Karl, 247
Valley of Slaughter, 365; *see also* Ben-Hinnom; Topheth
Valley of the Hyenas, 17
van Wolde, Ellen, 308
Vedas, 308
Venice, 185, 323
Venice (in U.S.), 185
Villalpando, Juan Bautista, 54
Virolleaud, Charles, 87
Vitae prophetarum, 344
Vritra, 281
Vulgate, 29, 53, 62–65, 85, 130, 168, 185, 184, 208, 287, 294, 301, 344, 346, 350; *see also* Bible

Yadaim, 70
Yahweh, 3, 5, 10–20, 22–26, 29, 31–42, 44, 46, 51–53, 55, 57–59, 62, 70–71, 73, 75–78, 81–90, 92, 94–100, 103–109, 113–20, 122–28, 130–32, 134–35, 137–42, 144, 150, 152, 154, 160, 167–79, 182–85, 187, 189–39, 253–55, 257–58, 262, 274, 281–83, 285–88, 290, 292–98, 300–304, 306–307, 309–10, 312–13, 315, 318–23, 326, 329–54, 356, 361, 363–65, 370, 378, 398; *see also* Adonai Yahweh; Elohim; Father; God; Lord; Omnipotent; Yahweh Elohim
Yahweh Elohim, 285–87, 292, 294, 302; *see also* Adonai Yahweh; Elohim; Father; God; Lord; Omnipotent; Yahweh
Yahwist, 111, 112, 307
Yarhibol, 378
Yerushalmi, Yosef Hayim, 261, 269
Yudan bar Simon, Rabbi, 136

Wandsbeck, 128
Water Gate, 356
Waters, 160, 188, 281, 334, 387
Wei, 324
Weil, Simone, 68, 110, 132, 296
– Notebook XI, 132
Westwest, Count (character in *The Castle*), 186
Wisdom, 3–5, 70, 72–73, 281; *see also* Hokhmah
Wu Yi, 323–24

Zachariah, 319, 344
Zadok, 46, 91
Zagreus, 323
Zaphenath-Paneah (Egyptian name of Joseph), 153
Zarathustra, 322
Zarephtah, 90, 376
Zebulun, 201
Zelzah, 11
Zephaniah, 321, 345, 382
Zerah, 237